HORSE
WATCH

HORSE WATCH

What it is to be Equine

MARTHE KILEY-WORTHINGTON

J. A. ALLEN

© Marthe Kiley-Worthington 2005

First published in Great Britain 2005

ISBN 0 85131 888 6

J. A. Allen
Clerkenwell House
Clerkenwell Green
London ECIR 0HT

J.A. Allen is an imprint of Robert Hale Ltd

British Library Cataloguing in Publication Data
A catalogue record for this book is available from the British Library

Designed by Judy Linard
Illustrated by Maggie Raynor and Rachel Tremlett
Edited by Jane Lake
Colour separation by Tenon & Polert Colour Scanning Limited, Hong Kong
Printed by New Era Printing Co. Ltd, China

Dedication

For all those horses, ponies, donkeys and zebras whose 'behavioural problems' I have been asked to sort out over the last thirty-five years. This is an effort to try to avoid more of you being in that category, by helping the humans to try to understand you all better.

To Druimghigha Oberlix and Chris, my partners and great pals, and, of course, the princess, Druimghigha Shemal, with gratitude and love.

Druimghigha Shemal.

Contents

Acknowledgements   9

Preface   11

Introduction to the individuals in the experimental equine herd   13

Introduction   27

1   Physique. The mind's and the body's landscape   37

2   The life-supporting behaviours of equines   83

3   Nature and nurture and how equines learn and acquire knowledge   107

4   Equine emotions and feelings   165

5   Equines' ecological knowledge and their need to become 'field naturalists'   218

6   Equines' need to become good 'natural psychologists'   241

7   Equine communication and language   276

8   What is consciousness and are equines conscious?   315

9   Can equines be 'reflectively conscious', or have emotions that indicate they are aware of others' minds?   337

10   Reflective consciousness. Other behaviours indicative of awareness of others' minds and self-awareness   365

11 Do equines have an aesthetic sense or appreciation and
    are they moral agents?   382

12 Applying equine lore to how we keep equines   392

13 Applying equine lore to handling and teaching
    equines   412

14 Conditional anthropomorphism revisited, and conclusions   436

15 Main summary of the different world view of equines:
    equine lore   441

Postscript   444

Bibliography   445

Index   459

Acknowledgements

Many people and animals have contributed to this book in many ways: our horses, in particular, who never cease to teach me. Members of the Department of Psychology, University of Exeter, Department of Philosophy, University of Lancaster and Department of Experimental Psychology, University of Cambridge are thanked for discussions and criticisms, in particular Stephen Lea, Alan Holland, Kate Rawles, Tony Dickinson and Tony Marcel. Those who have attended workshops in the UK, France, Switzerland, Belgium, Japan and Australia, who came from many backgrounds, have widened my thinking, as have the many students I have taught including Erica Shoise, Christine Nicol, Natalie Warren, Chloe Dear, Little Chloe, Lynne Webber, Katherine Ziegler, Nel Zweifel, Judith, Robyn Petrie-Richie, Bettina and many others.

Drafts were critically read by Caroline Rutter, Siobhan Ni Aisidhe, Rosie Brindley, Vicky Clink, Jane Jedwab, Maria Franchini and Kate Rawles, all of whom are thanked for their time and thoughts. Discussions with Mary Midgley over many years have been invaluable as has Hayley Randle's contributions to the research and data analysis. Without all of you, this could never have been written. As always, my partner Chris Rendle has been an enormous help as a sounding board for many of the ideas, and has helped to keep everything going

Caroline Burt of the publisher J. A. Allen has been particularly supportive and the editor, Jane Lake, has done a superb job rendering my oft times wanderings into a readable format.

Preface

This book is for those who are interested in equines, and other mammals, who would like to understand *their* world better and how to apply this understanding to improvements in horse, pony, zebra or donkey husbandry and education so that we can share our worlds and, as a result, enrich each others' lives.

To make the discussions come alive, examples and pictures are used, most of them from our own experimental herd of horses that has been studied now for thirty years, over six generations. The individuals are named and introduced and their stories unfold as a narrative, peppered with their individual skills and personalities: an equine soap opera. Many of the pictures at first glance may show little other than a horse or two grazing or standing, but look again, perhaps there is more going on than the unpracticed eye sees.

The up-to-date arguments about animal minds are complex, but fascinating and exciting, and key to developing constructive relationships between humans and animals. I have tried to simplify and shorten them. I also want to emphasize how much people, who have spent their lives with horses or other equines, have to contribute to these debates, provided they critically assess their own beliefs and experiences. The 'stuff' of these debates on the equine mind is not just what dreams are made of, or solely for the remote academic, but is what keeps many of us with our horses, and upon which we already ponder. I hope I will have clarified some issues, and pointed out the areas where we are still wallowing in a quagmire of unknowns about animals' minds, in order to help and enthuse the reader to cogitate further.

To help the equine caretaker or teacher who would like to improve the lives of the horses under their care, to understand better what it might be like to be an equine, have glimpses into a different world view, and different habits of mind, we have developed various exercises (which are in the relevant chapters).

The key features of these exercises are to:

1. teach people to observe;
2. give them personal experiences;
3. increase their awareness of similarities and differences in perception;
4. encourage us all to develop different habits of mind, particularly independent of language.

Some of these exercises will work better than others for different individuals, and there are many more that people will invent. This is only a start. These exercises have been selected as the most successful from many that we have tried out at workshops worldwide and which have encouraged participants to think and have fun as well as appreciate better what it might be like to be an equine.

Introduction to the individuals in the experimental equine herd

I t all began in 1959 when I was sixteen; we had recently returned from East Africa where I was brought up, and bought a farm in East Sussex. I bought a crib-biting, eight-year-old, 16.2 hh, beautiful chestnut Thoroughbred mare from a friend of my father's with my £40 Post Office savings. I later found out that her registered name with Weatherby's was Stirrup Cup (Kathiawar).

Kathiawar was an ex-racehorse who had been kept in an isolated box all her life, from weaning through training, and had become a crib-biter and unmanageable. I later discovered she had been sold on as dangerous and unpredictable. She had reared and come over backwards with various people and, as is often the way, had ended up in the hands of some unsuspecting novices who were not riders but had a horse to convince their shooting friends they were really country people. They never rode her and were relieved to have her taken off their hands.

I had had Somali ponies and Arab horses in Kenya where we had adventured with them in what would now be considered wild ways, but a large Thoroughbred was a new experience. I did not know much, but I had no fear, and could stay on no matter what she did. Kathiawar and I got to know Sussex quite well, and then started going to shows to jump, which I discovered she could do well. I had no money but managed to borrow a single-horse trailer from an aunt and my mother's small car to pull it and, between school and university, I spent a year helping on the farm, reading the classics and riding Kathiawar. We went to many shows and won gymkhana races and jumping classes, qualifying for national championships.

Kathiawar was not keen on getting into the trailer, particularly coming home and, as a rather shy teenager, I did not like to ask people for help, particularly since they had always been so rude to me during the day, seemingly because I could not afford the right clothes and equipment. This took me by surprise because I had never met that sort of attitude and behaviour in Kenya. No one ever offered to help me, few ever talked to me, but Kathiawar and I continued to win – and lead the field over fences the huntsmens' horses would not jump in our few forays out hunting. At the end of that summer, I vowed I would never have anything to do with these 'horsy people' again, at least until I were confident enough to give as good as I got. (It was twenty-five years later when I next went to a horse competition in the UK and, by then, I could stand up for myself but still did not have the right equipment or money!)

When I left for University in Scotland, Kathiawar visited a local Crabbet Arab stallion. The following year, when the syringa was out in May, she produced a foal I named after the fragrant plant. By then I was back in Africa researching wild animals, and my long suffering dairy-farming mother was looking after the two of them. Eventually, she rightly announced that I must sell one. I sold Kathiawar to a home in the New Forest, and when eventually I returned to the UK for further studies, babies intervened and Syringa visited another Arab stallion, Harwood Asif from the Harwood stud. The result was Baksheesh, an Anglo-Arab stallion (3/4 Arab, 1/4 Thoroughbred), one of my most important mentors.

I moved to the Cuckmere valley in Sussex and started an ecological farm where there was room for a small herd of horses. Sheba, a white Irish Draught, eighteen-year-old mare (who was said to have leukaemia) was bought for a song, and came to stay. I bought six Welsh mountain pony weanlings at an auction in Wales while my friends were in the pub. All but one, we sold on: Aderin, a section D registered wild Welsh mountain pony weanling joined our herd.

Sheba and Baksheesh produce a series of foals; we kept Shiraz and Shereen who became the important performing and breeding mares of the next generation. Baksheesh and Aderin also produced a string: Achmed, a gelding we retained for five years, and Alia and Aisha Evans among others. Aisha Evans we retained for her long life.

The first letter of the horse's name, refers to the mother's family, so relationships are evident. All the Ss relate back to Sheba, the As to Aderin.

After a few years of saving, my partner Chris and I decided to go to the Arab Horse Society auction to try to buy a purebred Arab filly, something I had wanted for many years. We bought Crystal (Crysthannah Royal), a sensible pretty two-year-old. But then Omeya, all slimness and bones, floating action, staring eyes and blowing nose, came in to the ring. We had no more money but Chris said he would buy her; we acquired the three-year-old for £700. It was only afterwards that I realized we would have to raise the money, but who cared, we had Omeya!

Crystal had four foals before my arm was twisted and she was sold on at the age of twenty to one of my ex-research students in Devon, but we see her still. Omeya stayed with us until her death at the age of twenty-four. Both Crystal and Omeya produced foals we kept. Crystal and Cherif (a purebred Arab for whom we were given a reduced rate for the covering because of our performance successes) produced Cariff, the next generation of our purebred Arab stallions who stayed with us until his death (aged fifteen). The C and O families were established. Crystal produced some foals with Baksheesh, (e.g Cara and Carma) but, unfortunately, we did not retain any of them, selling them on as performance horses at the age of three. Baksheesh and Omeya produced Osnan. Omeya produced Oberlix by Aboud who is a champion show Arab, now in Bahrein National Stud. We were given a free service by him, again because of our performance record. Oryx was Omeya's last foal (by a Friesland stallion).

Sadly, Baksheesh died in 1987 at the age of eighteen, on the Isle of Mull where we and all the livestock had moved in 1983. Cariff then became our main stallion and the next generation was founded. In 1989 we moved to Devon and there Cariff and Shiraz, Shereen, Aisha and Omeya produced a string of particularly able and enchanting youngsters, all of whom have been sold on aged three and are performing in many disciplines, some internationally. These include: Shere Khan, Shiera, Shirak, Shergar, Shella, Omen, Oscar, Amanita and Aroha. When Oberlix grew up, he produced Christmas Time with Crystal, and with Shiraz he produced Shemal, the 'princess' who features a great deal in this book, Shukrune and Shanti. With Shereen, Oberlix produced Shella and then Shindi, and young Oryx has now produced Shezam with Shereen and Shenandoah with Shindi. In total the stud has bred sixty-two youngsters. In 2000 we bought Lilka from the Lindsay's famous Polish Arab stud as a nine-month-old filly. She has now produced Luxor with Oberlix, and Liloni, a filly, with Oryx.

The horses run out all year around, but have some form of shelter in the winter. From time to time they are shut in yards for short periods when the weather is particularly wet or they are wrecking the fields, and they all learn to stay the odd night in a single stable. The mares run with a stallion and, if we have too many males, they form a bachelor herd which is kept separately. We often have two adult stallions at a time and, consequently, two small herds. We have been studying the behaviour of this group since 1976 (see Bibliography), but also compete on them, and educate the youngsters to secondary level, i.e. to be ridden quietly and do three-track work, before we sell them. We have specialized in long-distance riding, dressage and dance, but the horses can turn their hoofs to racing, jumping, cross-country work, competitive driving, Western, and almost any other sport we have tried. A synopsis of what they have done is given with each individual.

The main thrust of the stud has been to experiment with improved living and teaching conditions, from the equines' point of view. We have studied the economics, monitored closely distress and behavioural problems, and assessed fertility, longevity and soundness. The competitions we take part in are partly for fun, but mainly to test whether or not our horses kept and raised in this way can compete with others successfully, internationally if possible. Only by our good reputation earned by winning competitions will the changes to husbandry and teaching be applied more widely.

Having started this experiment to learn more about equine behaviour, we have learnt a great deal about the equine's view of the world in this thirty-five-year project, and demonstrated that improvement of equine lives is necessary, practical and of benefit to humans too. Now we continue with the research, focussing particularly on advanced learning and teaching: trying to find where the limits might be to what equines can learn, and answering some of the open questions in this book with at least Oberlix, Shemal, Shindi and Oryx. We are also establishing an educational centre and wildlife park in Africa to continue our research and to educate the local people about animals, working with traditionally wild animals, including zebras and donkeys, elephants, buffalo and eland.

Apart from meeting many delightful people and making the majority of our friends through our equines, the most valuable thing that the horses have done for me, is enriched my life by eternally opening my eyes to different world views; I hope they will start this process for the reader through this book.

THE DRUIMGHIGHA STUD PEDIGREES
From 1958 - 2004
(Only horses mentioned in the text are entered)

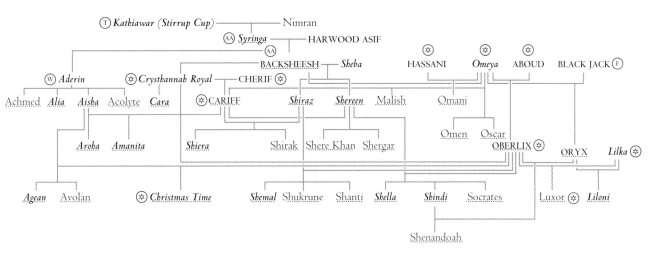

(T) *Kathiawar (Stirrup Cup)* —————— Nimran

(AA) *Syringa* ———— HARWOOD ASIF

(AA) BACKSHEESH —— *Sheba*　　HASSANI (✲)　*Omeya* (✲)　ABOUD (✲)　BLACK JACK (F)

(W) *Aderin*　　(✲) *Crysthannah Royal* —— CHERIF (✲)

Achmed　*Alia*　*Aisha*　Acolyte　*Cara*　(✲) CARIFF　*Shiraz*　*Shereen*　Malish　Omani

　　　　　Aroba　*Amanita*　*Shiera*　　Shirak　Shere Khan　Shergar　　Omen　Oscar

　　　　　　　　　　　　　　　　　　　　　　　　　　　　　　OBERLIX (✲)　ORYX (✲)　*Lilka* (✲)

Agean　Avolan　(✲) *Christmas Time*　*Shemal* Shukrune　Shanti　*Shella*　*Shindi*　Socrates　Luxor (✲)　*Liloni*

Shenandoah

Bold Italic = Mares/Females　　(AA) = Anglo-Arab　　(✲) = Purebred Arab

CAPITALS = Stallions　　(T) = Registered Thoroughbred　　(W) = Registered Welsh Mountain Section D

Plain text = Gelded　　(F) = Registered Friesland　　All the rest = Registered Partbred Arab

Underlined text = Home (Druimghigha) bred

Druimghigha Stud 1976 at Milton Court Ecological Farm, Sussex. From right to left: Baksheesh, Aderin, Sheba, Shiraz (daughter of Baksheesh), Omeya, Omani (son of Omeya), Alia (daughter of Aderin), Crysthannah Royal (Crystal), and Paddy (a long-term resident gelding).

Druimghigha Stud 2004 at our new centre in France. From left to right: Oberlix (Omeya's son), Shemal (great-great-granddaughter of Kathiawar, granddaughter of Baksheesh), Shenandoah (the seventh generation from Kathiawar, via Shindi (granddaughter of Baksheesh), Liloni (Oryx's daughter), Lilka (the new purebred Arab line from the Lindsay's famous Polish stud), her son Luxor (in the trees behind Oryx), and Oryx (Omeya's other son by a Friesland).

Kathiawar

The eight-year-old Thoroughbred foundation mare of the Druimghigha Stud. She had raced, but had reared over backwards with various jockeys. I bought her with my Post Office savings of £40 in 1959 and found she jumped, galloped fast, and was a delightful companion and friend. We won many jumping events, Foxhunter and Open, as well as gymkhana events, dressage and cross-country, but were thrown out of the hunt because of getting in front of the huntsman over some hedges!

Aderin

A section A Welsh mountain pony bought off the hill at auction when she was six months old. My children all learned to ride on her and she is pictured here aged thirty. Aderin is still going strong and winning veteran classes aged thirty-five. Mother of Aisha and all the other horses whose names begin with A.

Baksheesh

Baksheesh, one of the founding sires of our herd. He took part in the first ever Arab Horse Society race, coming third after leading the field all the way. He won the AHS marathon twice, once at near record speeds, and won many of the early 80 km endurance race rides. Baksheesh has been the foundation sire for some of the most talented endurance horses to date. Above all, he was a marvellous companion, taught me a great deal and was one of the most important influences on my life and interests.

Syringa

The Anglo-Arab daughter of Nimran (Arab stallion) and Kathiawar. We did not compete because I was having my children at the time, but I rode her a lot and we learnt together. She was the mother of Baksheesh.

Omeya

1977–1999. Purebred Crabbet Arab. Gengi x Zumana. One of our most treasured and talented friends. We bought her at an Arab Horse Society sale in 1980 as a wild three-year-old filly who had done nothing. She took part in everything with zest and absolute trust. She came fifth in the Summer Solstice International in 1987, was three times third in the Marathon, Arab raced at Aintree and Epsom, won fifty-mile races, worked in harness on the land, performed dressage, and came camping with us. She was a beautiful type with spectacular movement and was mother of our two recent stallions, Oberlix and Oryx. She features heavily in this book and is much missed.

Sheba

One of the herd's founding mares (1950–1980). She was an Irish Draught type and was twenty when we bought her. She was said to have leukemia, but in fact the woman who owned her could not catch her. We broke her to harness and she was with us until her thirtieth year. Mother of Shiraz and Shereen as well as many others sold on. We now have her great-grandchildren.

Crysthannah Royal

Born 1978. Purebred Crabbet Arab. Crystal King x Hannah of Fairfield. We bought her as our first purebred Arab filly aged two at an Arab Horse Society auction. She grew up to be a delightful all-round easy-going Arab, took part in many endurance rides, races and the Marathon. She worked on the land, in harness, danced, and is the mother of Cariff. We sold her to Hayley Randle in 1998 and she continues to take part in endurance and is a great companion.

Aisha Evans

Born 1978. Partbred Arab. Baksheesh x Aderin. Although she was only 13.2 hh, Aisha was almost unbeaten in long distance. Amongst her successes were the Scottish Championship 1987, best condition in the Summer Solstice 100 miles 1997, Red Dragon and many fifty-mile races. She inherited her father's competitiveness and often astonished us with her determination and endurance even when well into her twenties. She worked on the land and in harness and gave us foals. In 2002 she went to live in Belgium with one of our students with her foal by Oberlix.

Shereen

1978–2002. Partbred Arab. Baksheesh x Sheeba. Shereen won many awards including runner-up Scottish Long Distance Champion 1987, Red Dragon 1987, Marathon 1987. She was placed in Arab flat racing, won Versatile Horse 1993 and numerous fifty-mile races, was placed in affiliated medium dressage and took part in many dances. She worked in harness on the land and pulled vehicles. A big, strong, beautiful and talented mare who nevertheless preferred being a mother and aunt.

Cariff

1982–1997. Pure Crabbet Arab. Cherif x Crysthannah Royal. Cariff was our resident stallion and fathered many talented horses (see pedigree chart) for six years. He took part in many endurance rides and won Best Junior at the Summer Solstice with our son, Jake, doing sixty miles in 1996. He took part in few competitions but worked the land and was driven a great deal in harness. His speciality was dance, movement and performance. He was a real gentleman and could be taken anywhere and left with anyone.

Shebat

Born 1982. Trakehner stallion x Shereen. He was sold as a three-year-old, having completed his secondary education, and went on to do dressage.

Osnan

Born 1988. Anglo-Arab. Baksheesh x Omeya. Osnan was a talented endurance horse as a youngster, winning the novice award at Sherwood Forest in 1993. He was bought by a friend and has become a treasured companion.

Oberlix

Born 1989. Purebred Crabbet Arab. Aboud x Omeya. Oberlix features widely in this book. He is one of our current stallions and has excelled in endurance, including winning the marathon and 80 km race at the Red Dragon, various fifty-mile races and coming seventh in the 100 mile Summer Solstice Ride. He was tested and passed as a premium performance stallion in 1997, passing with flying colours in conformation, jumping, free jumping, cross country, gallop, dressage and general comportment. His offspring are doing very well in various disciplines, including his daughter, Shemal, who is still with us. As well as being one of the subjects with whom we have been studying equine cognition and language comprehension, he works on the land, dances, and travels with us. In 2001 I had the idea of using Oberlix to see if one horse could do well in international endurance and international dressage in the same year. We did just this, competing and doing well in international endurance races and at the same time competing up to Intermediare level (one level before Grand Prix) in affiliated dressage. We did not win, but we got above average marks in both disciplines. Oberlix is one of the individuals I have learned most from and continue to learn from daily.

Shiera

Born 1989. Partbred Arab. Baksheesh x Shiraz. Shiera was a delightful chestnut filly who was sold on as a three-year-old to become one of Britain's leading endurance horses, ridden in the British junior team.

Shere Khan

Born 1991. Partbred Arab. Cariff x Shereen. A big, solid horse, sold as a three-year-old having done his secondary education, he went on to excel in long distance with Pauline Morris in the West Country, and was then sold on to be ridden all around Ireland.

Shemal

Born 1994. Partbred Arab. Oberlix x Shiraz. Shemal features heavily in this book and has been one of our most studied horses since she was born. She has won the Man versus Horse race twice in Wales (twenty-three miles over mountains), the Arab Marathon once, and the fifty-mile race at the Red Dragon in a field of over fifty. She dances, works on the land, travels the world with us and is generally a delight. We hope she will have a foal by Oryx in 2005. Shemal's star role in ballet so far has been Aurora in Sleeping Beauty, which is why she is otherwise known as 'the princess', and she does behave like one!

Shergar

Born 1992. Partbred Arab. Cariff x Shereen. A big, talented Araby horse, he eventually excelled in long distance in the West Country. He is now ridden in the paraplegic UK Olympic team.

Oryx

Born 1996. Partbred Arab. Black Jack (Friesland) x Omeya. We wanted a heavier horse to be able to pull greater weights on the land, yet one with spark, good looks, great gaits, plus speed for enjoyable riding and competitions, so we decided to send Omeya to run with a Friesland stallion and see what they produced. Oryx is the result and resembles a Lusitano/Spanish horse, which points to the possible origin of these horses. He is an advanced endurance horse and is now beginning his tertiary riding education. He has lovely gaits, particularly eye-catching looks, and a delightful personality. He does everything and fits in everywhere, even though he and Oberlix are somewhat competitive.

Shukrune

Born 1996. Partbred Arab. Oberlix x Shiraz. A lovely big chestnut sold as a three-year-old gelding to Jackie who rode with us a lot. He is now in Devon and much appreciated as a companion and a delightful ride.

Shanti

Born 1998. Partbred Arab. Oberlix x Shiraz. A fine chestnut and the last of Shiraz's offspring. Sold as a three-year-old to Vicki, one of our students. We continue to see him and the idea is that Vicky will ride him to the other side of the world one day.

Shezam

Born 1999. Partbred Arab. Oryx x Shereen. Oryx's first foal, a large floppy character with a mild and delightfully co-operative personality. Sold as a three-year-old to be an older gentleman's ride and companion.

Shindi

Born 2000. Partbred Arab. Oberlix x Shereen. Shindi is the youngest of our equines of direct descent from Kathiawar and is pictured here as a two-year-old. By mistake, Shindi had a foal (Shenandoah) by Oryx last year and is currently being ridden and driven quietly. Sweet natured with the potential to panic, she has lovely action and conformation.

Lilka

Born 1999 at the Lindsays' famous Polish Arab Stud in Devon. Purebred Arab. Bought as a 'wife' for Oberlix, she arrived at nine months old and was very frightened of everything. Now she has two foals and is a quiet elegant ride, but has a spark of willingness and will climb almost any mountain – fast!

Introduction

'"After what I have seen of plants and fishes in the region of Naples, in Sicily, I should be sorely tempted, if I were 10 years younger, to make a journey to India – not for the purpose of discovering something new, but in order to view in my way what has been discovered". Goethe was indicating here that the discovery of new facts was of secondary importance to him. What mattered was the *way* of seeing, which influenced all the facts.'

Bortoft 1996, p 33

'Education is what survives when what has been learned has been forgotten.'

Skinner 1969

Even today, if you are a visitor, client, working pupil or student at a large competitive or training yard, you might be in awe, not only of the way some of the best competitors ride, but also of those who seem to 'know horses' and 'know how to handle and train them'. In these institutions and training establishments, we are all taught that the way they do things is the best way, and often that it is the 'kindest' way as well. Almost everyone will tell you that the equine mind is very limited, that equines learn very slowly and their behaviour is controlled to a great extent by 'instinct', and almost everyone will tell you how much they love the equines in their care. Generally, people really do care, but they have false beliefs about equines, how their minds work, how they learn, what they are aware of and can do mentally. The result is that, often, people's attitude to horses in the stable resembles that of a mother to a child: they care and protect, they do not allow the horses to make decisions and choices about their own lives in case they 'hurt themselves'; in other words, they overprotect, underestimate the equines' mental abilities, and end up trying to have a relationship with their horse like a human 'carer' (or, as stated, like a mother to a child).

This approach is not restricted to daft old ladies who love their horses 'to bits', it is widespread among professionals and competitors of all types and at all levels as well as the single horse or donkey owner.

Of course there is nothing wrong at all with caring for your equine, in fact, thank goodness, probably the majority of people now have equines *because* they care for them. But, should the human/equine bond be like a mother/infant relationship? This implies that equines lack the mental ability to have knowledge, make sensible decisions and choices and understand the world. I suggest that such an approach is neither helpful nor useful. Rather it undermines further questions about equine mental attributes and abilities; it is patronizing and undervalues the horse.

This is a question that I began to consider in my early teens, perhaps as the result of being the youngest, and having spent my childhood being irritated by the older human family members' patronizing attitude to me. What is it like to be an equine? Do we know? Can we imagine? I spent my childhood in the company of my pony, dog, cow and duiker finding them in many ways more rewarding company than the older humans of whose expectations I always seemed to fall short in respect of what I could do and how I did it, however much I tried! Watching and being with these animals as my close friends throughout my life has shown me how much more able and complex their mentality is than is usually assumed.

The new movement of 'natural horsemen' (interestingly, they all seem to be men!) recognizes that equines do understand some visual messages. Nevertheless it is still maintained that equines can never understand spoken language. These people believe that using the voice and language may be what some people do but that they are misguided, as it is only the *expression* that can be understood by horses. The 'natural horsemen' argue that it is 'unnatural' for the horse to learn to comprehend a verbal language. Such a position is confusing since the same people overlook how 'unnatural' it is for humans to live with, handle, teach, ride or drive horses at all ... or is it? And even if it is, is it therefore undesirable? These and many other questions confront any thinking student of equines (or other mammal).

We make a series of assumptions about the mind of the horse and consequently how we will train him, but are such assumptions real undisputed facts or just beliefs we have learnt from one another? How do horses learn to do all the things they undoubtedly do learn to do, and to live in environments that are so alien to those they have evolved to live in? Indeed, how could they have survived and adapted to a whole range of environmental conditions in the wild itself, if their behaviour was controlled exclusively by some pre-programmed inflexible mechanism which is called 'instinct'?

In the last decade or two, there has been a mushrooming of research in asking such questions about animals' minds, particularly those of apes and sea mammals and, as a result, there is a blossoming of ideas, at least on what the questions are, and how we might try to answer them. In any new science, there are many differences of opinion and discussion, which is, of course, what fosters further enquiry. In this book I will summarize the debates currently occurring among philosophers of the mind and behavioural scientists of many hues whose business it is to try to make headway in understanding further the minds of human and non-human mammals, and where similarities and differences lie. But, we must be cautious, and not let ourselves be carried away on the wind of desired belief. Such statements as 'my horse understands everything I say' or the holding of strong opinions concerning the equine's mental abilities without critically assessing the arguments for and against them, is very unhelpful and hinders progress.

I, like many others, have been obsessed by trying to find out 'what it might be like to be an equine' since I was a child. One ponders, wonders, discusses, reads and has experiences trying to get closer to this aim; it is a subject of infinite fascination. But, apart from this, there are other major reasons for trying to get a little nearer understanding what it may be like to be an equine: if we were to have a better understanding of equine behaviour and their mental abilities, then we would be able to structure their husbandry and education better, avoid problems, save money and have a better time together.

In the last few decades there have been major developments in our knowledge and understanding of how to educate humans but so far no one has applied this knowledge to 'educating' other mammals. In fact, the training of domestic mammals has shown very little progress over the last few centuries, although the modern natural-horsemanship movement has re-emphasized one or two important points that had been forgotten from time to time.

What is the difference between 'educating' and 'training'? Training is usually used to indicate the teaching of a particular skill, e.g. training the dog to beg, or 'training the nurse in midwifery', whereas educating is to 'give instruction in intellectual (cognitive or mental), moral or social skills' (*Oxford English Reference Dictionary*). It involves the development of a range of mental skills and introduces new or different 'habits of mind' which can then be applied in a whole range of circumstances. It can be thought of more as **the development of mental disciplines which will benefit the life of the subject**. By contrast, 'training' can be considered to be the development of a particular skill which will be of benefit to others rather than the subject, even though it may make him more employable and useful. If a human is to educate others it is crucial they have some mutual understanding of the students' mental life and abilities. Some horse owners may consider they do not want to educate their horse, they just want to train 'it'. However, if they are going to have any enjoyment in each other's company, avoid behavioural problems and if the human wants the companionship of a living being, rather than a robot, it is necessary to understand something about the horse's mental life, and to educate him.

In practice, educating involves teaching the subject to learn and to think about things, to make judgements, to have beliefs and to reflect on things. Many will argue that equines cannot do these sort of mental athletics. They argue that even if equines learn, they learn in a reflex-type way, pairing a certain stimulus with a particular response, and have no awareness of what they are doing, so make no decisions or choices. Effectively, such people believe that other mammals (except possibly some apes and sea mammals) do not experience most of the mental events we can identify in humans.

But, are equines just like motor cars where pressing one button results in a certain response, where there are no 'feelings' involved? There may be some humans who consider that equines are just like this, but they are few because the majority of human mammals who have to do with equines, know that they are not like robots or motor cars, they can be unpredictable, they make choices and, above all, they have feelings. They are, therefore, like us — mammals. However much someone has been taught that other mammals are rather like robots, when they come face to face with them and exchange some feeling with them, they know that this is untrue. To learn, or to pay attention and be aware of something, the individual has to have some motivation. Motivation is a feeling and without it there is no learning. We may debate the degree that equines are or are not aware of things (see Chapter 8) but we cannot debate that they learn to perform (or not perform) acts voluntarily. In other words, like us and unlike computers, they are living, feeling, learning beings.

Some of us have to do with equines because they will bring us fame and fortune, others for human social status, but the majority of us, however we justify it, are involved with equines because, although they may be useful to us one way or another, they are our companions and friends, sometimes even our enemies. We have them and like them because they react to us and respond to us with emotions and feelings that we can understand, because we also feel those emotions. Some equines might like us, some hate us, some are frightened of us, some are curious, others confused. They feel happiness and joy and show it and they can suffer, just like us.

Equines do learn to do or not to do things, they can make decisions and choices. They have to reason sometimes, and they have to learn about their environments and about the society they live in in order to survive and remain within the community. Indeed they can learn the difference between right and wrong, perhaps they are even moral agents and are capable of moral actions. Computers may be able to learn but, so far, no one has made a machine that feels and can do these other mental things as a result.

If equines, even when humans are not around, demonstrate that they do perform such mental tasks, then the job of the carer or educator is to encourage and develop these mental abilities, and perhaps to teach new ones. The job of the 'trainer' by contrast merely involves ensuring that the student can *do* certain tasks; it is not concerned with whether the subject has a mental life and what this involves.

Of course, many trainers have been interested in what is going on in a horse's head, if only to ensure that the horse begins to do what they are asking him to do, but the trainer's central concern is with the *doing*, not on *how it is done*.

My interest has for many years focused on what equines (not only horses, but also ponies, donkeys and zebras) do themselves, and why and how they are doing them. If we are to give them a life of quality and educate them better, in the first place it is necessary to study all aspects of how they have evolved to live, to begin to understand their mental lives. Only then will we be able to improve our keeping and teaching of them. They have of course also to learn something about us and our world so that they can begin to partake in it, as well as us learning about their world.

Initially, when having to do with equines, we use our own mental experiences to understand theirs, but we need to realize that equine minds, although similar to ours, are not just the same. There are differences in our 'world views'. The exciting thing is that when we do briefly understand their different point of view, we have glimpses of a different (but not inferior) world, our own point of view is modified and our lives enriched.

I do not pretend to have all the answers or to know all there is to know. All I can do is make some arguments for the way equine minds may work. These arguments are founded on a serious scientific study of them over some thirty-five years, represented by some empirical evidence and a scientific appraisal. But, unlike most cognitive psychologists or ethologists (scientists who study animal minds), I have included critically assessed knowledge acquired from close contact with, and experience of, equines.

The greatest difficulty here is to sort out the wheat from the chaff. For example, what is believed by the people who have horses about their mentality. What is, what we can call 'folk belief', that is, what horse people believe, but which may not be correct. It may rather be the result of preconceived notions (that which someone else has told you) or tradition (the way it has always been thought about and done, so therefore the right way). One of the problems with folk belief is that it can be self-fulfilling. For example, if someone says to you about an equine: 'be careful that one bites', you will be cautious in approaching him, and by your body language tell him that you are slightly wary and even afraid. He will read these signals, become slightly wary and afraid himself, and bite you, or at least threaten to, and the folk belief is confirmed, yet it does not mean that the equine is aggressive and nasty, it only reflects the fact that he is aware and sensitive to human visual cues and acts on them. Thus preconceived notions can often become self-fulfilling.

By contrast 'folk knowledge' is information that is proven to be correct (by the scientific method, or critically assessed experiences) and is also well known.

One of the curious things about people who have to do with equines is how strong their tradition or folk belief is, and how difficult to question. There are some things which are 'written', that is, everyone is told they must, or must not, do certain things which are, in fact, just silly, for example: 'never let a horse eat grass when he is being ridden or he will stop and eat any time'. This is silly because, just as he can learn when to eat, he can also learn when not to eat. Some folk beliefs are simply wrong, for example 'horses only learn by repetition', but in fact, they often learn, (usually to our cost) in one trial. Some folk beliefs cause the animal to suffer, for example 'horses must be kept apart in stables in case they injure each other', or 'foals must be weaned at six months'. Newcomers to equine keeping may ask the question 'why?' to start with but, after a while, having received the answer 'because it has always been done like that', and because often preconceived notions are self-fulfilled, they usually join the club and believe it all too!

Perhaps it all began with the cavalry, as demonstrated by Tennyson (1854) in 'The Charge of the Light Brigade':

> . . . Theirs' not to make reply,
> Theirs' not to reason why,
> Theirs' but to do and die . . .

But, horsemanship is no longer dominated by the military, it is time to start asking questions about many of our beliefs concerning equines and who they are.

Trying to understand another's mind, and to look after and educate him better is not a bed of roses. It is often hard and frustrating for both the student and the teacher. It requires commitment, hard work, serious attention and, particularly for the human, the ability to become a good observer, and act on what is observed. There is no way of getting away from it, it is tough, but the rewards are immense, resulting in the sheer delight in another's abilities, physical and mental prowess, amusement, companionship and mutual respect. But, perhaps the greatest reward is the enrichment of your own life as a result of having chinks of light shine through half-blinded windows into another's world. There are things for all of us to learn from equines. For me, one of the most important things equines have taught me is to be much more aware of the world around me at any moment, to be aware of the wholeness of it rather than the normal human approach which is to pay full attention to one thing at a time.

This book considers what we know about equines that is relevant to their whole beings. It looks at how this must be controlled by their bodies, their physical abilities, their learning, and the knowledge they have to acquire in order to survive without humans. This leads us onto questions concerning consciousness, self-awareness, whether they are rational, have aesthetic experiences or are moral agents.

Finally, I show how what we have learnt about equine lore can help us to design better environments for them and to teach them better. It allows us to develop a more complete picture of equines' physical, social, emotional and mental needs, and how we can cater for these in our husbandry, whether we have a large expensive stable yard, or a pony in a paddock. In this way, not only can we improve their lives, but also ours with them.

Throughout the book I have given examples and many pictures from our own stud or experimental work, to make it more relevant and alive to the reader. I try to develop the reader's interest in the equine subjects of our studies and to engage with their personalities, so that a narrative may emerge, an equine soap opera if you will. The examples and pictures are also included to help readers assess all the relevant circumstances more carefully, and not jump to unsupported conclusions.

Through the ages, many different approaches have been successful with equines, nevertheless some general rules emerge from our study of equine minds. There is no dogma, it is for every one of you to develop your own approach, and as long as you and your equine enjoy it, what could possibly be wrong with it?

Science is concerned with acquiring knowledge, and one of the ways of doing this (but by no means the only one) is by empirical measurement. Good science combines what the figures say with critical thinking, particularly when it comes to issues concerning minds, how they work and what they are. Consequently, it is positively unscientific, or bad science, to believe that similarities in behaviour between equines and humans do not exist until it is proved empirically in some way. We are all mammals, thus **a rational approach is to consider that we are similar until it is proved otherwise**, that is, we need to 'shift the burden of proof' if we are going to find out anything new about equines and their minds. If you believe that equines do not have a mind or mental events something like those of humans, your challenge is to prove it; it is not mine to prove they are similar, because this we already know.

But, this does not mean that they are just like me, or you, it simply gives us a starting point from which to begin to find out what their lives are all about and consequently how their husbandry and education might be better structured. It gives us a licence to use 'conditional anthropomorphism' (see Chapter 1), that is, consider our similarities with equines and how we would behave in that situation, and then mould this by our knowledge of our differences in world views. This does not mean we should not do certain competitions, or use the horse in certain ways (except if, by the nature of the work, they will suffer). By having this knowledge, and pursuing further the many unanswered questions, we can ensure the horse has a happy, healthy life and is an educated, delightful companion.

There is no magic. When people say to me 'you have never had a horse that did a, b or c, you just have horses that behave perfectly', firstly it is not true, but neither is it luck. We have had problems, like anyone has with other humans, but by thinking about them in this way, it is not difficult to put them right, nip them in the bud and correct our own behaviour or the type of life that animal is leading which may be contributing to the problem.

This book is written to clarify ideas on 'what it is to be an equine', not just a horse or pony, but also a donkey, zebra or mule, and then to outline how we can use what we know to improve our relationships with them, have more fun and even win more competitions, or allow them to work better and, above all, enrich our own lives by glimpsing new ways of looking at the world. This is not just for the high flyer and big yard, the same applies to the person who has a donkey in a field.

If you do not want to educate your equine but 'just ride him', he will be solely educating himself, and that may be to your disadvantage. For example, he may learn to perform a stereotype, such as weaving or wind sucking, in order to escape from the unacceptable environment he lives in. He may learn to spook, rear, bolt or buck thus becoming no longer fun to ride, whether you like it or not.

It is necessary, therefore, to take some trouble to try to understand his lore, cater for his needs *and* allow him to educate himself so neither of you suffer. Otherwise sell your horse and buy a Mercedes, which does not have emotions, an integrated physical and mental life, or learn!

1 Physique. The mind's and the body's landscape

'In reflecting on the diversity of animal minds, we come to recognise that even our ways of thinking about the world – on which we pride ourselves – are rooted in our species nature. The way that we divide the world into different categories of things, events and processes is a function, not only of how the world is but also of our own concerns. But it is difficult to understand what aspects of our thought reflect how the world is and what aspects are projections of our own nature.'

Bavidge & Ground 1994

THE MIND

We used to think we knew quite a lot about the mind and how learning worked in the brain, but when people tried to build robots that learnt, they found that it did not work quite the way they expected. Now, there are disagreements between those who are interested in 'minds' about how (or if) mental events are represented in the brain. Such discussions are the subject of frequent conferences and debates.

But, any animal of any type who can learn, perform voluntary actions and acquire knowledge, requires a 'mind', that is, something that does 'mental things': receives messages, analyses them, remembers, predicts, and so on. Most people who own horses, donkeys, ponies, zebras or mules believe their animal has a mind, but they do have trouble finding out where the similarities and differences between an equine's mind and that of a human might be.

In order to understand, keep and educate equines better, and consequently enjoy their company more, we must try to understand who and what equines are.

To do this we need to very carefully and critically study their whole being: their body and their mind. How the body and mind relate to each other is, itself, not always clear so we must look briefly at a little of the history of natural science.

One of the first questioning natural scientists was Aristotle (384–322 BC). He argued that the body and the mind were integrated parts of the individual which created the 'essence' of the being, whether a human or a horse. Through the ages there have been many people who have retained and developed this approach which is referred to as 'monism'.

In much of Western Europe this monism (the integration of body and mind) was overshadowed by an important seventeenth-century thinker, Descartes, who has had an enduring impact. He argued that we can be sure of nothing that we perceive because our senses are not reliable, they may get things wrong. In fact, there may be nothing there at all; the world may be an invention of the mind. The only thing we can be sure of, though, is that 'I think, therefore I am, I exist'; in other words, it is only the mind we really know exists. The way this idea has been interpreted is that the mind is separated from the body, thus what affects the mind may not affect the body and vice versa. In modern human and animal medicine this is often taken for granted. The body is treated for a physical illness without any attention being paid to the mind. In veterinary medicine, this has often been taken to an extreme where there is no concern with the effect that some physical problem may have on the mind, and vice versa.

This idea of a separate body and mind is called 'dualism'. The consequences of this widely held belief is that, until very recently, non-human mammals have been denied a mind because they are not able (so it is believed) to be aware of themselves.

Darwin, two centuries later, came up with the idea of evolution which involved both the body and the mind. In fact, evolution points out the similarities between human and non-human mammals. Darwin even wrote a book pointing out similarities in emotion between humans and non-humans (Darwin 1868). Despite this, many scientists and philosophers today still believe that there is no proof that non-human mammals have minds. Many scientists argue that *until we have undisputed empirical evidence that they are aware and can think and perform other mental tasks, we cannot assume that non-human mammals have minds.* But, in the last two decades a growing number of thoughtful scholars and scientists are wondering if this is such a logical position, or whether we should rather assume all mammals, at least, have minds and mental events, somewhat similar to human ones, since we are all mammals. If we take this position, which, as a result of much research, thinking and personal experience with equines, is mine, then we take for granted certain similarities in both bodies and minds between humans and other mammals. What we have to do is to find evidence for some of the differences.

Such recent understanding comes from a recognition that all mammals have similarities of body structure, of sensory receptors and of the brain, both in their anatomy and how it works, and their ability to experience mental events: to learn, to remember and so on. Consequently, it would seem more rational to assume that equines have a mind as well as a body, because they are mammals like us, until it is proved that they do *not* have a mind. This shifting of the burden of proof fits better with the horseperson's everyday experiences of and with equines.

Folk psychology

Those who spend time with equines generally attribute mental states to them in order to explain and predict their behaviour. Many people are also aware that the equine does the same to humans. As a result, equines often predict what the human will do next. This type of intuitive knowledge is sometimes called 'folk psychology', i.e. information that any normal person will have. We often use folk psychology successfully in our interactions with each other. The problem is that folk psychology can be seriously influenced by culture, that is by what one is told. Take, for instance, the example given in the introduction of how being told a horse bites can lead to him fulfilling this belief. So although we use folk psychology a great deal and much of the time it is helpful with understanding others, it can also be a hindrance. It may even stunt our study to better understand equines. Again, we need to be able to separate the wheat from the chaff and distinguish between the following.

Folk belief

This is where there is some human cultural input and something is believed and not questioned. For example, 'this horse is just trying to get away with it'.

Folk knowledge

This describes that for which we really do have some evidence concerning the mental state of the subject, for example 'he is rushing away at this time because he predicts frightening or painful experiences'.

In order to acquire folk knowledge we need to gather information in different ways.

- By critically assessing our own experiences and observations. That is our 'subjective' experiences.
- By acquiring knowledge from experiment, or detailed measured observation in an 'objective' way, that is 'science' which is assumed to be objective.

But of course, the subjective and objective are not completely separate because, although one has a subjective experience, its foundation may be based on generally held intuitive understanding of the world, for example 'the falling object nearby could fall on my head so I must move away fast'. Similarly, no science can ever be *entirely* objective since there is a human asking the questions, making the equipment and extracting the conclusions, and they have their own subjective point of view, which is particularly affected by the culture of the day. As Goethe said 'the history of science is science itself', science reflects its cultural/historical context.

To date, the trainers and writers about equines have generally concentrated on the subjective approach, and the scientists on the objective. But, neither one or other of these approaches alone will suffice to aid a greater understanding of any species, including equines. We need to try to mix them without drawing unsupported conclusions, or ignoring critically assessed experiences. It is this multi-disciplinary approach that this book uses to assess what it might be like to be an equine, that is, equine lore.

We generally have equines nowadays because we like them and, because we can exchange emotions and information of one sort or another with them (something we cannot do with motor cars which do not have minds). However, we must remain critical of our personal interpretations, and flavour them with knowledge gained from careful well-designed studies of equines, both experimental and observational. Similarly it is only too clear to many of us who have had to do with equines much of our lives that the empirical scientific approach to understanding better the whole being of an animal is not enough. Also, it may tell those of us who have had much to do with equines very little (if anything) we do not already know. So, if we want to learn more about horses, critically assessed personal experiences and folk knowledge must be added.

Conditional anthropomorphism

The recognition of our similarities with other mammals, rather than emphasizing our mental and physical differences, has previously been suggested by others in order to allow us to understand animal minds better. This approach has been called 'conditional anthropomorphism' (Burghart 1991, Fisher 1991) and it is this approach that we will develop in some depth to help us understand equines better.

Anthropomorphism is making judgements about other species based on our own human way of experiencing and interpreting the world. It has often been considered a very bad thing, an unscientific, improper, unthorough, and unjustifiably human position rather than an enquiring one. But other mammals, including equines, are not aliens from outer space, they are our mammalian relatives. We have similarities in our bodies and how they work, we all eat, sleep, defaecate, reproduce, look after our infants, have some social life, and we all feel and learn things. We have interwoven physical, emotional, social and intellectual or cognitive lives. Consequently, just because we are mammals, we already know something about 'what it is to be an equine', a great deal more than we know about 'what it is to be a spider', for example, because we are not arachnids. Anthropomorphism allows us to use, as a starting point, what we know (because of who we are) in our interpretation of what other mammals, at least, do and how they are.

But we must be very critical of making judgements assuming that equines are '*just* like us'. We must understand where the differences lie, in both what we perceive and how we analyse this information. To do this we need also to study equines as objectively as possible. To find out where our mental and physical differences lie, this is where the 'conditional' comes in. Thus, **'conditional anthropomorphism' allows us to recognize the similarities between all mammals, and use this to try better to understand another species but, at the** same time, to critically assess this and combine it with information from more objective empirical studies of equines so that we can understand our differences as well as our similarities.

Wittgenstein (1953) famously said 'if a lion could talk, we could not understand him', because he believed that his 'talk' would be so different from ours it would be incomprehensible. Another more recent philosopher, Nagel (1974), published a classic paper called 'What is it like to be a bat?'. He concluded that it was impossible to know what it might be like to be a bat because bats and humans are so different, it cannot even be a question worth asking.

Rather than taking this gloomy view, I will argue that we can, using conditional anthropomorphism, begin to understand what the lion is saying, and what it might be like to be a bat, or an equine. If we want to understand equines and have them learn about our world and do things for us, the first thing we need to do is to know 'where they are coming from', that is make an effort to begin to understand their world. However, this does not mean that we must open the stable door and let them all gallop off into the sunset in order for them to have lives of quality. It rather means we must recognize our similarities, but mould our approach with an awareness of species differences. In this way both the humans and equines will have a happy, healthy life together.

There is a growing group of alternative therapists who maintain they can 'whisper' or 'talk' to horses, or dogs, and that the animal will tell them their problems. There may be people with the special gift of being able to tune in more readily to another's state, however this is done. What detracts greatly from this approach is the persistence of the practitioners in assuming that these animals use only human concepts and ideas of time and space to explain how they feel. The other problem is that the practitioner tells us that the animal has diagnosed his own disease when, if a human were suffering from it, they would generally not be able to! Often an explanation for the practitioner's comments (which, nevertheless, may be helpful to the caretaker) is their ability to observe well, and react to their observations (even though they may not be doing this consciously), as well as their medical/veterinary knowledge. I am not suggesting that these people are con merchants (although there may be some of those among them) because they often sincerely believe that they can talk spiritually to horses, and indeed their therapy can have beneficial effects (for whatever reason). What I am suggesting is that their attribution of western European concepts and ideas to equines is often out of place, and they are missing the more interesting questions of how and where the equines' perception and interpretation of the world is different from ours.

Example
An alternative therapist was asked to look at Druimghigha Aisha Evans, a bright healthy fit little mare, standing in the barn. She is asked to tell us what the horse was saying to her and she said that the horse was healthy, happy and well. This was not too difficult to see by reading visual signs. She was then asked to give the age of the horse and she replied that the horse said she was ten years old. In fact the horse was eighteen years old but a very active athletic individual, and observation might have indicated that she was around ten. But, more importantly, why would the horse know about years in our sense, and about age? She may have a concept of time (see Chapter 8), but it is unlikely that she would divide it into twelve-month years, or know the number of years she has been alive!

The more interesting question is that she may have some other way of assessing time, and it would be exciting to know what this is. If only those people who 'talk to animals' really *could* talk to them, we would be able to find out. Oh, for my childhood hero, Dr. Dolittle!

What we must do is constantly criticize our own beliefs and review our statements to see if there is not a simpler explanation for what appears to require complex mental abilities. a couple of examples may illustrate this.

Example
Many owners talk about their horse being 'jealous' when they pay attention to another. Jealousy denotes a feeling felt when there is a redistribution of affection and intimacy from one individual to another. This involves an awareness of self, and that you have not received what is considered your 'just desserts'. We really do not know if the equine is feeling this.

A simpler explanation is that he would like the attention or food that is being given to another, so attacks the other, or the dispenser, in order to try and obtain those rewards. We do not know what is going on in the horse's head, but this simpler explanation for the behaviour – to obtain the reward – cannot be disregarded in favour of one that implies self-awareness and justice without serious study, not just 'opinions'. So far this has not been done.

One way of explaining equines' behaviour which avoids having to attribute mental lives to them is to say that it is 'instinctive'. Instincts are genetically pre-programmed behaviours which are usually inflexible and involuntary, consequently they do not require a mind, or making choices or having intentions, voluntary actions, pursuits of goals, memories or even sometimes having feelings. Instinct, is often used to explain behaviour that is otherwise difficult to explain: 'Oh well, it's instinct' or 'it's the breed [that is genetic or instinctive] what do you expect?' In this way it is used to excuse the human handler, caretaker or teacher from any blame for the behaviour of the equine.

The problem with this easy cop-out is that it explains nothing, because if we are going to use 'instinct' as an explanation, we need to find out how this genetically pre-programmed instinctive behaviour works. The causes of this inflexible type of behaviour must be discovered in the brain, and how and why it is *not* affected by environmental influences. We need to know how all these 'genetic traces' are made and how they are separated from learnt behaviour. So far no one has looked in any detail at this, but the vague term 'instinct' is still used to explain much of equine behaviour (see page 107)!

This is not to say that we do not all have **instinctive tendencies** to behave in certain ways. Our body/mind and behaviour is the result of the mixing together of certain inherited traits and the experiences during our lifetimes: **nature and nurture.**

Example

If either a young human or horse who has the genes to be big and strong are given insufficient food when they are young, they will be smaller and weedier than if they were fed well. Equally, if neither human nor horse are given enough to do and problems to solve when they are young, they will not be able to develop their minds to the extent they could be developed. Both may end up with a small and wizened body *and* an undeveloped mind. Today, the bodily needs of equines are often well understood and, if anything, many young equines are overfed, but their mental needs have often been grossly overlooked, resulting in large bodies and wizened minds. Luckily, however, although it often is more difficult to develop new skills of either body or mind when older, it still is possible with good teaching and appropriate experiences, to further the development of the mind of the adult.

In the developing countries, working donkeys may have the opposite development. They have had insufficient food and end up with relatively small and wizened bodies but, in order to survive, they have had to overcome a great number of mind problems and acquire much information about the world, for example where to find food, how to get hold of it, how to eat it, how to avoid overwork and so on. Thus, they end up sometimes with well-developed minds in small, wizened bodies.

So what happens to the genetic tendencies for either the body or the mind? The whole physical/mental being is the result of the genetic make-up but also the environment in which the individual grows up and lives. What, how, when and where these tendencies develop is moulded by the environment.

Example
A baby has an instinctive tendency to walk on two legs, a foal to get up and walk on four, but when where and how this is done is the result of the individuals' experiences, no two of the same species will ever do it identically.

Humans and equines learn, and they learn to do things voluntarily, that is (as we all know to our cost) our equines can do, or not do, what we ask; they can decide. Thus, learning is not some curious reflex-type affair over which the individual has no control and the performance of which occurs without any choice. Equines, like humans when they learn to perform voluntary acts, have to have mental events: make decisions and choices, remember, assess and predict outcomes, often they also have to have an idea of cause and effect. Equines, like humans, acquire information all the time; they learn. As a result we must be aware that they, like humans, have mental/cognitive or intellectual needs: 'mind needs', that is a need to have experiences, acquire knowledge and solve problems through their lives. If these mind needs are not catered for, both humans and equines develop abnormal behaviours, one of the easiest to recognize is stereotypes (a repeated activity constant in form).

Example
Stereotypes were found and studied first in one-year-old babies who were isolated from humans for much of their lives and strapped to high chairs. They were unable to explore, move around and learn from the world, they had little social contact with others. They developed stereotypic head tossing and nodding which were performed more and more as

time went on. As they grew up, the children found it difficult to learn new things or to integrate socially with other humans.

Think then of the conventional way of allowing a young colt destined to race to grow up. He lives with his mother, often isolated from the rest of the group for the first few months of his life. He has no experience or contact with others but his mother, and little experience of the world since he lives in one small field. He then suffers severe trauma as he is separated from his mother, the only other equine he has known, at 4–6 months old. He is then kept shut up in a stable for all but about one hour a day. He is isolated from others and unable to explore and learn about the world, or move much. He has no unsupervised contact with other equines, and little contact with any other living being. He starts crib-biting his box in order to give himself something to do, and to escape from the difficult world in which he has been placed. As time goes on, he spends more and more time crib-biting and it becomes more complex; he sucks in air and swallows it while biting something to support his head, and contracts his neck muscles. Gradually this crib-biting 'generalizes', that is it is performed in almost any situation when things become too exciting, too dull, too frightening, or when he expects either good or bad things to happen. Now he has what has been called a 'vice'. His value and his believed usefulness will be reduced. (This is a real case.)

Humans and equines (and other mammals) develop stereotypes for very similar reasons. We know the function and the cause of stereotypes in all mammal species today as a result of studying them in human children. Although there are probably four research projects a year financed (often by charity money) to study stereotypes in equines, this is really not a justified expense. We know why they are caused and how to prevent them arising – if we want to – the problem is we really do not want to change our ways of looking after horses very often, so we continue to try and justify it by concluding that a piece of research is 'inconclusive'!

On the other hand we must not lose sight of how adaptable equines and humans are. They both can live in an enormous range of ecosystems, and can adapt to changes remarkably well.

Examples

1. Tropical zebras can adapt to freezing climates in European zoos and to being kept in restricted and semi-solitary environments. They grow long winter coats, and not all of them show evidence of suffering mentally (distress) in the zoo.

2. Thoroughbred horses imported to run races in Namibia from temperate Europe have adapted to life in the Namibian desert. They cope with the very high temperatures, they have learnt how to find food and water in the desert and breed there.

3. Donkeys, although predominantly grazers, can adapt to live on rubbish tips, eating and remaining healthy by consuming cardboard, fruit skins and other organic waste (Figure 1.1).

Fig. 1.1   Donkey on the rubbish tip in Lamu, Kenya, living on cardboard and odds and ends of organic waste.

Perhaps the most dramatic testament to equine adaptability is their ability to survive and sometimes even breed when kept in conditions where their physical, emotional, social and cognitive (mental) needs are very far from fulfilled in many domestic environments where they are:

1. weaned from their mothers;

2. kept isolated from others;
3. restricted in their movement to a solitary prison (stable);
4. restricted in their access to appropriate food;
5. often in environments where there is little for them to do most of the time;
6. made to travel in motor vehicles, in aeroplanes, in ships;
7. made to run races, work on the land, jump jumps, gallop distances, charge into war, pull vehicles, carry people for great distances and for long periods even when there is little to eat or drink.

It is quite remarkable how they manage often to remain healthy and sometimes even happy; a great testament to their adaptability, just like that of the humans by whom they are kept!

But, although many of them are able to cope with such extremes in life style, some do not. To ensure that they can all have a life of quality, whatever we ask them to do, we need to understand much more about what it is like to be an equine.

SUMMARY TO DATE

To summarize so far. In order to give equines better lives and understand them better, we can start with six basic premises which apply to both humans and equines.

1. They have interrelated mind/bodies and brains, as far as we know.
2. They are 'sentient', that is they feel and 'mind' about things. They have subjective experiences.
3. They have instinctive tendencies to behave in various ways, but how, what, when, why and where they do these things depends on their lifetime experiences, that is, what they have learnt.
4. They learn, they can perform voluntary acts and consequently have mental events.
5. They are very adaptable.
6. If we want to know equines better, we need to understand the world in which they live, and how similar or different it may be from ours.

➔

By putting together information from our own critically assessed subjective experiences and information from a more objective approach, that is from empirical and scientific studies, we may be able to learn more about 'what it is to be an equine'. This approach is called 'conditional anthropomorphism'. It can help to improve our lives together, even if there are many questions left to answer.

THE BODY'S LANDSCAPE

Because of the interrelationship between bodies and minds, the body's landscape has an important role to play in the human's or horse's world view. Every aspect of an individual will affect who they are. So, here, we will point out some similarities and differences between human and equine bodies, some of which may be obvious, but the effects of which on their behaviour and minds may not have been carefully considered.

The first point of similarity to re-emphasize, because it is often forgotten, is that humans and equines are all mammals. First then let us define a mammal, what characteristics do they all have in common, and how do they differ from other vertebrate species.

Potted characteristics of mammals
(after Young 1950 and Grove & Newell 1942)
1. Warm-blooded so able to survive in a range of temperatures, and consequently have environmental 'freedom'.
2. Have to have appropriate behaviour to disallow large changes in the body temperature. To achieve this, sense organs and a central nervous system have evolved which encourage flexibility and 'enterprise' in adapting to different environments.
3. Waterproofed skin which includes sweat glands and sebaceous glands.
4. Heart with four chambers.
5. Lower jaw with teeth.

6. Secondary palate to allow breathing while eating.
7. Larynx (for sound production) and epiglottis (shuts or opens canals to either the lungs or stomach) are always present.
8. Always have similar internal skeletons consisting of long bones, ribs, skull, backbone, and pelvis and pectoral (scapular) girdles.
9. Show care of the young, produce milk and are active and exploratory, highly perceptive and mobile with large well-developed fore and hind brains.

A comparison of the physical characteristics of humans and equines and their adaptability

Homo sapiens (humans) are primates. Primates are predominantly tree-living terrestrial mammals whose evolutionary ancestry is partially known. Humans are, according to DNA profiles, very closely related to the great apes, particularly the chimpanzee; however there are no known cases of inter-breeding to date! Primates branched off from their rodent and carnivore ancestors some 70 million years ago, although *Homo* – the human family – branched off from apes only 2–3 million years ago. Their teeth are specialized for an omnivorous diet, and people have argued (although this is presently disputed, e.g. Leakey 1981) that the rotation of the eyes to the front of the skull, and the opposable thumb led to their specialism in manipulating the world, and tool making. This in turn, so it is argued, gave rise to greater brain development, and cognitive (mental) skills, including in particular the evolution of human language.

Hoofed mammals (ungulates) are herbivores (plant eaters) that separated from the common ancestral stock some 80 million years ago. Equines are descended from *Hydracotherium*, a four-toed forest-living animal that lived at the beginning of the Eocene, about 50 million years ago. The history of equines showing the specialization of their legs is one of the classic evolutionary stories.

The *Equidae*, the horse family, are true ungulates. Ungulates (hoofed mammals) are a very diverse group of large terrestrial herbivores and include all the horses, pigs, camels, cattle, antelopes and deer. The *Equidae* belong to a relatively small group, the odd-toed ungulates: the perissodactyls. These include the tapir and the rhinoceros (both groups now under threat of extinction). We have studied the Black rhino (*Diceros bicornis*) to look at behavioural similarities and differences from the *Equi*. Despite their apparently very different-looking

Fig. I.2 A rare relative of equines. Rhinos have many behavioural and bodily characteristics similar to equines. Here our son, Jake, handles a young black rhino who was captive bred.

bodies much of their behaviour is surprisingly horse-like. Thus, interestingly, the body classification currently used (which has been based mainly on the similarities of skeletal structures) also reflects similarities of behaviour, for example in their gaits and their communication. Rhinos lie down to roll like equines (which the split-toed ungulates, the artiodactyls, do not). They have mobile ears and no horns on the tops of their heads so their ears are very conspicuous and have evolved elaborate movements to communicate with others, unlike many other ungulates. (Figure I.2.) Also like equines, rhinos snort when surprised or frightened; many other ungulates do not (Randle & Worthington 2001).

The equine family includes the zebras — three species of which are still extant: *Equus burchell* (plains or Burchell's zebra), *E. zebra* (mountain zebra), *E. grevyi* (Grevy's zebra) — and the wild asses: *E. africanus*, a few of which are still

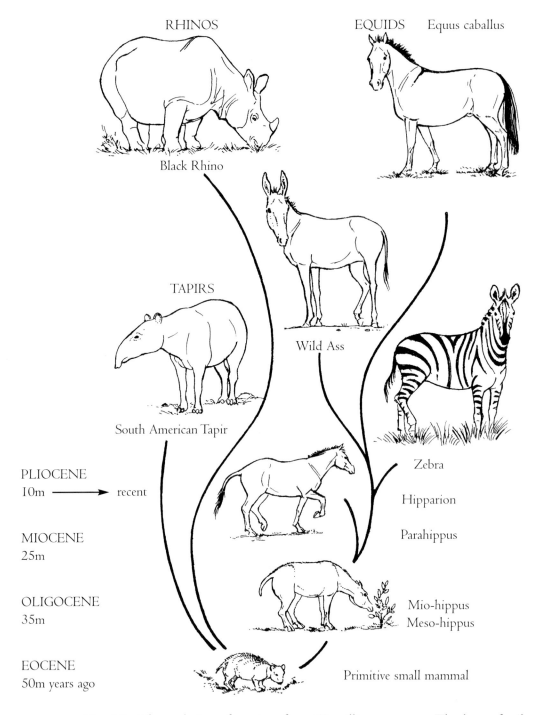

Fig. I.3 The evolution of equines from 50 million years ago. The horse family (*Equidae*) belongs to a small group of odd-toed ungulates: the perissodactyls.

alive. The domesticated offspring of the wild ass is the donkey, the most numerous working non-human animal in the world today.

Equus caballus, the horse, it is thought originated in the European steppes and spread to grasslands throughout the world (Figure 1.3). These steppe horses are represented today by a few Przewalski's horses which have been bred from a very small gene pool from the last truly wild Przewalski's horses which were caught and placed in zoos at the end of the nineteenth century. This zoo breeding has been a success, and they have been brought back from the brink of extinction to the point where semi-wild herds are being re-established in Russia, and recently France. The domestic horse, from the Shetland to the Shire, is generally considered to be the descendant of the wild-roaming Przewalski's horse, *Equus caballus*. The variation in size, build and colour is partly the result of selection by humans over the last, approximately, 7,000 years, and partly the result of the different places they were living in and the lives they led. The Exmoor pony is said to be the oldest indigenous equine in Britain and one of the closest to the Przewalski's horse, but its wild uninterrupted life on the moor now hardly exists; it has been turned into a show pony.

The members of the genus *Equus* are closely related (like the apes to which man belongs). In fact, they even interbreed, giving rise to mules, hinnies and zebroids. However, because the offspring of these unions are not generally fertile, they are still considered separate species. Recently, however, some of these hybrids have produced young, so this idea is also being disputed.

Mammalian evolutionary success has often been the result of their ability to adapt to a variety of environments. There are perhaps three ways in which the adaptability of a species can be enhanced.

1. By **manipulating** the world to fulfil your own needs ensuring that it is warm enough and there are other resources such as food, water, shelter and so on. Human primates predominantly do this.
2. By being able to **physically adapt to great changes** in temperature and availability of resources by such strategies as hibernation (which slows the metabolic rate reducing the need for resources) or by insulation, such as putting on fat, or growing winter hair for adaptation to cold, or losing hair,

sweating and panting to adapt to heat stress. Equines do all of these (except hibernate) while humans share mainly the abilities to pant and sweat.

3. By **learning about the world**, finding and remembering where resources are (or might be) as a result of becoming good 'field naturalists', and by acquiring information from others, becoming good 'natural psychologists' (see Chapters 5 and 6). Both equines and humans have a tendency to do this; whether they do it well depends on their lifetime experiences.

Species that are highly adaptable usually combine all three of these methods, although they are often better at one than another. For example, primates were not originally found all over the world. They were restricted to the more tropical areas where the first real humans – *Homo sapiens* – and his ancestors arose. But with the development of Neanderthal man, human primates began to seriously manipulate the world, and were able, as a result, to invade other more difficult climatic zones.

Some populations became good field naturalists (learning a great deal about the natural world they lived in in order to survive), such as the Bushmen in Southern Africa, or the Aborigines in Australia who, like zebras, brumbys and mustangs can survive in the deserts by having **knowledge about the environment** rather than **by changing it**. Modern humans with their heating and cooling systems, availability of all foods throughout the year and so on, have followed the road of **manipulating the environment, that is creating their own, rather than adapting to the existing one.**

Before humans appeared in the fossil record, equines were found all over the tropical and temperate world, except Australasia. This wide distribution is evidence of their adaptability, and one reason why some were domesticated. That the domesticated equines have retained this adaptability is illustrated by the rapidity with which they establish feral populations even in difficult locations (see page 47, Example 2).

Perhaps the most dramatic testament to equines' adaptability is their ability to survive, and even breed, when kept by humans in conditions where their physical, emotional, social and intellectual needs are far from fulfilled (Kiley-Worthington 1987, 1990, 1999).

As with the chicken and the egg, the body and the mind arose together to allow adaptations to different niches.

The skeleton and muscularisation

Although human and equine bodies are different in size and shape, nevertheless, they are **fundamentally** and **anatomically similar**. The same bones are recognizable in every mammal: a 'humerus' is identifiable as a humerus whether it is one from a sheep, an elephant, a human or a mouse. But also, each species has its own slightly different characteristics, (for example the femur of a horse is longer, larger and has more solid, rounded protuberances than that of a human). Figure 1.4 shows the structure of the skeletons of these two species groups, and identifies some homologous bones.

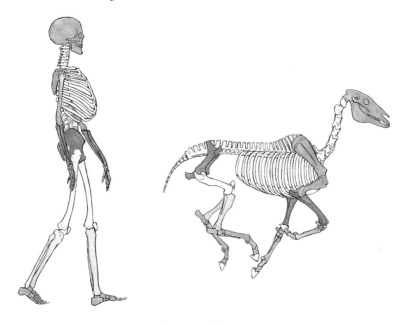

Fig. 1.4   The skeletal similarities of man and horse.

This structural similarity is also demonstrated in the muscles and internal organs. Differences relate to their ecology, for example humans manipulate the world largely by using their hands; consequently they have retained a relatively primitive type of limb with five digits (a structure recognizably similar to a frog's foot) but with considerable muscular specialization. Equines are not world manipulators, although they can investigate and move objects with the ten pairs of muscles in their almost prehensile noses (Kiley-Worthington 1969). They are greatly specialized 'perceivers of the world', look at the complexity of the muscularisation and innervation of their ears, allowing each ear independent movement in almost any direction (see Figure 1.5). Equines are also movement specialists, their body, limbs, muscles and cardiovascular system reflect this. Humans are talkers, the muscularisation and innervation of the larynx, glottis and pharynx reflect this. Equines will never learn to talk verbally as we do; they do not have the physical body equipment. It would be like asking a human to lift a tree trunk with his nose (something elephants can do with their trunk and tusks) or to run at 30 km (19 mls) an hour for 30 km (19mls) or 10 km (6 mls) an hour for 160 km (100 mls) as some horses can.

Fig. 1.5 The muscles of the equine head. There are thirteen pairs for each ear, ten pairs for the nostrils, lips and mouth. A great many movements are possible for visual messages. There is an equivalence here to the number of muscles we humans have controlling the larynx, mouth and tongue, so we can talk.

Size

The donkeys are the smallest of the equine family, varying in weight from around 150 kg to 300 kg (330–660 lb), and in height from 1 m to 1.5 m (39–59 in) zebras are slightly heavier, and horses vary in height and weight even more than humans, ranging from around 150 kg to 2,000 kg (330–4,400 lb) in the case of the large shires, and from 1 m to 1.9 m (39–75 in) at the withers.

One of the most common domestic horse sizes is around 500 kg (1,100 lb) and 1.5 m (59 in) at the withers.

Horses can pull something 4–5 times their weight for long distances, whereas the humans can pull something only 2–3 times their weight.

We do not know if horses perceive size very differently from us but relative size, weight and strength must have some bearing on the species and individual's world view.

The following table summarizes some of these body comparisons.

A COMPARISON OF HUMAN AND EQUINE BODIES (similarities are shown by the dotted lines)		
	Human	Equine
Size	Adult from 50 kg to 100 kg (110–220 lb).	Adult from 150 kg to 2,000 kg (330–4,400 lb).
Shape	Two legs and upright. Specialised climbers and manipulators.	Four legs which are long and specialized for speed and distance.
Sexual differences	Considerable. Secondary sex characters pronounced.	Relatively small differences between sexes. Secondary sex characters small.
Genitals	Male: external penis and testicles.. Female: vulva	
Teats	Two... Greatly enlarged at puberty.	Enlarge a little at puberty.
Limbs:	Muscular power in the limbs. anterior limbs have manipulative fingers and opposable thumb. Hind limbs specialized for bipedal walking.	Limbs elongated. Muscular power in the body. Anterior limbs carry most weight but all limbs specialized for speed and endurance.
Neck	Short.	Long, helps with balance and feeding. →

Head	Round, small, flat in front.	Long, broader at the top and tapering to the nose.
Tail	None	Long with long hair, used for reducing skin irritation and for communication.
Feet	Flat and primitive. Five divisions. Skin covered.	Hard hooves, specialized for movement. Large weight carried on small surface area.
	Develop hard soles when appropriate	
Teeth	Two sets during life	
	Cease growing when adult.	Continue growing through-out life.
Skin	0.5–2 mm thick.	0.5–4 mm thick.
	Well supplied with sweat and oil glands	
Hair	All over body. Longer hair on head, under arms and on genitals.	A thicker growth all over body, which thickens in cold weather. Longer hair along neck and on tail.
	Different colours in subspecies and individuals	
Infant develop-ment	At birth not well developed. Take 1–2 years to walk.	Precocial (well developed) at birth. Take 1–4 hrs to walk.

The shape of the body

This is markedly different in the two species groups. From the bipedal, upright and relatively small structure of the human, to the long, quadrupedal equine. The human primate walks on the two hind legs, freeing the front legs – the arms and hands – for other things, particularly feeding. Unlike equines, humans can clamber about in the third dimension. The body proportions of both species can be pleasing, at least to other human primates! Many humans and equines, particularly domestic horses, are distinguished by their grace and symmetry of proportions. Equines have been admired and coveted by humans for these characteristics, as well as their usefulness, throughout history.

There is no very obvious overall body difference between the sexes in equines. Horse and donkey stallions are slightly bigger and heavier than the mares of the same race, have thicker necks and canine teeth, but the sexes of all the equines are difficult to tell apart at any distance. Humans show more sexual dimorphism, the males, again, are bigger, with facial hair and often more body hair than females, a deeper voice and a more muscular body with broader shoulders and narrower hips. Females are generally smaller, with a somewhat different-shaped body: narrower shoulders, wider hips and large teats even when not lactating.

Since individual equines stay in the same family groups for long periods, they are very well known to each other, as in monogamous pairs (e.g. swans) consequently there may be no need for the male and female to be very obviously differentiated. The great sexual dimorphism displayed by humans may indicate the males' promiscuity rather than monogamy; although monogamy is a cultural development in some societies (see Chapter 6).

Similarities and differences between humans and equines in how the body works

There are very obvious similarities in the physiology (the way the body works) in mammals. They all have the same organs: brains, lungs, heart, spleen, digestive tract, kidneys and so on, which function similarly, to a point where one species' organs, for example the heart, can sometimes be inserted into another species when the heart has been extracted (e.g. pig into human). The way nerves and muscles work and their basic structures are the same. Almost exactly the same hormones are produced by all mammals, although the amount produced varies. Again this similarity is used to harvest some hormones for human use (e.g. progesterone from pregnant mares for human use; there are large intensive farms in the US supplying the market by taking urine from pregnant mares fitted with catheters). Superimposed on these overall similarities in how the organs work, there are some differences. We will briefly examine these.

Digestion

The differences in the anatomy of the alimentary canal, the eating habits and resulting knowledge of the world between these species groups, is discussed in Chapter 2. It is noteworthy that they all produce the same enzymes, although more of one or another depending on what they eat. Both primates and equines have a range of bacteria in the gut to aid digestion of various components. In particular, the large herbivores have numerous cellulose-digesting bacteria. The host then digests the bodies of the bacteria, thus converting the indigestible cellulose into easily digestible proteins and carbohydrates. Without this symbiotic association, equines are unable to live healthy lives. These bacteria are acquired by the foal from eating fresh, warm faeces usually from the mother. A shortage of minerals, or indigestion, a change of diet, and other forms of physiological stress, can also cause adult horses to eat another's fresh faeces (coprophagia). But persistent eating by adult horses of another's, or their own, faeces, is an abnormal behaviour practised by animals kept in inappropriate environments (Kiley-Worthington 1998).

Humans also have symbiotic relations with gut bacteria, but they are less able to digest cellulose, and consequently unable to live on the high cellulose diets that equines thrive on, although they can live healthy, long lives as vegetarians.

Equines cannot vomit so they are vulnerable to poisoning and digestive problems that are rare in humans who vomit easily when inappropriate food is eaten (see pages 84–88).

Equines produce little bile (used for the breaking down of fats) but, nevertheless, they seem able to digest some fats although their natural diets are normally relatively low in them.

Temperature control and dehydration

Mammals have to keep their blood temperature within limits (between approximately 30–40 °C). They keep it warm with fat, hair, clothing and exercise; they cool it by harnessing the latent heat of evaporation of water from the body surface. How they do this varies somewhat between mammals, but equines and humans are similar in relying on sweating through glands distributed over the majority of the body surface to reduce their body temperature.

If there is a significant loss of body water, there is a risk of dehydration. This can cause collapse and death. Experience in living in hot dry areas will reduce the risk of dehydration for these species since, given time, both the human and equine bodies are able to adapt, up to a point.

Equines can adapt to large temperature changes, for example feral horses in the very hot Namibian desert (temperatures over 50 °C), or in the Canadian winters where the temperatures can drop to below −50 °C. To do this, they need to have the opportunities to make behavioural adjustments, e.g. find and choose sheltered spots or cool places (see Chapter 5).

Movement and Exercise

Equines are specialist movers and can run fast and far. They do this, in part, by having a long, well-developed and well-packed intestine, a small stomach (much smaller than cattle for example), an extraordinarily well-organized and efficient cardiovascular system, with a large heart and lungs well supplied with blood, and the equine spleen which is able to supply an instantaneous supply of red blood cells to carry oxygen around.

The bodies of both equines and humans can also adapt to living at high altitudes with little oxygen by increasing the lung capacity, or by increasing the efficiency of oxygen absorption by the red blood cells.

If oxygen is in short supply (i.e. it is being used more quickly than it can be absorbed), then equines can switch to anaerobic respiration which allows specialized parts of muscles to continue to contract using stored products in the muscles for energy. These types of muscles are generally used for short fast runs, i.e. sprints (Morel and Davis 1993). Humans can also use anaerobic respiration, but they use it less efficiently and cannot go on as long, although, as in equines, different individuals appear to have different capacities for anaerobic respiration. This individual variation in adaptability is the result of both experience and genetic tendencies (see Kiley-Worthington 2004).

Equines, particularly domestic horses, are specialists at being able to tolerate severe prolonged exercise without showing any physical signs of distress. This does seem to be something that has been selected for by humans over their 7,000 years of domestication. The domestic racehorse can run faster than any wild equine (sprinters can reach 56 km [35 mls] an hour), and can go further (up to 175 km [110 mls] a day) than the wild equines, particularly zebras.

Having said this, however, we must be cautious as, to date, those who know how to train horses to be fit for such distances have never trained a zebra.

Over the last two decades a great deal of information on equine exercise physiology has been gathered, much of this learnt from human exercise physiology. The strategies to achieve different sorts of fitness have also been developed from those of humans. The result has been that the average speeds in long-distance competitions have increased dramatically. Over distances of 160 km (100 mls) a day winning speeds have increased from an average of 10 km (6 mls) an hour to 18 km (11 mls) an hour (Endurance Horse & Pony Society and Federation Equestre Internationale records). Interestingly, though, the speeds at which flat race and steeplechase horses complete their shorter distances (up to 5 km [3 mls]) have not improved over the same period. It has been argued that this is because the speeds the horses reach are as high as they can be, given the horses' particular morphology and physiology (Budiansky 1996). This seems unlikely since the human running speed records continue to improve. It may be that it is as high at it can be with *the current practices in racehorse husbandry and training* which have changed very little over the years. It is doubtful that they are the most suitable (e.g. Kiley-Worthington 1998). Whether or not equines or humans are faster over rough hilly ground, such as over the North England fells, is often debated. The Arab Horse Society marathon (36 km [23 mls]) and the Man versus Horse race in Wales (35 km [22 mls] over the Welsh mountains) both originated because a bet was waged that a human could finish the distance faster than a horse. The results are that the horse, carrying a rider, finishes the distance at an average speed of around 29 kph (18 mph), in 1 hr 30 min, the runner in no less than 2 hr on relatively flat terrain. Over the erratic, tough, wet Welsh hills, so far the horse and rider have won everytime, except in 2004 when Shemal was not there, and the runner won by a narrow margin.

Perception of space and distance by equines
This is likely to be different in equines from that of humans as a result of the equines' abilities to move further faster and more easily than us. But perception of space and distance varies greatly, even within one person, as illustrated by the following example.

Example
Most of us have had injured legs at one time or another, and found how large the garden
was, which, when we could move normally, we found far too small.

Moving across a valley may be perceived as a great distance for a human, whereas
a horse, who can cover the distance in much less time, may find it close. Forty
kilometres (twenty-four miles) is a three-hour trot for a reasonably healthy horse
but, for a healthy human, it is a day's march.

How tired an individual gets will also affect their conception of space and
distance. For example, a tired but hungry horse (assessed from physiological
criteria) when presented with desired food several yards away, will behave like a
tired human in similar circumstances: looking at the food, looking away, and
finally walking towards it, sometimes stopping in between, rather than rushing
at it as he would if not tired but hungry.

Thus the perception of space and distance changes with the species, the
individual and how the individual is feeling. For healthy, fit horses, we are fairly
safe in assuming that distance to them appears to be less than to smaller humans
who do not move so fast or so far. Consequently, if distances are smaller, then
space, to them, must be larger. They may feel they are near another individual
and still part of the group, when for us, it would appear they are quite separate.
They may feel crowded and cramped when we would not, they may feel restricted even when in smallish paddocks, when we would not. A lot of this, however,
will depend on the past experience of an individual. I have heard tell of army
horses who, normally kept in stalls in London, when taken on their summer
holidays and put out to grass for a couple of weeks, do nothing but stand close
to the hedge, trying, apparently, to regain the security of their restricting walls
in, what to them, is a vast uncharted territory. This is of course a behavioural
pathology, indicating that the animal is psychologically sick and not an
argument for keeping horses in restricted places all the time, but it does
illustrate the extraordinary adaptability of equines.

Gaits
Humans normally use only two different gaits: the walk and the run,
although they can learn others such as skipping or hopping on one foot.

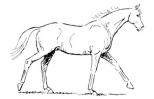

Fig. 1.6   Three different phases of the three-beat canter. The left lead: 1) following the moment of suspension, the outside (right) hind leg meets the ground first; 2) the inside (left) hind and outside (right) fore come down together; 3) the inside (left) fore comes to the ground prior to the moment of suspension and the sequence starting again.

Equines generally have four gaits: a four-beat walk, a diagonal paired (two-beat) trot, a three-beat canter (Figure 1.6) and a four-beat gallop. They can also learn, and some have been selected for, one gait (e.g. Icelandic ponies, four-beat all-purpose gait: the tölt). Others 'pace', a lateral trot, some perform a four-beat canter, and there are various other gaits which 'throw' the legs in different ways. Many of these curious gaits are not genetic, but encouraged by restraints and sometimes painful procedures. For example, pacing in harness-racing trotters is controlled by straps and chains, and the Tennessee Walking Horses have special shoes fitted which cause pain and make them lift their feet to achieve the stylized running walk. Some other gaits are taught, such as collected, short-strided gaits, or the long trot with a suspension, i.e. the passage, the piaffe (trotting on the spot with a slow rhythm), the Spanish walk and trot (an exaggerated lifting of the front legs), flying changes in various rhythms and going sideways etc.

The animal may occasionally perform these gaits naturally in his untutored state – just as human ballet dancers, or break dancers all perform movements that may be done naturally occasionally – but *the individual learns to perform them in a particular way at particular times as a result of being taught by humans.* However, because equines form habits quickly (see page 133), they may also teach themselves to do strange gaits or movements at particular times which may or may not be welcomed by the humans around them. Both equines and humans can learn to dance, sometimes they develop these steps themselves, such as a stallion courting a mare, or a bunch of colts playing, but sometimes they are taught different steps by humans, used by humans to develop various forms of equine performance.

Sex and reproduction

This is controlled in equines, as in all mammals, by the production of a series of hormones which are produced as a result of both external stimuli, such as temperature, length of day, presence of the opposite sex, and internal ones such as maturity, and a healthy being. The pituitary body, a lobe of the brain, has an important role to play in the production of the various hormones. There are many texts on reproduction in equines but it is important to realize that there are many controls on reproduction that are the result of changes in mental states, such as whether or not the opposite sex is present, and whether or not there are affectional bonds between reproducing partners. Successful reproduction is not always the result of mechanistic phenomena.

Fillies first come into season and ovulate at about eighteen months, and can become pregnant soon after this. They come into season in temperate climates every three weeks during the lengthening days, and then less often through the rest of the year. In the tropics, they seem to come into season throughout the year, although zebras show a peak breeding season at the beginning of the rains when food is widely available.

Oestrus is diagnosed in equines mainly by smell, through smell messages (pheromones) particularly in the urine. The urine testing is often denoted by flehmen. This allows for a more thorough investigation of the smell/taste (see Figure 1.8).

Colts are usually able to produce sperm at around a year old, but in feral or wild populations, they are unlikely to be able to have sex until around three years old because older stallions will prevent them from doing so. The males of many species have been shown to have changing levels of testosterone (the male sexual hormone) with seasons and day length through the year. The breeding season when the males' and the females' sexual hormones are highest, corresponds to favourable environmental conditions for the survival of the young after they are born.

Pregnancy lasts eleven months in equines. The mares remain very active and it is often difficult to detect visually until a couple of months before parturition.

The behaviour during reproduction is discussed further in Chapter 6.

The anatomy and physiology of the brain and sensory receptors

Although many scholars and scientists will agree that there are great similarities in the anatomy and physiology of the bodies of human mammals and other mammals, it is in the anatomy and physiology of the central nervous system – the brain – where they believe there are profound differences and, consequently, human infants must be considered and treated differently from other mammals, because, it is argued, they have greater mental potential.

Example
'The neocortex is not primarily or exclusively a device for tool making, bipedal walking, fire using, warfare, hunting, gathering or avoiding savannah predators. None of these postulated functions alone can explain its explosive development in our lineage and *not in other closely related species*.' [My italics.]

Such statements concerning the uniqueness of the human brain are frequently made and rarely examined. It is clear that humans are very skilled at language and manipulation of the world, that is, technology. But, whether this is the *only* type of explosive brain development that has occurred within living systems has not been investigated; it badly needs to be.

The brain is where the information picked up by the sensory receptors is analysed, and is the seat of other mental activities. One of the general beliefs in biology has been that as the collection of nervous tissue called the brain becomes better defined, bigger and more anatomically complex, the more 'intelligent' the species becomes.

Different areas of the brain have different functions to some extent, although it is now understood that it functions much of the time as a whole, and that the functions of certain parts are plastic, that is they can change somewhat. Nevertheless, large differences in the development of the different parts of the brain are still considered to give some indication of the importance of the skills a particular part of the brain is associated with.

Example

The difference in size and development of the olfactory lobes of the dog, horse and human seems to indicate the declining importance of smell from dog to horse to human. (Figure 1.7).

The difference in the development of the forebrain (cerebral cortex, [Figure 1.7]) has been used to define the relative 'intelligence' between species, (as in the quoted example above) but there are problems with this approach as we shall point out (see also Intelligence, on pages 108–22).

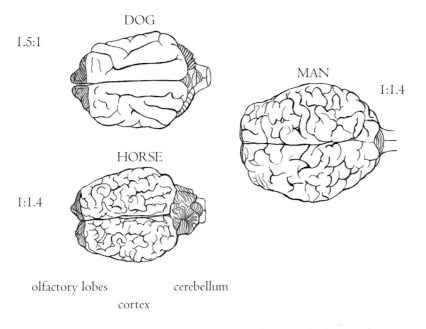

DOG

1.5:1

MAN

1:1.4

HORSE

1:1.4

olfactory lobes   cerebellum

cortex

Fig. 1.7 The dorsal view of the brains of a dog, a horse and a human for comparison. The numbers refer to the scale (the dog's brain is enlarged by 50%, the others reduced by almost half). Note the difference in the development of the olfactory lobes (red) and the cerebellum (yellow) which deals with balance and movement. The forebrain or cerebral cortex is strikingly differently developed in these three, with few convolutions in the dog's brain, but as many in that of the horse as in the human's. It is this part of the brain which is usually equated with intelligence and general mental development.

The size of the brain

Equines, although they have brains that are not much smaller than an adult human's, with a very well-developed and convoluted cerebral cortex (Figure 1.7) are not considered as cognitively able as humans because they have a large body and it is generally believed that the larger the body, the more nervous tissue is required just to service the body, consequently the bigger the brain. It is not clear why this must be the case, since nerve fibres from individual muscle cells, for example, join together before feeding into the brain. Thus, the presence of more body cells does *not* necessarily mean that there must be more brain cells, since every body cell does not have an individual brain cell representing it.

The problem concerning the relationship between the body and brain size has been much investigated but is still debated.

Example

Some people considered to be very intelligent have been found to have rather small brains with not very many cell layers. It is generally believed that there is often a great deal of spare tissue in the brain which is not used by most individuals. In addition, smaller people do not appear to have smaller brains.

The brain/body-weight ratio was considered to relate to 'intelligence', but when this was calculated, rather than humans coming out ahead, it was the tree shrew that topped the list! This approach was subsequently dropped. Instead the attention was shifted to the ratio of the body-weight to the brain volume where humans do come out on top – just – with elephants a very close second (Jerison 1973).

Another idea is that it is the size of the surface area which controls 'higher cognitive activity', that is 'intelligence'. This can be assessed by looking at the number of convolutions in the forebrain, in particular. Figure 1.7 obviously shows the difference: there are relatively few convolutions in the dog's forebrain, but a large number in the forebrain of the horse and the human.

Perhaps, rather than the size of the whole, or even bits, of the brain being the focus for assessing different species or individual mental abilities, *it is the degree to which each piece is used that is important.* How we measure this has yet to be worked out.

Sensory information

A species world view will also be controlled by its sensory receptors, what it can taste, smell, feel, hear and see, or any other sensations it can receive. We will discuss what we know of each of these for equines contrasted to humans.

Taste The taste buds, which are distributed over the tongue function in much the same way as they do in humans (Kiley-Worthington 1998). Equines are particularly cautious of unfamiliar tastes. We do not know much about taste in equines but what we do know and its effect on behaviour is discussed more fully in the next chapter. Its role for communication is discussed in Chapter 7.

Recently there has been much discussion about the role of the varonasal gland which is at the back of the mouth (e.g. Watson 1999). Some maintain it allows a more careful assessment of a smell uniting it to other mental events (memories and experiences).

Smell Smells are picked up and sent to the olfactory analysers in the brain in the same way by all mammals. How this happens is well known (see e.g. Kiley-Worthington 1987). However, the role of smells in the life of different species has been less considered. Smells appear to be much more important to equines than to humans, who if they cannot smell are hardly considered handicapped. Their use by equines is further discussed in relation to communication (see Chapter 7), but some of the ways in which they are used by equines are outlined here.

In the first place it is important to understand that smells to equines will not necessarily be identified with a particular object, although they may be, rather they may conjour up a particular memory or moment, and consequently it will be this and the circumstances around it that will be associated with a particular smell. In fact we are able to do this too as is well known, although more usually when presented with a particular smell, the human approach is immediately to try to identify it rather than to let the imagination and memory soar. Try these exercises to help you appreciate the different way in which equines may be perceiving the world.

Fig. 1.8 Flehmen. This lifting of the upper lip, head and neck, allows the smell/taste in solution to run down to the vomeronasal gland at the base of the pituitary body for further investigation.

Exercises
SMELLS AND TASTES

1. Try giving different substances to your equines by squeezing some dilute juice into the mouth: lemon, garlic, salt, vinegar, or anything that will not burn him or cause him to have an unpleasant experience. The close relationship between smelling and tasting will become evident, his nose may start to run, and he may flehmen (Figure 1.8). He will also demonstrate his interest, his dislike, or even his delight. Repeat the same substance several times and record what you think his response is. After a while you may have to review how you interpreted it.

2. Try giving equines with different experiences (old and young) new things to eat and see whether or not they will try them and, if they do, how they smell and taste them before they eat.

SMELL

1. In order to try to awaken the perception of smells and their importance, try this exercise. Have a friend collect a bunch of different smelling plants, not necessarily particularly strong smelling, blindfold someone and let them smell the plants, one at a time, and without touching them. Try to get them to say *not* what it is and its name but, rather, what *experiences* that the smell conjures up, and to describe the picture that presents itself. If there is no picture initially, just get them to keep trying and gradually there will be for every smell, a situation, an experience, a moment. This may help you realize how important smells may be to equines. This exercise can be quite fun to do in a group, each person taking a turn to smell and describe, but remember, try not to be affected by the picture

that someone else paints of the smell, an equine will not have an account given to them, they will have to make up their own!

2. Observe how your equine smells you when you approach him. Wear someone else's dirty clothes, or rub some stallion faeces, or a little urine of another equine on you and see how this attracts attention. Do not use synthetic cosmetics for a day or so prior to this experiment or they may mask the smells and if you normally wear them, he may have learnt not to bother to smell you.

Rather than a smell identifying a particular object for equines, individuals may have very different interpretations of the meaning of the smell messages as with the people in exercise 1 above. However, they may also have some general rules attached to the interpretation of smells.

Familiar smells These may be important for the identification of a sense of place, a 'home', or a safe place.

Strange smells These are of two kinds: 1) unfamiliar smells, and 2) familiar smells out of context.

These are discussed more fully in Chapter 7.

Different sexes and smells Although there may be little difference in the importance (or lack of it) of smells to different sexes or ages of humans, we see a great difference in equines. This may be just that stallions show more obvious behaviours associated with smelling than mares tend to. All equines however will be assessing others first by smell: smelling them on the wind, their trails, urine or faeces, before contacting them visually or by touch.

Interesting smells may also take precedence for stallions even when they are frightened and running away from some object.

Examples

1. (From email, Equine Behaviour discussion group, Nov 2000.) A reported incident where a stallion who was running away from a helicopter, but stopped in order to investigate faeces. This behaviour has not been recorded when mares are frightened.

2. When our two adult stallions are brought near each other in the barn, until one of them

urinates or defaecates, they may only acknowledge each other visually and with the odd shout. But once one of them urinates or defaecates, or they even get the smell of this without visually seeing the other horse, they will become agitated and start pawing, defaecating, staring, leaping about and shouting at the other. One behaving like this, will spark the other off to become even more excited, leaping around and kicking out. Here, the smell seems to have the effect of changing the emotional level of the other and causing a spiral of growing excitement.

Smells associated with defaecation and urination These have strong odours bearing messages. The place where equines defaecate is generally chosen, particularly by stallions who defaecate in piles. Equines will investigate their own and others faeces, and presumably gain considerable information concerning the other individual who left them, such as who, when, what sex, age, direction of movement, state of sexual cycle, what they have been eating and so on (see Figure 7.5b).

It is well known that smells (and perhaps tastes) which have been associated with frightening, aggressive, or unpleasant situations will tend to spark off these emotions, or avoidance. Some are also associated with other emotions such as excitement, conflict, frustration, happiness and joy and they can be cues for behavioural changes, but we need more information here.

To summarize, it seems we know little about the smell world that opens up to those who are very 'smell aware'. As a result, the type of world we perceive, and our knowledge, will be very different from a mammal that is smell aware. In one sense we could be considered handicapped. It is possible to improve your own 'smell awareness' and in this way perhaps gain a little more of an idea of the equine world.

Exercises
1. Take a little time daily for a smell exercise. For three minutes concentrate your mind just on the smells around and the images they may conjour up. Start with easy strong smells, such as cooking smells, but then begin to notice the less-strong smells that are around, gradually performing the exercise when there are fewer and fewer strong smells around. You will in this way become much more aware of smells and may be able to tune into the responses of your equines a little better from time to time. Becoming very smell

aware is not always a good thing though, it is surprising how many human smells there are around!

2. Watch the nostrils and breathing of your equines when they enter the stable or the paddock, or a new environment, the twitching of the nose, moving of the lips and nostrils all indicate that smells are being perceived. The nostrils function almost like the ears in the way that they move around to pick up smells.

Tactile sensations: feeling Equines, like humans, are sensitive to being touched all over the body although there are more and less sensitive areas (Kiley-Worthington 1998). They investigate by touch largely like cats, with the vibrissae, the large hairs on their noses which are very well supplied with sensitive nerves, relaying messsages to the brain. It is fashionable to cut these vibrissae off for showing and competition. This must have particularly unpleasant consequences for equines and is an entirely unnecessary practice.

Exercises
TOUCH
1. The importance of weight changes and touching with the hands or the legs is all part of ordinary riding, so a good riding instructor will be able to point out many different things you can do to begin to tune into the individual sensitivity of your mount.
   a) Just sit relaxed on the equine, close your eyes to try to feel his breathing.
   b) Feel, and be aware of, each of his legs as they come to the ground. You should be able to feel exactly where every leg is at any time.
   c) With no reins or rope, even around his neck, try with very slight changes of your leg positions and weight on your behind to ask your mount to move in a particular direction. Practise this and eventually you will be able to do all the normal school movements with the legs or weight changes only. It is wise to start this in an enclosed space of course.

2. The importance of touch to the equine in his everyday life.
   a) Touch the vibrissae with your hand, and then gradually move it away until the equine seems no longer to feel it and does something else. Alternatively, gradually bring your hand, or an object, nearer the nose and the vibrissae and note when he appears to make some slight twitching of the face or mouth, or movement away or towards the hand/object, showing he is feeling it. It may help to have him

blindfolded but, remember, he will have to get used to the blindfold, so do not rush in and expect him to accept it in just a few minutes.

b) Repeat this with other equines, and you can even do something like this with a blindfolded human, how far away from their face and top lip can they 'feel' something?

3. Another exercise is to test each of your equines sensitive touch zones with different brushes, and draw diagrams of these. Make sure that any people handling or grooming them look at the diagrams before they rush in to scrub them with brushes that are too hard, or you will end up, as many stables do, with horses who hate being groomed, and who have to be tied up or they bite and kick the people grooming them!

Hearing/audition The ears of all mammals have a homologous structure and function in the same way, although some animals are able to pick up a greater range of sounds or particular frequencies better than others. The sound waves are picked up by the small bones in the inner ear. These are some of the first bones to ossify and begin to work in the foetus, consequently it is now believed that sounds are picked up by the foetus. A man sang to his pregnant mare and believes that this had an important affect on the foal who, when born, recognized his voice! Try it and see.

The sound is relayed to the labyrinth which is lined with auditory sensitive cells. These react to particular frequencies and activate neurones that take the message to the auditory cortex where the sound is analysed. The auditory cortex has close links to the neocortex, the thinking part. No tests on equine auditory sensitivity have been conducted to date, but they appear to be able to discriminate sounds differing by a semi-tone (tests with key changes and response to melodies, Eco Research Centre), and can hear sounds at least as high and low as humans. They do seem to have more acute hearing over distance, often picking up auditory cues and showing this with orientating responses (involving turning the ears, head and body in the direction, pointing and extending the nostrils twitching the nose and staring with wider-open eyes), when humans cannot.

This ability has been used from time to time by the cavalry, and others in war, and resulted in early warnings and saved lives. It is also useful when you are camping out with equines who will often pick up sounds from intruders before you do yourself, and sometimes before the dogs do too.

Equines, like many other mammals, have also been reported responding to earthquakes before there are any signs humans can pick up. Here it may be that they are picking up vibrations from earth movements.

Equines can move silently, particularly when they think they are being followed or stalked, but when in a safe place, they are remarkably noisy: groaning, sighing, sneezing, breaking wind, chewing, breaking sticks on the ground, making noises with their hooves as they move, and so on.

Exercises
HEARING
1. Acuity of hearing. Arrive at the stables one day before the normal routine feeding time and watch the horses to see when they pick up the sound of others arriving. It will probably be before you do. Warnings of vehicles coming, or other horses, or strange events can often be picked up from the equines' responses of ear pricking, turning to look in the relevant direction and remaining still while listening. Begin to tune into these in your everyday interactions with your equines.

2. Hearing pitch range. Try blowing a dog whistle which is pitched above the normal hearing level of adult humans and see what response you get from different equines, old and young. Infrasound (very low sound) is more difficult to test without specific equipment though.

3. Equines are very sensitive to rhythm.
1. a) Play a metronome to them in the rhythm of one of their gaits (whichever you choose). After only a few days you will be able to make the rhythm slightly faster or slower and they will gradually follow it.
1. b) You can then substitute some music for the metronome with a good beat close to their own rhythm and they will quickly follow the rhythm, even if you find it difficult. They may also syncopate.

Rhythm Equines appear to be particularly sensitive to rhythm, one reason why they perform to music so well. They seem to be able to pick up the rhythms of the gaits of other horses they know when they hear them, and they can certainly learn to respond to different rhythms played on different instruments (Eco Research Centre unpublished experiments). Cariff, and now Shemal and

Oberlix, have been taught to match the rhythm of their gait to the rhythm of the music and change it as the music changes. It is surprising that more use is not made of this ability by people doing dressage to music, quadrilles, dances and displays where usually, rather than letting horses develop their own rhythm to the music, they have been taught to respond to the humans aids reflecting the human riders' idea of the rhythm, which is sometimes not very good!

The use of audition for communication is discussed in Chapter 7.

Exercise
Walk, trot and canter your equine loose in the school, or a round pen and, with a metronome, record the speeds of the different gaits. Then as he walks, start the metronome beating out the trot and it will not be long before he trots, once he has learnt to listen to the metronome of course. Reward him when he does what is required and he will soon be able to do this at any gait. The next phase is to find some music at the appropriate speed for each gait (use the metronome to choose it) and work him to the music. Then you can develop it as you will. Just remember that he may not be 'out of time' rather he may be playing with the rhythm by syncopating, i.e. putting in double beats here and there. It is surprising how much equines can teach us about rhythm and music I have found!

Visual acuity The eyes of all mammals have the same structure and operate in the same way, that is, the light passes through the iris and forms an inverse image on the retina, which is lined by light-sensitive cells. There is a translucent lens in front of the retina and, by changing the curvature of the lens, objects at different distances from the eye can have focused images falling on the retina. The muscles for this change in the curvature of the lens are less well developed in equines than humans; as a result it is often believed that they are not good at changing focus rapidly, this may or may not be correct. They are however, extremely sensitive to movement.

When light falls on the photosensitive retinal cells, the neurones in the optic nerve are activated. These run to the visual cortex in the forebrain, through the optic chiasma. In the optic chiasma, a portion of the neural fibres cross over from right to left and a portion from left to right, thus the information ends up in both sides of the brain. In the visual cortex the information is analysed and matched up with other information in the cortex (e.g. auditory, smells, past experiences etc.). There is a curious belief among scientists, and consequently now among certain sections of the community who are interested in horses (e.g. followers of Parelli), that every learning procedure has to be performed on both sides of the horse as they do not have the facility to pass information from one side to another. This seemed so curious that it encouraged me to look much more carefully at the anatomy and physiology of the equine brain, and talk to those who might know more. The dissections of the horses' brains that I performed showed very plainly that they have a corpus callosum (the part of the brain where information crosses from one side to the other). It is just as well developed as in humans or other mammals so there is no reason to believe that information acquired from one side does not pass to the other in equines.

Visual information analysis has been researched for some decades. It is extremely complicated, with the individual possessing an extraordinary amount of information and being able to make a range of visual assessments without knowing it, for example assessing the speed of travel of a ball, or the distance apart of two objects, or recognizing a face. This is not unique to humans; equines and dogs, as well as other mammals, just as frequently make these types of visual assessments.

Example

An experienced horse when jumping loose judges the distance and the size of a jump, and decides when to take off. A zebra judges how far the lion is behind him, and when to turn or dart sideways to ensure he does not get caught.

Equines *are* able to see colours, we know this from the pigments in the retina which have been recorded (Gregory 1958) although whether they see the same shades as we do is unknown.

They can discriminate between different shapes and are particularly visually sensitive to movements or changes, picking up subliminal cues (very slight visual changes) which we humans often do not see. They can also see well in poor light at night. Shining a light at night on the eye of an equine will show up the trapezium which, acting as a mirror behind the retina, reflects the light, and in this way doubles it to help night vision. There are some indications that equines were originally nocturnal, they have very large eyes characteristic of nocturnal animals, larger than those of elephants!

Thus, equines are extremely visually aware, and can see further and in poor light with more acuity than we humans (see Chapter 7).

The eyes of humans, cats and other primates are placed towards the front of the head which means that there is a large binocular visual field, but a relatively small monocular field of vision and nothing can be seen behind. By contrast, the eyes of equines are at the side of the head, consequently there is a large monocular field of vision, almost 360 degrees when the head is up. This means that there is an enormous amount of information being sent into the visual cortex, a different view from each eye. We humans with a more restricted visual field, and most of this binocular, have difficulty imagining what this must be like. The horse is able to see clearly to the right and left of himself, behind and in front all at the same time. How they analyse the two different views from the two eyes we do not as yet know. We humans can only do this by focusing our eyes on one, then another object which often also involves turning our heads and sometimes our whole body. The result is a linear temporal visual assessment of the world; we look at an object, look away and then look back at it to see what has happened to it in the meantime. Equines will be seeing the whole world around them all the time. However, if they then need to look in detail at one part of it, they can do this by turning the head and focusing the object immediately in front of them in their binocular visual field, but the majority of their visual information will be two continuous simultaneous monocular world views of all the things around them.

Exercises

Sight

1. The position of the eyes on the head gives a different view.

   a) Hold your arms up to the side and, while looking straight forward, draw them back until you can only just see your hands out of the corner of your eyes. This tells you how wide your peripheral visual field is.

   b) Get someone to hold an object in the peripheral visual field of one eye and without moving you eyes, tell them what it is. This will demonstrate how relatively poor the peripheral vision is.

   c) Now cover up one of your eyes with one hand, and place the other hand vertically against your nose, with the little finger forward. This gives you an idea about the separation of the monocular visual fields, with the barrier created by the hand in front of the eye.

d) Next, close your eyes and place the fingers together in a praying position then, holding that position, place the base of the thumbs against the nose with the fingers pointing forwards. Open both eyes, and see what a barrier this creates to the binocular visual field; there is a blind spot in front where your fingers are and, if things are nearby, it is easier to see them by turning the head sideways. This helps you understand something about the equines' visual field and head movements when watching things, particularly their teacher.

2. The equines' ability to pick up very small visual cues. Various games can be invented here between people to increase their powers of observation of visual cues.

a) As a start for beginners, get one person to try to get some simple message across to another by not making any movements, but just using the eyes.

b) The next test will be making only small movements of one part of the anatomy, the feet, for example, to put across messages concerning intention.

c) A more difficult variation of this exercise is to have someone try to imagine feeling a particular emotion (acting it without making any particular movement or facial expression), and for the others to try to tell what the emotion is that they are feeling.

3. Try writing down what you see while watching an equine in an enclosed space in order to be able to predict his next likely actions. Discuss this with others. Gradually you will get better at this, but not if you just listen to others, because they may be making mistakes. Concentrate in turn on:

a) the face, eyes, ears, nose, chin, mouth movements or tensions;

b) then the body and tail;

c) finally the legs.

Whether equines have other receptors, for example a sensitivity to vibrations, electric messages or thought transfer, or whether there is a 'collective unconsciousness or morphic resonance' (see, e.g. Lovelock 1991, Sheldrake and Fox 1997, and Watson 1999), we do not know, but it would be foolish to assume there are no other sensory modalities and ways of communication at this stage. However, so far there is no firm evidence which does not have other possible explanations for such communication in equines.

Humans intuitively use the physical characteristics of the animal to assess by sight their 'essence'. Size, presence of claws, teeth, tusks, horns, and so on, will predispose you, in the most obvious case, to be afraid or not. Superimposed on the obvious physical characteristics of the animal will be cultural beliefs that humans have learnt from others concerning a particular species or individual (see pages 246–250).

Examples

'Lions are dangerous', (epitomised in law in the 'dangerous wild animal act' UK 1978), 'horses bite and kick', 'donkeys are stubborn', 'zebras and African elephants are difficult to train'.

These are examples of 'folk beliefs' as a result of making a visual assessment. 'Folk belief' involves preconceived cultural notions in determining our apparent understanding of it. Equines can also have preconceived notions. One preconceived notion that equines generally have is that 'strange things are dangerous'. Knowing this helps us considerably with understanding their behaviour which otherwise may appear mysterious. We need more 'folk knowledge' to enable both humans and equines to live in the world and to see it as the other sees it.

SUMMARY

1. In the first place, similarities between equines and humans in terms of their adaptabilities are striking. They are able to adapt to a large range of domestic conditions as well as maintain breeding populations in areas both physically and socially very different from those they evolved to live in.

2. a) Despite their disparate appearance, the overall structure and physiology of the bodies of equines and humans are similar.

   b) The differences in size and shape will have an effect on their world view. But even differences in the development of the structure and use of the limbs are sufficiently similar for it to be possible to have some idea of what it may be like to be the other.

   c) Differences in equine and human size and their different abilities in the types and speed of movement outline the different world views in relation to space and distance that these two species may have.

   →

---

3. a) Although the different sense organs of equines and humans have similar structure and physiology, there are differences in what is perceived and how this is analysed. Equines are better at smelling than humans. Smells can outline a very different world view.

b) Equines are very visually aware, even in poor light; they are sensitive to visual changes and movement and consequently pick up cues that humans miss. They have two simultaneous monocular world views most of the time. This allows them to have a continual 'world visual view' unlike humans who tend to look at particular objects rather than being constantly visually aware of the whole environment.

c) Equines also have an acute sense of hearing and touch and consequently are extremely aware of all around them at any time.

4. The differences between equine and human world views are not necessarily a result of equine inability or mental inferiority compared to humans. Rather they are the result of their different bodies, the way in which they are able to perceive the world, and their assessment or analysis of it appropriate to their lives. For example, horses have a sensitivity and assessment of tactile, taste, auditory and visual information which has its own sophistication although sometimes of a somewhat different kind from that of humans. With proper study and practice, it is not impossible to be able to learn more about this different world view, and even, perhaps, to be able to have experiences more similar to those of equines.

5. It is important not to be blinded in the search for what it might be like to be an equine by human preconceived notions and cultural trappings, that is folk belief as a result of what is generally believed and taught whether this comes from people who have horses, or even what has been called science. Such beliefs affect both the questions we ask, and our interpretation of the results. The first stage is to become aware of this.

→

6. Studies of the integration of the body and workings of the mind, and the similarities in the mammalian body and how it works, suggests that in order to understand equines better, the first stage is to use anthropomorphic judgement. Put yourself in their place and imagine how you would behave if you were them. The next stage is to understand more about the differences between humans and equines integrated bodies and minds in order to understand their different perspective and world view.

Much remains to be discovered, but this is a beginning.

2 The life-supporting behaviours of equines

'. . . a man has no better thing under the sun, than to eat, and drink and to be merry . . .'

Ecclesiastes ch. 8 v. 15

'. . . there is proclaimed, as a fundamental right, the right of free movement . . . and also the right to a dignified life.'

Declaration of Human Rights 1948

In order to live and remain healthy, mammals, including humans, have a variety of behaviours they must perform: they must eat, drink, sleep, rest, move around, keep their skin healthy, and keep their body at the right temperature. Consequently, such behaviours have been described as 'essential for life', as opposed to behaviours such as socializing with others, or dust bathing for hens, swimming for ducks, galloping around for horses, or gardening for humans which are examples of behaviours that have been described as 'luxuries' (Dawkins 1993). Such 'luxuries', it has been argued, are not essential for the survival of the individual.

This is a fine distinction (and one that not all thinkers on this subject, myself included, go along with). Be that as it may, the first task is to consider all the behaviours that are essential for life. Without eating or drinking, for example, the individual would die, without reproducing, the species would become extinct.

It is these behaviours, and how they are similar or different between equines and humans, that we discuss in this chapter in order to further our understanding of equines and draw some conclusions about how similar or different our world views are. We concentrate on describing these behaviours in equines, making only passing reference to the differences in humans.

There are, as we have already stressed, inborn tendencies to perform these behaviours in certain ways, but how, when and where they are performed is learnt. Consequently, these behaviours, like all others, are moulded by life experiences.

EATING

Equines are herbivorous and predominantly grazers but, if grass is short, unpalatable, or they seek a change, they will browse bushes and trees, particularly at certain times of the year. As we know, humans are omnivorous and evolved as omnivorous scavengers, stealing others' leavings wherever they could.

Selection

Equines are extremely selective. They select what to eat by recognizing the species, but also the part of the plant, stage of growth, and length (Kiley 1977). They prefer short, quick-growing, high-protein, green swards (Figure 2.1), although all equines, wild, feral and domestic, can survive and grow on dry high-fibre swards.

Equines are in particular very cautious about new foods, even if other horses are eating them around them. This appears to be related to their inability to vomit and the consequent risk of poisoning, or blockage in the intestines, which even if these are temporary, result in an accumulation of gas. If stabled, they can learn to eat whatever is presented and are, therefore, prone to stomach pains, that is colic: the result of many types of digestive upset which is one of the major causes of death in stabled domestic equines.

Possibly because of the risk inherent in eating, and having to acquire a great deal of information on what to eat, observational learning and social learning — learning by observing others — (see Chapter 3) is of particular importance to equines. Nonetheless, provided they have time to learn from others, equines can survive and breed on very different types of food: donkeys on cardboard (see Figure 1.1), horses on lichens in the arctic or blood and milk in the deserts.

Fig. 2.1 Shemal selects flowers and high-protein clover from rich organic pasture of great diversity. Note the dandelions which horses select some of the time in the spring.

Mammals, including humans, have what is called 'nutritional wisdom' which is an innate ability to select a diet rich in the particular nutrients that are needed for healthy body maintenance (Kiley 1977 for review). In this case, a scarcity of a particular type of substance required by the body is relayed biochemically to other parts, including the brain. Somehow a 'need' for it is established subconsciously, and the mammal will then select food high in the required substance. Children, when presented with a whole range of foods including their favourite chocolate and sweets, will first gorge themselves on their favourite food but, within a couple of days, they will be choosing a balanced nutritive diet. The same is true for equines. But, the problem is that this 'nutritional wisdom' can be overruled by large changes in the taste or texture of the food available, and also by learning to eat the wrong thing (e.g. anything in the manger for equines, or fast food for humans). This can result in many physical and sometimes behavioural problems for both humans and equines.

Cultural and social influences on learning what to eat are important for both humans and equines. Eating different unknown foods can be less of a risk to humans or dogs because they can easily vomit, which, as stated, is not the case for equines. Nevertheless, the cultural food habits established by social learning can be so strong in humans that populations have been known to die of starvation when surrounded by unfamiliar food. Sometimes even in equines, inappropriate food cultures can be learnt from others.

Example
Horses that were kept in a field in South Africa where there was much ragwort (*Senecio jacobeas*) and little grass, developed a culture of eating the ragwort (a plant poisonous to most grazing stock) and some died. The younger horses had learnt to eat it from observing their seniors. The population ended up with what amounted to a self-destructive culture (personal communication from S. Mariner. South Africa). Normally, equines learn not to eat growing ragwort, 1) by having plenty of other things to eat, 2) by observing its avoidance by others in the group, and 3) as a result of trying it in small quantities, and becoming slightly ill: this is called ' learnt food aversion' (see below).

Because of the risk to equines of eating new foods, they are particularly careful about trying them, even when others are eating them.

Example
Try giving a young horse who has never had a sweet a piece of sugar. Even when his neighbours greedily devour it, he will be pushing it about with his nose, and spitting it out.

Learnt food aversion
This is a particularly interesting phenomenon. It consists of the human or animal making an association between a particular food that makes them sick hours after consumption and, consequently, thereafter avoiding the food, even if they are very hungry. The important thing here is the time lag between the cause and the effect of what has been eaten which indicates that some sort of mental events must have taken place, even though they may not have been 'conscious' ones.

Example
After a human has become sick after eating seafood, even the smell of seafood will induce retching.

When a horse has had a bout of colic from eating some particularly mouldy grain, it may take months before he will take any grain again.

Clearly, because of their curious digestive tract, learnt food aversion is particularly important for equines.

Learnt food acceptance

There is a great risk when feeding equines from a manger, or out of a recognizable container, that they learn to eat things presented in this container by associative learning (see page 142). It is possible in this way for equines to eat foods that they would otherwise reject, such as slightly rotten or mouldy grain. This behaviour can generalize (see page 121) so that the equine will eat almost everything that is presented to him in the stable. The risk of eating something inappropriate can be increased by the fact that the horse may also be hungry because he does not have access to food all the time, and a diet low in fibre (that is little or no fodder such as hay, horsehage, silage or straw).

What this 'learnt food acceptance' means is that the human caretaker must take full responsibility for everything the equine eats. The problem here is that it is very difficult for us humans to make appropriate judgements on what is good, or unfamiliar, for the horse, he is much better at doing this for himself!

Consequently, this is another important reason why the equine should not be confined to stables for the majority of the time where he is restricted in terms of what he can eat: it increases the risk of colic. Colic is much less common in animals who are able to make their own decisions on what to eat, even though there may not be much of it, or the quality may not be good.

This is not something that has been taken into account so far by equine nutritionists whose aim is to sell particular products for their company. It is wisest for the horse owner to give the animal the options to make his own decisions to learn about what to eat, when and where.

The wild or feral equine has a great amount to learn about eating and where to find his food, and he is born with the abilities and tendencies to do this. (See example 1, page 91, and Chapter 5).

Time budgets

Equines spend a lot of time eating, around sixteen hours out of twenty-four and, interestingly, this varies relatively little depending on the availability of food (only by about three hours a day). Thus, even if they can eat all their nutritional requirements in a couple of hours, they will continue to eat for around fourteen hours.

If they are fed high-quality food in stables which takes little time to eat, provides for all their nutritional requirements, and they have nothing else to eat or to do, they often develop behavioural problems and show signs of distress such as performing stereotypes: weaving, box walking, crib-biting etc. (see Chapter 4).

By contrast, if they have a great deal of good food available and nothing much else to do, they will eat more than they should to fill the time. Consequently, they may suffer from obesity or laminitis (a metabolic upset). Humans of course have the same problem with obesity and a whole series of medical disorders as a result of overeating high-quality food.

If the grazing is scarce or unpalatable and they are unable to move away, instead of increasing the eating time above around nineteen hours to ensure they have enough, they lose weight and become malnourished. These physical/mental problems are the result of inappropriate equine husbandry, that is, not understanding the importance of equine time budgets (Figure 2.2).

If you wish to improve the life of equines, understand them and be able to educate them better, it is very important to allow them to eat for as long as they like each day by giving them access to food, high-fibre food usually (for further discussion of this issue see Kiley-Worthington 1987 and 1998).

The amount of time spent standing doing nothing increases in equines stabled on their own, but, with a little redesigning of the environment, it is easy to ensure that the appropriate time budgets (that is those that the equines have a tendency to want to fulfil), are achieved (Figure 2.2, diagram B).

Since humans were omnivorous scavengers, and hunter/gatherers (like pigs), their staple foods were grains, vegetable matter, insects, small mammals, reptiles and fish caught by chance, as well as scavenged kills from other carnivores. Interestingly, even in very difficult terrain without much obvious food available, hunter gatherers such as the K'hung bushmen in the Kalahari desert or the

Australian desert Aborigines, rarely spend more than about two hours a day searching for food, although another two hours may be spent on preparing it (Leakey 1981).

How horses spend their time

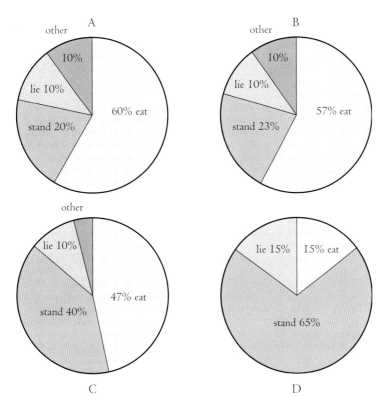

Fig. 2.2   How horses spend their time.

A. Feral horses in the Carmargue.

B. Similar time budgets for our yarded horses, recorded over three 24-hour periods. This proves that it is possible to maintain the appropriate time budgets of feral horses with domestic equines.

C. Three of our horses in individual stables where they had access to *ad libitum* hay and straw from their beds. They were also able to see and touch one another, but the time budgets are quite different from A and B.

D. The normal time budget of stabled competition horses who are fed rationed hay, a lot of concentrate feeds, and kept in the stable for around twenty-three hours a day. These significantly different time budgets are one of the major reasons why these horses show so much distress, and many behavioural problems.

Food processing

Humans spend much time processing their food, that is washing, chopping, squashing, cooking and so on. By contrast, equines spend time selecting their food, but little time processing it although occasionally one may toss the hay about before eating, or shake the earth off a sward before chewing up the grass.

In other words, good equine husbandry and the individual's education ensures that the equine has had the appropriate experiences to learn *what and how much* to eat, and where to find it. But how can this be done?

Appropriate education of the equine on how to select food

In order to ensure less behavioural and physical problems for the equine (and consequently for the equine carer), the most sensible thing is to ensure that the young equine has access to the type of information he will need to ensure that he does not eat the wrong things.

The first thing is to allow the youngster to learn the choices to be made about what to eat both in pastoral and stabled situations by watching others. To learn in this way, it is necessary for him to have free social contact and not be isolated in individual stables. Then he must also be allowed to make trials of what to eat and not to eat for himself. To do this, the youngster must not be hungry or have had his eating time budget disrupted.

In a pastoral situation, access to various different types of plants must be made available to the youngster and his friends and relatives, the more different types the better, even if there are some poisonous plants there, ragwort for example. But, it is very important to ensure that there is sufficient grazing of the preferred and desirable type of plants for the equines to eat so that they do not eat something they should not because they have nothing else. The more access to different plants he has, will increase the chances of him learning how to make the appropriate choices. In other words, the greater the species diversity of the sward and the more different places the youngster visits and has to feed himself the better, particularly if accompanied by an experienced adult. This will increase the chances of him learning how to make the appropriate choices.

In a stabled environment it is not difficult to provide sufficient fodder at all times (including choices) and access to other adults to learn from. Firstly, the equine must have access to fibrous food for twenty-four hours a day. This is just as important to him as having access to water twenty-four hours a day. If he eats too much, then make it difficult for him to eat a lot in a short time by, for example, using a hay net with very small holes, or some other way in which he has to work for the odd piece of hay rather than mouthfuls at a time. Give him choices of hay, straw, silage or haylage to ensure that if one or other of these is not quite as it should be, he will not be so hungry that he will eat it anyway. In this way he will always be able to keep himself feeling full and not eat undesirable foods because he is hungry and restricted in his choice. If he has hard food, feed him in different containers in different places in the stable, or in the field on the ground. It is surprising how often he will leave the hard food preferentially for good fodder (when you thought the food was of a good quality).

Overprotection

In terms of disallowing the equine to make his own choices and decisions on what, how much and where to eat, overprotection will only increase the problems he suffers. It underestimates an equine's abilities to acquire knowledge. Consider, for a moment, the notable fitness and health of almost every feral population of equines from the Arctic to the tropics. Even at the end of a severe winter with access to little food, they look healthy and rapidly put on weight when the spring comes. Feral or wild equines in the tropics, such as zebras, are renowned for their plumpness and health, even where there are no predators to eat the less healthy ones, so they must be able to feed themselves well. The outdated approach of overprotection, when the equine is considered similar to a new-born child, should be recognized and *equines given the opportunity to learn about what, where, when and how to eat.* Remember though, they have to learn, so start the education today whether it is in a racing stable, a competitive yard or for horses kept just for themselves.

Examples

1. One of the major causes of colic in stabled equines is the gorging of corn or other concentrate food by an animal who breaks into the food store. Here the animal is demonstrating learnt food acceptance for foods which have always been rationed, and fed in particular containers; so he gorges himself.

2. When working very hard, some equines may not retain their weight as well as others, and

their appetites may need encouragement. We have used free access to a concentrate food for several of our equines when getting them fit or taking part in long endurance races (160 km [100 mls] in twenty-four hours). In particular, Omeya, the mother of Oberlix and Oryx, a slight, pure-bred Arab, always needed every encouragement to eat when she was in training for endurance races. At competitions in particular, therefore, we used to leave a sack of food open in the corral for her to help herself whenever she wanted. In this way, she used to help herself to slightly more than she ate in her eight small meals a day we were giving her. Curiously, at one international event, we were reported to the technical advisor for 'cruelty' for doing this! It is a shame that people do not ask questions before jumping to conclusions when they see something different occurring. The technical advisor soon came to see us and had to apologize for the reporter's behaviour, however much she was trying to help; I never did manage to meet her and discuss this with her though, which is a pity!

DRINKING

Equines are extremely fussy about the water they drink, for the same reason as they are fussy about food: they cannot be sick. Consequently, they, again, need to learn about what water to drink and what not to drink. Some stabled equines who have never had proper access to running stream water, will *only* drink water from the mains which has a particular taste, usually of chlorine. Whereas others, our own for example, who have rarely had mains water, will not drink it easily. On the other hand our horses who have had access to water from many sources: troughs, streams, lakes and springs, as we encountered them in our travels, remain very fussy about the water they drink. Sometimes they, curiously, choose to drink from a rather dirty puddle when there is, what looks to us, a nice running spring adjacent.

Example
When riding around France, we would often visit the *lavoires* (where the village women used to do their washing) still present in almost every village, which are usually fed by a clear bubbling stream. To our surprise, the horses would sometimes not drink from these. When, because of their refusal to drink, we made enquiries concerning the source of the water, on several occasions we found that there was a history of high levels of herbicide or pesticide application upstream, and the locals would not drink the water which had been shown to be contaminated. After a while we only drank water when the horses drank it, and we all remained healthy throughout!

Stabled equines will become accustomed to drinking water from buckets or automatic waterers and will only drink from them (**conditioned water acceptance**). This severely cuts down your options of where you can go with the horse and, on endurance rides, also leads to the particularly ludicrous practice of having support vehicles carrying water around for the horses to drink, when there is plenty of good-quality, acceptable stream water, and even water troughs available.

If, on the other hand, treatment for diseases, or exhaustion etc., are to be administered through the water, then teaching the equine to drink from buckets only can be an advantage.

The overall risk of water poisoning an equine, *provided he has gathered the necessary knowledge and can make choices*, are slim. If he has not had the opportunity to do this, the risks are very high.

All the equines, with the exception of the wild ass and occasionally the Grevy's zebra (*E. grevyi*), drink daily. This means they have to stay within daily travelling distance of a watering hole. But their ability to travel far extends their feeding range at difficult times of the year (e.g. up to 60 km [37 mls] from water) and consequently allows them to survive and breed in dry areas where less mobile grazers such as the Cape buffalo cannot (Prins 1997).

Equines can dig shallow holes in dry river beds by pawing, but zebras often use watering holes dug by elephants. Wild equines have to be particularly cautious at water holes as they are good hunting grounds for predators but, when the opportunity arises, they also play games in the water: pawing and splashing themselves and each other, rolling, chasing and trotting with a very elevated trot.

Equines swim well and fast without practice at about 6–8 km (4–5 mls) an hour (personal experience) thus they can often colonize islands or obtain access to areas that are otherwise difficult to get to. It is fun swimming with them, but do not remain on their backs as they then end up vertical and when their ears get wet they become very distressed. Hold onto their manes and float alongside them and they will pull you along. If you let go, you will soon be on your own as they can outswim the best of you!

Humans generally have to drink daily. They show many cultural drinking habits, such as drinking particular substances at particular times of the day.

Both equines and humans can adapt over a period to drinking less frequently than once a day, provided they do not have to do too much exercise.

STANDING, LYING AND SLEEPING

Much of equines' resting time is spent standing around (4.5 hrs a day when living in a feral-type situation). They have a locking mechanism in the knee which allows them to stand almost without effort and, at the same time, take the weight off one of the hind legs. A typical dozing pose for an equine is with one hind leg resting on its hoof tip, the head lowered and with the eyes half shut (Figure 2.3). One of the problems with stabling equines, which probably contributes considerably to lameness and leg problems (as well as to behavioural ones), is the increase in their standing time, from 4.5 hrs to 15.5 hrs a day. (see Figure 2.2, diagram D).

The normal equine adult who has choices, will lie down for around 2.5 hrs a day, the very young and the old tend to stand less and lie more. When Sheba, the foundation mare of our stud, was observed for 24-hour periods when she was over twenty-three, she lay down for 6.6 hrs a day. Foals may lie for as much

Fig. 2.3 Cariff (left) with Shereen and Christmas all dozing in the evening light.

as 15 hrs a day and, for the first few days of their lives, find it difficult to stand still at all when on their feet.

Equines find it relatively difficult to get up once they are lying down, and it takes time. Consequently, for a prey species whose escape from predators is to run, they are vulnerable when they are lying and tend not to lie down in unfamiliar places, or where they feel at all insecure. Equines lie with their front end first, (Figure 2.4a) and get up with their front end first (Figure 2.4b), which may be quicker than the other way around (cattle with their less muscular quarters lie front end first and get up back end first), nevertheless, it requires considerable effort. Equines with severely damaged hind legs have been known to learn to get up like cattle, but some do not manage to get up at all.

Equines can learn to lie down when asked, but they have to have confidence in the handler and the place before they will willingly do this (Figure 2.5).

Whether or not they lie down in their stables is a measure of the degree of comfort they have in them and how familiar they are. Only very experienced travelling horses will lie down in unfamiliar places. Figure 2.6 shows Omeya (an older mare) and three of the youngsters lying flat out in the deep-litter barn which they can come in to, or go out of, at will.

Humans may sit or lie for hours at a time, resting, talking and socializing

Fig. 2.4a Shezam about to roll, lying down front end first. Note the compressed grass where others have rolled.

Fig. 2.4b Oberlix getting up, rather slowly, after rolling. Raising the hindquarters requires some effort.

Fig. 2.5 Chris asking Oryx to lie down: he collapses his front legs first.

Fig. 2.6 Omeya, the senior mare (standing) eats hay while the youngsters lie in the deep litter yard from where they have access to fields when they wish. Two lie flat in deep sleep and Shemal is dozing on her sternum, probably in REM (rapid eye movement) sleep.

without sleep for up to a total of around twelve hours a day. Perhaps this is why they often believe that equines will not suffer from, indeed may need, similar periods of 'rest'. This is an example of the inappropriate application of 'anthropomorphism' to equines.

Like other mammals, including humans, equines have deep sleep and REM (rapid eye movement) or paradoxical sleep. Dreaming is said to occur in REM sleep (see Chapter 9). Exactly how much they sleep as opposed to doze has not, as yet, been properly measured, but they appear to sleep for around 5–6 hours out of twenty-four. As in humans, the time spent sleeping can increase when the animals are restricted or in dull environments, that is they switch out of the unacceptable present by switching into sleeping more.

Equines will doze standing or lying on their sternum. They may fall into REM sleep for short periods when standing but most of this occurs when they are lying on their sternum (Figure 2.6). Deep sleep is usual only when they are lying flat out (Figure 2.6), which, because of the need for their digestive movement to continue and the risk of an accumulation of air in the gut, they usually only sustain for up to forty-minute periods. Veterinarians performing surgery have a problem here as their patients cannot lie flat out for longer.

Sleep is now considered particularly important for humans in allowing the individual to consolidate any information or mental events that have happened during the waking time. Again, there is no reason why this should not be the case also for horses. Many people have had the experience that the horse they have been teaching one day, will often perform the movement much better the following day, after a period of rest and sleep which, apparently, helped the individual understand what was required, and consolidated the learning. At present we do not know if this is in fact the case, or just the result of preconceived notions and expectations in the human handlers; another area for further research.

By contrast, humans generally lie for 8–12 hours a day, sleeping for around eight hours although they can become conditioned to both sleep and lie for shorter and longer periods. Some humans can train themselves to sleep much less, particularly when under some form of stress, a sailor on lookout duty for example. Some individuals also teach themselves to catnap, i.e. have very short sleeping periods whenever they have the opportunity through the day, which is what equines do most of the time. Equines who have had long periods of work and less access to food (such as cab horses, cavalry horses, and today's modern stabled equines) can change their sleep and rest patterns, but, judging from the frequency of distress behaviour in stabled equines (see Figure 4.4) the limits of their adaptability are often overstepped.

MOVEMENT

Equines spend around 15% of their day moving around (that is continuous movement of more than five steps, as opposed to movement while grazing), unless migrating when it may be more. Humans spend rather less than 8% of the day moving. Equines move while grazing, browsing or socializing, and occasionally when having to run away from predators. They have evolved to move around more constantly than humans or dogs, both of whom have a 'feast and sleep' strategy, as opposed to the equines', 'move and eat' strategy.

We have already mentioned that equines are speed and endurance movement specialists. But, in addition, they can bounce, leap about, buck, rear, even walk on two legs when they wish. They can alter each gait, changing the rhythm, the elevation and length of stride quite dramatically.

Both equines and hunter-gatherer humans, even without special training, can cover large mileages if they have to, particularly when searching for food or water. But, it is a sobering thought that before the recent interest in understanding equine exercise physiology better (started in the 1970s) most of the horses who were ridden extraordinary distances at high speeds, such as Black Bess (London to York in twenty-four hours) died (Lawrence 1980). Carriage driving horses, though, were expected to be able to continue work for years, and they usually covered around 40 km (25 mls) at up to 20 km (12 mls) an hour most days. Such horses must have been as fit as many of the top endurance horses today.

As a result of the recent research on human and equine exercise physiology, and the rise in popularity and competition in endurance races, when it is the veterinarians who are the judges, our knowledge on how to improve and measure the fitness of both humans and equines has grown over the last few decades. Both the distances covered and the speeds have increased dramatically in human running and endurance riding competitions, and horses no longer need to be put at risk from exhaustion, provided the rider knows something about how to assess their horse's fitness.

Racehorses cover short distances, with or without leaping obstacles. These animals can run at over 56 kmph (35 mph), but their speeds have not improved recently. Other equines, zebras and asses usually do not run faster than 40 kmph (25 mph) and that for only short distances.

Because of the importance of movement in the life of equines, and the fact that they normally move around for much of the day (slowly during the sixteen or so hours eating, and more vigourously for other periods each day), the limbs and mentality of the equines have evolved to cope with almost constant movement, and sometimes the need to run fast.

The modern stable management practices of restricting movement to short periods each day is counter-intuitive, and likely to cause serious damage to both the physical and the mental attributes of the equines. This indeed happens, with lameness being extremely common, and early death (often euthanasia as a result of limb damage of some sort). Restriction of movement of equines for long periods is one of the most important restraints causing a whole variety of behavioural problems (Animal Behavioural Consultancy Records). It is important, therefore, that if you are going to successfully improve the education of the equine, if stabled, he must be able to move about unrestricted in an area where he can take at least ten strides without restriction for the majority of the time he spends there. This rules out most looseboxes, but suggests that yarding horses may be more appropriate, from the point of view of fulfilling physical needs as well as mental and social ones (see Figure 2.2 and compare diagrams A and B).

GROOMING AND SCRATCHING: MAINTAINING THE SKIN AND COAT CONDITION

Humans can scratch themselves with their hands almost all over the body, except the back, which they will rub on other things. Through history, humans have spent much time on self-grooming, including washing, dressing, hair styles and so on. It has become an important part of human culture. Nevertheless, they still scratch and groom themselves similarly to other primates.

Equines can scratch themselves all over, with their mouth or feet, or by rubbing on things (Figure 2.7a). Maintaining skin health is an important part of the equines' behavioural repertoire. But, just as in humans, such behaviour and movements have acquired all sorts of extra meanings, for example for communication (see Chapter 7). They may also be important in the identification of a common 'culture', that is, showing a belonging to a particular group

Fig. 2.7a Lilka rubs herself on a fence post, while Shindi (aged one year) watches.

Fig. 2.7b Affection and familiarity. Oryx and Shukrune grooming each other when they were foals.

by demonstrating familiarity and even affection between individuals, as in equines' mutual grooming (Figure 2.7b). Attachment and affection is often demonstrated by mutual grooming in both humans and equines when, for example, mothers and their babies stroke, lick or tickle each other. Patting, hugging, and grooming goes on among adults too.

Equines are particularly prone to skin itches, presumably because of their thin skin. They can twitch their skin, lift and wag their tails, stamp their feet and kick their bellies, rub their heads, back and sides, roll, and bite their sides,

Fig. 2.8   Oberlix and Aisha keeping the flies off one another.

Fig. 2.9a and b   Lilka rolls, watched by Shindi, then gets up and shakes.

back and legs to get rid of itches or help wounds heal. They can also scratch the front part of their bodies with a hind leg. They will use another's tail to thwart a persistent insect attack, by standing head to tail. (Figure 2.8). They will lick wounds and seek out water or trees to relieve themselves of insects, or to cool themselves, and they habitually roll where others have rolled, particularly when sweaty after exercise, when joining a new group, or entering a new field. Rolling may have a function of anointing themselves with a group smell, as well as relieving irritations (Figures 2.9a and b).

Activities related to skin irritation are interesting as they often become activities to convey information to others, that is for communication (see Chapter 7), in both humans and equines. Equines are more visually able to spot movements and changes, and use activities connected to skin irritation to communicate each others' feelings a great deal. They also, presumably, acquire information about their human handlers feelings in the same way.

Example

When both humans and equines are in conflict over whether to approach or to avoid something, or when they are frustrated, they often scratch or perform movements related to self-grooming. This, when witnessed by others becomes a 'displacement activity' (see Chapter 7) and can acquire a particular meaning.

SPARE TIME, LEISURE, TOO MUCH LEISURE AND OVERPROTECTION

At many times of the year equines and other mammals, including humans, have more time than they need to do all the behaviours they have to do to survive. At such times, they have what can be called 'spare time' or 'leisure time'. One of the situations in which equines often have spare, or leisure, time is when they are kept in domestic situations.

In humans, this spare time is often used to perform hobbies, which are defined as 'doing things which interest but are not immediately essential for the maintenance of a life style'. Equines also have hobbies defined in the same way. These may involve playing many sorts of games with each other, or alone, investigating and exploring, even just lying sleeping or standing staring (see the discussion of play on page 365). Of course such behaviours may ultimately have a use for the individual by allowing him to develop his body, skills, or acquire knowledge which may benefit him in the long run, just as human hobbies might. But, the immediate reason for doing them is 'fun': it gives the performer pleasure, it is what he chooses to do with the time and energy available. Indeed he may, even when there is little spare time in certain seasons, *make* time 'spare time' in order to do things for fun.

One of the major problems for equines, and humans, particularly in institutions or captive environments, is too much spare, or leisure, time. This is often the result of overprotection because the carers have provided for all the individual's physical needs in such a way that the equine is unable to use his own knowledge and decision making to maintain himself, and may never have had the opportunity to acquire the information to be able to do this. Here the human, or other mammal, is deprived of making choices and having experiences as a result of his environment.

Example

Horses are often brought inside because it is raining and they might get cold, or, they are not allowed to mix freely with each other because they might hurt each other.

Carers usually overprotect because they care, but, nevertheless, the result is that those being cared for show evidence of deprivation and suffering. This is often the case in poorly designed domestic or captive animal environments, or in some human institutions (e.g. in some prisons, schools, old-people's homes) where there are insufficient choices of behaviour available as a result of imposed restrictions (Figures 2.10 and 4.6a and b). Unfortunately, this has not, to date, been properly understood by the establishment.

In such environments the humans or animals are unable to engage in simple cognitive decision making (e.g. when, where and what to eat, when and where to shelter, and so on). As a result, their intellectual needs are not catered for, they become bored or distressed, and display this by developing behavioural pathologies, often performed in order to increase the stimulus in the environment in one way or another (see Chapter 4 and Fox 1968, Kiley-Worthington 1987 and 1990, and Wemelsfelder 1993).

Fig. 2.10 Cages for horses. A modern stable block at a university department teaching Equine Studies and an example of overprotection and restrictions. Anti-weaving bars are installed as a fixture since it is assumed that the horse is bound to weave (if he does not develop crib-biting, when electric wires may be fitted to stop him!). Some serious thinking about equine husbandry is necessary if things are to improve for horses, if behavioural problems are to be reduced, and horses are to be kept in environments conducive to learning, which would result in their human caretakers and teachers being safer and having more fun with them.

If individuals, whether human or equine, are kept in an overprotected way for a long time, they may become unable to make simple choices and decisions. These 'institutionalized individuals' are often, alas, encountered in the smartest of modern competitive stables, children's homes, hospitals and old-people's homes.

This leads to the question of what is the optimal amount of 'difficulties in living' which will ensure a flourishing life for individuals of either of these species. There has to be a delicate balance between too much or too little, a question that requires research for the welfare of many humans as well as equines.

One thing this points to clearly, is that because both humans and equines acquire knowledge throughout their lives concerning life-supporting behaviours, they have a cognitive need to do this. If this need is not fulfilled in one way or another, then they may show behavioural abnormalities and pathologies.

SUMMARY

1. Behaviours such as eating, drinking, resting and scratching are performed by equines and humans as the result of an inbuilt tendency to perform them. But, how, when, where and what is performed is the result of the individual's lifetime experiences, that is what they have learnt. If they are to be performed with the least risk and maximum benefit for a long life, then the individual must acquire much knowledge. This involves, in particular, learning to take decisions and make choices.

2. There is little evidence that there is a great deal of difference between the amount of knowledge equines or hunter-gatherer humans have to acquire in order to support their lives; both species groups are selective feeders and have to find and eat their food, find good drinking water, look after their skin and coats, rest and sleep, find shelter, and fill their spare time.

3. One of the distinctive differences between large herbivores and humans is that the former spend a great deal of their day finding food and eating (around 16 hrs) whereas hunter-gatherer humans spend only around 4 hrs a day. Their type of food is different too, equines requiring high-fibre diets to ensure long and healthy lives. They are often fed diets that are said to fulfil all their nutritional needs which can be consumed in only 3–4 hrs a day, this causes behavioural and physical problems.

4. Equines, when allowed a choice, spend less time being inactive and sleeping than humans. Their bodies and minds have evolved to ensure this so that they are able to be almost constantly aware of what is going on around them, which is a successful antipredator strategy.

5. Both these species groups acquire and use information concerning these behaviours. If they are unable to do this then they become

→

vulnerable, by, for example, eating or drinking inappropriate material. The conventional horseperson will say that there is no difficulty here, provided the human carer takes the right decisions in providing the right things.

But the problems are:

a) The carer is not a horse and is not going to be able to make the right decisions for the horse as well as the horse, who has learnt how, can.

b) The horse remains vulnerable to any mistakes that the human carer may make.

c) A lack of opportunity to make decisions, choices and employ their cognitive abilities to acquire knowledge on these matters, leads to behavioural pathologies including distress and boredom.

6. In order to improve our lives with equines, their education and ensure they have a long life of high quality, and are well prepared to acquire more information from further learning or teaching, it is essential to give them an environment in which they are able to develop their abilities to support themselves, have choices and can make decisions to do this.

How to do this is discussed (together with other aspects) in the concluding chapter. How equines acquire the necessary knowledge we have discussed here is outlined in the next chapter.

3 Nature and nurture, and how equines learn and acquire knowledge

'Hominus dum docent discunt.' (Even while they teach, men learn.)   Seneca

It is vitally important to understand current ideas on both instinct and learning if we would like to understand and educate equines or humans better. We all know that equines learn but, nevertheless, there is a belief that the way they learn is not the way humans learn, and that it is always tempered by 'instinct'. In fact, much of their behaviour has been (and still is by many who are not conversant with current understanding of animal behaviour) described as 'instinctive' rather than 'learnt' (see Introduction). It is very important to understand the intrinsic combination of both **nature** (that is instinct) and **nurture** (that is past experiences) in all behaviour. There are of course, in man or beast, instinctive tendencies to do many things, but how, when, where and, even, if these behaviours are performed, is the result of the individual's lifetime experiences, as we have already stressed (see page 44). The degree to which the behaviour of equines or humans is controlled by instinct is therefore not an easy (or even interesting) question to answer.

Most of us know quite a lot about learning and teaching, simply because we practise it with our children and in all our human relationships, so it is useful to employ what we can call 'common sense', and is not always necessary to understand all the terms. However, sometimes we need to examine our understanding to ensure that we have not taken up some preconceived notion which is not helpful. One of these is the widely held belief, that needs to be dispelled, that equines (and other animals) learn by 'conditioning', believed always to result in some reflex response which the animal has no control over; a sort of instinct-like learning. This means that an equine will not perform actions voluntarily, but like a motor car, that is it is just a question of 'pushing the right buttons' and the right response will result. Learning is a great deal more complex and interesting than this and it would be a great benefit to all those involved with equines if they had some serious understanding of how it works. As early as 1956, learning was categorized into different types with an emphasis on the overlap between the categories and the complexity within them.

In order to sort this all out as simply as possible and also to be properly up to date (because, as with all science, things change fast), we will first discuss the types of learning both equines and humans display and give some examples. It is important to remember that how learning works was originally studied in rats and pigeons because they were cheaper and easier to keep in laboratories (e.g. Watson 1919, Tolman 1932, Skinner 1938). The findings of such people and their later modifications have been successfully applied to learning and teaching humans. In other words, it has long been recognized that learning works in the same sorts of way, for all mammals, although some may be better at certain types than others.

First we need to define what learning is. It has often been defined as: having occurred in any situation where behaviour is modified by experience (Figure 3.1). This definition has been used because the behaviour can be measured. But learning can also occur that does *not* make any immediate, or perhaps even long-term, difference to a behaviour that we can measure.

Learning is influenced by the individual, the species and the environment. Are horses, donkeys, zebras and mules intelligent? This is a question that is often asked, and most of us have strong views on this, particularly with regard to our own horse. Let us discuss this.

INTELLIGENCE

If I had £1 for every time I had been asked 'are horses intelligent?' I would be (financially) rich. The relative intelligence of each species, or even individuals

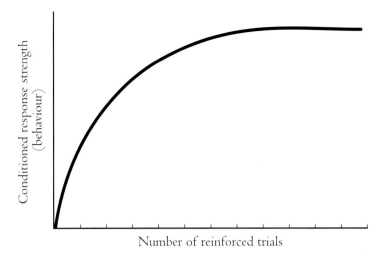

Fig. 3.1 An idealized learning curve. The desired behaviour (vertical axis), becomes stronger as it is modified by experience and time (that is, the reinforcement) along the horizontal axis. The flattening at the top indicates that learning has taken place, and the required behaviour occurs each time.

within a species, is a subject of endless discussion. Horse breed societies will recommend their breed by claims that they are particularly intelligent. Comparative intelligence is something that some psychologists are now discussing (e.g. Ristau 1991, Macphail 1998). However, the most common position taken on this issue is that each species will have a different physique, different receptors, different emphasis on emotionality and socialization and consequently live in different worlds. If this is the case, then comparisons between species are meaningless, each species will be the best, the most intelligent at living in *their* world. A comparative cognitive psychologist's stock response when asked about the intelligence of one species relative to another is: 'Each animal is likely to appear very intelligent in the environment for which it evolved and may appear very stupid when faced with other kinds of demands. Comparing animals' intelligence is like comparing their abilities to move. Do fish move better than horses?' (Roitblat 1987)

One of the major problems here is that there is no agreed definition of what intelligence is. The common use of this term relates to 'ability to learn' or 'to solve problems' or 'to perform IQ tests', but IQ tests given to humans are generally based on language ability and consequently irrelevant to non-humans. In any event, what IQ tests measure and whether they are worth the paper they are written on remains highly disputed (e.g. Howe 1997). It is beginning to be realized that there can be more than one type of intelligence even in humans (see *The Times* headline: 'What does David Beckham have in common with Albert Einstein?', 23/11/99, quoting work by Howard Gardner, Harvard Univ.). But, between species, intelligence is often used to indicate similarity to the observing human and his interpretation of the world. In other words 'how like humans is he?'

So what could the general rules be for one type of intelligence, say the ability to think and act rationally, to learn fast, to remember and to be able to put information together from different areas to solve problems? Speed of learning might be one, but if we are trying to measure this, how is it possible to be sure the act the subject is learning is equally difficult for different species, and can we be sure that they have similar motivations? In the 1970s there was a fashion to test farm animals in mazes to see how their performance compared one with another (e.g. Houpt 1979). On this reading, horses scored badly; this confirmed the general folk belief that horses:

1. learn very slowly, so everything has to be repeated again and again;
2. have to learn everything on both sides of the brain because they do not have a corpus callosum (the part of the forebrain where information is transferred from left to right and vice versa) but this is untrue (see page 77);
3. will not be able to learn anything at all difficult because they are 'stupid'!

But there were many reasons why the horses might not have performed well in the maze.

1. They were not interested in solving the problem.
2. They were more easily distracted and cautious.
3. They may have known the solution but simply not felt like rushing there.

Learning in the real world goes on in a constant interaction between others of the same, and different, species and the environment. Testing animals in an isolated alien laboratory environment might be expected to cause changes.

Indeed it is interesting that humans are not tested in such alien isolated situations, in fact laboratory ethical committees would not allow it!

So before having opinions concerning the intelligence of your equine, remember, making this judgement is rather complicated; perhaps it is only another equine who might be able to make it. In just the same way it is not possible to consider donkeys more or less stupid than horses, who are more or less bright than zebras; and mules, well we all know they are stubborn . . . or are they? Perhaps this is just the way we like to interpret their behaviour. On looking through some of the military history where donkeys and mules have been used, you cannot but admire these particular equines for, not only coping with every type of terrain, putting up with every type of harsh physical condition, their extraordinary toughness, but also their ability to come to terms with those conditions, and to learn about the physical, emotional, social and cognitive trappings and difficulties of human wars. Is this intelligence or adaptability?

In order to peruse the aim of this chapter which is to describe as simply as possible, what we now know about learning in order to be able to use this knowledge in our understanding of equines, it is divided into three parts.

1. We need to start by **clarifying the meaning of some of the terms** that are widely used, but whose meanings are not always clear. Unfortunately there is a tendency to use these terms too loosely, and then for others to use them without having much idea of what is meant. Thus rather confusing language often emerges which puts people off trying to understand how equines learn. This is not at all helpful for clarity or understanding.
2. The next step is to outline **the different types of learning** so that you can have more of an idea about why an equine behaved in a certain way in a particular situation, as well as what a teacher may have done right or wrong.
3. Finally, we outline some of the **co-operative teaching research** we have been doing with our equines and other mammals over the last few years. The central idea here was to see if our subjects could learn to understand human language by using a similar interactive approach to that used when teaching young children to talk and understand language.

If we wish to understand 'what it might be like' to be an equine, it really is necessary to have a more complete understanding about how learning works, and it also helps you to think about what is going right and wrong when teaching, and analyse your own behaviour.

CLARIFYING THE MEANING OF TERMS

We will discuss only the most important and commonly used terms.

Stimulus and response

A **stimulus** is something that arouses an activity. A **response** is the activity of the subject. This can either be internal in the body (such as changes in hormones, heart rates etc.) or external (such as doing something) but it will be related to the situation with which the responder is faced.

The stimulus can be **unconditioned**, that is, nothing (in relation to what is being learnt) has so far been associated with it, or **conditioned**, that is it has been linked to some outcome, i.e. reinforced (see below).

Example
Shindi, our yearling, comes into the ring for her first free-school lesson. She has never seen the whip before (unconditioned stimulus) and when it is raised behind her, makes no response. She is touched by the whip and leaps forward (unconditioned response). Next, she is asked to walk on with the voice, an upright body and the whip raised behind her (conditioned stimulus), she leaps forward as the whip is raised (conditioned response). That is, in one trial she has learnt to go away from the whip (the reinforcer is to avoid being hit and frightened by it).

Extinction and habituation or desensitization

Gradually, if there is no reinforcement (see below), a conditioned response will occur less and less frequently, until it no longer occurs at all, this is called **extinction**.

Example
Naïve equines do not like having their legs touched or held firmly because, presumably, as prey animals if their leg is trapped, they will be much more likely to be caught by a predator. Consequently, the normal response of a naïve equine to having the legs touched

by a human, is to withdraw it. If he is frightened or hurt while his leg is being held, then he is confirmed in his tendency not to allow his legs to be touched or held. If, however, nothing nasty happens or, even better, something nice happens, such as being given a food reward when he allows his legs to be picked up and held, then his tendency to withdraw the leg will become extinct.

Habituation or **desensitization** are a type of extinction where there is a gradual decline in the strength of a learnt response the more times the stimulus is presented (Figure 3.2).

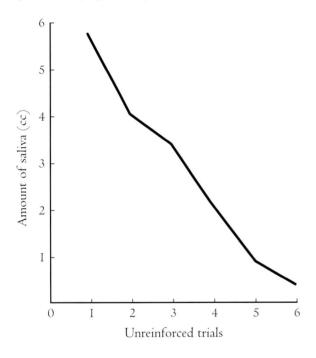

Fig. 3.2 Extinction. Pavlov's measurement of the decrease in the amount of saliva secreted (the conditioned responses) with an increasing number of trials when the conditioned stimulus (i.e. the gong which has been associated with the food) is presented. (Adapted from Pavlov 1928.)

Examples

Police horses are habituated or desensitized to crowds, traffic and bombs. Cavalry horses were habituated to the noise of guns. Horses who live where there are many low-flying aircraft, or very near motorways, become habituated to aircraft flying nearby or constant traffic, respectively. Humans too become habituated to traffic noise; often people who are, find it difficult to sleep when there is no traffic noise. The same may well be true of equines.

Habituation to a stimulus may require no remembering or processing of the stimulus but, equally, there are occasions when it may.

Examples

1. Humans or other animals may be habituated to a particularly loud noise. When the noise changes tone the subject's attention is aroused, this is because comparisons are made with the previous noise, and it is recognized as not being the same. In other words, mental events have taken place to compare the noises, even though the individual may not be aware of this.

2. Lack of habituation to traffic of many ridden horses is the cause of many accidents and behavioural problems (Animal Behaviour Consultancy records). To become habituated to traffic, the equine must overcome his 'instinctive' tendency to flee (unconditioned response to fear). To do this, he has, initially, to be consciously aware of the object (see Chapter 8) and of his own immediate response in order to be able to make a decision to change this, that is *stop* himself from leaping away. After some repetitions (provided this behaviour has not been accompanied by some form of negative reinforcement: an unpleasant experience such as a fright or pain), standing still in traffic does not require a great deal of attention or decision-making. Here the equine is described as 'habituated' or 'desensitized' to the stimulus.

Reinforcement

A **reinforcement** is the trigger that motivates (makes the individual do things) when behaviour has been conditioned. It can be **positive** (a reward) which will encourage the animal to do something for which he 'has an appetite', or **negative** (that is, do something in order to avoid something aversive or unpleasant). When training equines, although **positive reinforcement** (food and reward) has sometimes been used, generally it is much neglected.

Example

A horse moves about when someone is trying to mount. Instead of scolding him for moving, which will be a negative reinforcer and cause him to be more unsettled and consequently to move more; use positive reinforcement: reward him with some food and voice praise when he stands still. If he does not stand still all the time, do it again and again using the same approach until he does. Remember, however, that you must always praise him *after* he has stood still after mounting. Do not, initially, do it in difficult or scary places or he may not be able to resist moving around. A good idea is to give him a food reward and praise him before moving off, then ask him to move. After a few trials he will have learnt by positive reinforcement to stand still and not to move off until he has had a food reward and praise.

Equines are, unfortunately, today, more often trained by avoiding something nasty happening to him, that is **negative reinforcement**.

Example
The naïve horse is chased around in a round pen by the person throwing out a lunge line along the ground. The horse moves away from the lunge line in order to avoid being hit and having an unpleasant or frightening experience. This is negative reinforcement used to get him to move away. If the lunge line continues to be thrown out after him, he may become so scared that instead of running forward, he rears up and tries to climb the side of the round pen. The wise approach at this stage is to stop throwing out the lunge line (i.e. stop the negative reinforcement). Failure to do this will result in the horse learning that the round pen is a scary place, and to try to get out of it or avoid going into it. This is not the lesson you are trying to teach.

There are also **secondary reinforcers**. A positive secondary reinforcer would be praising the horse verbally for doing the right thing because, in the first instance, he performed this act to get something he wanted: usually food. Then the food should be paired with the voice saying particular things, 'good boy', for example. After several trials it will no longer be necessary to give food, the word itself is reinforcing. In this case it is often the voice conveying not only the right word, but also a pleasant emotional response from the teacher: pleasure or approval. This speeds up learning because the equine responds to the teacher's emotional responses displayed by her body, often accompanied by gestures and smiles.

Traditional training of equines often does not emphasize how important it is to praise the horse for doing the right thing, it is often taken for granted, whereas the animal is scolded or worse, for doing the wrong thing. This is one of the most important reasons why so many horses learn to do the wrong thing and thereafter have behavioural problems related to training.

A slightly different secondary reinforcer, which is becoming very fashionable, is the 'clicker'. Initially, the clicker is used at the same time as a food reward is given, then after a time, the noise of the clicker itself becomes reinforcing (a secondary reinforcer). In order to encourage the animal (or it could be a human) to do something different or new, the clicker will be used as soon as he begins to do what is desired, until the final response is performed.

Example
To get a donkey to walk across the stable and touch a bucket, the clicker (which has already become a secondary reinforcer by being paired with a food reward) is clicked when he starts

to move towards the object. Clicking continues as he moves towards it, but stops if he turns away. When he touches the object he will have to be given a food reward otherwise the reinforcing value of the clicker will gradually decline: it will become extinct.

Clicker training has an important contribution to make to equine education for someone who is confused about learning. What clicker training does is to train the teacher *to observe carefully, and respond appropriately.* If the clicker is clicked at the wrong time, or too late, then it will have a reinforcing value for a response that is *not* desired.

Learning to observe and act on observations when teaching equines is essential. If you are having trouble with this, or making the wrong decisions when interpreting the students' behaviour, or having preconceived notions (that is, thinking that this animal is difficult, or stupid etc.) then a session or two with a clicker will help. However, the use of the clicker as an important training aid from the equines' (or dogs') point of view has disadvantages.

1. It is not possible to direct the student to what is required with the clicker. This might be done with gestures, facial expressions and the voice as well as using the clicker. If this is done, then what is the point of the clicker at all? Why not just concentrate on the appropriate use of the voice, gestures and facial expressions without the clicker? A more useful lesson for the teacher that we use when running workshops, is to have teachers say 'yes' to the animal when they would be using the clicker, having first rewarded the animal when they say 'yes'. In this way, teachers learn to observe, but the equine is also learning to listen to the voice and to watch the teacher and interpret their emotion. In addition, a teacher uses as many gestures as necessary to start with. Finally, it is possible to simply say 'go and touch the bucket' or whatever it is, without either gestures, clicker, or other physical restraints or aids, because the equine has learnt to listen to the voice. With the clicker this is not possible, all you can do is click or not click.

2. Another serious problem with the use of the clicker is that it tends to confirm the user in the belief that emotional interchange between the student and the teacher is unimportant, that learning, even operant or instrumental learning (see page 139) is just a sort of automatic series of responses

without mental events taking place. This is an outdated approach that takes us back to the behaviourists. Skinner (a famous behaviourist) could eventually (using hundreds of trials) teach his rats to do a long series of agility acts or chickens to dance. He even maintained he could teach pigeons to fly aeroplanes or chimps to drive trains by clicker-training-type conditioning.

The trouble with this clicker-training approach is that it is mechanistic; it denies the importance of any emotional input on the part of the teacher. The teacher is of no real importance, it could be a robot doing the teaching, and usually it is in laboratories. It takes very much longer for the animal to learn what response is desired than to listen to the voice (see page 141) and watch the gesture. It also results in the subject going through a large repertoire, trying things out to see which one is right, which may be mildly amusing (although I find this distinctly distasteful).

It is very easy, in fact *a lot easier*, just to say to the animal, 'yes, yes, well done, good' when he does the right thing at the time the clicker would be used, and at the same time direct him with a gesture (especially as horses use such a great deal of visual communication, as discussed in Chapters 1 and 7) and particular words. In fact those who use clicker training *do* use gestures and the voice as well, in which case the clicker introduces a 'tertiary' reinforcement step which is unnecessary. Inevitably the voice and gestures will be used to direct the animal anyway, so use the voice to show approval as a secondary reinforcer (Figures 3.3 and 3.20).

Partial reinforcement
Partial reinforcement is when the response is only reinforced some of the time. There are two characteristics of partial reinforcement.

1. It tends to reduce time to extinction. If the individual does not know if he is going to get a reward or not, he is more inclined to try rather than not to bother, particularly if he is working for a reward (positive reinforcement).
2. It increases the speed of learning new things because the outcome is not predictable (Figure 3.4). This may be one reason why, with horses, we can often get away with some very confusing teaching: we have not reinforced wrong actions because we have not noticed them. Initially, when teaching a new act to

Fig. 3.3 The use of primary (food) and secondary (an appreciative voice praise and chuckle, and a pat or stroke) reinforcement. The importance of the voice used consistently and appropriately to help a horse learn quickly. The two tasks the three-year-old filly, Shemal, learnt were to stand on a pedestal and to paw with one front leg. The number of instructions required from the beginning was four.

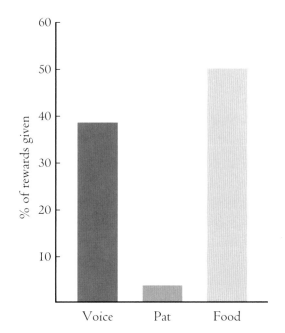

The use of primary and secondary reinforcements when teaching Shemal

Fig 3.4 The effect of partial reinforcement. There were two groups of rats whose speeds of running down a runway were measured. The black line indicates those that were reinforced every time, and they stopped running much sooner than those that were reinforced occasionally (grey line). (After Weinstock 1954.)

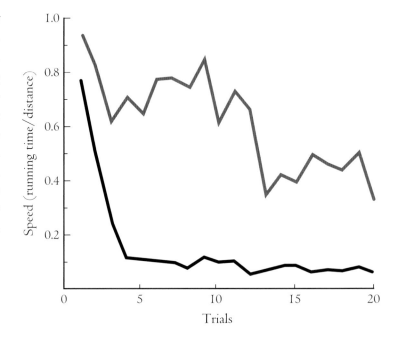

an equine it is important to motivate him to want to do it, consequently,contin-
uous reinforcement (perhaps in the form of a titbit) is important. However,
once he expects a reward, often verbal praise or a pat is sufficient.

Example
Shemal is learning the Spanish walk. To start with, each time she lifts a leg she is rewarded
with a titbit and praise. After half a dozen times, when she does it well, she is only
rewarded with the voice, and finally she must do at least ten strides correctly before she is
rewarded even with the voice.

Delayed reinforcement

One of the characteristics of effective reinforcement is that it needs to follow
the response immediately. If there is a delay before the reinforcement is
acquired, then the subject will learn less fast (Figure 3.5).

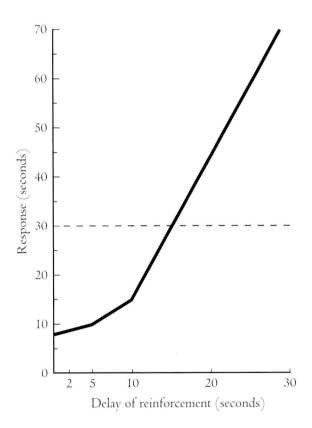

Fig. 3.5   This graph shows the delay in response by a group of rats pressing a lever which gave them a food reward following delays of 0, 2, 5, 10, 20 and 30 seconds. The rats show less delay in response when the delay in reinforcement (reward) is short. When it is longer, they can hardly be bothered to do it at all. (Adapted from Perin 1943.)

Example

In an equine-learning workshop, the participants are asked to teach an equine the simple movement of lifting the left leg to a word command. They have ten minutes to do this in. They have been instructed to give the food reward as soon as the equine subject, initially at least, begins to lift a leg or even change his weight to the other leg. In one group, one person has the cubes that are being used as the positive reinforcer in a pocket from which it is difficult to extract them. With each trial there is a delay of around one minute before the horse has his reward. After ten minutes, the horse has more or less given up paying any attention, and does not perform the required response when asked at the final display. A horse who was immediately rewarded with food by his group, lifts his leg quickly when asked in the display.

Punishment

This is when something unpleasant happens or is done to the individual *after* they have performed an act (a response). We all know about punishments in human education (a child being hit after he has run in the passage when he was supposed to walk, or criminals going to prison, that is having their freedom taken away from them). We also know that the effects of punishment are more unpredictable than those of rewards for doing the right thing. In fact, partly for humanitarian reasons, but also in order to improve learning, corporal punishment in schools is now frowned on in most European societies. It is less effective in improving learning than using rewards. But, punishment is still very widely used when teaching horses.

Example

If a horse shies or refuses a jump, he is whipped, rather than being rewarded when he *does* approach and praised when he *does* jump a jump, however small.

The use of punishment at the wrong time can result in the equine *learning to do the thing you are trying to teach him not to do.*

Example

A horse spooks, so he is kicked, shouted at and whipped to try to get him to approach the object he shied at. In this case the first thing to consider is why did he shy? Generally this is because he is excited and afraid. If you hit him or kick him as he looks at the object or shies, then you are negatively reinforcing him, that is he is learning that the object he was slightly frightened of is, indeed, frightening and causes some pain or unpleasantness. If you hit or kick him after he has shied, he is also confirmed in his belief that the object is frightening, and consequently continues to try to escape. The more you do this, the more he learns to spook or shy.

The rider will often say that he cannot be frightened, he knows this place or object very well, and he is just being 'difficult'. He may indeed know the object or place very well because he has had similar experiences there in the past, that is unpleasant ones. It is often tempting to try and explain his behaviour in this way, but take a moment to let him stop and look and, nine times out of ten, you will find he has a high heart rate and is unable to stand still, all evidence of fear (see page 198).

Consequently, *the great majority of shying horses have been taught to shy by their unsuspecting riders.* A little understanding of learning, and thought, can go a long way to help correct and avoid such problems.

A common explanation of why the horse is shying or spooking is that he is 'trying to get away with it', or 'trying the rider out'. This explanation must be examined with evidence *which does not have another simpler explanation* before you accept it. If it were the case, then why would he bother to do anything with you, he is bigger and stronger and can avoid doing anything required when he really wants to. Why would he be trying to 'dominate' you and 'get away with it'; these are rather complex cognitive manipulative ways of interpreting a competitive world. This may be the way some humans view the world, but it is very unlikely to be the way that equines do from what we know of them today (see Chapter 9 for further discussion).

Very often the equine is 'misbehaving' because he has been taught to by the human handlers and riders by inappropriate use of punishment, negative reinforcement and lack of reward for doing the right thing. Thus, in effect, he has outdone you, but only because you taught him to do it, and he thought it was the right thing. The fact that you have taught him to do the wrong thing is hardly his fault!

Generalization

In the real world, the stimulus is never identical each time. The horse can learn to respond, for example, to come when you call his name, but each time you say his name, it is slightly different. Provided it is sufficiently similar to the word he has already learnt, he will come. This is called **stimulus generalization**. The closer the stimulus to the one he has already learnt, the more likely he is to respond. The more different it is, the less likely he is to respond. Figure 3.6 shows how this evens out in experimental situations, this is called a **generalization gradient**.

The relevance here, when teaching horses, is that initially, at least, it is important to be consistent with the stimulus, do not use different gestures or words to mean the same thing. This is something that we may often do without thought, even when teaching a child to talk. At least at the beginning of something new, it is important to *make things very clear.* After he has learnt what is required to one set of stimuli, it is possible to use generalization so that the same response will be performed to a variety of slightly different stimuli.

Fig. 3.6 A generalization gradient of a 'classical' conditioned response (see page 112): the blinking response in rabbits. The conditioned stimulus was a tone of a certain pitch: 1,200 hertz. The conditioned response was to blink. You can see that the more the pitch changed (either higher or lower) the lower the percentage of trials that caused a blink in the rabbits. The nearer the pitch was to 1,200 hertz, the more the rabbits blinked. The blinking response had 'generalized'. (After Moore 1972.)

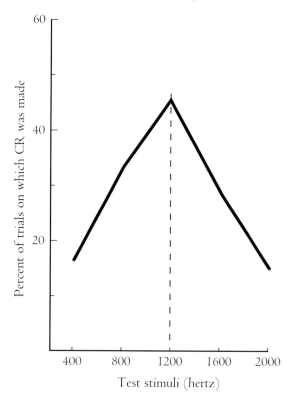

122

Example

In our experimental work we taught all the subjects to do five simple tasks to 1) a physical cue, or a gesture, 2) imitation and 3) the voice. Now they will do it to any one of these stimuli. (Figures 3.7a and b.)

Type of instruction used per simple task (all subjects)

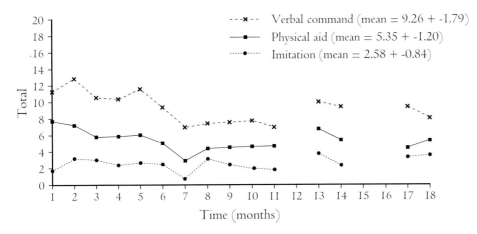

Fig. 3.7a Types of instruction and frequency of use. The three different types of instruction were used for all four subjects (heifer, filly, puppy and guanaco baby) being taught to do five simple tasks in the co-operative teaching experiments. Even from the start, the number of times an instruction was used was relatively small. For example, the vocal instruction only had to be used twelve times before the subject performed the exercise.

Fig. 3.7b Shemal putting her head down to the word command and the gesture.

Equines and humans generalize responses, and perform them with more or less speed and enthusiasm to different stimuli.

In this regard, consider, for a moment, how confusing we can be to an equine.

Example

The use of the arm and hand with equines. We put our arms and hands out when we want the horse to come up to us, or to touch him. But we also raise our arms and hands as a signal, sometimes accompanied by the whip to tell him to go away (in the free-school for example). Now how is he to know when it means come here and when it means go away? You may think that you use many other gestures as well to make this clear but, if you video yourself one day, you will see how this is by no means always the case. It is again much easier to use the voice, paired initially with very obviously different gestures, postures and so on and then, eventually, just the voice: 'come here' or 'go away'. There can be no confusion once he knows the words; they are too different to generalize – even if your gestures and body movements are confusing.

Many horses are blamed for the human's inability and clumsiness in this regard. After a period of such confusion, he may give up responding at all and you may have to be rough; for example, making a riding school horse, (who has been kicked and pulled about daily, often for years) go forward will initially require some rough encouragement. However, even an equine with years of such experiences can often relearn to respond quickly and easily when things are made clearer.

The human, who does not understand how equines learn, usually just increases the strength of the stimulus.

Example

When a horse does not stop or put his head in the right place, harsher bits or pieces of leather to prevent movement such as martingales, and drop nosebands to keep the horse's mouth shut, or spurs and whips to inflict discomfort/pain, are used to try and 'improve the response'. These are all negative reinforcers used because the horse has learnt not to respond in the required way, and it is, of course, the teacher's fault in one way or another.

Shaping

Shaping can be called **successive approximations**. This is what you do when you say 'yes, yes, good boy' or click the clicker before the animal has performed the final response. Thus, he is rewarded for an approximation to it. Gradually the reward is only earned by a closer and closer approximation. Shaping takes place in most of equine teaching (Figure 3.8).

Fig. 3.8 Shemal being taught to cross her legs in front by 'shaping'; the teacher rewards her when she has performed the action more correctly each time, first lifting the leg, then gradually learning, by shaping, to put the leg over the other one and stand still on it.

Example

Teaching a piaffe (trotting on the spot with the back legs well flexed and an elevated stride). First, the horse has to learn to have his hind legs right under him, then to trot, gradually moving forwards and then with less and less forward movement until the trot is on the spot. The successive 'approximations' are: to ensure that he positions his head correctly without it being held there, to gradually increase the height of the lift of his legs, particularly his hind legs, and then to spring off the ground more so that the trot becomes more suspended; there is a split second when no legs are on the ground. Each of these stages must be taught one at a time successively shaping the movement. There is no way he will understand all the concepts involved in this movement at once, but he can if they are presented one by one, like a human learning algebra. Almost any equine can get there with good teaching, but not all will do it well (Figure 3.9).

Fig. 3.9 Oberlix learning to piaffe in-hand. The stick is to encourage him to lift his hind legs up a little more – 'shaping' the movement.

Moulding

This is a type of shaping where the response (the leg for example) will be helped physically into the desired placing or movement. It is employed a great deal when teaching children and primates to use AMSLAN (American Sign Language) which is a gestural language used by those who are deaf without speech.

Example

Teaching an equine to stand with her front legs crossed (Figure 3.10). Shemal lifts her left leg when asked so, first, she is asked to do this, and then to 'cross your leg'. The teacher places the left leg in front of the right and, initially, holds it there, while praising her vocally, and telling her 'cross your legs'. After around twenty trials, she will be putting it there herself with only a gestural or word command.

Imitation

This is frequently used when teaching children, and we found it helpful when teaching animals (Figures 3.11a and b). It is discussed further on page 145.

Fig. 3.10 'Moulding' Shemal's leg across the other one. Here the teacher places the leg in the right place and tells her when she has it right, and to keep it there. She is rewarded when she keeps it there for a second, then two or three, and so on.

Fig. 3.11a Imitation. Here Shemal imitates the action performed by the teacher. We discovered by chance how good the horses were at this, and use it now much as you do when teaching a child. It works well, but have a horse who has learnt to listen and to perform something when asked before you start.

Fig. 3.11b Shemal imitating a leg lift.

Memory

How memory works in the brain is not very well understood yet, but what is clear is that it is all interwoven with perception, past experience and possibly, imagination. In all types of learning where voluntary acts are performed, memory has to be involved.

Retention of information, or memory, is now divided into **short-term memory** and **long-term memory**. Short-term memory is used to manage the immediate environment, for example by remembering a series of recent events, decisions can be made on what to do next.

Examples

1. A zebra remembers the distribution of the acacia trees at the edge of the water hole that he has frequented recently. As a result, he can dart through and around them to escape the cheetah chasing him.

2. A human remembers the location of a book, put down five minutes ago, which they now wish to read.

3. The pony remembers that the last time the reins were dropped onto the ground five minutes ago, he stood on the end of the rein as he tried to walk away, so he stands still this time.

There is very little experimental empirical information on the extent of equines' short-term memory, but we do have information on this from studies of the ecological and social knowledge they need to live as they do (see Chapters 5 and 6).

Short-term memory is very important when teaching equines.

Long-term memory is stored, often for years. Equines have good long-term memories. They can remember locations, food substances, individual horses and people, places and situations over many years. The importance of long-term memory, i.e. the amount of information they need to remember and what this is in order for them to survive and live the way they do in wild or feral populations, is outlined in Chapters 5 and 6. One thing is sure, that we do not need experiments to demonstrate this, we already know how profound their use of memory must be, because of the lives they live. Consequently it is no surprise to find that a mare recognizes her offspring years after they have been parted.

Equines will remember particular unpleasant experiences all their lives, and may require to be retaught, with care, before the undesirable response can be changed, even years after an event. This is called 'episodic memory' at which equines are very able, as we often know to our cost when they remember particular unpleasant episodes.

Example

One winter's day we rode up onto Dartmoor, found one of the rivers was flooded, and decided to ride across a clapper bridge (a bridge made of a large lump of stone). Crystal was cautious but followed one of the older mares onto the bridge, but then, looking down into the swirling water, panicked and fell off. We helped her out and she was not injured. However, she remembered this incident for years, and even generalized to make a fuss before crossing any bridge thereafter. Eventually she unlearnt this experience, but it took us some serious reteaching over two years of exposure to non-dangerous bridges, accompanied only by positive reinforcement, before she happily crossed bridges, even quite wide ones.

Memory is selective (you do not remember everything). There has to be some form of 'reflection', that is some events, situations or behaviours of others are remembered as a result of thinking about them.

It is probable that memories will, in the first place, be **'autobiographical'**, that is memories of what the subject has done, or what has been done to them, and where they have been. It is difficult to understand how equines could learn without first of all having some autobiographical memory. After the establishment of an autobiographical memory, a **biographical memory** might develop. This involves a memory of what others have done or might have experienced. The social behaviour of equines indicates that these animals will have to have some form of biographical memory as well.

Different species as well as individuals will remember different things, depending on who they are and what their lifetime experiences have been. Sometimes individuals, even of different species, have similar experiences, at other times different ones. Sometimes this is the result of the combination of a selection of past experiences they have had or have witnessed, interwoven with previous information, (not all information is experience) so that outcomes are predicted. This is what is called **'imagination'**, which is discussed more fully in Chapter 9.

Motivation

This is the energy/will/emotion/need to do things. It is at the heart of learning, nothing can be learnt unless there is motivation to learn it. What motivation is and how it works is a subject of deep debate at present among scholars of learning and behaviour. Here all we will say is that motivation is necessary in some form for learning to take place, even if it only involves paying some attention and noticing things, and therefore to have learnt silently (see page 147). Motivation is most obviously important when understanding reinforcement: the motivation for learning to do something voluntarily is either to have pleasure as a result (positive reinforcement) or to avoid pain, fear, or displeasure (negative reinforcement).

Because of the general belief that if you use jargon you know what you are talking about, the use of these sorts of terms often seems grand and tends to give credence to certain statements, or methods employed with teaching equines, without any proper explanation or understanding. It is important to understand the terms and the types of learning.

Remember, if in doubt, think how you might behave in that situation, or how you might try to get a child to do this or that, that is use **conditional anthropomorphism**. You may never have to use any of these terms, but if you do, let us ensure that we are talking about the same thing or wires can get crossed, often with very unhelpful consequences, and it is usually the equines who are the losers.

The next stage is to identify the different types of learning, because there are a host of beliefs about them which cause confusion.

TYPES OF LEARNING

Avoidance learning

This is where an equine, or any other species, learns *not to do* particular things because it will hurt, give pain or problems of one sort or another. It is usually the result of negative reinforcement.

Examples
A child learns not to put his hand in the flame of a candle because it hurts. A horse learns not to go through a gateway because it hurt last time when the human let the gate bang on his hips. The subject then generalizes this response to all candles or all gateways.

Many undesired behaviours are of this type in equines but, with thought, avoidance learning need not occur or it can be encouraged in the right circumstance because it can, of course, be useful too.

Examples
A harness horse learns to keep to the side of the road because he is hooted at when in the middle, and this frightens him. An endurance horse in the Western Isles of Scotland learns to avoid falling into bogs by observing the vegetation where he places his feet (having previously been frightened by either himself or another horse falling into a bog).

Both humans and equines may use avoidance learning quite constructively much of their life, but if they have a bad or traumatic experience, then they may develop a **phobia**, and as a result end up with elaborate strategies to avoid going to certain places, or doing certain things, even if the original frightening stimulus has long since been removed.

Example
A horse hurts himself while being loaded into a trailer. He develops a phobia about entering trailers and becomes more and more hysterical the harder people try (using negative reinforcement, such as pulling him, ropes behind his legs, noise and excitement) to make him enter, and the more he resists.

What has to be done here, is for him to unlearn his aversive conditioning, relearn slowly and quietly that all is well, and that going in can be pleasant. This may take many hours, *but is practically always possible.* Whether the human handlers will have the motivation and patience is another matter. It is important not to try to frighten him into the vehicle, this will just enhance his fear of going in next time.

The halters presently being marketed which cause pain when the horse pulls back, use avoidance learning. The problem is that once it has worked, the horse will often use other avoidance strategies such as either not having the halter fitted, or not going into the trailer. His existing phobia may have been enhanced.

Since equines are so easily frightened (see page 198), the problem is to stop them 'learning to avoid' the things you would like them to do, or the places you would like them to go.

Reversal learning or unlearning

This occurs when some response which has been learnt (and may even have become habitual), is reversed: the human or other animal learns to do something different, sometimes the opposite.

Example

A young horse has learnt, by instrumental conditioning (see page 139) to rear (stand on his hind legs) when the rider gets on. The *reinforcement* for rearing was that the rider fell off, or got off, and the horse was put back in the stable (which he preferred, as he had had unpleasant and frightening experiences when he had been ridden). He now needs to learn (be taught) *not* to do this when the rider mounts.

Most importantly, the people handling and riding him must not be frightened. A team approach is useful here, when at least one person who is not frightened at all is there to reassure the horse, talk to him and reward him. It is important to be relaxed and to have 'bonded' with the horse, which means that you must like the horse, and both of you must recognize and have some confidence in each other. It is also useful to use a mounting block initially. Ultimately, the job is to teach him that being ridden is pleasurable rather than scary, and does not have to involve fear, roughness, and general misery all around.

First, the reteaching is made pleasant by giving him food, pleasant tactile attention, and reward to remove the fear. He is praised and rewarded with food when he remains relaxed. Gradually over several trials, mounting is started. To begin with, the rider does not complete the mount and sit in the saddle, but each time he is rewarded with food and then returned to the stable. This continues, until he stands all the time while being fed, and fully mounted. Gradually over the next couple of weeks, the food is withdrawn but verbal praise continues and, slowly, moving forward bit by bit, the goal – the horse standing still while being mounted – is achieved with voice praise. Eventually, movement around the yard following another horse is possible: being led while relaxed and calm. After that, movement away from the stable can begin, again with another horse. There may be progress one day, and retrogressive steps the next, but he never goes back to his stable until he has remained relaxed even if this is only while someone stands beside him. Common sense will dictate how fast you progress, but the central idea is to rebuild his confidence in the exercise. The voice is invaluable here to help the horse relax, provided, of course, that he is already familiar with its use. When he does not rear, he must be praised and rewarded.

Shouting at a horse, jagging his mouth, and putting on more and more restraints will only confirm his worry and fear (negative reinforcement). Force does not work very often because: 1) the horse is stronger than you are; 2) someone may get injured; 3) it will re-establish the problem. Anyone who is nervous should be sent off to make lunch, because they may, by their body language, frighten the horse further.

Habit formation

After the initial learning process, **habit** can become an important component of learnt behaviour, and can obliterate the conscious processes (see Chapter 8 and page 324). Once a more or less satisfactory way of doing something, or even thinking about things is established, it tends to be repeated in the same way. The more it is repeated, the more it becomes resistant to change. Some species and individuals acquire habits more easily than others. Equines acquire habits very rapidly which would seem to be a sensible strategy for a prey species. If a series of actions allowed the individual to escape once, even though it might not be the best possible series of actions, at least it has achieved the aim, and will be likely to be repeated. Trying a new series of actions might fail, and the subject would be caught by the predator. Consequently, you would expect habits to form quickly in prey species and also expect this tendency to be selected for, up to a point.

Example

If when free-schooling or lungeing a horse, he sees something suspicious at one point on the circle, and cuts in at that point, a voluntary action; the goal is to avoid the frightening object or event. The next time around, he is very likely to do it again, even though he has had no reinforcement to encourage this behaviour, that is he has not been frightened, and he may well repeat this at the same place every time he goes around, even when the strange object has disappeared.

The way to change this habit is to do the following.

1. Remove the stimulus that started it first, if possible. If it cannot be removed

take the equine up to it and let him investigate it slowly and quietly, and wait until he approaches it by himself before allowing him to move off.

2. Walk him past the place on the circle four or five times on both reins. Praise him with the voice, and give him a titbit when he does not jump or when he comes in less on the circle.

3. When he is walking past easily and quietly every time, start free-schooling or lunging him past it. If he comes in, say 'no' and frown. Predict that he might do this, and raise your whip as he comes near that place on the circle.

4. Always praise him when he goes quietly past it until he has done it properly at least 8–10 times.

Strong habits are common in humans too. Try cleaning your teeth, or getting out of the bath and drying yourself a slightly different way from normal: it is difficult. Unless there are very important reasons to change the habit (such as having an injured arm, for example), the old way of doing it will constantly be re-established. In this way, habits tend to inhibit innovations in the way familiar things are done.

Because equines form habits quickly, bad habits can also be formed quickly, but let us not forget how many good habits are formed very rapidly too. Without this quick habit formation, we would find it much more difficult to look after and teach equines.

Habits of mind (forming mental habits) are also very important for understanding an individual human or a horse (discussed in Chapters 8 and 9).

Imprinting

In order to survive, a foal must quickly learn to find a teat and suck some milk. To do this, he must rapidly learn who mother is. The term 'imprinting' was invented to outline this early learning which consists of the newborn having an innate tendency to get up and follow a moving object. The first object approached is usually the parent: the mother in the case of equines. The newborn foal then searches for a teat, and if he finds one and receives a milk reward, he learns rapidly to discriminate between his own mother and other mothers by using all his sensory modalities: vision, hearing, touch, smell and taste, and to stay close to her, follow and suckle her thereafter (Figure 3.12).

In the earlier days of ethology, much was made of imprinting as a particular type of learning (e.g. Lorenz 1935); however, it has since been demonstrated that **imprinting involves rapid associative learning** (e.g. Hinde 1970, Bateson 1966, and see page 142) although it does have one particular characteristic: there is a critical period after birth during which it is likely to take place. This in equines appears to be up to twenty-four hours postpartum.

Originally, it was also considered that, unlike other types of learning, imprinting was irreversible, but this has now been shown not to be true.

Fig. 3.12   Shereen, aged twenty-two, with her latest foal, Druimghigha Shindi (by Oberlix) at one week old. They have mutually imprinted, and the foal is sticking very close to mother.

Example

If after imprinting on their mother, the mother dies or disappears, the young of many mammals, including equines, can adopt another individual as their mother, although this may need some encouragement, skilful handling by humans (if they are involved) and relearning by the infant.

135

Imprinting a foal on humans (e.g. Miller 1999) has become a popular idea. Be warned, however, there can be many problems attached to this. We have had a number of youngsters people have tried to do this with presented to us with behavioural problems. The most serious problem being that the foals have not imprinted on their mothers and, consequently, are not receiving milk and growing properly. Miller's idea was that if humans handle the foal very early in his life, that is within the first hour if possible, the foal will imprint on humans and not be afraid of them in the future, because, he erroneously maintained, imprinting is not reversible and imprinted experiences are not forgotten.

One of the dangers of interfering with the foal very early in life is that it interrupts the development of the relationship with the mother. This can cause considerable problems for both the foal and the mother. There are, in addition, many examples now where the foal handled immediately after birth and therefore supposed to be imprinted on humans does *not* behave differently towards humans from others who have been handled for the first time later in their lives. This illustrates that imprinting *is* reversible.

Learning about humans is better done gradually by the foal associating with a sympathetic non-frightening human after he has already established his relationship with his mother, is feeding well and has been exposed to other equines. This is some days after birth.

A week or so after birth, if you have the time and inclination, is a good idea to begin to familiarize him with humans by fondling, handling and talking to him for short periods as frequently as you like. Remember, equines, like humans, continue to learn throughout life, although the speed at which they can acquire information tends to reduce with age. Consequently, early familiarization of the foal with humans and even starting to learn not only about humans, but also with humans, is a very good idea if the foal is healthy, has a normal relationship with his mother and is learning about other equines. The handling must be done well though, or he will learn to avoid humans rather than have much to do with them (see Kiley-Worthington 2004, Chapter 4).

Examples of experiment results

Druimghigha Osnan was handled all over (non-invasively) for two hours after birth, stroked, talked to, and rubbed. For the next two days he approached a human when the human approached him in the field and he continued to be stroked, but after three days he became wary, and only after handling his mother for ten minutes would it be possible to touch him without him withdrawing. His handling continued for 5–10 minute sessions every other day for the next three weeks. By the end of this period he was familiar enough to come up and investigate and be stroked. He had had to learn and become familiar with the humans even though he had been handled shortly after birth and had never had a rough experience with humans. During the summer we were too busy to handle him regularly. When the winter came and we had more time, he was as wary of humans as any of the unhandled foals to begin with. Once he had begun to eat from the hand and a bucket, he progressed rapidly.

Two other related foals were not handled until two weeks old, and behaved in much the same way, progressing rapidly once they had had the same initial handling experience. These foals could not have been imprinted on humans. Finally, one foal was not handled until he was four months old, and he took longer to become relaxed enough to eat from the bucket or human hands, but this has made no difference to his long-term response to humans as far as we can see.

Mismothering is a type of **malimprinting** when things go wrong in early learning between the foal and the mother.

Example

Druimghigha Baksheesh was his mother's first foal and was born in a stable. Although after one hour he was standing and attempting to suckle, his mother had sore teats, was young and inexperienced, and kicked out as he tried to grasp the teat. Within another two hours he had learnt not to try to suckle her, and was suckling a bar in the stable. After we expressed some of her milk, which was causing pressure in her udder and increasing the soreness of her teats, she was then held and fed food while someone else manipulated the foal onto her teats. This was continued every three hours for the next twelve hours, by which time, the pressure in her udder had been reduced, he had learnt where to suckle, and she allowed him to do so. Thereafter things progressed without our interference.

Baksheesh became an easy stallion who was relaxed with humans and took part in almost every type of equine activity. Nevertheless, we have no evidence that this was related to his handling at this early stage as he was quietly handled regularly as he grew up in his first summer, rather than left untouched by humans.

Malimprinting describes the imprinting of one species on another, usually as a result of the infant being bottle reared or suckled by a mother substitute from another species. After this, the individual will preferentially associate with the other species rather than his own kind, and even direct his sexual behaviour towards them when he matures. This can be embarrassing, or dangerous, and it is important to ensure that young equines, particularly hand-reared or orphan foals, do not become malimprinted onto humans.

Examples

1. A friend of mine in Kenya brought up a young orphan giraffe on a bottle. When, after a year he was 3.6 m (12 ft tall), he started to direct play-sex behaviour: mounting, neck twisting and turning, at my 1.5 m (5 ft) friend. When you have a giraffe this size jumping on top of you and trying to embrace you with his long neck around your body, you begin to wonder if raising him was such a good idea!

2. One year we placed duck eggs under a bantam. The mother bantam looked after the ducklings with all her considerable skill, but one thing she found extremely agitating was when they paddled off into the pond. She would run back and forth, screaming and panicking, as their yellow forms bobbed happily out on the muddy broth.

There are many examples of bottle-reared equines who become serious problems to humans, because horse play is rough play. It is very rarely aggressive, just overexuberant affection from a rather larger mammal than yourself, and the fault of the rearer. It is very important if hand rearing a foal to ensure that he has contact with other equines for the majority of the time, and to teach him your rules.

Pavlovian learning

This is the conversion of an unconditioned stimulus and response to a conditioned one as a result of reinforcement (see page 114).

Pavlovian conditioning has often been taken *not* to involve the subjects' voluntary participation. The classic example is Pavlov's dogs who were conditioned (i.e. they learnt) to salivate when they heard a gong. However, when the dogs were released from the experimental restraint, it became clear that they were 'expecting' food as well as salivating (Hinde 1970). To 'expect' necessarily involves some form of awareness; it is not a reflex. Thus, this example of classical conditioning appeared to be able to draw on some form of mental awareness or conscious control, involving expectations and decision making.

Example

A better example of this type of conditioning which is *not* under voluntary control, is eye blinking when a gong is sounded because the human or animal has previously been presented with a strong light accompanying the gong. Here there is a physiological response of the eye to blink to protect itself, and neither humans nor equines can voluntarily control this. However, they *all* can learn *not* to blink the eye voluntarily on other occasions by instrumental conditioning.

Instrumental or operant conditioning

This is defined as conditioned learning where the subject does something voluntarily, and the behaviour is thus under some conscious control. Instrumental conditioning is goal directed and the subject decides either to do it or not. The instrumental behaviour is the means to achieve the goal (the reinforcement). This type of learning is common in humans and other mammals, and is used when learning to perform any particular movement. It is the most important type of learning used in teaching both equines and humans. By definition, **instrumental conditioning** involves a series of mental events having to take place.

Example

A zebra following a human when a lead rein is attached (Figure 3.13). Here, the zebra has had an experience of pulling against the lead rope and found it was not pleasant. He has an 'expectation' a 'belief' that if he pulls against the rope it will be unpleasant, so he follows.

Fig. 3.13 Instrumental conditioning. The most important type of learning for equines and humans. This zebra was an eighteen-month-old wild stallion and the photograph was taken twenty-four hours after his capture.

Once voluntary actions have been learnt, then the individual who has learnt has some idea of cause and effect (MacPhail 1998, Dickinson 1994). So they **believe** tightening the rope is unpleasant, they **remember** what happened last time they tried, and **decide** to follow. The **goal** is to avoid being frightened or hurt.

Figures 3.14a and b show the performance curve: the learning curve for Shemal learning by instrumental conditioning to do some simple actions (Fig. 3.14a), for rewards, and some more complex ones (Fig. 3.14b).

Learning does not stop there, however; secondary reinforcements, generalization, habituation, extinction, and all the other things we have discussed, sometimes occur so that learning one thing, can lead to learning another, or result in different behaviours being performed or things being unlearnt.

One area of possible confusion here is that instrumental learning (otherwise called operant conditioning) can become automatic so that it does not need direct attention.

Example

When you have learnt to type or drive a car, or a horse has learnt to be ridden and respond to certain aids, these behaviours have been instrumentally conditioned, and required voluntary decision making by the learner. But, thereafter they can be performed without this conscious decision making as a result of becoming **habitual**, i.e. well practised, they are performed without attention or apparent consciousness.

But, if there is a problem with the response for some reason, the conscious attention will be redirected to the doing of the action.

Examples

1. When driving your car while thinking about your latest boyfriend, you are dangerously overtaken near a corner; your attention is immediately directed away from your thoughts to your driving, which previously had been on autopilot.

2. A horse pulling a milk cart around a well-known route stops and starts at the appropriate houses in an automatic way, 'without thinking about it'; but if the road is obstructed by a lorry, which has to be negotiated, the well-known route is brought back into conscious control, he becomes aware of where he is on it, and where to stop next after negotiating the problem.

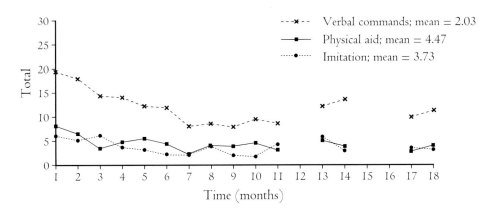

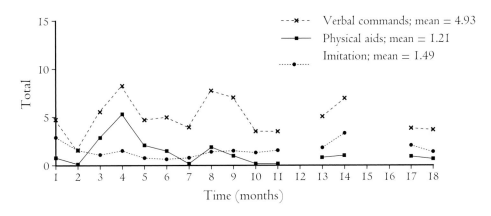

Figs. 3.14a and b   The performance curves for the filly. a) Shemal when performing five different simple behaviours (lifting the right and left leg, shaking the head, putting the head up and down) and b) four more complex behaviours (pawing with the right and left leg, standing on the pedestal and kicking the ball). The different lines indicate the type of instruction used.

I am stressing this here as there is much confusion about this 'part-time' conscious doing, and incorrect assumptions are made which imply that animal learning is always of this unaware type (see Chapter 8 for further discussion).

Associative Learning

This is **S-S (stimulus-stimulus)** learning rather than **S-R (stimulus-response)** learning; it involves associating one object, or situation with another independently of the observer making any response. This involves causal links, that is some understanding of cause and effect (Macphail 1998). In other words, there has to be a recognition of an association of *this* situation or object with *that* situation or object.

Example

In the winter, our horses are kept in yards from where they can come and go to the field. In the morning some of them (the young, the pregnant, the old, and those working hard) are given a small feed with some minerals in it. The feeds are made up in the food store, in view of the horses from the yard, and then presented in buckets. When they see me coming out in the morning, they all call, and stare at me over the rails, that is they have an expectation of having their food and they associate me with giving it to them.

These associations may be formed without any consciousness; but, when necessary, the association *can* be brought to the conscious attention such as when voluntary acts are performed.

Example

Oberlix is tied up outside the tack room as usual before working. He is aware that he will be doing some form of exercise at this time and will be tacked up accordingly. He sees the collar being prepared and sighs. It is put on and he moves off quietly to the garden to do some hard work pulling a spring-tyne cultivator. He returns and we untack him. Next we bring out the small racing saddle, he perks up, looks at the saddle and begins to jink about as it is fitted. Here, he has made an association between: 1) being kept outside the tack room at that time and going to do some work; 2) the harness and hard, slow work in the garden which requires pulling and walking only, that is going quietly and slowly; 3) the small racing saddle which requires short bursts of fast work. He has already done some hard work quietly. Subsequently, he is not just excited to be doing anything, he 'understands' that the small saddle means fast exciting work. He demonstrates this by the difference in his behaviour associated with the different tack.

Equines are particularly good at associative learning, but it can take some analysis of what has happened to that animal before the range of associations can be disentangled. It may not be just stimulus-stimulus, but may be stimulus-stimulus-stimulus-stimulus and so on.

Observational learning, social learning and culture

Observational learning is a type of association learning and involves the ability of an animal to acquire information, or skills, by observing. This can be watching events, even those not involving other equines.

Examples

1. Equines have to grasp simple physical principles, like gravity for example. Shemal hears a noise on the roof, looks up and sees a tile slipping. She leaps away, knowing that the tile will fall down and if she stays where she is it may hit her.

2. Equines often observe things in the natural environment which give them information on where to go or what to do. For example, if they observer a landslide or a rock fall in one area, they will be very cautious of visiting it even days or weeks later.

More commonly, observational learning is used when one equine is watching another and learns something from this. This type of observational learning is called 'social learning'. It is extremely important to a social mammal as much information necessary to survival can be acquired by observing others: for example, how to behave in certain unfamiliar situations, where to go, what to eat and so on (see Chapters 5 and 7).

Example

Druimghigha Shereen's mother, Sheba, was when we bought her aged eighteen, difficult to catch, particularly for the students. Shereen learnt the same behaviour from observing her mother, although she had never had a worse experience of being caught than any of the other horses we have bred and owned, all of whom have been easy to catch.

Social learning has often been harnessed by humans to help equines learn.

Examples

1. To familiarize a horse with draught work on the land (or many other things) an experienced horse will be used while the youngster walks beside them and watches. Because one equine will often follow another, having one equine who is familiar with the routine will

Fig. 3.15 Lilka having one of her first lunge lessons with Chris, watched by Shezam and Shanti. Instrumental learning, with positive reinforcement from Chris when she does the right thing. When she pulls against the line she receives negative reinforcement from the line, so she has learnt to keep it slack.

make a great difference to how easy it is to get others used to a routine or to enter a certain place. The follower, by observation and association has learnt that nothing terrible happens (see Example 1 below and Figure 12.2).

2. Figure 3.15 shows Lilka learning to be lunged, watched by Shezam and Shanti.

Social learning gives rise to differences in behaviour between populations, this is called 'culture'. There is now much evidence that animal societies, including equines, have different cultures just like humans have (e.g. Bonner 1980).

Examples
1. Shereen has had five foals, all of whom learnt from her to be difficult to catch when they were with her. So we took them away at nine months and put them with some of the other older mares and stallions who were easy to catch. These youngsters then learnt the 'approach humans and be friendly' culture, rather than the 'keep away when the humans have a headcollar' culture.

2. On the stud we do not like horses with bad manners, such as stepping on feet, barging through gateways, kicking or biting a human, or another horse when a human might get

hurt by being in the way. We taught the first youngsters these simple manners with care. However, four generations later, we find we hardly have to teach the new youngsters, they appear to have learnt how they behave in relation to humans from their elders. A culture has been established.

3. Each yard/stable/stud which has had some residents for at least a ten-year period will have its own culture, the result of a) the behaviour of the humans, b) a horse's expectations of the other horses, and c) the horses' expectations of the humans. All of this is social learning from their own and other species. It is worthwhile understanding that social learning is occurring in order to help understand the horse's point of view, and establish the equine culture you like.

Proving whether or not different species learn by observation and social learning is a current vogue in ethology. Although having some empirical results here is interesting, particularly to find out where the limits are to what can be learnt in this way, nevertheless, it is also important to remember they have to learn from and about each other for their societies to work (see Chapter 6).

What is particularly interesting is that social learning also works between species: different people will learn to behave in different ways as a result of their contact with different equines; and different equines will behave in different ways as a result of their observation and contact with different people.

Imitation

A particular case of observational learning is **imitation: learning to do something novel by copying another.** Imitation has been much discussed among those interested in animal minds because of its relevance to whether or not various species have an awareness of themselves (true imitation, rather than just imitating as a result of learning to do this by instrumental learning: see Chapter 8). Records are only just beginning to be kept of cases of true imitation in equines (see example below).

Example

I took a visiting scientist into the field where Shemal (one of the experimental subjects with whom we had been studying learning) and Shukrune (a yearling gelding at the time) were living. I asked Shemal, verbally, to paw when she came up to me. She did but, most surprisingly, seeing her paw, Shukrune pawed too. Shemal had been taught to do this but

Shukrune had had no teaching at all of this type. It was out of context, since he had no expectation of a reward and was not frustrated (a time when pawing can take place naturally). He was performing a novel act by imitating his elder sister.

The subjects of our studies learnt to perform leg lifts, head shakes, head up and down, to paw, and many other behaviours, partly by imitating the teacher. At the beginning of the research programme I performed the act I was asking for, as one does when teaching a child for example, and found that this was a helpful teaching aid, together with gestures and a verbal command. As a result we used imitation to help with the teaching. The interesting thing here is that the subjects were learning to imitate not just another horse, but a similar movement made by another species. This means they had to be aware of what bits of my body were equivalent to theirs. This does imply a considerable amount of self-awareness, and it was the first time that it had been reported with equines. We discuss the implications of this more fully in Chapter 8.

Trial and error learning

Thorpe (1954 and 1963) places this in a different category of learning because it combines both associative learning and instrumental learning, or operant conditioning. He defines it as: 'The development of an association, as the result of reinforcement . . . between a stimulus or a situation and an . . . action'.

The classic examples of trial and error learning are rats learning to run mazes or to open problem boxes. Rather than the stimulus leading to a particular response (S-R) as an explanation for learning a maze, a simpler explanation could be in terms of the animal having what is called a 'cognitive map'. This implies some form of understanding of 'what leads to what' (Hinde 1970), and the need for some form of conscious involvement by decision taking and memorizing (see Chapter 8).

Example
A donkey is presented with a box with a lid on it in which there is some relished food. Only by pressing a button on the right side of it will he be able to open the box. He pushes it with his nose and attempts to lift the lid with his prehensile upper lip, unsuccessfully. Finally he pushes and bashes the box so hard that it breaks. He eats the food. The next

time he is presented with the box, he immediately breaks it and eats the food. He has learnt by trial and error to break the box, which was not the intention of the experimenter!

Cognitive and silent learning

This is a type of associative S-S (stimulus-stimulus) learning which allows information about the world to be acquired. As an individual travels through the world, he notices things in it. This may be done by directing conscious attention at those objects or just by cues being picked up about objects and their places in the world. There is a recognition of objects, shapes, places, species and individuals without any stimulus attached to any particular response and without any immediate reinforcement. Silent learning is often involved particularly in route finding and ecological knowledge (see Chapter 5).

Some maintain that cognitive learning is a different, more complex, type of 'reflective learning' than associative learning (e.g. Savage-Rumbaugh et al. 1996) but, as we have emphasized, the boundaries between each type of learning are moveable, one drifting into another.

Examples

1. A zebra, walking on her familiar way to the water hole, sees a peculiar shaped acacia tree with a 'rock' at its base. That evening as she walks back towards the centre of her home range with her family, the 'rock' has disappeared. She snorts, ears pricked towards the tree, showing a recognition that it is different.

2. The stallion Oberlix has previously been ridden once over part of the island of Mull to the other side, a distance of some fifteen miles over which there is no marked trail. Two years later he is ridden over the same route and allowed to choose the way. He follows almost exactly the same route as before, even remembering a particular stream crossing which we had had to choose carefully the first time.

Insightful learning

The solving of problems, not as a result of trial and error or any of these other types of learning, but as a result of demonstrating that they have taken in some understanding of the problem in order to solve it, was demonstrated first in animals by chimpanzees, in a classic experiment designed by Wolfgang Kohler (1951). He placed the chimps in an area where there were some hanging bananas that they could not reach by jumping, and some pieces of furniture. They solved the problem by 'insight', having a) some idea of the problem (can't reach the bananas), and b) its solution (pile the furniture underneath until they can be reached). Previously, it was considered that only humans would be able to do this.

Examples

A young stallion can understand the problem and behave appropriately so that he is not attacked by an older one when they are living together. He must: a) show that he is not a threat to the other stallion even though he may be a mature male; b) show he is not sexually attracted to the stallion; c) never show he is attracted to any of the mares and behave sexually to them when he can be seen by the other stallion.

If he manages all this — behaves like a much younger colt when he sees that the stallion is boiling up to try and attack him and chase him away, and manages to reassure him that he is no threat — he may be able to continue to live with the group, and even, if an entire, occasionally copulate with one of the mares, provided the stallion does not know (see Deceipt on page 359).

2. When riding on Dartmoor we had a two-year-old gelding, Druimghigha Shirac (now an international endurance horse), running loose with the three mares and a stallion we were riding. We rode across a clapper bridge over a deep small river. The youngster had been left behind as we came to the bridge because he was grazing. He came rushing to catch us up, but went past the bridge along the wrong edge of the ditch. After following the ditch for 300 m on the other side, the rest of the party turned away from it. Shirac neighed and became frustrated rushing up and down the ditch. Instead of turning back, we left him to it. After around two minutes, suddenly he turned and galloped 300 m back away from us to the bridge, came across and joined us. He had apparently had a flash of 'insight' of how to solve the problem.

Sometimes it is difficult for us to leave the equines to try and solve the problem themselves, and it may well be that the motivation has to be very high before they do have these flashes of insight, but of course in the wild situation, there is no human there to help them out, and it may be that it becomes quite common, at least in some individuals.

Insight learning has been neglected to date when considering equines and what they may be able to do mentally. But, we must be very cautious not to jump to conclusions when there may be simpler explanations. It would be out of place to consider that equines use insight learning a great deal, but it would be equally out of place to say they *cannot* solve problems in this way.

SUMMARY TO DATE

There are, of course, a number of controversies among learning theorists concerning all this and I have tried to be accurate but simple. The main controversy which is relevant here, is the degree to which these types of learning may require mental events and what these are. Are non-human mammals, in this case equines, conscious or not, and if so when? Many people have argued that consciousness does not need to be involved in learning and consequently, there is a profound difference in what humans and non-human mammals, including equines, can learn. I have pointed out that there are some types of learnt behaviour which occurs in humans and non-humans alike, which could be performed in a way which requires little, if any, mental activity (decision-making, memory, awareness), for example true Pavlovian conditioning, or when behaviour has become a 'habit'. The problem here is that even habits have to be learnt in the first place.

One thing that must be considered is that the main type of learning that we use in teaching our children or our equines, is instrumental conditioning, and this is a clear cut demonstration of the necessity for conscious decision making, because it involves voluntary action; the individual has a choice to do something, or not do it. If your equine demonstrates choices, then he has some awareness of the environment and what he is doing within it. This is one of the most teasing problems confronting our understanding of 'what it might be to be an equine'. It is discussed further in Chapters 8 and 9.

Another important point I would like to emphasize is that even though we have compartmentalized these types of learning, and indeed tried to define the terms involved, it is very important to realize that learning is generally not so simple. All types of learning are occurring at any time in most situations, although one or other may be most important at any one time.

Example

Shemal is having one of her lessons in learning how to kick a ball. First, it is crucial to obtain her attention, this may not always be easy as she is going to be aware of and absorbing information from all around her all the time. For example, the sparrows in the barn are making a racket as usual and she is clearly aware of them; when there is an obvious change in the noise, she reacts. Chris is also about to go and turn the hay with the tractor that is parked outside the ring, but first he has to fix new blades on the mower, so she is also aware of him, and to some extent watching him (silent learning) at the same time as listening to me trying to teach her by instrumental learning. She kicks up some dust when she kicks the ball, and after a couple of times, as she kicks the ball, she shuts her eyes and turns her head away (Pavlovian conditioning).

To start with I kick the ball and say 'kick the ball'. She watches me kick the ball, and then has a go (imitation), and she has also been watching Oberlix who had just kicked the ball (social and observational learning). After a few trials all I have to say is 'kick the ball' without gesture and she goes to the ball and kicks it (associative learning). Then I say 'kick the ball to me', and when it comes somewhere in my direction, I praise and reward her. After another five tries, she has more or less got the idea of the meaning of 'kick the ball to me' rather than just kick it randomly anywhere (further associative learning of direction). She listens to my words and the emotion involved in them, and although she would like to follow her sister, Shindi, who is going back to the field, she continues to remain calm and get on with the work required (cultural learning). (Figures 3.16 and 3.17.)

There are some **Basic Rules of Learning** despite this complexity. To make it simple:

1. In order to learn, there has to be motivation, that is, an awareness or a need/want/desire — a feeling or wish to respond appropriately. Learning thus has to involve emotions or feelings.
2. There must be directed attention. Attention by definition involves some form of awareness and recognition of objects or situations.
3. In the case particularly of voluntary behaviour, there are decisions to be made: to do this, to do that, or to do nothing.
4. During learning, the behaviour may be modified by experience, thus there must be experiences. Experiences in their turn require perception

→

(things to be perceived), and analysis (things to be ordered and related to others in some sense) and some form of personal feeling as a result, in other words some form of 'conscious memory'.

5. Although some forms of learning may be able to be induced without any conscious involvement of the mind (by Pavlovian conditioning for example), most learning requires memory. But some learning will be done at a conscious, decision-making level, but may afterwards be transferred to a less conscious level from which responses, even quite complex ones, (such as performing a dance routine for a horse, or typing for a human) can be performed in an automatic way (see Chapter 8).

6. Since there are clear individual differences in behaviour both between species and within one species, as a result of the different sensory information they acquire and different physical (see Chapters 1 and 2) emotional (see Chapter 4), and cognitive (see Chapters 5–9) experiences they have, there are differences in the way and amount these different types of learning are used by different species, and even different individuals of the same species.

7. One thing that is clear is that learning inevitably involves the interplay of the physical, emotional and cognitive worlds of an individual, and a recognition of the causal links between events.

How can we apply this information in our dealing with equines? In the first instance, we should now be better aware of why an individual may be doing something unexpected at any time, and it will help us understand equines better.

These are general rules of learning which apply to all species, including of course humans, and they do not depend on obtaining information from others through language, although language may help the acquisition of more information about the past or the future.

Shamal ball kicking: type of cues

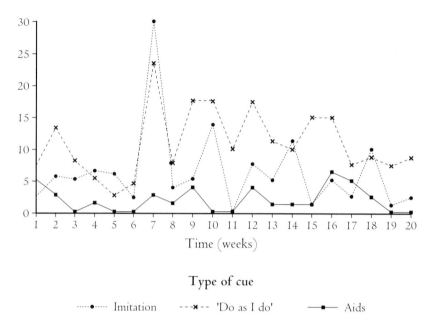

Time (weeks)

Type of cue

········•········ Imitation   ---✕-- 'Do as I do'   ━━■━━ Aids

Fig. 3.16   Shemal, the filly, knows what to do and how to do it from the beginning, the problem is, she does not always feel like doing it. In this case, imitating the teacher has been the most used cue.

Fig. 3.17 Shemal kicking the football. She is not being led to the ball but is actually following it and kicking it forward and away from her.

KNOWING OR LEARNING 'THAT' AND 'HOW'

Ryle (1949), a philosopher of mind, made an important distinction with regard to acquiring knowledge, or learning, which is very relevant here. This is the division of the task into two phases or types of learning. The first one is to learn 'that' or 'what to do'.

Examples

1. Teaching an equine to lift his left leg: **'knowing that'** is that he knows he should lift his leg when asked. The second part is **'knowing how'**. He may know what to do, but not how to do it. With this simple example this seems curious because, lifting a front leg for an equine is very easy, but example 2 is Ryle's classic example that illustrates this point more clearly.

2. A human riding a bicycle. You may know that bicycles are for riding: 'that'. But can you ride one? Do you know 'how': the practical side of how to do it?

3. Teaching a more complex movement to a horse, e.g. the Spanish walk. The front legs are to be thrown forwards in an exaggerated way, one after the other, and the hind legs follow as the horse walks forward. Now the equine may quickly learn 'that' with the appropriate words and gestures, including imitation and watching others, so he knows he has to lift his front legs right up as he walks. But can he do it? What usually happens is the novice horse finds it difficult to do in sequence while continuing to move forward; the hind legs keep getting left behind! (Figure 3.18a.) This demonstrates learning 'that' for a horse is one thing, but learning 'how' to do it, is another (Figure 3.18b).

Figs. 3.18a and b   a) Learning the Spanish walk. Oryx has learnt the 'that': lift the front legs high up and walk forward. But the 'how' is more difficult – he has forgotten his hind legs! b) Now he understands both the 'that' and the 'how' although I am still having to use a gesture (pointing the whip at the next leg), as well as a voice command.

An understanding of this distinction can be very helpful when teaching equines. Generally, a horse will not manage the 'that' and the 'how' all at once, any more than a human will. He will have to learn 'that' first, followed by 'how'. If you take account of this and structure the teaching to allow for this: praising when first the 'that' and then the 'how' is acquired (rather than just being disappointed that it is not happening right), it makes a great difference to what can be learnt and how fast it is learnt; it helps with the 'shaping' of the response (see page 124).

Example
Recently Oberlix has been doing advanced dressage tests. In his learning of the various movements and how they are to be done, I omitted to teach him the 'that', of lateral movements: that is 'go sideways, and cross your legs', thinking (as most are taught) that this would just come out of other exercises. His low marks and the judges' comments brought this to my attention. Thus, we did exercises going sideways, almost anyhow, but without going forwards (i.e. learning 'that') so that he grasped the concept of the movement ('go sideways and cross your legs'). The next step was 'how' the movement had to be done for this discipline. This requires that the horse bends in the direction of movement, keeps going forward as well as crossing his legs and not leaving his quarters behind. Once he had the concept of 'go sideways', it was relatively easy to teach him the rest, although we do not always do it very well of course! This learning took three sessions not three months or years.

With equines though, there is a third type of distinction to be made. This is 'knowing that and how, but not feeling like doing it'. Equines do not always tell us in an unambiguous way (like humans may) that they do not want to do it. So, it is sometimes difficult to understand if they have understood 'that' and 'how' but just do not feel like doing it, or if they just have not understood. The only way out of this, is to try to increase the motivation so that they do want to do it. Sometimes stopping or having a break doing something different is useful, or sometimes rather more harsh methods involving negative reinforcement for being idle are utilized, which, in my view, should be avoided if possible. Many of the old masters of equitation suggest that the best reward for a horse is to get off him and take him back to the stable (Podhajsky 1967, Burger 1959). This is a sad reflection on their teaching. Despite the teacher's efforts, the equine still does not like doing whatever it is, presumably because he was taught mainly by negative reinforcement (whips and spurs and pulls in the mouth). If he dislikes doing it and consequently the reward is to stop, it cannot be co-operative teaching.

There are by contrast many horses who became frustrated and excited when asked to do things they do not understand, and may indeed even panic. If negative reinforcement is continued here, far from them learning what you are teaching, they may learn not to do it, and panic more and more. For this reason it is always sensible to assume the horse does not understand the 'that' and/or the 'how' before assuming that he just does not want to do it.

Examples

1. Teaching Shemal to piaffe. She is asked to collect, something she already knows, but then not to go forward at all, but continue trotting. She finds this difficult and begins to jump and become very excited. Rather than continuing when she will get into a greater panic and then not settle down to do anything right for a while, the solution is to recognize this, and take her very slowly through it all, praising her for the slightest improvement. If the person riding her is too bossy and firm, this will result in her becoming panic stricken, not because she does not want to do what is asked, but because she does not understand.

2. By contrast, Oberlix is extremely laid back about learning new things but he really does not want to do flat work with any enthusiasm for more than around ten minutes, and his piaffe will be performed on the spot with the minimum of effort. He knows the 'that' and indeed the 'how', but does not really feel like putting the effort in. Touching him with the whip makes little difference to his energy and enthusiasm, all he does is kick-out backwards. The only way I have found to motivate him to put more effort in and lift his legs higher is to scold him verbally. If I get very cross, verbally, he usually begins to make an effort, but of course I cannot do this too often or his response to this will be extinguished!

The distinction between 'knowing that' and 'knowing how' will apply when the equine (or human) is learning a mental skill, a 'habit of mind'. There may initially be difficulties with learning both 'that' and 'how' here.

Example

Learning to comprehend some simple human language. First the horse needs to learn that a) he must listen, b) he must learn the meaning of individual words and c) he must learn the meaning of the combination of words presented to him. This is an area we have been working in, and there are some remarkable results coming out of the short periods of time we have been able to spend with the subjects who have been learning in the same way as we generally teach pre-verbal infants. Once they know that they must listen, then they have developed a 'habit of mind', at least up to this point (see page 320).

INTERACTIVE OR CO-OPERATIVE TEACHING OF EQUINES AND OTHER ANIMALS

At the research centre, we determined to set up some learning experiments for a variety of species, including equines, not in isolated experimental boxes, but in an interactive teaching situation (Kiley-Worthington & Randle 1997) such as that used successfully with children. Such interactive teaching situations are sometimes used traditionally for equines, but the point of our experiments was to try to measure the performance of the different species, and to learn more about how the animal learns and the similarities and differences between the species.

Of course these differences might be related to the different behaviour of the teacher with the different species, so we were particularly interested to measure the behaviour of the teacher and see if this were the case. We also wanted to see if we could develop some 'general rules' for improving the teaching of equines.

Because of their physical, emotional and social differences, finding problems of similar difficulty for different species is awkward, even when teaching them simple actions.

Example
Horses do not have hands, trunks or paws and rarely fetch, lift and carry things around like humans, elephants or dogs. Consequently, it might be expected that teaching them to hold, lift and carry objects would be difficult. It may be like teaching an elephant to trot, or a human to canter on all fours.

There are also the problems of what are the limits of their minds, what can they learn? Making assumptions about the way animal minds work and the inability of certain species to learn certain things has been shown to be highly suspect (see, for example, concept learning and language learning, Chapters 6, 7 and 9). If only one animal of a species can learn to do whatever is being tested, it means that we can no longer conclude that that species *cannot* learn that task. Tests indicating that a species cannot do it (negative results) may just prove that the experiment has been wrongly designed and, with further tests, the results may be shown to be incorrect. Haangi (1994), for example, showed that equines 'transfer learn' (transfer some general rules about shapes to slightly different shapes); previously it had been concluded that only primates and humans could do this. We have shown that equines can learn to perform new acts by imitating a human, something that was not considered possible before.

To try to overcome these problems, we chose to teach our experimental animals of five different species (a filly, a heifer, a puppy, a young guanaco, and a young African elephant) some very simple movements that none of them should have had much difficulty performing to a word command. The activities were: 1) shaking the head, 2) lifting the right or left front leg as asked, 3) moving the head up and down. The teacher accompanied the use of the words with a) gestures, b) physical restraint to stop them walking off, c) shaping, and d) imitation, much as if the subjects were children. No negative reinforcement was to be used in any of these experiments, and food as well as verbal ('good girl' etc.) physical (patting, scratching and stroking), and gestural praise (smiling and laughing etc.) were to be used as positive reinforcements to help motivate the individual towards the correct response. In addition to the responses of the animal student, the behaviour of the teacher was recorded to see if there was a difference in the way she responded to one animal in comparison with another, and whether this affected the subjects' learning.

After these simple movements (which were relatively easy for each subject), we went on to teach more complex ones such as, 1) pawing the ground, 2) kicking a ball, 3) standing and turning on a pedestal, 4) lying down, and 5) picking up and holding an object in the mouth. This is where the species differences emerged. It was easy for the filly to learn to paw when asked (something that they often do when in some form of frustrated situation), but difficult for her to learn to kick the ball forwards; kicking the leg out forwards is not something that comes naturally to an equine, but is something that comes naturally to guanacos who will use their front legs to attack. Lying down was something that was much more difficult for the filly, because equines have to feel very secure before they are happy to do this, whereas it is something a puppy or guanaco will do frequently and easily. Standing up on the pedestal was a simple task for the filly, but more difficult for the puppy to learn. But, very interestingly, the heifer had little trouble learning to paw, even though bulls are usually the only bovines who paw (normally as a threat, but cows may sometimes do it around calving time). Some results were unexpected though, for example, Shemal found head tasks more difficult than leg tasks. A full report of these results is given in the centre's publication (Kiley-Worthington & Randle 1996).

We were interested in the speed of learning these first simple acts to a word command and, interestingly, it was not the puppy (who had much more contact with us humans and language because he lived in the house with us), but the filly and the heifer who were the quickest to learn. The puppy and the guanaco coming a poor second and third. The elephant was, as expected, quick and good at these simple tasks, and also good at manipulative ones like learning to pick up a straw bale by its strings so as not to break it, and put it somewhere else (Figures 3.19a and b).

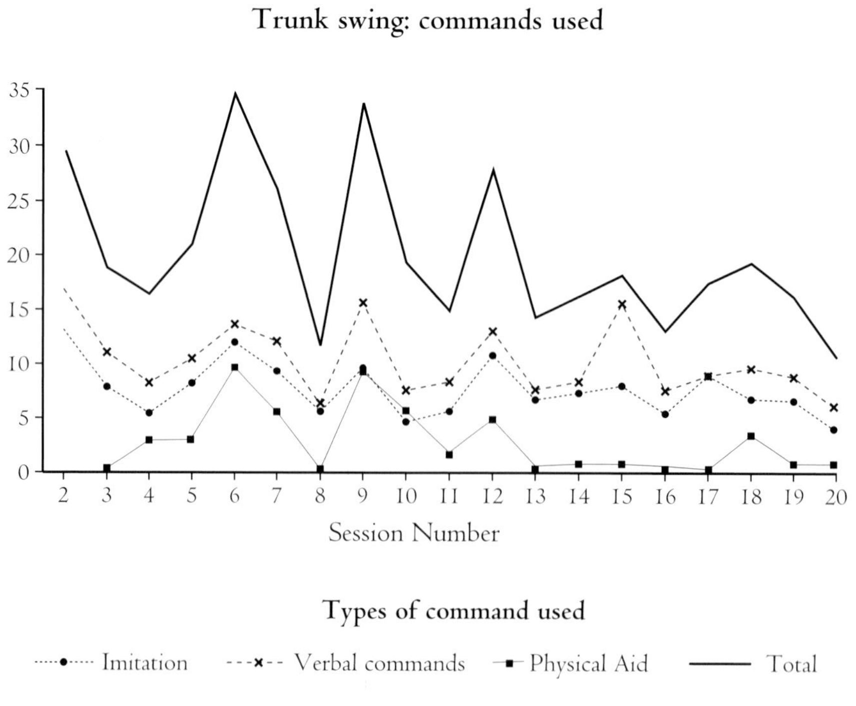

Trunk swing: commands used

Types of command used

······•······ Imitation   ---×-- Verbal commands   -■- Physical Aid   ──── Total

Fig. 3.19a   Chaka had no clear idea of the 'that' for swinging the trunk to start with, but after the fourteenth trial he grasped it. The 'how' in this case is very easy as trunk swinging is a little like arm swinging for us, it is not anything any normal elephant would find difficult.

Fig. 3.19b Chaka has to learn to pick up a bale by its strings so that it does not break. He grasped the 'that' right away and kept trying to pick up the bale but without success as the string kept breaking. He took some time to learn the 'how'. Chaka's part in the research was conducted in Zimbabwe.

The overall results of this work indicated that there were, indeed, some expected results from comparing the learning abilities of these different species, but there were some unexpected ones too, that is, often preconceived notions need to be examined.

As far as a difference in treatment by the teacher to the different species was concerned (which was expected because inevitably the teacher may like one better than another and make particular allowances or give extra help in some way), there was in fact very little difference. Since I was the teacher, and I was aware of this problem and tried to overcome it, I must say I was particularly pleased with this result, it shows that with a little concentration it is possible to overcome the preconceptions that we all have.

Another very interesting thing was that all the subjects learnt to work for an appropriate verbal and/or tactile praise (secondary positive reinforcer), rather than just for food. In other words, if the use of verbal-gestural and tactile praise is restricted to the appropriate situation, it *will* be used to help learning; there is no need for the 'clicker' or other gadgets (Figure 3.20). In fact the heifer, Ramblie, was not keen on taking food during the summer, so

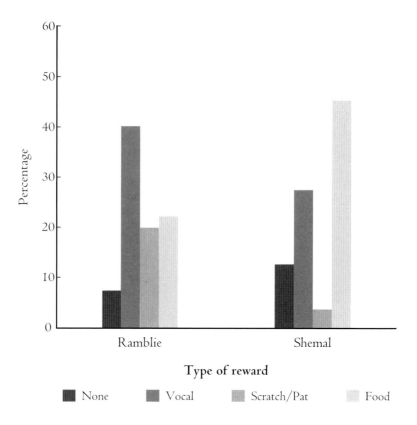

Fig. 3.20 We used food (22% for Ramblie and 45% for Shemal) and vocal reinforcement: telling the pupils, Ramblie the heifer and Shemal the filly, when they had got it right. Patting and scratching were used much less: under 10% for Shemal, but 20% for Ramblie.

first we used just a scratch at the base of her tail which she liked, associated this with the verbal praise 'good girl, well done, brave' and she learnt the rest of her tasks in this way.

This, of course, is only a beginning of the 'science of animal educational psychology', but the results are interesting and, together with information about learning that we have already covered, allows us to outline a list of 'general rules' for good teaching of equines, and other animals, including human infants, (see end of chapter).

People who have thought about these things often make remarks such as, 'This is all very well, equines may be able to learn a lot more than we thought, and even learn some simple human concepts, like some numbers, the use of symbols and so on, but what they *never* will be able to do is to understand some of our uniquely human concepts' (but see Chapter 9 and Figure 9.2). The jury is still out on this issue. We have only just begun to consider what the mind/body, 'the being', of the equine might be and what it might be able to learn with good teaching, although I am prepared to admit that equines could probably never design a space shuttle or send a man to the moon; let us not jump to conclusions at this stage.

One thing is clear, that studying learning and teaching in equines will give us a much better grasp of the world they live in and the knowledge they have of the world, as well as helping us to improve our teaching to help them to become better educated.

Exercise
Learning to concentrate the attention on the subject rather than on human company
The first and often the most difficult cognitive jump that has to be made, by any animal teacher is to learn to concentrate 100% of the attention onto the individual equine student, rather than (as we normally do) the other humans who are around watching or talking to the teacher about the student. Learn to concentrate on the subject rather than to talk about him.

Mental exercises of changing the consciousness can be useful here, as practised in yoga, shiatzu etc. However, the aim is not to concentrate the mind on 'nothing' as in yoga, or on 'energy' as in shiatzu, but rather on the 'equine subject'.

Stage 1 Spend five minutes (time it) holding or standing near your equine subject while he is just standing resting or not doing very much. Look at him, concentrate on him, not what he is doing, why he is doing it, or what adventures you have had together, but concentrate on him just there as he is right now. Again, do not try to concentrate on nothing either. Look him in the eye, look at all aspects of his body, without assessing him or reminding yourself to do this or that to improve this or that, just looking and enjoying without judging. No talking to others must take place.

Stage 2 When you have managed to spend a good five minutes doing this alone, then do it when others are watching you; this is more difficult. Discussing how you managed to put your mind in a 'neutral concentration zone' on the subject may be useful afterwards for the others.

SUMMARY

1. All behaviour is the result of both nature and nurture, that is both the genes and the past experiences of the individual. To describe equine behaviour as 'instinctive' (genetically programmed and consequently unalterable) is unhelpful and wrong. We all have 'instinctive tendencies', but how, when, where and if they are performed is the result of the individual's lifetime experiences. This applies to all mammals, including humans.

2. It is helpful to have a good grasp of learning theory to teach any mammal, including humans. To do this we need to agree on the meaning of words that are used when discussing learning as well as how it works. This has been outlined and an attempt made to simplify it and, in particular, make it relevant to equines.

3. How learning operates is often divided into a series of different types, these are outlined and examples given relevant to equines. However, it is very important to understand that these types of learning interweave and overlap, they are not mutually exclusive.

4. Learning to do voluntary acts generally involves complex mental events. These include an understanding of cause and effect, having goals, desires, beliefs, memories, making decisions and choices.

5. Mammals, including humans, learn to do voluntary actions by reinforcements of various types, but also by acquiring information from the social and physical environment in which they live.

6. The measurement of 'intelligence' between species is fraught with difficulties, but not impossible to overcome. Different species will have different mental skills as well as physical ones. There may also be some general rules concerning 'intelligence', used here to outline the ability to have complex mental events.

7. One important aspect of learning is to be aware of the difference between learning 'that': learning what to do, and learning 'how': how to do it. An understanding of this is particularly important when teaching more complicated actions or mental skills to equines.

→

8. Early experiments with 'interactive teaching' of equines and some other species involving teaching animals in the same way as children are: a) by emotional involvement with the teacher, b) by the use of associative, observational, silent learning and imitation as well as instrumental conditioning, which has shown promising results. Equines learn very fast when this method is applied and, in particular, when they are taught carefully, can begin to comprehend not just commands, but language. This has considerable relevance for improving their teaching and education.

9. The limits to what equines can learn are not clear. Further investigation of improving teaching methods is a major area and can reduce the large number of behavioural problems equines exhibit as a result of bad teaching.

Fig. 3.21 We do not know the limits for what equines can learn. Here Oberlix yawns when asked to just for fun. Imitation is the key but if nothing happens do not assume the pupil has not understood. Sometimes I wait five minutes before we even get the beginnings of it. Plenty of encouragement is required to ensure a full-blown open mouth response.

RULES FOR GOOD TEACHING

'More Pleasure Attending Accurately to Very Consistent Clear Instructions For Horses'

That is:

1. Motivation of the equine.
2. Positive reinforcement is the best way to learn, use it.
3. Attention of both the teacher and the equine is crucial.
4. Associative learning is one of the easiest ways for equines to learn.
5. Voice is very useful and can be used to express emotion and for words with particular meanings.
6. Consistent cues are essential.
7. Clarity, and creativity in teaching is important.
8. Innovation in what and how you teach is very helpful.
9. Familiarity of the equine with the situation will reduce fear.
10. Habits form fast in equines.

4 Equine emotions and feelings

'Scientific humility tells us that we will probably never understand other animals completely. But if we do not begin by insisting that we already know what characteristics they do not have, we will understand a lot more. To learn about other animals, we must take them on their own terms, and these terms include their feelings'.

Masson & McCarthy 1994

One position often taken today is that equines are almost exactly like us, although some may also maintain that they are 'better' and have a greater 'spiritual' dimension. But probably the majority of people, including scientists, take a different view. They maintain that the emotions that animals feel, if they feel any at all, are extremely limited, like the rest of their mental experiences. This is because many people believe that:

1. Without human-type language it is not possible to feel or convey an emotion to another (Carruthers 1996), that is, emotions are 'language dependent'.
2. In order to be able to feel and interpret emotions, it is necessary to have an awareness that others have minds and emotions too. We have little evidence that other mammals have an awareness of others' minds, although they may be aware of others' bodies and what they are doing (Bryne 1998).

One of the most important considerations that has led many researchers to more or less ignore the problem of animal feelings and emotions is that, in all of us, emotions, feelings and sensations are personal, private things and there is no way in which we can ever experience what another may be feeling. Since, therefore, we cannot measure emotions, they are best left alone. However, it is possible to record and measure behaviour which looks 'as if' the animal may be experiencing a similar emotion to that which the observer feels when he performs similar behaviour. In other words, although emotions are private, they have, nevertheless, some things in common between individuals, as well as between species. Today it is now widely recognized that unless we try to appreciate the feelings of different individuals and species, we are not going to get very far with trying to understand another, whether human or non-human, mammal. (Masson & McCarthy 1994, Bekoff 2000) One of the major reasons for this change of heart among the scientists in particular is the reawakening of the debates on animal welfare where the key argument is, if they suffer (that is experience a feeling and, therefore, are feeling beings: are sentient) then we must be concerned about their welfare.

Even those of us who do have much to do with equines tend to believe now and then (particularly when we cannot understand why an animal is behaving in a certain way) that equines are so different from us that they do not have similar feelings.

If we want to progress in our understanding of equines and consequently improve our relations with them, we need to have more clarity about their emotional experiences: what emotions/feelings they feel, which ones they may not, and how important their emotional life is to them. In this chapter we address these issues. As usual we need to assess information from every possible source to be able to assemble some valid, up-to-date understanding. This includes experiments, detailed measured observations, as well as critically assessed 'folk knowledge', that is, people's experiences.

Emotions are of course involved with every aspect of our and equines' mental and physical lives, for example we have seen how interlinked the emotional life is with learning (see page 130): motivation. Some form of feeling is required for any human or non-human animal to learn to do a voluntary act. Thus, wherever learning or information is being acquired, there must be some sort of feeling involved. Learning and past experiences are intimately interwoven with everything the animal or human does, so emotions must also be interwoven with everything that the animal does and experiences.

Not all feelings are entirely private affairs though, there are shared experiences. We may not experience *exactly* what another human or horse is feeling, but we will know, more or less, how another human/horse is feeling because we personally will have similar feelings in the same situation, or when we are performing similar behaviours (running away from something frightening for example). We can interpret another's feelings, at least a little, from their behaviour, using 'conditional anthropomorphism' (see page 41). However, to do this we need to know about similarities in our behaviour with another species so we may assess when an individual may be feeling a similar emotion. This is relatively easy even with little experience.

Example
Some city children came to visit the farm and research station. Initially, they were very frightened of approaching the horses who were, to them, large and scary. However, our older horses who were used to different people did not react to the children's body language which indicated fear, so the children began to run up to them holding bunches of grass for them to eat. Then a very low-flying aircraft came over the field, and the horses and the children bolted off. I asked the children afterwards what they felt, and what they thought the horses felt. There was no doubt at all in any of their minds, they were frightened of the noise, and they knew that the horses were too because they did the same thing: ran off and stared at the aircraft as it disappeared.

But there are other times when it is not so clear what equines might be feeling, unless you know them very well and understand much about their behaviour and communication.

Example
When the two stallions, Oberlix and Oryx, are in fields adjacent to each other, one will defaecate, turn around and smell his faeces pile, then start pawing. The other does the same thing. This causes the other to do this again, and paw with more vigour, and then the other does it and starts throwing his front legs out and shouting. Soon they may have worked themselves up into a frenzy. Unless you know stallions well, it will not be at all obvious that this normal defaecating behaviour in these circumstances is often attached to emotional excitement: interest, threat, fear and attack all rolled into one.

It is here that the 'conditional' part of 'conditional anthropomorphism' comes into play, that is the differences between us and equines. But to disentangle this, we still need to make comparisons with our own basic feelings. In the above example, 'excitement, threat, fear and attack all rolled into one', may not be what the stallions are feeling exactly, but it is good enough for us to be able to predict their actions, and understand something more about them as a result of observing and making comparisons with our own feelings.

Many will consider that this is bad science, making assumptions without justification. But, since we are all mammals and have feelings, we should surely start from the premise that we will have similar feelings in similar situations and behave as a result in similar ways, at least until we have evidence that this is *not* correct. In other words, if we want to prove that equines (or another species of mammal) feel quite differently from us, the onus will be to *prove that they **do not** have similar emotions, rather than prove they do*. The two major arguments for the existence of emotions and feelings in other mammals can be summarized therefore by:

1. **Evolutionary continuity**, which indicates that all mammals are similar in many bodily and behavioural respects, as we have pointed out (see Chapters 1, 2, and 3). If we think evolution is the best explanation to date of different species' relationships to one another, then, to be rational, we must assume that equines have emotions that will be something like ours, since we are closely related and they show similarities in both their bodies and their behaviours to us humans who do feel emotions.

2. **Behavioural evidence and folk knowledge**, which indicates that mammals (elephants, rats, humans, equines and so on) show the same type of physiological and behavioural responses in similar situations. A horse will respond in a similar way to a human when frightened. His heart rate will go up, he may shiver or sweat, he will have increased chorticosteroids and adrenaline in his blood, he will try to get away and run fast if he can, be unable to stand still, leap around if prevented from moving, call more, etc.

Other emotions are also similarly displayed in both humans and equines (as well as other species): aggression, sexual desire, frustration, uncertainty, for example. Darwin pointed this out in 1868.

Despite the lack of studies on emotions in animals, it is clear that anyone, even those who have had nothing to do with another species, can recognize when another mammal is feeling frightened, sexy or aggressive at least. It is these similarities in response that have allowed us to identify more or less what the horse is feeling, and consequently to be able to domesticate and teach him. We have some folk knowledge about what the horse is feeling, because we ourselves would feel the same thing in a similar situation, and we use this knowledge daily. Some of us are better at this than others, some of us get it wrong some of the time, but then, of course, we get it wrong trying to interpret what other humans are feeling some of the time too.

There may be problems with our everyday interpretation due to preconceived notions as a result of a particular cultural education. One of the most obvious examples of this is the development in the Western United States of 'rodeo' breaking on which Sherpell (1986) remarks: 'The emphasis on gratuitous domination and cruelty has been aptly described as the modern equivalent of a public hanging.'

This approach of treating other mammals either as robots without feelings, or brutalizing them, is deeply ingrained in some human societies. Treating animals in brutalising ways transforms the individual animal into what he is perceived to be by, for example, heightening his fear and aggression. The result is that the individual animal responds aggressively, which is what is expected, and fulfils the preconceived notions of the human witnesses. This is not because these animals are 'red in tooth and claw, brutish and aggressive', but often because they are scared. Another example of this is the bullfight where the bull usually has to be hurt until he panics with excitement, fear, defensive threat and aggression by being prodded and poked in the neck with knives as he stands in a pen *before* he enters the bullring. There is nothing romantic about this, however much one may admire the athleticism of the bullfighters.

This brutal approach has *not*, however, been the general interpretation of horses' emotional responses in the classical schools of equitation in either Europe or India through the ages (e.g. Xenophon 1972, Podhajsky 1967, de la Gueriniere 1994, Pluvinel 1989, Imam 1987). Xenophon in 350 BC mentions how important it is to *understand the horse, and encourage his trust, rather than subduing and dominating him by terror.* Those who live with animals, use anthropomorphic judgements to explain the emotions which they believe the animals experience.

This is done not only by observing their behaviour, but also as a result of having some knowledge of the individual animals' past experiences (e.g. Hearne 1994, Johnson 1995, Podhajsky 1967) and generally it works.

Since emotions often fade one into another, and can be of different intensities, 'identical' emotional experiences or feelings are unlikely even for one individual. The differences in emotional experiences between species are likely to be greater, nonetheless we will attempt to critically outline the feelings of equines. To begin, however, we need to point out the difficulties with trying to do this.

OBSTACLES TO THE UNDERSTANDING OF FEELINGS OR EMOTIONS OF OTHERS

Preconceived notions resulting in self-fulfilling prophecies

If you believe that a horse will react very excitedly in a certain situation, this is very likely to be fulfilled, as it often is with humans. This is not the result of any mystical phenomenon, but simply because the messages concerning the human's own emotionality will have been conveyed by body positions, movements, smells, touch and so on to the sensorially aware equine who will then act appropriately. This can also go the other way, the equine may have his own preconceived notions about the human which the human may read and then it affects his behaviour (see Anticipation, page 193; Suspicion, page 198).

This is recognized between humans too. There are now particular schools 'teaching' people to behave happily and react positively to others, that is show pleasure, in order to have pleasant responses returned. A similar approach is successful with equines, elephants, buffalo and dogs (e.g. Roberts 1992; Rees 1983; Club Hippique Foret Mouliere, Poitier, France; Druimghigha Stud; Imire Safari Park, Zimbabwe; Zimbabwe Veterinary Research Centre, Mazowe; Johnson 1995; Mugford 1992).

Cultural differences

In humans there are well-known cultural differences in the degree to which it is expected that emotions will be displayed: the Latin races, and many African

Bantu tribes, are renowned for showing high levels of emotion: fear, sexual arousal, aggression, excitement, grief and so on, while other cultures in Northern Europe, for example, are encouraged not to display emotions but rather to show a 'stiff upper lip', i.e. to maintain composure, in almost every type of situation, although this does not mean that the individuals do not feel the emotions. Cultural effects on emotionality also exist in equines, for example Thoroughbred or Arab horses in one racing stable may be much more nervous and over-reactive than in another, even though they may all be related (see page 145).

Individual differences

There are individual differences in emotionality as there are individual differences in anatomy, physiology, and mental skills. These may be, in part, produced by the individual's body, and/or past experiences. A knowledge of an individual human's or horse's past experience is, therefore, pivotal for gaining greater insight into their feelings.

Genetics: the breed

There are different breeds of horses which are renowned for being very reactive and emotional, they are called 'hot blooded', and include the Thoroughbred and Arab, whereas the heavy horses, cobs, some ponies and donkeys are renowned for their phlegmatism. Zebras are believed to be so emotional that they are untameable and, when they are captured, inevitably aggressive. This emotionality, or lack of it, is considered to be genetic, but it may also be the result of the folk belief held by the handlers. Most likely (as we have found with our experimental herd of Arab horses and teaching wild zebras) there is a genetic tendency controlling emotionality, but this is greatly affected by lifetime experiences. You can have very laid-back Thoroughbreds or pure-bred Arabs, even stallions, and very wild over-reactive cobs or donkeys depending on their lifetime experiences.

Do animals always show what they are feeling?

It is often believed that animals, unlike humans, always show their emotions and feelings. They never emotionally 'lie' (e.g. McIntyre 1999), that is display behaviour not related to what they feel. There are doubts about this too. Is the emotion *never* controlled, repressed or absent, and how would we know, particularly with another species? Only very recently has anybody been considering this question and collecting evidence to try to answer it.

Examples

1. When teaching our Arabs to work the land with often a dangerous implement behind them, we first teach them that when they are frightened they must stop and stand still. Oberlix, can get extremely upset by noise behind him, or when he has overstepped the trace. He now knows that when things are really scary he must stand still and we will sort it out. He will stand there immobile with a very high heart rate. He is very frightened, but he has learnt to behave differently from the way untutored horses behave in this situation. He has repressed his typical behaviour associated with this emotion, that is to run, whether or not he has repressed his fear.

2. Shemal has often caught her shoe in a fence when pawing at the fence, and has taught herself not to pull back and generally try to get away, but rather to stand still and call, and eventually someone will hear her and come with the pliers to release her. When we appear she appears to be extremely relaxed but, on taking her heart rate, it is much higher than it would normally be, thus, again, her behaviour is not reflecting her emotional state at that time.

3. We had a quiet Arab mare, Crystal, who we had owned since she was two. She always behaved as if she was unexcited, relaxed and quiet when taken to places where our other Arab mares would be behaving in exuberantly excited ways: moving around, calling, pawing, head shaking and so on. When we recorded the heart rate of Crystal and the other demonstrably excited horses, however, we found that although she was showing no behavioural sign of excitement, her heart rate was as high as the others: 65 beats per minute compared to 60–68 bpm for three others. The heart rate at rest of all these horses (which we would have expected from her behaviour) was between 36–42 bpm, so she was indeed feeling excitement, but not showing it.

It is likely with equines, and humans, that there are individuals, and cultural groups, who show their emotions less than others, but this does not mean they are not feeling them. Humans can tell us in words if this is the case, but they may also lie and pretend they are feeling a different emotion from the one they really are, so we are no nearer understanding their emotions sometimes.

Not showing an emotion that is felt is one form of 'emotional lie'. Another example of this may sometimes be when an equine ignores attacks directed at him (see Chapter 7). Here he may be feeling irritated or slightly fearful but does not display it. So, although emotional honesty may be more common than emotional lying in equines, the latter cannot be ruled out.

Different emotions as a result of different perception

Another confusion is that there are different and subtle behaviours displayed by different species depending on their use of the different senses. For example, humans use language and consequently have, compared to equines, neglected the sophisticated use of visual cues to convey messages or emotions (see Chapter 7). Using different senses in different ways may result not only in different sensations, but also different feelings and emotions which, to date, we cannot identify.

Example

Slight changes in smells may indicate various emotions which equines will be more able to pick up than humans (see page 287), for example the smell of sweat on a slightly frightened human.

By increasing our awareness of the subtle cues indicating different emotions, we can learn to become more sensitive.

Example

Experienced humans can pick up high heart rhythms when riding a metre or two away from an excited horse. Equally, equines who have experience with humans can read our emotions and next intended action better than those who do not have this experience.

Different, unknown emotions

There may be emotions experienced by other species which we just do not experience.

Example

It is difficult to outline the feeling that is behind the 'snake face' driving by the stallion of mares (Figure 4.1), or emotions generated by equines smelling their own faeces (see Chapter 1 and Figure 7.5b).

(See also 'champing' on pages 200 and 201.)

Fig. 4.1 Oberlix 'snake faces' Lilka to keep her away from Oryx who is on the other side of the camera.

Differences in threshold at which emotions are felt

What may be different in these different species, or individuals, are not the feelings themselves so much as the thresholds at which they are sparked off in the different situations. But individuals can have experiences which will change the threshold for feeling a particular emotion, by habituation or 'desensitization', or learning (see examples above and on page 112).

Example

The threshold for feeling caution and fear may change. This is illustrated by police horses working in crowds with bangers going off around them, donkeys pulling carts in crowded Cairo, zebras in zoos living near lions' cages. They have all had experience of adapting to changing and potentially frightening situations, and the threshold at which they feel anxiety and fear has consequently been raised. For humans an example is familiarity with driving a small car among big lorries on crowded motorways. This is initially frightening, but may become routine.

Mixed emotions

One of the other problems with emotions and feelings is that they overlap and intertwine with one another as well as with other mental events, so identifying one or the other is not always easy, even for the individual experiencing them.

SUMMARY TO DATE

At this stage of our knowledge in trying to identify the different emotions/feelings of equines, a sensible approach is to:

1. Recognize the likelihood of shared experience as demonstrated by similar behaviour, but, at the same time, be sceptical and aware of the effect of preconceived notions.
2. Individuals of one species may be having very different emotional experiences, and either show them or not, but a knowledge of the species' and individuals' past experiences will give greater insight into their emotions.
3. There are cultural effects (social learning) on the degree and types of emotions or feelings which may be shown by an individual's behaviour.
4. You must be aware of possible genetic tendencies.
5. Emotions are often mixed one with another, so are not easy for others to identify, or even for the subject sometimes.
6. Emotions or feelings are intertwined with all aspects of mental function so cannot be ignored.

In the rest of this chapter, I have selected some emotions to discuss in order to better understand what it might be like to be an equine emotionally.

I have divided emotions into primary emotions which it is generally considered mammals do feel and are discussed here. There are also reflective emotions which, it has been considered until recently, only humans can feel. Whether equines feel these emotions is dependent upon a level of consciousness and self-awareness. They are discussed later in Chapter 9.

PRIMARY EMOTIONS

Primary emotions are subdivided:

1. **General emotions/feelings** which occur in many situations and are difficult to associate with a particular feeling.

Example
Excitement can be identified as a physiological and behavioural state, but may involve a mixture of different 'feelings' such as pleasure, fear, aggression, anticipation and so on.

2. **Specific emotions/feelings** are more easily related to one type of feeling.

Example
Fear/terror, or aggression/fury.

This division is used to try to clarify thinking, rather than to make them exclusive categories. Let me stress again, emotions and feelings interlink, cross over, change and intermix with each other and all other mental functions.

General emotions
Excitement
There is no doubt concerning the existence of a feeling of excitement in humans and equines. It is generally only identified by behavioural changes. These involve doing more things more often, with more activity and movement, and switching from doing one thing to another (e.g. Kiley 1969). There are also physiological changes, such as an increase in heart rate, an increase in postural tonus and changes in blood steroids, among others (Selye 1959, Kiley 1972). Whether the animal (or human) is very frightened, very aggressive, very joyful, or very sexually excited, they will tend to show these responses. The function of such behavioural and physiological changes, this feeling of excitement, is, as Selye argues, to prepare the body for exertion. These responses to 'stress' are to help the being to adapt, consequently they are all part of what he called the 'General Adaptive Syndrome'.

   The differences in behaviour as a result of the different emotions felt, are superimposed on this framework, although it is not always very clear from the behaviour (particularly at low levels of excitement) whether the subject is just 'excited' or feeling a particular emotion. Which particular one of these emotions might be felt will come from cues in the context. Thus, mistakes can be made in interpreting the specific feeling and intention, particularly between species.

Example
A stallion comes to greet a human at an elevated trot with his head and tail up indicating that he is excited and interested in seeing the human, but the human interprets this as a threat and runs away. The stallion then chases because he reads the running away of the human as the beginning of a game of chase. This is interpreted by the human as attack.

The behaviours that identify different levels of excitement involve an increase in the anti-gravity tonus of the body posture so the head and tail are raised more as the level of excitement increases. The individual will move more and faster; and he may also vocalize more and the calls will become louder and longer and often of higher frequency (Kiley 1969).

   Many of the displays (e.g. the calls, the positions of the tail, the head positions and so on) are used as an analogue system to tell the receiver about the general excitement level of the individual, rather than giving a message about his specific emotional state. The behaviour itself signals *only* something like 'I am at a particular level of excitement', rather than a specific, 'I am going to attack you', or 'I am very fond of you'. This type of context-dependent communication may have disadvantages (such as specific messages are dependent on context, so there is no particular unchanging meaning to almost any behaviour) but also advantages (see Chapter 7). One of the great advantages, particularly for a prey species and very different from verbal language, is that to interpret the message there must be a greater awareness of the recipient's total environment, both the physical and the social.

Frustration
This is another general emotion or feeling which is often difficult to discriminate from excitement as the individual will tend to do the same things. Frustration is interesting in terms of mental events as, in order to be frustrated, the individual must recognize a goal that is unobtainable.

Example

I conducted many tests with equines and other species to see what behaviour they performed and how frequent each behaviour was when they were presented with food that they could see and smell but not obtain. All the different mammals I tested (pigs, goats, cattle, horses, cats and dogs) behaved in similar ways. They all moved around more and performed more activities more often than when they were not frustrated in the same place. They also tried to obtain the food by pawing, biting, pulling at the obstruction separating it from them: that is they worked to try to achieve their aim (Kiley 1969).

Behaviours shown by both humans and equines that are characteristic of frustration include **'displacement activities'** (e.g. Morris 1956). Here the subject is unable to perform the behaviour they would like to, so they perform activities that appear often to be out of context and incomplete (Tinbergen 1956).

Examples

1. A hungry horse or human will scratch and rub himself when he can see some food but cannot reach it ('displacement scratching').

2. A mare would like to approach another one, but is frightened of being kicked, so she starts to graze, grabbing a mouthful but not chewing it properly (displacement eating).

3. Your horse waiting in his stable for his supper, paws at the door (wanting to move towards the food but cannot). When he is given his food, he continues to paw, often holding his leg up in the air and waving it to and fro, an 'it is so good, but I cannot eat it fast enough' type of frustration.

4. Pawing (an incomplete movement associated with movement) is characteristic of frustration in equines. It occurs in different situations. Figures 4.2a and b show pawing in two slightly different contexts.

Another frequent group of behaviours that can become 'displacement activities'are those related to skin irritation. both human and non-human mammals may scratch, rub, shake or nod their heads, sneeze, and wag their tails or flick their ears if they can.

Displacement activities are also often related to eating: grazing (often without chewing), or to moving around: swaying, pacing back and forth, pawing (a human child might stamp), (Kiley-Worthington 1978, Manning & Dawkins 1998).

Figs. 4.2a and b   Pawing. a) Kaloon, a purebred black Arab with us for educating, pawing when he is tied up. The rope and all the equipment around him are part of his education to help him get used to all sorts of things and not panic when, for example, he paws the rope and it moves about. b) Oberlix, pawing in the field when close to Oryx, is frustrated because he is unable to get closer.

Individuals also often vocalize more when they are frustrated. The more frustrated and excited they get, the louder and longer are the calls.

Relaxation

There are a number of similar behaviours between humans and equines which indicate that the individual is feeling relaxed (these are the opposite of those indicating excitement), that is a lowered head and tail, and other parts of the body, including resting a leg. The equine's ears will be still and neither pricked nor back. The mouth and chin will often be relaxed with the lower lip hanging down (in the equine and elderly human). The eyes may be closed or half closed, and the tail lying relaxed (see Figure 2.3).

There are also common physiological responses such as a low respiration and heart rate.

Relaxation is not difficult to identify in equines, but confusion can arise when the equine is not relaxed but immobilised, 'frozen', with fear (see page 199).

Distress

Welsh (1964), a psychologist working with the army, suggested that there was an 'optimum level of environmental stimulation' for all individuals; too much or too little for too long leading to physiological stress and behavioural changes related to this. Distress is not, perhaps, an obvious feeling, but it is a 'state of being' where negative emotions or feelings are experienced for long periods of time. It results from the prolonged activity of the General Adaptive Syndrome (see page 176). The result is non-adaptive changes in the physiology and behaviour: for example, a reduction in the immune responses of the body, an increase in corticoseroids, ulcers, heart problems. Behavioural changes related to prolonged stress, that is 'distress', include an increase in aggression and rapid mood changes. Behavioural distress and how to assess it, has now received a considerable amount of attention in farm animals (e.g. Kiley-Worthington 1977, Hughes and Duncan 1988, Schmidt 1987), pets, zoo and circus animals (Fox 1968, Kiley-Worthington 1990) (Figure 4.3).

Fig. 4.3 A list of behaviours characteristic of 'distress' in horses. The same measures are used for assessing the welfare of farm livestock, zoo and circus animals. The only difference is that they are not so common as they are in stables (Kiley-Worthington 1990).

- Evidence of physical ill-health (including poor nutrition, wounds etc.).
- Evidence of frequent occupational diseases.
- Need for the use of drugs and/or surgery to maintain the system of husbandry.
- Behavioural changes:
  a) performance of abnormal behaviours (that are not normally in the animals' repertoire, and which appear to be of little benefit to the animal, e.g. running at bars, pacing up and down);
  b) stereotypes, i.e. the performance of repeated behaviour fixed in all details and apparently purposeless (e.g. crib-biting, wind-sucking, weaving, head twisting);
  c) substantial increase in inter- or intra-specific aggression compared to the wild or feral state;

→

d) large differences in time budgets from the wild or feral animal;

e) substantial increases in behaviour related to frustration or conflict (e.g. often behaviour relating to locomotion and/or skin irritation).

f) substantial characteristics of a very different time in their development e.g. calves of sixteen weeks walking as if they were a day or so old).

- Behavioural restrictions – this is the inability to perform all the behaviour in the animals' natural repertoire which does not cause severe or prolonged suffering to others (see pages 183–185).

It is important to understand that distress can result from two different types of environment.

1. Where there is too much stimulus for too long. Such as in overcrowded, noisy, frightening or frustrating places.

2. Where there is too little stimulus for too long. Such as in isolation from others, where there is little action, routine is too strict and change in the environment minimal.

Generally people are now becoming aware that equines can become distressed in over-stimulated living environments but less attention has so far been devoted to under-stimulation in the equines' lives whether they live in stables or in paddocks.

The behaviours characteristic of distress in equines are given in Figure 4.3. As long ago as the 1960s (Fox 1968) it was recognized that humans and other mammals, including equines, who are confined, behaviourally restricted, and have dull unchanging environments, or, alternatively, are overcrowded, overworked and pressurised in various ways, will show similar physiological and behavioural changes.

One indication of distress comes from the amount of **behavioural restriction** that the individual has to suffer. If it is chosen not to allow an equine to perform some of the behaviours that are in his repertoire, the effects must be very clearly considered.

Courtship and mating are complex social activities in equines (as well as in humans). They involve the individual making choices and developing bonds between the male and the female. Not allowing courtship, the necessary excitement and development of bonds causes distress to individuals, particularly females who are restricted and raped instead. This results in the female's anxiety about sex and consequently an increasing likelihood of her injuring the stallion. The caretaker's response is to restrict the mare further using drugs and physical restraints. This increases the risks further, and reduces conception rates as a result of the distress caused.

Examples

1. The physical restrictions normally used in the majority of studs for breeding mares include a) twitches and hobbles; b) unpleasant manipulations: internal examinations by a human hand usually daily; c) the use of drugs: steroids to encourage libido (testosterone in stallions), and ovulation in mares (oestrogen). With all this manipulation conception is low, on average 68–70% (Rossdale 1983) compared to 95% when the mare and stallion are allowed to run together, and even when there are several mares in oestrus at once. It is often agreed that since there is a restricted breeding period for stallions, if he were to run with the mares and court them he would be unable to cover that many. However, Bristol (1982) showed that this was not the case when he synchronized the oestrus of thirty mares, they were all covered – and became pregnant – by the one stallion.

2. Foals are usually weaned between four and six months old. This causes profound trauma, and distress to both the foal and to the mother. Since the attachment between mother and foal has been selected for and is moulded by the lifetime experiences of the animals, it seems foolhardy to break this bond in a sudden way when the foal is so young. In fact, our recent work indicates that it is at this time that the foal may begin to exhibit stereotypes, that is 'vices' such as crib-biting, weaving, head throwing etc.

3. Preventing animals having contact with each other or even moving about freely or making their own decisions about simple things such as when to shelter from the weather, or how to cope with flies are very frequent in modern stable management. Although the animals are overprotected in such ways with the best intentions (that is people do not want them to be cold, or irritated by flies), the results on the welfare of the horse are often much worse than if they had been left alone. Such management often results in evidence of distress, and reduces the quality of life as well as affecting how the individual learns and his relationship with humans (Kiley-Worthington 1998).

With a little thought it is quite possible to reduce the behavioural restrictions dramatically, for even stabled equines. A helpful project is to assess the amount of behavioural restriction in the way you keep your equines, or those kept at the stable where you ride, Figure 4.4 shows one way of measuring this.

Distress and trauma can also be the result of experiences with people in training or handling where the equine has been frightened or had some other unpleasant experiences. If this was sufficiently strong, it may generalize and occur in many situations.

In Figure 4.4 we have made an effort to quantitatively assess the **behavioural restriction** of equines kept in different ways. There is obviously much leeway here, thus the behavioural restriction when keeping a horse in a loose box for twelve hours a day will be much less than keeping one for twenty-four hours in a small pasture alone. Indeed even keeping equines in stalls for part of the day can be much less overall behaviourally restricting and consequently cater better for their various needs than keeping an animal in a large loose box, or even a yard, without access to high fibre food or being able to associate with others.

It must also be realized that the 'wild' or feral situation, although it gives us a clear view of the type of life equines have evolved to live, and consequently how we can improve our husbandry to cater for their various needs, is not the best of all lives as there are often behavioural restrictions and problems. Such animals have no veterinary treatments and may die, they also from time to time may be very hungry or thirsty, cold or hot etc.

The thesis here is that we should be able to improve on the environments that our equines have from those in the wild, but if we are going to fulfil all their needs, this needs more thought than it has previously been given, otherwise the animals do show evidence of distress. Having said this, however, it is not necessary to just open the stable door and wave your equines goodbye, or even to ensure that they are left roaming around in fields. Even in urban areas it is possible to keep equines (and humans) in environments that are acceptable and where they show no sign of distress, but rather that of pleasure. This is achieved by using substitution and ensuring that, 1) the needs are known and understood, and 2) facilities in one way or another are provided to allow for these. One of these can be educating and teaching equines new things. Repeating things they already know may not be sufficiently stimulating.

Fig. 4.4 The amount of behavioural restriction and lack of fulfilment of needs (quality of life) for equines in different enviroments. The types of environments chosen for comparison here are:

Feral = wild or semi-wild animals living their own uninterrupted lives.

Pasture = groups of at least five animals of different sexes and ages together in an area of over one hectare with water, shelter and access to fibre foods or grass at all times.

( ) = the same plus no artificial weaning and running with a stallion (Druimghigha stud summer husbandry).

Yard = group of mixed sex and ages with stallion and no artificial weaning (Druimghigha stud, winter husbandry).

Pasture alone means that a single animal is turned out alone.

Loose box + fibre is a single animal kept in a stable in a block, able to look over the door, has others around and access to fibre food at all times. The stable allows three strides at a walk in either direction and the partition between boxes is either a bar, or a low wall allowing individuals to touch and groom each other.

Encl. box - fibre is a single horse in a box within a large barn, able to see others but unable to see outside or to touch others through bars or netting. The fibre is ration fed, and the horse able to walk three strides in either direction.

Stalled is a single animal in a stall adjacent to others, tied by the neck or head but with access to fibre food at all times.

A constant group is at least three members who remain together for at least one year.

NB It is assumed that all the animals being kept in these conditions have:
1) sufficient nutrition; 2) access to clean water at all times; 3) shelter; 4) good veterinary and farriery care.
0 = non 1 = some 2 = much 3 = complete. Thus the higher the score, the more restricted the animal is.

ACTIVITY   TYPE OF HUSBANDRY

	Feral	Pasture	Yard	Pasture alone	Loose box + fibre	Encl. box - fibre	Stalled
Physical needs							
Sufficient exercise/ move as far as is wanted.	0	0	1 (1)	1	2	2	3
Perform all gaits.	0	0	2 (2)	1	3	3	3
Feed at all times.	1	0	0	0	0	3	0
Always water available.	1	0	0	0	0	0	0

Never unenclosed.	0	I (I)	2 (2)	3	3	3	3
Self-groom all parts of body.	0	0	0	0	0	0	2
Shelter always available.	2	0	0	0	0	0	0
Diseases etc. treated.	3	0	0	0	0	0	0
Social needs							
Free contact with others.	0	0	0	3	2	3	3
Mixed aged groups.	0	0	0	3	3	3	3
Constant groups.	0	I (0)	I (0)	3	3	3	3
Sex possible, with entire males.	0	3 (I)	3 (I)	3	3	3	3
Maternal behaviour and being mothered; no artificial weaning.	0	I (0)	I (0)	3	3	3	3
Total	7	7 (2)	II (6)	23	25	29	29

ACTIVITY   TYPE OF HUSBANDRY

	Feral	Pasture	Yard	Pasture alone	Loose box + fibre	Encl. box - fibre	Stalled
Emotional needs Ability to experience range of emotions.	0	I	2 (I)	3	3	3	3

No constant fear or frustration.	2	I	I (I)	2	2	3	3
Cognitive needs Opportunity to learn.	0	I	I (I)	2	3	3	3
To make choices and decisions in complex enviroments.	0	I	2 (I)	2	3	3	3
To become a 'natural historian'.	0	I	3 (3)	2	3	3	3
To become a 'natural psychologist'.	0	2	2 (I)	3	3	3	3
To solve problems and use all types of learning to acquire information.	0	I	I	2	3	3	3
Total	2	8	12 (9)	16	20	2I	2I

Examples

I. A horse was placed in the round pen and chased around by someone throwing out the lunge line. The horse panicked, and tried to climb out of the pen by rearing. The person, concentrating so hard on throwing out the lunge line, and believing that at all costs she must make the horse keep moving around, thus continued to frighten the horse with the lunge line. The next time the horse was frightened by someone entering his stable unexpectedly, he immediately tried to climb out by rearing up on the wall. (Personal observation.)

2. An Arab mare who had been thoughtlessly handled previously, and is nervous around people, refuses to go into her stable because she is frightened of something she sees within. The handler hits her hard with a stick, she rears around, kicks out and panics. The handler

calls others to help and continues to shout, hit her, and generally excite her more. She becomes hysterical, and they let her go by mistake. She gallops off and falls on the concrete at the end of the yard, gets up and rushes back, they continue to chase her while trying to catch her. Finally she is caught. With ropes and restraints around her hocks, twitches on her nose, and hobbles fitted onto her front legs, she is forcibly marched into the stable. For months afterwards, she either attacks humans when they come into the stable – out of defensive threat (see page 202) – or retires quivering to the back of the stable and lashes out with her heels. She is 'dangerous', and is not taken out of her box anymore. The equine behaviour consultancy is called in, and eventually uncovers the case history. It takes three months of careful, quiet, scheduled relearning to reduce her fear. She is handled very carefully in order to ensure she is not frightened at any stage and gradually begins to trust people again, and even becomes demonstrably affectionate to those she knows well, her distress is eventually alleviated. (Animal Conultancy case.)

A distressed equine may be dangerous, have a low quality of life and not be easy to deal with or teach. It is vital to have the living conditions right for your equines if you wish to have them enjoying themselves and learning fast.

Boredom

Boredom is defined as a state of distress characterized by insufficient environmental stimuli (Kiley-Worthington 1977). This is a state which many animals in restricted husbandry or captive environments may be prone to. It is recognized by their performance of abnormal behaviours of one sort or another, or by the individuals increasing their time doing nothing (Kiley-Worthington 1990, Broom & Johnson 1993). Although the way in which distress is shown by equines may be similar, whether they have too much or too little stimulation in their environment, which is the cause is not usually difficult to assess.

Stereotypes, (which are defined as repeated actions, constant in form and apparently purposeless) are very common in humans and equines kept in environments which lack sufficient stimulation (over 31% in stabled equines from our surveys) (Figure 4.5).

Example
It has become standard practice in the UK to fit 'anti-weaving' bars over the stable doors in many major competitive and teaching stable yards as it is assumed the horses will weave (see Figure 2.10).

	Racing stables		Teaching stables*	
No. of establishments	5		12	
No. of horses	76		150	
Drugs and survey	number	%	number	%
No. on phenylbutazone	5	6.5	43	28
Denervated	20	26.5	6	4
TOTAL	25	33	49	32
BEHAVIOUR				
Wood chewing	70	92	50	33
Crib-biting or wind sucking	6	7.8	9	6
Weaving or stable walking	12	15.7	10	6.6
Head throwing or tossing	10	13.1	20	13.3
Stable kicking	8	10.7	15	10
High aggression levels	30	39.4	35	23.3
Stable neurosis	26	34	47	31.3
TOTAL	162	212.7	186	123.5

*= BHS approved

Fig. 4.5 The frequency of stereotypes and other methods of measuring distress in a survey of top racing and training yards.

Figures 4.6a and b show internal stables that have become fashionable and another new stable yard at a university teaching a degree in Equine Studies! Here the horses are kept in loose boxes, but there is evidence of wood chewing on all the doors. Normal equines healthy in body and mind do not go around chewing wood. Here again, it has been assumed that the animals *will* wood chew, and pieces of metal are fixed over the doors to stop them. No effort has, apparently, been made to confront the cause of this behaviour and change the conditions under which the animals are kept, despite the fact that one of the important courses taught in this degree is Equine Behaviour and Welfare!

Because stereotypes are very obvious, they have been the subject of much research, particularly in farms, zoos, circuses and stables, as well as in human

Figs. 4.6a and b   The types of stable yards that many aspire to. However, from the horse's point of view, neither of these are satisfactory unless the animals are either turned out or working for many hours each day. a) The internal, or German stables that have become fashionable. Here the horses are unable to see out, and the only activity they see is when people come and go or animals are taken in or out. In such stables evidence for distress can be as high as 100% (as observed in a show stable of this type) even in a half-hour period. b) This English-type stabling is better from the horse's point of view because they do, at least, have some view of the outside and can feel the wind. But again, although it is very neat with pretty flowers, if the horses are confined for many hours, it leaves much to be desired. Marks on the doors indicate how the horses have been attempting to chew the wood. However, if the horses are out of the stables for much of the day, fed *ad libitum* hay or silage, and given a serious amount of exercise, such stables can be acceptable to both humans and equines.

institutions. By giving the animals more to do, stereotypes can be reduced. Various toys can be introduced to the stables where equines are kept: suspended tyres, objects to manipulate and even voluntary tasks to perform. One commercially available 'toy' is a 'horse ball'; this ball can be filled with a desired grain and has holes in it. As the ball is rolled around, small amounts of grain fall out, so the animal spends more time feeding. However, such 'toys' do not cure the stereotypes. There are many changes that need to be made within such environments in order to stop the equine performing them, but it can easily be done.

Captive zebras frequently have a problem with boredom and pace up and down, weave, and head throw repeatedly, often arousing public concern. It is curious that this public concern has not yet been applied to racing, competitive and teaching yards where the problems are very common and the causes obvious.

It has been reported that the performance of a stereotype induces the release of opiates and consequently is an adaptive mechanism to allow the animal to continue to live in boring or otherwise unacceptable environments (e.g. Dantzer 1986). Even if this is the case, the question needs to be asked whether we should keep our animals (or our children) in conditions where this is necessary much of the time.

When bored, one adaptation is to switch out of the environment by, for example, increasing sleeping or dozing time, or switching onto self-stimulation (e.g. performing stereotypes), or perhaps even entering into a different type of consciousness (see Chapters 8 and 9). We know how much normal feral equines rest and sleep by looking at their time budgets, and we can compare this with the time spent sleeping or standing doing nothing in stabled environments (see Figure 2.2, and Kiley-Worthington 1987 & 1998).

Example

Working horses, such as cab horses, and those working on the land in the nineteenth century were often kept in stalls where they had more restrictions than in loose boxes. However, because they were out of the stall, often for up to fourteen hours a day working, when they returned, they had just sufficient time to eat and rest and rarely showed evidence of stereotypes or behavioural distress (in this respect these animals were 'better off' than many horses today, even though there may have been other aspects of their husbandry that was poor). By contrast, 90% of horses at teaching yards in the US kept in stalls, from which they are taken out only two to three hours a day, perform stereotypes (Animal Behaviour Consultancy records).

Boredom is not always alleviated by giving the animal a toy or a loose box instead of a stall. Equines' mental needs are more complex, just as they are for humans.

Humans, like other mammals, are from time to time bored: they have not enough to do, or they have done one thing quite long enough and want a change, but this does not become a psychological pathology.

Example
I am now bored with writing, which I have been doing for four hours, and intend to go and cook some food and have a stiff drink; this is not indicative of pathological behaviour (unless I am an alcoholic, of course). Equines often appear to be feeling the same way when they have been performing the same thing for a long time, e.g. going around in circles, or jumping jumps. There are no pathologies exhibited but they show a lack of energy and no interest in doing the same thing again.

If equines are then permitted to change and do something else for a while, they will often show renewed energy and enthusiasm, and even be able to return to the original task with refreshed vigour. This has been well known by those who have thought about the teaching of equines (Podhajsky 1997, Fillis 1969) and important to bear in mind.

The threshold for boredom varies with the past experience and age of the individual, as well as the external environment. Young humans or equines are bored more easily than older ones. If jobs are either easy and repetitive (like working on an assembly line or, if a horse, giving a beginner a riding lesson) or very difficult (having to repeatedly jump a difficult jumping course), the human or equine generally becomes bored more quickly. Performing jobs which keep the attention and interest, but are not too demanding and stressful, reduce the onset of boredom.

Examples
1. If the horse and rider are having trouble keeping an even cadenced trot around a circle, ask them to canter straight, try a shoulder-in or a half pass, and then return to the original exercises.

2. If a donkey has to walk around in circles to pump water, changing the pace and having other activities happening around him will reduce his boredom and increase the time he does it willingly.

3. Zebras kept in zoos may have to remain in the same environment for years. The good keeper's job is not only to spot when they may be ill, and to keep the area clean but, more importantly, to change the environment by bringing in different things daily to allow the zebras to investigate and play with them. The keeper can even begin to teach the zebras to be handled and to tie up so that they can have their feet trimmed and their diseases attended to without the trauma of restrictions and restraints, whether these are chemical or physical.

There are different thresholds for boredom, between different species, but we do not know much about this yet.

The use of 'conditional anthropomorphism' (see page 41) is useful to help predict when the animal might become bored. Many so-called behavioural problems of the horse encountered by the teacher (for example, lack of obedience and leaping around) are the result of boredom. The belief that equines must have things repeated often before they learn is just wrong (see Chapter 3). The equine may perform undesired behaviour as a result of boredom, not because he does not understand. This is easy to correct. A more difficult problem, which many good teachers remark on, is to keep up with the equine's learning and understand how necessary it is to invent new activities, rather than repeat the previous action.

It is quite likely that wild equines occasionally become bored. But, one of the defining characteristics of the wild or feral state is that individuals have options on what they can do, and space in which to do it. They can therefore make choices. Consequently if they become bored searching for food for example, they can switch to doing something else: standing dozing, or playing with a friend. When equines have less space and fewer options, signs of boredom are common both in stables and at pasture.

Just as with humans, the provision of an appropriate environment which is sufficiently complex, with plenty of options, choices and work to be done ensures that there is no evidence of pathological prolonged boredom even in restricted environments.

A feeling of boredom in human and non-human mammals may have been selected for in order to ensure that individuals do not continue with the same action for too long as this might reduce their chances of acquiring and using other information. An ability to suffer the subjective state of boredom, and consequently to try to avoid it, will ensure that the individual is constantly gathering new knowledge. Prolonged boredom can therefore be considered to have a similar type of function for the mind as pain for the body: it is a sign of lack of health which will put the individual at risk, therefore efforts to avoid it must be employed.

Anticipation, anxiety and expectation
These emotions must involve some concept of time: knowing that something specific will be happening in the future, and deciding whether or not it is desirable. Equines show evidence of a feeling of anticipation from their behaviour which is similar to that of humans when anticipating things: pleasure (see page 210), for the anticipation of pleasant things, and anxiety or fear for the anticipation of unpleasant ones.

Example
If a horse expects to be fed at around 8 a.m., by 7.50 he will be waiting at the stable door, or paddock gate, watching (head pointed in the direction from which the feed will come, ears pricked, head up and possibly neighing), that is, anticipating.

Before an unpleasant experience he will behave differently.

Example
He sees the white coat of the veterinary surgeon (who caused him pain last time he came) and becomes anxious, retreating to the back of his stable, box walking or circling or leaping, that is trying to get away. He may even start shivering with fright, or attack out of 'defensive threat' (see page 202), that is bite or kick.

These responses are widely reported in the literature and well known among animal minders and scientists. They involve associative learning but also mental abilities that are considered advanced, such as having some concept of the future, and a belief (see Chapters 8 and 9 for further discussion).

If these animals show evidence of operant conditioning (see page 139), frustration and anticipation, then they are capable of **expectations**. It is also possible that equines and humans have expectations without showing behavioural changes. It would be curious if they did not, since there must be a motivation, a 'feeling' before there is a response. Because these species groups also learn by silent learning, without showing obvious responses (see page 147), they may show expectations as a result of information acquired.

Example
When following routes, they may have an expectation of arriving home. This is very common in equines where the slowest old donkey can turn into a veritable racer when turned towards home!

How far their expectations or anticipations go into the future no one knows, but since they follow routes, make migrations and act on ecological knowledge in various ways when the outcome may be weeks away (e.g. to find food, shelter, avoid snow storms etc., see Chapter 5), although they may not always be consciously aware of this, whether human or horse, there must be some form of expectation/anticipation of the end goal, even when it is relatively remote in time.

It is likely that humans' expectations are more complex and go further into the future because they are often language dependent. But we must be careful about assuming non-language users cannot have future expectations and the emotions that go with them. They may be using their senses in different ways.

Example
Olfactory cues can be very complex, and may communicate about the future or the past (see page 282 and Chapter 7).

These, then, are what we have called 'general emotions' felt by both equines and humans. When teaching an equine, it is important to be able to recognize these general emotions by the animal's behaviour, although exactly which of these are being felt, and the cause of the behaviour, may not be obvious since the equine may behave in similar ways when he is either frustrated, excited, expectant, distressed, or bored. The first step is to recognize these general emotions from the equine's behaviour and then assess the context he is in, to try to understand the particular cause. What must *not* be done is to assume that the equine is somehow at fault when he behaves in these ways even though they may be dangerous, or inconvenient.

One set of behaviours that can be easily recognized and be a helpful indicator of emotional state for the equine carer or teacher are the movements and actions that often tell us when things are changing for the equine, in particular the end of a strong general emotion.

Indications of the end of strong general emotions

When a tense emotional situation of almost any type is resolved, equines and humans behave in the same way, they will perform one or several **transitional activities**. For example, if the horse has been anxious while being lunged because he was perhaps not familiar with the situation and was having to learn to keep out on the edge of the ring and so on, when the anxiety is removed, he relaxes, lowers the head and tail, and may chew, or sigh. Thus, when the horse chews while you are teaching him in the free school, you know he has relaxed and overcome an anxiety, and can progress to the next stage. But, while chewing, sighing, stretching, scratching, yawning or even sneezing can be indicative of such moments, they can also be **displacement activities** performed as a result of *not* being able to perform what you would really like to do (see pages 178 and 297–298).

Example
Chewing can become a habit which is performed whenever the animal is anxious, hence constant chewing of a bit, or when they see someone coming. This can generalize and occur in all sorts of situations for prolonged periods. Bit chewing, teeth grinding or tail swishing in horses performing dressage tests demonstrates that the equine is not working in harmony with the rider.

It is important to observe well and be able to tell a relaxed transitional chewing activity, from a tight, anxious chewing.

Specific emotions or feelings

Pain

Pain is the feeling that has attracted most attention in relation to animals. Although some argue that animals do not feel pain (e.g. Descartes 1641, Kennedy 1992), others have criticized their arguments at length (e.g. Clark 1982, Midgley 1978, Rollin 1989, Singer 1976).

The type of pain that has attracted most attention in animals is physical pain. Mental pain has not been considered of much importance for animals to date. This is now changing, and mental pain may be assessed behaviourally by indications of distress (as above). Physical pain, because of the integration of body and mind, will be indicated behaviourally as well.

Behaviour indicative of pain is often similar to that shown by humans (unease, groaning and vocalizing, shivering or sweating etc.). Chambers (1993) has outlined the typical pain behaviour for horses. Evidence for equines feeling pain also comes from the effectiveness of using the same pain-killers on horses and humans. Ironically, the similarity in animal and human pain is tacitly recognized as animals are often used to test analgesics!

There are a host of different levels and types of pain and many of these we may not be able to recognize in equines (or indeed in some humans) from their behavioural or physiological criteria. However, generally, sickness can be recognized relatively early before behavioural signs of pain are evident by taking the heart rate at rest and comparing this with the individual's normal healthy resting heart rate. When an equine is in pain, the resting heart rate will be increased.

Example

You may notice what might be considered early behavioural signs of colic: unease, wandering around, occasional looking at the flanks. It might be that the individual is not behaving as he usually does. One way of checking quickly at this stage is to take the heart rate with a stethoscope. If it is over 60 beats per minute, ring the vet. If it is the normal resting rate of the horse (from around 38 to 44 bpm) there is probably nothing to worry about.

Investigation, curiosity, interest and exploration

These emotions will have been selected for (particularly in prey animals) in order to help them survive. It is vital for the prey to be familiar with the objects and places around them. It is also vital for them to acquire more information, to be mentally active. It is an active searching for knowledge.

Example
Foals in the first six months of their lives spend approximately 10% of their waking time investigating things in their home environments, adults approximately 2% (Eco Research Centre, unpublished data). Normal healthy equines spend time investigating (between three and fifteen minutes every twenty-four hours). To do this, they must be extremely aware of the 'familiar' compared to the 'unfamiliar'.

People's lack of understanding of this can cause the horse to perform behaviours that become a problem to their handlers or riders, such as shying, spooking, refusing to move, and so on.

The behaviour indicative of curiosity and interest is similar in equines and humans and includes: approach – a high postural tonus, ears pricked forward, nose advanced to touch and smell the other (or hand advanced to touch), sniffing, moving of the facial muscles particularly around the mouth, chin and lips, gaze directed at the object of interest, sometimes turning, raising or lowering the head to have a different view (Figure 4.7).

Fig. 4.7 A zebra in a wildlife reserve in Zimbabwe has approached quite close and is watching us teach the elephants.

Equines do a great deal of visual exploration, often watching objects from a distance. The placing of their eyes at the side of the head means that they do not have to turn their head to watch. Thus it may appear to an unobservant human that they are *not* taking information in.

Startle and surprise

Startling occurs as a result of a sudden unexpected environmental change: a loud noise, or a sudden visual change. A sudden strong smell can also induce startling. There is a series of reflex responses called the '**startle reflex**' which is used by all mammals. These responses are:

1. A sudden increase in postural tonus by contraction of the anti-gravity muscles. As the muscles suddenly contract, the head and tail are raised, there is a contraction of the larynx, and a sudden intake of breath and sometimes resulting jumps occur.
2. Noises made by most mammals when startled tend to have characteristics in common, for example a gasp or a snort; a short sharp noise the result of a sudden inspiration or expiration, often accompanied by a sudden movement, an increasing attention to the surroundings and fear of the unexpected.
3. The heart and respiration rates will increase, and adrenaline will begin to be excreted from the adrenal glands.

Surprise results from an environmental change which is not expected: a mismatch between what is expected and what is observed although it might not be registered by a startle reflex.

When objects have been removed from, or their position changed on, a familiar route, horses will often shy: stand and stare with ears pricked, snort, suddenly stop or jump away. In fact this shying or spooking can become a behavioural problem when the horse has learnt (or been taught by inappropriate human behaviour) to 'be surprised' and shy, wherever there has been a slight change (see page 133).

Caution, suspicion, fear and terror

Equines are prey species and, consequently, tend to be cautious by nature. They must be particularly aware of their environment and changes in it, and therefore have a low threshold for fear (that is be easily frightened). They have physiological responses accompanying fear that prepare the body for stresses. These include an increase in the heart rate and respiration rate, and sometimes sweating and shivering.

If an individual has had a slightly fearful experience before in a situation, then he may be suspicious, that is have an expectation of something unpleasant, and this can change to fear.

Fear can arise from unfamiliarity or a sudden change and the first thing equines do is try to escape by running. Thwarting of escape can lead to terror and panic. Both equines and humans will behave without any consideration of the consequences of their actions when panicked by terror or fear and may injure or kill themselves, their infants or any others by leaping or throwing themselves about.

Example
Equines terrified by low-flying aircraft gallop hysterically into fences or, terrified by the sudden appearance of something strange, rear over backwards and knock themselves senseless.

An alternative response to terror, is to freeze, that is to become immobile. This is a strategy often used by young and trapped individuals: they may stay upright and rigid, or even collapse and feign sleep.

It is particularly obvious with caution, suspicion, fear and terror that if, even in doubt, we assume that the equine is feeling frightened, and make efforts to reduce it, it works.

The behaviours associated with caution, suspicion, fear and terror are:

1. **Caution** is an awareness of potentially frightening things in the environment, a 'nearness of fear' and this is shown by a heightening of attention and awareness, training all the receptors onto the stimulus, watching, listening with ears pricked, sniffing, a tensing of the anti-gravity muscles in the body ready for flight, and often immobility.
2. **Suspicion** is distinguished by caution but with more fear; the animal will run away or freeze more quickly.

3. The heightened level of **fear** may be shown by leaping away and running, often with exaggerated upright strides, then stopping and turning to watch, then snorting. If the equine is restricted or restrained, fear will induce leaping about kicking, rearing, trying to escape in some way, often with neighing.

4. **Higher fear** is characterized by further leaping and trying to escape. If escape is possible this will involve running as fast as possible with a more streamlined body away from the frightening object or place. This may be followed by stopping, snorting, trembling and sweating, breathing very fast (respiration rates over 60 per minute, and high heart rates even over 200 bpm).

5. **Terror** is characterized by immobility. The animal (or human) freezes and is unable to move, the eyes protrude, the heart rate is very high, and the breath may be held. If this continues the individual may fall into a 'catatonic sleep state'; some people interpret this as 'feigned sleep or death' but it is not feigned.

The calming effect of the presence of an experienced equine who is not afraid will help to reduce fear and flight in others and has been used for centuries when training horses (see page 143, Social Learning). It is equally important that the humans handling naïve or easily frightened equines are not themselves frightened as this will increase the equines' fear. Relaxation of the body, and an awareness of things going on around them helps here.

A particular display of fear and lack of aggression, perhaps a form of 'respect', is shown by 'champing' (Figure 4.8). It is usual in youngsters when meeting a more mature and/or unfamiliar individual: the head is raised, the mouth corners are withdrawn and the mouth opened and closed frequently while the rest of the body may squat down and the tail be withdrawn; in some cases, the youngster will urinate and even completely collapse on the ground!

An individual to whom this display is performed, will smell and touch the performer, and may even take a playful nip, but will very rarely attack. All youngsters may do it to older equines of either sex. Fillies, and more particularly colts, will do it to adult stallions even after puberty. If they remain living with the mature stallion, they may continue to champ to an older resident stallion for years after this. This is one of the behaviours sparking an emotion

Fig. 4.8 Shindi 'champing' to Oberlix who has just moved over to the gate. Shindi moves away, not taking any chances; she was ten months old here.

which we as humans may find some difficulty identifying. It may be a feeling something like, 'I am just a hopeless little guy who admires you enormously, is slightly afraid of you, and hopes you will not attack, because I am not worth it'!

It seems that one of the most important things an equine needs to know is what he must do to avoid being frightened. Reassuring him that doing a particular thing will not be frightening, or cause him to be hurt in any way is essential, and the equine has to learn that the teacher is trustworthy and will not frighten him. The good teacher will try *not* to use fear or pain as a motivator to ensure equines do different things because it is less effective than a policy of reducing fear and working for a reward: a positive emotion.

As with all the emotions, it is possible that fear or anxiety is sometimes felt without any behavioural change (see page 171). Any good teacher will be aware of this, particularly when things are not going according to plan.

Defensive threat

One of the difficulties with assessing the specific emotion of equines is that defensive threat is common in frightening situations, particularly where the animal is trapped. This is confusing and often leads to an incorrect assessment of a horse as being aggressive, when in fact the cause of the behaviour is fear. Defensive threat involves feeling fear, but results in aggressive behaviour. It is often displayed as a last ditch measure: when the individual is restricted or confined and unable to escape, he attacks. If the frightening situation is no longer frightening, attacks decline, this has been shown to be the case with humans and equines (Blake 1975, Rees 1991, Skipper 1999, Kiley-Worthington 1998). However, since the behaviour is not always easy to distinguish from straight aggression, confusion in reading the other's feelings is common in both equines and humans.

Defensive threat shows evidence of protective responses rather than pure aggressive behaviour: the ears are flat, mouth corners withdrawn, head projected forward, the nostrils reduced in size, biting, tail withdrawn and then swished, and kicking with the hind legs.

It may be that the majority of aggressive actions between mares are not serious aggression, rage or fury, but defensive threat. It is common when equines are not permitted to form stable bonds with others, or have not had the opportunity of learning to become 'natural psychologists'. Consequently, rather than showing curiosity and interest, they are frightened when they come into contact with other equines and attack out of defensive threat. They learn that defensive threat removes the frightening object, consequently the solution to a frightening situation becomes one of attack.

There are also postures and movements that appear to indicate a lower intensity of feeling, milder threats. These are often intention movements, displays to indicate to the other that unless they move away, they will be attacked (see Chapter 7). These involve behaviours more characteristic of a slight feeling of defensive threat, a mixture of fear and aggression: ear withdrawal, nostril withdrawal, tense chin, swishing of the tail, turning of the quarters towards the intruder, and lifting of the hind leg.

Such movements have quite clear messages, even for other species (see Chapter 6). They are usually employed by mares and are directed at each other, at youngsters who annoy them and sometimes at the stallion. The stallion rarely directs them at other equines, but he might at humans.

There is a great deal to be learnt about how the feelings of aggression and fear interweave in equines (as well as humans).

On a practical level, when in doubt, treat these types of threats or movements as motivated by fear rather than aggression. This has frequently been successful in reducing aggressive behaviour (Eco Research Centre Animal Consultancy records, Mugford 1992 with dogs, Rees 1983, Roberts 1998 with horses).

Aggression

Aggression includes: rushing at another, ears flat, often roaring or squealing, biting, rearing and striking with the front legs, attempting to bite the front legs of the other, boxing with the front legs, occasionally turning and kicking out behind at the other.

Attacking and showing irrition are not very common in equines, as far as we can tell from their behaviour (0.07/horse/hour observed, Kiley-Worthington 1997). Detailed studies of other species also indicate that aggression is rare (de Waal 1996).

These acts are also performed as games in play (see page 365), particularly, but not exclusively, between males and youngsters. The rules of where the game ends and the serious aggression begins are not at all clear and have not been studied.

Serious aggression shown by anger, rage and fury in equines and humans, is confined, generally, to fights between well-matched adult males when one challenges another. Fights between equine males are characterized by attacks head to head, involving trying to bite the head, face, neck or, particularly, the front legs of the other. This often results in both rearing up and boxing each other with their front legs as they try to bite each other. Injuries after fights between adult stallions are common in wild or feral equines, and deaths do occasionally occur.

The stallion who lives with a group of mares has an emotional advantage when challenged by another stallion: he will be more highly motivated to fight since he has more to lose. If he has to move away, not only does he lose his breeding partners but also his friends with whom he has strong emotional bonds. Thus, unless seriously sick, old or injured he is less likely to give up than the intruder. A stallion who is senior will attack younger colts and geldings with pronounced, exaggerated ear flattening, head extending and biting, similar to defensive threat in mares. In this case however, it appears to be related entirely to aggression, rather than mixed with fear (Figure 4.9), and the youngsters have to get to know when and where they will be at risk from attack, and act accordingly.

Fig. 4.9 Oryx, the other mature stallion is in another field off to the right. Oberlix is angry because the mares have strayed down there and is attacking Shindi. This is an unusual situation but illustrates how important it is to allow horses to become 'natural psychologists' so they can predict behaviour and get out

of the way quickly as Shemal and Lilka have done here. Oberlix is angry and showing it, but he is unlikely to hurt Shindi as she squats, champs and indicates her fear and lack of aggression.

This way of attacking inferiors is different from the 'snake face' employed by the stallion to herd the mares back to the group and away from a competitor. The difference is predominantly in the movement of the head and neck. As shown in Figure 4.1, the stallion displaying the snake face projects his head out with the nose forwards, and twists his head around with his ears completely flat, resembling a snake in the movement of his head and neck.

This snake face is, usually, employed only by stallions, and may indicate a type of aggression unfamiliar to humans. Nevertheless, we may have some idea of what it might feel like; perhaps something like: 'darling, do go back with the others, you belong there with me, and your friends and relatives. I do want you to stay, I am very fond of you, but I really want you to do what I ask. I will stop you going, even attack you if I have to, you will stay away from him whatever', but conveyed rather faster and more effectively!

The similarities of the behaviour in many fearful and aggressive situations outlines how complex it is to study emotions, and one reason why most ethologists have steered clear of it. But, let us not be deterred, if we are seriously interested in understanding equines, we have to be committed to trying to understand the relationships between different emotions or feelings.

It is important to remember that learning about aggression, who is likely to attack and when, is an important part of becoming a 'natural psychologist' (see Chapter 6).

Hate, dislike, iritation and annoyance

Equines, like humans, are all individuals. Some may be more popular than others, that is, more generally liked as shown in Figure 4.10. Some individuals may be generally disliked, or choose not to be social and keep away from others (see Kiley-Worthington 1997, figure 6.5 page 141).

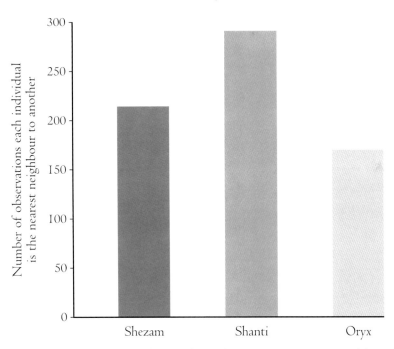

Nearest neighbours

Fig. 4.10 Some individuals are liked more than others. Here two young geldings (Shanti, aged two years and Shezam, aged one year) and an entire (Oryx, aged four years) show that of 681 observations – one taken every fifteen minutes over a 173 hour period – Shanti is significantly more often the nearest neighbour for Shezam and Oryx. He also tended to be nearer Shezam (between 1 and 5 m) than to Oryx (5-15 m on average). Thus Shanti was 'liked' by both of them, and Oryx tends to be the least often chosen as nearest neighbour and thus the least preferred by both of them. (*From Eco Research centre unpublished data with thanks to A. de Cartier and H. Randle*).

Stallions in particular will take 'hates' against certain other stallions even in the absence of mares, whereas others they tolerate. Stallions will chase colts out of the maternal group (see page 260). Some will learn how to appease the stallion and at least be tolerated, while others do not. Certain mares will do the same, although they are usually not so violent. However it is not unusual to see the equivalent of 'fisticuffs' between two mares who, quarters to quarters, kick out at each other.

Stallions tend to try to get rid of fillies born in their group, mothered by the mares they live with, as well as their sons. This may be some form of 'incest taboo', not necessarily because the stallion has any conscious awareness that they are his infants but, more likely, because he has become very familiar with them as they have grown up and, consequently, does not feel sexually attracted to them. A similar effect is found in normal human families where fathers are not sexually attracted to their daughters. Even where children are raised in groups, the males are usually not attracted sexually to female members of the group (e.g. in the Kibbutz in Israel). Interestingly, a filly whose mother died and was subsequently hand reared but continued to live in the herd *was* accepted by the resident stallion, her father, and had a foal by him (personal communication from Beck, North Island, New Zealand).

Mares protect their fillies from being attacked by kicking out at the stallion if he comes too near them, even after weaning when the fillies become sexually mature. Why he tries to get rid of them when he tolerates others in the group to whom he is not sexually attracted (foals and the old, for example), is an unanswered question.

Example

Druimghigha Shiera and Druimghigha Cara were daughters of Druimghigha Cariff who was the senior stallion at the time. They lived with the stallion and their mothers, D. Shiraz and D. Crystal, respectively, and some other mares and foals, until they were over one year old. At this time Cariff started attacking them. They would run around their mothers, but sooner or later he would try to attack them when they were separated from their mothers. In the end they left the group and joined up together in a different part of the field. We then took them away from the group, and put them with D. Osnan, an older gelding who had been kicked out of the group the year before by Cariff.

However, if after puberty a stallion and his daughter are made to live together, it can work well.

Example
Oberlix and his daughter Shemal have lived, travelled, competed, and generally done many things together for a period of seven years, on and off. The result is that although they may not be particularly sexually attracted to each other (although we do keep her on contraceptives when they are travelling together), they are close companions and friends and may show slight annoyance but never dislike, hate or serious aggression towards each other. Shemal does flirt exuberantly when near other stallions (and does not tolerate sexual advances from Oberlix). This infuriates Oberlix who will then herd her around using the snake face, but he very rarely tries to flirt or court her.

Again, this may be a feeling that most humans do not experience, although we can have some understanding of it. For example, the sexually developed filly feels much less attracted to her father, than to other stallions; he, perhaps, has similar feelings.

Dislike is indicated by: avoiding another, or moving away from them or an unpleasant situation.

Irritation or annoyance are indicated by mild defensive threat acts: ear withdrawal, tail swishing, hind leg lifting, swinging the head towards another, or even away from another, moving away and avoiding another.

Equines, like humans, quite frequently show behaviour characteristics of irritation and annoyance.

Annoyance and irritation are demonstrated clearly by a stallion who may be grazing peacefully. All of a sudden, he catches sight of a particular colt he does not like and, after a moment, lunges at him. This behaviour resembles very closely that of a human who behaves in a similar way when annoyed. The sight of the other individual the stallion dislikes suddenly becomes too much and he rushes at him to attack. When the other has gone, or his attention is directed elsewhere, the stallion returns to normal peaceful occupations, until he again suddenly catches sight of the annoying individual and lunges at him.

It is important in your relationships with equines to recognize these likes and dislikes, and to know what is likely to annoy and give pleasure.

Example

When an equine is being touched or brushed in a place that he does not like, he will show irritation, either by moving around, shaking his head, moving his legs, or trying to avoid the person doing what he does not like. If the irritation continues, he may turn his head around and bite or kick, either another object or the person responsible. If the handler believes the horse is 'just being aggressive' then they may continue with this annoying attention, disregarding the horse's objections. This will annoy him more, and he will be more likely to attack. In this way, he may well learn that being brushed is so unpleasant and annoying, he will try and avoid it always. This is the result of a lack of understanding and sensitivity on the part of the human in assessing when the animal was uncomfortable and irritated. Once this error is recognized, it can be changed.

Of course different equines, as a result of their different experiences, will have different thresholds for showing fear, irritation and annoyance. Simple observations can make an enormous difference to the quality of an equine's life with humans.

Redirected irritation is shown in both humans and equines. This is where some other individual or object in the environment is used as a scapegoat on whom, or which, to vent the irritation or aggression. Redirected irritation occurs when an individual of your own or another species annoys or irritates, but the irritated animal (or human) dares not attack, knowing that the consequences might be unpleasant, so attacks another (sometimes younger or smaller) or even an object.

Examples

1. Crystal, who hates having her girth done up, will lay her ears back, turn her head and attempt to bite the person doing this, however she knows she must not bite a human, so she attempts to bite another horse who is nearby, or failing this any fence post or rail in reach.

2. The young stallion Oryx, would like to attack the stallion Oberlix, who is coming too near to a mare whom Oryx is with, but he is frightened of the consequences, so he rushes at a nearby foal and attacks him.

The remarkable thing about equines is that, *if* there is sufficient knowledge and sensitivity about what annoys them in their associations with humans, and efforts are made to reduce the irritation, they become extraordinarily co-operative. Instead of being passive sufferers having to perform particular tasks by domination and fear, as many believe they are, they can become willing volunteers, participating in activities together with humans with enthusiasm, sometimes even making informed judgements to improve the way to achieve certain goals (see Chapter 10). If however, no effort is made by humans to recognize and to try to reduce the cause of irritation, they will quickly become more and more difficult and uncooperative – just like humans.

Depression and grief

Equines may suffer from depression. They show this by: lethargic behaviour, loss of appetite, lack of interest in others and the world as a whole. They perform few behaviours, sleep more and will often avoid even their close social partners. They sometimes die as a result without an identifiable physical disease. Prolonged restriction or isolation in dull environments can induce this, as can the death or separation from a social partner. This is particularly the case when two equines have been kept together without others for long periods and become emotionally dependent on each other.

One of the problems with depression and grief is that the obvious demonstration of these emotional states is the exception rather than the rule. It is difficult to know if the animal is depressed, or just very relaxed and lethargic. It may be that we humans miss the message as we are unable to read the visual signals.

It is often argued that since humans cry, demonstrating their grief very obviously, they are the only mammals who feel such emotions. Such a view, held despite other explanations, reflects the current cultural view that non-human mammals have an inferior emotional life. This then justifies the use of them in ways which would be unacceptable if it was universally recognized that they do feel many emotions very like us. In other words, it is a **'belief of convenience'**.

Another explanation for crying in humans is that they have had to develop such an obvious display of an emotion because of their *inability* to be able to tell what emotions others are feeling by observing them, or even by listening to what they are saying. The human may have to demonstrate grief very obviously and noisily before it is noticed. Human children in particular use this to manipulate others by drawing their attention.

Learnt helplessness

This involves giving up, that is learning not to try to extricate oneself from a difficult situation. It is the result of emotional and physical traumas of one sort or another and involves a 'switching out of the world'. It is the result of prolonged illness, pain or distress caused by physical or mental stressors such as a severe accident, loss of friends, or isolation in domestic or captive equines and humans. The more reliant the animal (or human) becomes on a form of help or protection, the less they make an effort for themselves. This can get to a point where animals refuse to get up from a lying position when they are capable of doing so, refuse to eat unless fed by hand, refuse to suckle, or refuse to make an effort to get out of a bog or difficult place.

A lack of an understanding of the normal self-help and self-reliance in equines, results in **overprotection**. This prevents equines from learning how to make decisions and is a form of institutionalisation of the equine, and also occurs in humans. It is a type of learnt helplessness.

Examples

1. Not allowing horses access to different plants in the pasture to learn what to eat, or always cutting up and cleaning food, (e.g. processing the food of zebras in a zoo) rather than allowing them to learn to pick out the bits they like, results in their inability to make choices.

2. Bringing donkeys into shelters to avoid the flies, instead of allowing them to choose whether or not to come in, together with many other manipulations of equines, results in them being less able to make their own choices and decisions on these and other things.

Overprotection is one of the most common and, from the equines' point of view, unhelpful management practices used in modern equine husbandry.

Such husbandry underestimates equines' mental abilities, and treats them like infants. This patronizing attitude, although practised with the best intentions, is one that has particularly common long-term problems for the equine, and can give rise to a type of 'learnt helplessness'.

Positive emotions
Pleasure, happiness and joy
If these animals can feel pain, depression and grief, then they can also feel

Fig. 4.11   The pleasure of movement as youngsters gallop about in the spring air.

positive emotions such as pleasure, joy and happiness since one is complementary to the other. The types of behaviour which indicate pleasure in equines include: leaping, kicking the legs in the air as they run, galloping around, jumping about, play investigating, then snorting and progressing at exaggerated gaits, nickering, touching and smelling each other, mutual grooming, moving, or even standing resting, as a group, and playing social and object-directed games.

Horses, who are deeply involved with movement, appear to take much pleasure in moving: galloping, leaping, jumping and cavorting, rearing and bucking as they dash around, particularly in groups (Figure 4.11). Healthy horses will display this behaviour almost without fail when released from enclosures or stables, particularly in cold weather. They appear to be galloping around for the sheer pleasure of moving.

It is quite likely that they also take pleasure in various group movements that they do with other equines, but also with humans, such as racing, or chasing about with other horses, humans and dogs (e.g. hunting). Maybe a certain amount of jumping also gives them pleasure and even learning and performing intricate movements and dance. We know when they are apparently taking pleasure in these activities because of the voluntary energy and enthusiasm displayed and their frustrated behaviour when forbidden to take part (see also Play on page 365).

Performing to audiences who show appreciation of the horses' performance can apparently cause them pleasure. Circus trainers are particularly aware of

Fig. 4.12 Companionship and enjoyment of each other's company: the stallion Oberlix with yearling Shindi and two-year-old Lilka.

Fig. 4.13 Mutual grooming and touching is relatively common within and between species. Here Oliver grooms Shemal, who in turn begins to groom him. This helps to cement bonds between individuals, and instills confidence in humans.

how the audiences demonstrating their pleasure improves many of the animals' performances. Our young filly, Shemal, who was 'Aurora' in the multi-species ballet of Tchaikovsky's Sleeping Beauty, quickly understood the audience's appreciation of her, and elaborated on this by darting and turning around, leaping and cavorting in the ring. The more she did it, the more they applauded, and the more she continued! (TV Farm Fantasia 1996. Channel 4.)

Equines will also demonstrate pleasure and happiness out of affection for their own kind (Figure 4.12). or others, including humans (Figure 4.13). One index of this is whether your horse or donkey approaches or calls to you when you approach, not when you are going to feed him, but just when you go to see him.

One of the interesting empirical results we have from our teaching research was that the tested animals would be motivated to learn to perform a task if the human showed approval and pleasure by praising them using the voice, smiling and laughing (see Figure 3.3). We have used this approach more and more in our teaching, with quite dramatic results. The fact that a pleasurable emotion was displayed by the teacher acted as a reinforcer for the equine pupil. This indicates that the equine must be aware of the behaviour indicating human pleasure, something that is often disputed (see Chapter 8).

It is more than likely that equines, just like humans, will also have moments of joy and happiness, just from being where they are: the sun is warm, they have a full stomach, are with others they are fond of, and can either admire the view, doze, commune with the others, or switch their attention to being a part of the world they are in at that moment.

Making distinctions between pleasure, joy and happiness is something that humans rarely agree on. No doubt the emotions may be slightly differently felt in equines, but then they are between humans too. What is not in doubt is that, like humans, equines feel positive emotions as well as negative ones.

Affection, individual preference and love
We have already mentioned that individuals discriminate between individuals of their own and other species: some they like, some they do not. They show affection towards some, particularly their young, their social partners, many of the members of their group, and even members of other species. For equines,

the whole of their social group becomes part of their deeply cared for emotional circle.

Behaviour demonstrating affiliation or 'liking' includes: approaching to touch, nibble, rub, smell, lick, nose to nose smelling and touching, licking and rubbing the neck and other parts of the body, smelling parts of the body, grooming each other, nickering in greeting, neighing when parted (see Figures 4.12 and 4.13); and they are relatively common in horse societies (0.02/horse/hour – 65% of the performed interactions).

Equines often form life-long associations demonstrated by affection (see Chapter 6).

Courtship, sex and lust

Mares remain in season for up to ten days, much longer than most species. Courtship is a prolonged affair and involves the male courting the female sometimes for days before she will stand for him. The length of the oestrus period may well have been selected for because it ensures that a strong affectional bond has developed between the mare and stallion which will, in turn, increase the chances of conception and, if the stallion stays around, survival of the foal. Careful observation of normal equine courtship emphasizes tenderness rather than the usual 'brutish' interpretation of courtship and sex in animals (Figure 4.14).

Rape may occur occasionally among wild or feral groups, but it is normal practice when humans breed equines by restraining the mare, often with hobbles and twitches. In this artificial breeding situation (often, ironically, called 'natural breeding', as opposed to 'artificial insemination'), the stallion learns to jump on the trussed-up restrained mare and copulate without having to make any effort to convince the mare of his desirability for sex, that is courtship. It is nothing short of rape where the female is sexually violated against her wishes.

Homosexual courtship and mounting (if not copulation) is relatively common among wild and domestic bachelor groups of equines. They smell, touch, rub, have erections, chase and mount each other not uncommonly, and from two to three months old, although complete intromission is not often reported.

Sometimes sex may be directed towards other species (**malimprinting**, see

Figs. 4.14a, b and c   Courtship and pleasure, affection and sex. a) Oryx says 'hello' to a visiting thoroughbred mare. b) There follows a chase, squeals, leaps and general fun. c) Finally, when she is receptive enough, he mounts her. The mare ran with Oryx for four weeks, conceiving on her first season, although she had a history of 'not being able to breed'. Emotional attachment helps with conception in equines and humans and is another example of the interweaving of mind and body. No need for drugs, manipulations, restraints or rape, just good clean affection and sex!

page 137). It can happen, however, even when individuals are brought up by their mothers and with other members of their own species. For example it is not unusual to find bulls trying to mount mares, guanaco males trying to mount cows or heifers, or stallions having erections when being groomed by human females. Bagemehl (1999) argues that such behaviour is not 'abnormal', but rather the result of a 'natural exuberance'; the result of the existence of life being easier than expected, the availability of plenty of energy and enthusiasm leading to different sexual experiments, if you will. This is an interesting idea which is worth serious exploration. It also questions the current evolutionary paradigm emphasizing the constant struggle and competition for life, the lack of leisure and time for experiment, and for fun, although this is beginning to be challenged today.

As in humans, sex may have a lusting violent aspect from time to time, and result in forceful copulation. But it is more difficult for a stallion to rape a mare than a human male to rape a human female, since the mare can just keep moving even when he has mounted her and he then cannot achieve intromission. Normal sexual relationships in equines, who are allowed to behave in normal ways, are founded on the establishment of affectionate bonds between the male and female. These are often long term.

In equines, there may also be many **reflective emotions**. These are emotions that require an idea of self, and what others are feeling, such as jealousy, embarrassment, loyalty and so on. However, before considering whether or not they may be able to feel these emotions, we need to know whether there is any evidence that they are 'reflectively conscious' or aware of what others might be feeling, so these emotions will be discussed when we consider consciousness (see Chapters 8 and 9).

SUMMARY
1. Understanding the feelings of equines is fraught with problems, but it is crucial to try. Since we are mammals, it is sensible to assume, initially, that another mammal's feelings and emotions are something like those of human mammals: in other words to use a conditional anthropomorphic approach. This must involve good observation and careful study of behaviour without preconceived notions, so that we can identify various feelings that we know, as well as others that may be unfamiliar to us.

2. There remain many problems with understanding emotions. The first one is that different emotions are not always easy to identify, and one human may not feel them the same way as another human, never mind another species. Often, there are interpretations which are the result of cultural belief or preconceived notions, rather than examining the similarities and differences in how equines might be feeling and displaying emotions. Another problem is the possibility of undisplayed emotions, and/or emotional lies which occur in humans, and may in equines. The fourth major problem relates to differences in world view, whether human or equine. Nevertheless, a conditional anthropomorphic approach may set us on the right path to understanding equine emotions better.

3. To try to simplify the emotions/feelings, they are first divided into a) general emotions or feelings, which are not related to specific situations, and b) more specific emotions which are usually related to specific situations and more particular feelings.

→

4. There may also be emotions experienced by equines which, because of their differences in body, being and lifestyle are not experienced by humans. It may be possible to construct an understanding of 'something like' what these feelings are; the champing of the youngsters and the snake face of the stallion herding mares are in this category.

5. Without some idea of what the equine may be feeling, it is difficult, if not impossible, to keep or educate him well. A critical assessment of what you think the equine is feeling is crucial for a better understanding of equine lore, however difficult it may be.

6. One very important applied aspect is to understand the importance to equines of reducing fear. Much of equines' inappropriate behaviour in relation to humans appears to be the result of fear. Reducing fear improves the quality of their lives. When in doubt about his emotions, assume he is feeling frightened, it is more likely to help than hinder in any situation.

5 Equines' ecological knowledge, and their need to become 'field naturalists'

'Consider migrations, pregnancies, seasons, brief harvests and the constant need to anticipate the movement of prey and predators. Many animals move continually from one food source to another, often with their young to provision, and sometimes with responsibility for a whole pack or herd. They have to be able to think how long this or that will last, or when it will recur. If they had not enough memory and anticipation of order to fit their plans into the probable train of events, with alternatives for altered circumstances, they often could not survive.'

Midgley 1978

To most ethologists as well as others who have some folk knowledge of animals, Midgley's statement would seem self-evident. However, many eminent philosophers (e.g. McDowell 1996) disagree, and argue that 'mere animals' are not capable of memory, anticipation and even simple plans. Animals live in a world of 'nothing but responding to a succession of biological needs' (McDowell 1996); they live in an environment, but not the world: 'The point of the distinction between living merely in an environment and living in the world is precisely that we need not credit mere animals with a full-fledged subjectivity, an orientation to the world, at all.' (McDowell 1996 p.116).

Another philosopher maintains that 'an environment is essentially *alien* to a creature that lives in it.' (McClelland 1972).

This is often believed by scientists too, who maintain that, until we have some empirical evidence that equines have an awareness of the environment, we *must* assume they do not.

But, this seems irrational since, if we study the way mammals live and what they do in the wild, it is evident *that to survive they have to have not only an 'awareness of the environment' but they need, as well, to acquire considerable knowledge about it.* Consequently, we do not have to do experiments to prove or disprove this, we can just study the way they live and what they do, when they are allowed to.

Most people who have horses, if they have thought about this at all, are inclined to consider that the world is 'home' to their equines, not 'alien', and that making a distinction between 'humans' and 'mere animals' in this regard is faulty.

In Chapter 2, we outlined how equines perform behaviours essential for a healthy life, and touched on the knowledge they must acquire to do this. In this chapter we will outline what knowledge and awareness of the environment equines must have in order to survive. Surprisingly, this is a subject that has attracted little attention from researchers. This is probably because the knowledge they acquire about and from others has won the interest of researchers, up to now.

It has long been argued that it is living in a social group that encouraged the development of a large brain and the mental abilities of humans (e.g. Jolly 1966, Humphrey 1976). This belief has been helped by modern western culture which has emphasized the importance of 'getting along with others'. Unfortunately, this is often at the cost of acquiring knowledge about the living world and the necessary skills to be able to live within it, that is 'ecological knowledge'.

Previous tribal societies who lived in the natural world, such as the pastoralist Masai, and hunter gatherers, such as aborigines and bushmen, had to acquire such knowledge to survive. Ironically, today it seems as if it is not the wild equines who find the world 'alien', but rather, modern urban-dwelling humans!

A hundred and fifty years ago no one in Europe could have avoided some experience of the living world and, in particular, horses, but now such experiences are often confined to the imagination and represented in films or books. Today there are many humans raised without any idea of common animals or plants. The equivalent limitations of experience and understanding can be seen in equines raised and living in highly protected confined stables or in zoos. As a result of these humans' or animals' lifetime experiences, they have not had any opportunity to develop their skills as 'field naturalists' to be 'at home in the natural world'. They have not lost the ability to be 'at home', but it is a very different home involving very different knowledge.

Becoming a 'field naturalist' involves acquiring knowledge about the natural world you live in. Some idea of space and time must be developed as well as observing, remembering, learning, analysing and assessing things, both living and non-living, in the environment.

As stated, there has been little attention devoted to research into this aspect of learning, that is the **how** and **what** animals learn in the constantly changing world in which they live, rather it has been their social learning, that is, learning from and about others, that has been concentrated on. But, inevitably they must have acquired the necessary information about the living world they live in, in order to survive and reproduce. It is irrational and non-scientific to assume they have not acquired a considerable amount of ecological knowledge until we prove they have, because we already have the proof: they can live and reproduce within the world.

In order to learn more about 'what it is to be an equine', we need to examine exactly what ecological knowledge has to be acquired, and how, by the wild or feral equine. Once we know this, we will know more about the mental equipment and tendencies to develop certain mental skills that they are born with. This in turn will help us to be able to develop quality environments for them, to improve our lives with them and to be able to teach them better.

HOW ECOLOGICAL KNOWLEDGE IS ACQUIRED

One of the simplest explanations of how **'knowing that'**, (declarative knowledge, see page 153) is acquired by the foal is observational learning (learning from watching how others behave, see page 143) from group members. However, seeing that a plant is being eaten by mother, is different from actually seeking it out and eating it, and the **'knowing how'** (procedural knowledge) must be acquired by trying, that is, trial and error and operant conditioning (see page 139). The individual will also need to acquire information from silent learning (see page 147).

Consequently, in the first place, wild or feral equines must learn to become good observers to notice things around them, and store this information to use at a later date in order to allow them to make appropriate decisions (see Chapter 1). As individuals mature, they will become more independent and start making their own decisions about how and where they go. By the time they are fully mature, they will be good field naturalists, if they have survived, and will be passing on knowledge to others, including infants, who observe them. Eventually, one individual will become the most knowledgeable naturalist in the group, leading to, for example, becoming the senior mare, or, if a human hunter/gatherer woman, the principle food provider who leads the other women to gathering points.

Mothers in particular must be good field naturalists if their infants are to survive and prosper. As a result, it is not surprising to find that it is the females who play the leading role in acquiring ecological knowledge (e.g. Turnbull 1982, Waring 1983, Kiley-Worthington 1997). Perhaps then, at least for females, it is the skills involved with being good field naturalists which spurred the further development of 'mind skills'. The male humans and equines, by contrast, once mature, require less resources (as they only have to maintain themselves) and are not inextricably bound up with supporting and bringing up infants. For them (given that they become enough of a field naturalist to survive growing up in their natal group), it might be more important to concentrate on becoming good sociologists or 'natural psychologists' in order to mate and leave offspring (see Chapter 6).

WHAT ECOLOGICAL KNOWLEDGE IS ACQUIRED?

Geographical knowledge

Geographical knowledge is crucial. Initially some form of topographical map of the area must be learnt. Each species has a 'home area' where they spend most

Figs. 5.1a, b and c   A knowledge of topography, that is 'knowing where you are' is essential for equines. When moved to a new home there is a great deal of 'natural history' to be learnt. Our three locations: a) Isle of Mull, b) Dartmoor, c) France

of their lives and which they need to know well. Wild equines, such as the zebras, have home areas of between 600 sq km (375 sq mls) and 2,000 sq km (1,240 sq mls). Wild horses home areas vary between 400 sq km (250 sq mls) and 2,000 sq km (1,240 sq mls). Within these areas the terrain is well known and the adult individual is aware of where he is within it as he can quickly find others, food resources, water, shelter and so forth. There is a lot to learn and remember over such an area (Figures 5.1a, b and c).

Young equines have to start to collect spatial information, that is form a 'cognitive map' to remember where things are, shortly after birth. In human babies it is some months before they form a type of cognitive map. There is much discussion about how this is done, but we can say with confidence that equines do form cognitive maps because they know their way around in their home areas, and can even re-find their home areas from a distance.

Example
When doing a training ride on Aisha Evans on Dartmoor, the mist came down very thickly when we were a good 8 km (5 mls) away from the edge of the moor. I was lost, but left it to Aisha to choose the way. Even though she had only been living in the area for two years at that time, she never faltered and took us directly back to the edge of the moor, finding a ford over a particularly difficult river surrounded by bog which I could not remember having encountered before.

That this is not some form of pre-programmed knowledge is illustrated by the fact that individuals make mistakes.

Example
Riding back across Dartmoor one day, I left Oberlix to choose his own way. He chose to take a direct line towards home (which we could see from the Tor at the top of the hill). However, he omitted to remember that there were only three gates off the moor. Consequently, we arrived at a fence rather than a gate, and he had to follow along the fence until he came to a gate.

There has over the last two decades been a blossoming of interest in how animals find their way around. In a recent review, Shettleworth (1998) concludes that they use different methods in different situations: dead reckoning, route learning, instrumental learning, responses to landmarks, stimulus generalization between familiar and unfamiliar views, magnetic fields, celestial cues such as the sun compass, and stars. Some equines also make migrations learning routes often over hundreds of kilometres (e.g. zebra in the Serengeti in Tanzania, and zebra and feral Thoroughbreds in the Namibian desert). Blocking migration routes by fences, drains or pipes causes severe confusion to these animals and because it is now recognized that migrating animals are following known routes, some forward-thinking conservation authorities in Africa are keeping migration corridors open.

Horses often route learn, but are extremely sensitive to environmental changes on familiar routes.

Example

Shemal shied at a log which had been moved on a familiar route and Oberlix shied at a road sign erected on a well-known road, that is they recognized a slight environmental change; sometimes these changes are not noticed by humans.

They appear to respond to landmarks, correctly locating or relocating themselves after viewing a landscape. They may also be using a sun compass or magnetic fields as they can correctly relocate themselves to travel homewards even after travelling 50 km (31 mls) in an enclosed vehicle (Eco Research Centre experiments, unpublished). As well as visual cues, equines may be using sound cues from ultrasound or infrasound of, for example, water or earth movements.

Recent animal responses to volcanic activity indicate that they often predict an earthquake. Equines, as we have mentioned, also use a great variety and richness of olfactory cues to map read, following trails by scents.

Long-distance riders have had the impression that experienced horses will learn to follow routes as a result of learning to follow the markers (often small coloured plastic flags attached to convenient objects) but we do not know if they are doing this, or following scents left by other horses, or the person or his motorbike laying the trail.

Different species and different cultures have a different idea of space, as we have discussed.

Example

While studying animals on the open Athi River plain in Kenya, when driving around in a

Landrover over a distance of around 25 sq km (16 sq mls), we kept coming across giraffe browsing the tops of the flat acacia trees, and believed them to be disparate individuals. Only when we were mounted on horses, and being higher up able to have more of a giraffe's eye view, did we realize that these animals were all part of the same group even though widely dispersed. They were able to see each other, and were responding to each other's movements and gestures. With their high heads, long sight and ability to move easily over great distances, they have a different idea of space, recognizing themselves as part of a group although dispersed over an area some ten times as large as our human group recognition would be.

Equines acute visual awareness and long vision coupled by their ability to move quickly over great distances point to their more extensive idea of space, although this will also be partly the result of their lifetime experiences. Horses that have always been confined in small areas may have a different idea of space and how close they need to be to others. We see the same thing when urban humans (who are not used to much space), visit rural populations who are: they have different ideas about distances.

Example
Throughout rural Africa when asking how far is 'x', the answer is (in Swahili) 'karibu sana', 'very near', which it is to those people, but might mean an afternoon's hot march to an urban westerner.

When designing environments for equines to live and learn in, it is very important to assess what the individuals' understanding of space may be. Turning Thoroughbred horses who have always been confined in stables out into a large field may be traumatic for them at first, although they will probably be able to acclimatize after some months. Keeping adult wild-caught zebras in stables or small paddocks may be very traumatic for them, like restricting a group of humans to one room, although, again, with thought, design and education, they may (up to a point) be able to get used to it.

Exercise
Ecological knowledge Watch an equine doing things for ten minutes (time it, it is quite a long time!). He can either be in a stable wandering around eating or (and this is preferable, and easier for the observer) take him for a walk on a headcollar to look at things and eat something along the verges or wherever is convenient. Watch him carefully, and in detail.

Use the way of concentrating on him that you learnt in Stage I of the exercise on page 161 to critically assess what he may be feeling. Take him through woods, rivers, around trees, along roads, up and down banks, whatever you have available, and make it as varied as possible.

The easiest behaviour to look at in detail is eating. Look carefully at what he is eating, how he is using his nose and what he is selecting. Find out which plants he is eating, which he is rejecting, what stage of growth of the plant he chooses, how he selects, what movement he makes, what he spits out and how. It will be a lot more interesting than you think. If you do not know what the plants are, then it is a good opportunity to learn something about them, and become a good natural historian yourself, after all, your equine is. This does not mean you have to look them up in books (although having a name *does* help you remember) but it does mean you have to look at them very carefully, and remember them.

There are more exercises that can be done in relation to his knowledge about geology, topography, the weather, other species (zoology), that you can observe closely either as you walk about with your equine or ride or drive. Set up little experiments testing his knowledge and learning about, for example, different substrates (gravel, cement, tarmac, grass, tufted grass, boggy areas, surfaces in an arena, sawdust, soil in the woods, or ploughed land etc.) Watch and learn about his knowledge. This can then be developed to help him learn more about different aspects of the environment: a learning environment. You will be surprised how much you learn too, as well as learning to look and watch.

Field geology

The mammalian naturalists' knowledge will involve learning some geology, that is what the substrate is like: differences in the character of the rock, and whether it is possible to climb the mountain safely up a particular scree, negotiate a particular sandbank, or jump up onto particular rocks while ascending a mountain.

We know that this knowledge is acquired by equines from studies of their wild lives and from teaching and working with them (e.g. Jackson 1992, Rees 1983, Welsh 1973, Kiley-Worthington 1987). It is not difficult for an equine to recognize a similar type of rock or substrate to one on which they have had an accident before, even if it is in a different place. They can also learn to distinguish between rock which will not be slippery (by crumbling) and rock that is slippery, ground that is boggy, mud that is suspiciously deep, even concrete where they may slip or rubber where they may not, and so on.

Part of this knowledge will be acquired by trial and error: trying, feeling, touching and smelling as well as looking, just like human geologists! Equines

Fig. 5.2 Shermal stands on granite. Whilst living on Dartmoor she learnt that these rocks were hard and, unless icy, not slippery, and so she would clamber about on the tors.

become extremely good at discriminating between safe and unsafe substrates, where there is ice, sinking sand or a hard surface on which they can climb (Figure 5.2). In some cases it is not easy for humans to see what features the equines have picked out to make these distinctions.

They need not only to be familiar with water to cross rivers, but also to know when they need to be very careful of the surroundings and substrate, when they can walk through it, when they cannot and need to jump and so on (Figure 5.3). All horses when first presented to the sea with breaking waves, tend to be frightened, but after a while they can learn to trot with confidence through the breakers. They also generally will try to drink the sea sooner or later, only to learn that it is not drinkable after which they make clear distinctions between trying to drink from the sea or from fresh water which may be adjacent (Figure 5.4). They can also learn to negotiate different types of sea floor when walking in the sea: pebbles, sand, rocky outcrops, uneven rocks and pools. It takes some experience, of course, but they certainly become aware of the difference in carrying their body in water or out of it, or confidently stepping off a rocky edge to swim.

Fig. 5.3 Oberlix carefully crossing an unknown river with steep banks and rocks in the middle. Pepsi, the collie, has no trouble crossing with his smaller lighter body.

Fig. 5.4 Horses must learn what and where to drink. The moorland streams near their source are popular, but Shezam (centre) watched the others before she tried it on a winter's day on Dartmoor.

Some equines who live in very dry areas will occasionally dig holes in dry river beds to find water, picking the place to do it, thus indicating some awareness of the substrate. In some cases this will be recognized from a previous dig, but not always; they must be making some judgement concerning the geology. Only western humans write books about geology, but the aborigine and the feral or wild equine may, nevertheless, be good practical field geologists.

This will not be the case for those who have had no exposure to rocks and geology, or a need to acquire such information. The horse raised in an urban riding school, who is used solely for riding lessons or dressage, or the urban human, will have little such knowledge. But each species can learn, and there are courses available for all of them!

Examples

1. A horse who has learnt to compete in cross-country events (where they have to gallop at speed over different terrain and jump fixed obstacles), or go hunting, will in the course of his training have gained much knowledge of the types of substrate and soils in order to avoid falling. That is he will have had a course in learning about the substrates, as well as balance, speed, and so on.

2. To a desert-living aborigine, different rocks and soils may indicate the possibility of water, this may also be the case for wild desert-living asses. An urban human or horse may be able to learn how to do this, if they have enough time before they die.

Field botany

A knowledge of field botany is crucial to the survival in the natural environment. Learning to distinguish different plant species, parts of the plant, quick-growing material from fibrous and woody material, which have prickles and thorns, which taste nice, which make you sick, is vital in order to learn what to eat, and how to eat it (see page 86). There is a wealth of floral species out there, even in an enclosed area, not all are edible and some are poisonous (Figure 5.5).

Example

Despite the thorns, Exmoor ponies on the moor during the winter live mainly on gorse (*Ulex europeus*) which they have to eat with great care to avoid pricks, but gorse in their field will not be eaten by racing Thoroughbreds. Many horses kept in paddocks learn to eat the prickly flower heads of thistles (*Carduus spp.*) – which presumably are particularly delicious

Fig. 5.5 Equines must become good botanists. Here Lilka experiments with a plant she has not come across before.

(they are related to globe artichokes) – by curling up their lips and picking them off with their teeth. Youngsters take time to perfect this tricky operation, often initially being put off by pricking themselves. If their companions continue to eat them though, they usually go on trying until they manage.

They must also learn where to go to find different plants at different times of the year, and have some idea of the growing and flowering season of different plants.

Example

Dartmoor ponies travel to where they can reach birch-tree branches when they are in bud in early spring, or to the grassy lawns scattered between the bracken fields as they start to grow.

There is thus a considerable amount of botanical knowledge these animals must acquire in order to eat. This will of course vary between habitats, depending on what is available and what the animals have had experience of eating. In addition, as with humans, food habits arise that are peculiar to different populations: that is 'cultural food habits' (see Chapters 2 and 3).

Examples
Extreme examples are some Arab horses who will, in the desert, drink milk and blood when very hungry and thirsty, or the Lamu donkeys in East Africa who live off the town's rubbish (see Figure 1.1).

Both equines or humans who have lived only in their own societies and travelled little, will have had little exposure to the vast cultural range of foods available and, consequently, find it difficult to eat unfamiliar foods. We had farming students from Kenya who even after five months, would not eat cheese as they traditionally do not make or eat it. Equines who have only been exposed to a few types of food will take a long time to try new types, whereas those who have had a range of food types will often tuck in more quickly, provided they see others eating it.

Botanical knowledge, a recognition of species and their ecology, is important, also, for identifying particular types of terrain: where to find plants useful for other purposes such as shelter, shade, presence or absence of other animals, water and bogs.

Example
We took our horses (born and bred in Sussex on the chalk downs, which are characterized by no surface water, and alkaline-soil-loving plants) to the Isle of Mull in the Hebrides, characterized by much surface water, steep larval deposits, acid-loving plants and peat bogs. The plants were very different in the two areas, and it took the horses and ponies a year to adjust to the different food species. A problem at first was our, and their, lack of knowledge of the indigenous flora which indicates bogs. Both horses and humans initially plunged in without due caution.

Since horses are heavier and carry more weight on small carrying surfaces (see page 58) they quickly sink through the surface layers that can carry humans. Consequently, they have to combine knowledge of botany (the plants) and the substrate (geology) in order to eat, travel and cross rivers and streams (Figure 5.6). With exposure to the bogs on Mull, both our horses and we learnt how to discriminate at a distance between wet, but reasonably solid, ground and serious bogs. The horses, like the humans, must have been recognizing the different species growing on them since they made judgements to avoid such places at a distance of 10–20 m (33–66 ft) or more. The deep bogs are often covered in the moss *Sphagnum spp.* with has a characteristic growth and varying colours. Some areas can carry the weight of the horses, but have sphagnum mixed up with rushes and cotton grass. In this case they would carefully approach, trying the surface with their feet, and assessing the area by smell and touch before attempting to cross. As a result of such knowledge, hill ponies and any equines who have had enough experience can travel safely and at speed over boggy rough country.

The horses became very skilled, often better than the experienced humans, presumably because it was more important to them and they lived in the environment all the time. At the end of six years, when gathering the sheep and having to concentrate on finding them (and working the dogs who were bringing them in), the riders would leave the horses entirely alone to choose their way across boggy areas and expect them to travel at speed.

Fig. 5.6   Knowing/learning where to trot through the stream on Dartmoor.

Exercise

Food selection/botanical knowledge. Again, watch the horse for a period of ten minutes, but this time you are trying to assess his choices in one particular sward or piece of verge. So count either the number of different plants he eats, or the number of times he selects one of them, and make a note of this, then try it again a month or two later and see how things have changed as a result of the changing seasons. The idea here is, again, to make you look and concentrate closely on the animal, not on other humans or other animals around, and also to begin to appreciate the complexity of his selections. This can be done with hay, silage, haylage or straw in the stable too, if it is too wet or cold to go out.

If this becomes a human social exercise, that is, several of you chatting together while trying to do it, it misses the point. This is not to ignore the importance of humans socializing with horses, but just to suggest that in this case it may be better to disperse to the tack room and drink a coffee and chat after the exercise. This is an important part of stable life, but not the only one!

Having learnt to concentrate on the individual, without your mind jumping back to communicating with humans every now and then, and having begun to understand his understanding of botany and food selection, the next step is to try to begin to concentrate on how he might be perceiving and interpreting the equine social world, his awareness of what is going on there, in other words his ability to be a natural psychologist (see Chapter 6).

Field zoologists and ethologists

The 'field naturalist', whether equine or human, will recognize the other animal species in the area, or those passing through, whether they are prey animals or predators, and how each species is likely to behave. Recognizing other species and their behaviour will give them important information, which may mean life or death.

Example

Burchell's zebras in East Africa often live with gnu (*Connochaetes taurinus*, Figure 5.7a), Thomson's gazelle (*Gazella thomsonii*), Grant's gazelle (*Gazella granti*), and impala (*Aepyceros melampus*) to name a few. This is partly because they are all grazers and prefer to graze young growth which is often restricted to areas such as those where there has been a recent fire, or close to permanent water. However, they can also use each others' skills to improve their spotting and identifying of predators as they creep up on them. They respond to each others' warning signals, becoming alert, and flee at times as a result. For instance, the zebra responds to a gnu orientating and intently watching an object by doing the same thing, or a Thomson's gazelle will spronk (leap in an exaggerated way) away after hearing a zebra snort.

Prins (1997) found that zebra preferred to graze with buffalo (*Syncerus caffer*). The buffalo live in very large herds, and were vigilant, so the zebra benefited from early predator detection, even though the buffalo were grazing long grass which is not the zebras' preferred food.

Most people who have equines, are aware of how they react to strange species of animals.

Example

1. We were running an endurance race and long-distance event on the Isle of Mull. Zanape, our llama, decided to attend the vetting and, as was his wont, he jumped effort-lessly over the fence to converse with a visiting Thoroughbred cross who was being vetted. The horse leaped about, snorting and cavorting (his trot up was very flamboyant) being followed by a confused Zanape who lived most of his life with our horses who took little notice of him!

2. Oberlix and I were doing a long-distance competitive ride and had found ourselves alone on the Dorset downs. We were trotting along quite relaxed until, rounding a corner, both of us saw a herd of ostrich. We both froze and Oberlix, less familiar than I was with ostriches, snorted and cavorted around. Presumably he recognized their similarity to other birds (two legs, wings, beaks etc.), but they were very much larger than even geese and turkeys, and ran about flapping their wings.

Because they live closely together, different species may benefit from each other, become tolerant of each other, and even enjoy each others' company (Figures 5.7a and b). There is a considerable amount of interspecific communication and certainly tolerance of other species in both feral equine populations and tribal humans. This tolerance is sometimes even directed towards predators, or others who might compete for resources or be dangerous: for example, zebra may graze near lions who prey on them, and the pasturalist Masai or Karamajong tribes in East Africa do not try to exterminate either the predators (who may kill their livestock) or the prey animals (who compete for grazing with their stock).

Studies on interspecies tolerance and co-operation are in their infancy. That species, including humans and equines, will voluntarily associate with each other (or even avoid each other), indicates that , if nothing else, there is a recognition of one by the other.

Figs. 5.7a and b   Field zoologists and ethologists. a) A typical group of antelopes living together in Zimbabwe. These include: waterbuck (white stripe on backside); blesbok (in foreground); eland (brown, in background on left) and gnu. All species I have studied. They often choose to live together to benefit from other species' response to predators. b) Here a human, Esme, one of our students, has become part of a domestic multi-species group. She is with Ramblie (the cow in the foreground) some llamas and horses. They all choose to be close to each other in a 4.5 hectare (10 acre) field.

Example
If an equine has been attacked by another species, cow, gnu or buffalo for example, he will be very cautious of contact with any cattle, gnu or buffalo until he has learnt that not all do this. After this, he will discriminate between that particular animal and another which did not attack.

There is a fashionable belief that because a horse, for example, has lived with a goat who is his companion and friend, or a dog has lived with a human, that somehow or other, the horse or dog 'does not know he is a horse or dog', but 'thinks' he is a goat or a human. Unless the animal has been malimprinted on the other species (see page 137), there is no question that this is the case, but just as some humans prefer horses or dogs to other humans, they may prefer associating with their friend the goat or the human, while knowing full well that (although they have many experiences and knowledge in common, and are companions and friends) they are not the same species.

Meteorological knowledge

Equines and hunter-gatherer humans must also have some meteorological knowledge. They need to have some idea of what the weather is likely to do, at least in the near future, so that they can predict where to be, to avoid being washed away in a flood, or at risk because of avalanches, ice, water, wind, volcanic activity and/or being deprived of food or shelter. Simple decision making like where to go in order to be sheltered from the rain, given that the wind is in a particular direction, is acted on daily.

Examples
1. Ponies or donkeys make a beeline for the sheltered side of the field when they are put out in the wind and rain. They have learnt where the shelter is when the wind is in a particular direction.

2. When studying equines on the Isle of Mull, we had to stay with them for eight-hour periods and soon learnt that, in winter, the way to be as warm and sheltered from the wind as possible, was to stay as near as possible to the group. They would choose curious slopes or slight dips as shelter, which at first sight would appear to be exposed, yet would prove to be well protected.

Combining all these types of knowledge and learnt skills allows both equines and humans to become good **field naturalists** (Figure 5.8). Such ecological knowledge is vital for remembering the location of resources in apparently featureless locations such as the prairies or African savannahs.

Fig. 5.8 Lilka learning about mountain sheep tracks in France. becoming a better 'natural historian'.

Examples
Water holes must be found and remembered and the appropriate water hole visited at the appropriate time of year; the best places to shelter; where to dig for food in the snow; where to go to avoid very heavy rain, or being caught by lions, outrun by cheetah, or shot by humans; and remembering where different food resources are at different times of the year.

This ecological knowledge and much more, has to be acquired by at least some members of the population, if the group is to survive and prosper.

Examples
1. The importance of this knowledge, and how it is passed on from one generation to another, has been demonstrated by the killing of the old female elephants in Amboseli in Kenya. They were the only individuals who had this knowledge, and now the young are unable to locate the water holes during the dry season (Moss 1975).

2. In just the same way, the aborigines are no longer able to survive in the areas of Australia their forebears came from because they do not have the geographical knowledge of the resources in the area, particularly water.

Such crucial field-naturalist knowledge died with their mothers and fathers, although, given enough time, it can be redeveloped, as in the case of the wild Thoroughbreds who survive in the deserts of Namibia.

More evidence that large mammals need to acquire appropriate ecological knowledge comes from the difficulty now being experienced with reintroduction programmes of zoo-bred animals. Captive born and raised individuals are unable to survive (unless very carefully supervised) in the habitats they are thought to have evolved in, even though they have only been absent for one generation. When they are given courses on local ecology and how to become field naturalists, some of them, at least, reacquire the knowledge and skills – it is possible to regain these skills during an individual's lifetime.

The importance to humans of having a serious understanding of the depth and breadth of the ecological knowledge that wild equines must acquire is crucial in designing appropriate environments and education for them. The ability to acquire such a wealth of knowledge about their environments ensures that the equines have the capacity, indeed the need, to use and develop their mental abilities in order to have a life of quality and avoid suffering.

This is not something that, to date, many have realized. An interesting idea is that it is perhaps this necessity to acquire so much ecological information in order to survive, that has led to the development of many mental skills.

Sometimes equines' ecological knowledge is extremely surprising.

Example

We were with a three-year-old Thoroughbred mare, and a twelve-year-old trotter gelding camping together in the West Australian Margaret River forests. These are well populated by indigenous birds, including groups of different parrots (particularly green ones shouting 'twenty-eight' much of the time; these parrots are called twenty-eights!). One evening we played a recording of some English birds. The young mare, Spice Girl, immediately pricked up her ears towards the sound, and became extremely disturbed, walking around, and attempting to get out of the corral. We played the tape again the next day and had a similar reaction, although not so violent. Scotty, the older horse who had much experience travelling with humans, paid attention to the unfamiliar bird songs by pricking his ears and looking in the direction of the tape recorder, but was not so disturbed. Although the changes in the bird song were not something that other humans would have particularly noticed, unless they were bird experts, it was dramatic how Spice Girl and her older companion had tuned-in to these unfamiliar bird noises, and how disturbing Spice Girl initially found the unfamiliar songs of sparrows, thrushes and wagtails.

This awareness of changes, which would hardly seem to have any useful value to horses, underlines how much information they do acquire about the environments they live in.

When considering different species of mammal, it is important to realize that those living in a particular ecosystem will tend to have similar knowledge; that is there will be considerable common knowledge between species as a result. Although different species may have slightly different needs, they will nevertheless, if they live in the same neighbourhood, have much knowledge in common.

Example

All those who live in a desert, from mouse to human, need knowledge concerning the whereabouts of water, the types of plants and animals around and where they are; that is, the ecology of the area. They also need to know when the weather might change, how to keep cool, where and when to shelter or move to avoid being too hot.

Arctic species learn how to: keep warm; look and dig in the snow for food, and lick or melt snow for water; where to walk on the ice; be aware of different kinds of snow; and when and where to hole up or migrate. Those in the warm tropics, where food and water is always available, may require other knowledge: how to keep away from biting insects and snakes, for example.

The implication of this is that the K'hung bushman or woman may have more knowledge in common with the elephants, zebras or impala with whom they live, than with another *homo sapiens* from, say, New York. This can also be relevant to those of us who live directly with our animals. Mrs X living with her four cats and two dogs in her bungalow on a Devon farm, has many common emotional experiences and more common knowledge about the area with her cats and dogs, than she has with a man from Ethiopia or London. In other words, if we and our horses share much of our lives, we may have much more knowledge in common than we thought we had, and in some respects more in common than with members of our own species from very different areas. This is demonstrated by some of the writings of people who have travelled long and far with their own horses (e.g. Tschiffely 1933).

The fact that both humans and equines have spread almost worldwide indicates their ability to adapt and become field naturalists. Of course, the amount of knowledge about these different facets of the environment may vary between species.

SUMMARY

1. Both equines and hunter-gatherer humans acquire ecological knowledge and have to become good field naturalists in order to survive and prosper. This knowledge is often more detailed than we usually suppose. Its wealth and depth has, to date, largely been ignored when assessing what equines can learn.

2. Equines, just like hunter-gatherer humans, need to become good geographers, geologists, field botanists, zoologists, ethologists and meteorologists, in other words, natural historians.

3. The acquisition and retention of this breadth of knowledge requires considerable mental skills and abilities and therefore would have been at least *as* important an incentive for mental development as acquiring social knowledge and being a 'natural psychologist' (see Chapter 6). It may be particularly developed in females whose responsibility is to look after the young.

4. Different populations from different ecosystems will acquire different knowledge.

5. Since species who live in a common ecotype will have to acquire much common knowledge, it is suggested that there can be **much shared knowledge between species**, and that this could, in some cases, be greater than the ecological knowledge acquired by the same species living in different habitats. We could have more knowledge of the natural environment in common with our horses, if we share their environment, than with members of our own species who may come from very different environments.

6. The importance of having a serious understanding of the ecological knowledge equines can acquire, the complexity of the necessary mental events and, therefore, the importance of giving equines opportunities to acquire such knowledge (or some replacement mental exercise), is emphasized if we are to understand and educate them better.

6 Equines' need to become good 'natural psychologists'

'The meeting of two personalities is like the contact of two chemical substances: if there is any reaction, both are transformed.'

C.G. Jung 1931

A question that has exercised the minds of many thinkers is why do so many species, including humans and equines, live in societies, why are they social, how does the individual gain from living in a society? One of the first reasons given was that by living in a group, it may be possible to find resources that otherwise you might miss.

For example, by being relatively close to and aware of what others are about, an individual can follow and home in on food.

Example
Vultures keep an eye on the sky and the other vultures around, and follow them when they descend to eat a carcass. In this way they can find carcasses over a very large area which they would otherwise miss.

But for some species of grazing mammals, including equines, particularly wild or feral animals, food is *not* found in patches; rather it is spread around. At certain times of the year it may be plentiful for all the grazing animals, such as during the rains in Africa or the European spring. At other times, during droughts or in winter, it may be scarce for all. This means that there is nothing to be gained by competing for food, since it is either available or not available for all.

Another reason often given for living in groups is that the risk to individuals of being taken by a predator will be lower in a group.

Example
If zebras live in a group of say 100, and have foals around the same time, there will be 100 new-born foals rather than one here and there. Consequently the risk to each youngster will be 1 in 100 when a predator turns up. If the mare and foal are on their own when a predator appears, the risk is 1 to 1.

But since a large group is easier to find than the odd individual, it is likely to attract many more predators, so the odds for the survival of an individual are reduced. If there are, say, 100 lions around ready to hunt during the day, then the odds are the same as if the zebras were living alone!

Life is not as simple as this and rarely are answers either black or white, so neither one nor both of these explanations is good enough to fully explain why a species is social.

The socialness of humans has often been attributed to their 'higher cognitive' abilities, including their language which allows them to pass on information from one to another and, consequently, to explain *their* social living as necessary in order for knowledge to be transferred. Indeed, because of this, it has become generally believed that social living is essential for the development of 'higher' mental activities. It has even recently been suggested that the more social a species, the bigger their brains will be (e.g. Dunbar 1998). A rather extreme position which, even if true, does not demonstrate that large brains reflect greater mental ability! (See page 68.)

Nevertheless, an important reason to be social for any species of mammal will be that **living with others allows more knowledge to be acquired by observing and imitating** (even without a human-type language). The youngster learns how to be a good field naturalist partly from watching others. Those who acquire the necessary information survive, those who do not, die. As a result, social living (which is not the only factor, but which does help with the acquisition of knowledge) has been selected for.

But, for the group to remain together, **there must be some form of 'social contract'**. This requires:

1. Innate tendencies to be social and to be able to pick up ecological and social information from others, that is to 'socially learn'.
2. To be flexible in order to adapt and acquire different ecological and social information, depending on the place and group.
3. To learn how to behave to ensure the continuation of the group, and not to be thrown out.
4. To learn about the individuals in the group: who is worth learning from, who to follow and watch.

All of this requires the individual to develop a number of social skills and to become a 'natural psychologist' (e.g. Jolly 1966). The differences in behaviour between populations is called **culture** or **social tradition**. As we have already argued, animal, as well as human, societies have cultures (Rendell & Whitened 2001). Humans pride themselves on their cultural differences, but these *also* exist in equine societies where the young learn particular ways of behaving, places to go, things to eat, what to do to whom. As a result, their behaviour and knowledge varies between populations.

Exercises

1. **Being a natural psychologist, the equine's social knowledge.** Take your equine, on a headcollar perhaps, somewhere where there are other social equine things going on: horses or ponies are coming or going, members of his group are around, or strange equines are around of different sexes and ages. Look at his social interactions with the other equines. These may not be immediately obvious; it may appear as if he is ignoring another, but subtle clues will be there, for example, in which direction he is pointing and progressing when grazing, the tensing or twitching of the nose or chin, movement of the head and where he appears to be looking. Try, without preconceived notions from other humans, to piece together the relationships he may have or be putting together with the others. Meeting others may be a time of squeal-and-throw-a-front-leg-forward, so do not stand in front of him, and use a long lead line so that you can stay clear while they play out their greeting.

There will be times when you jump to conclusions about his relationships with another which are wrong or the result of something someone else has said to you or that you have decided yourself, such as 'she hates him' or 'she is boss'. Critically analyse how you have interpreted the social relationships afterwards, you may find there are other explanations, and perhaps it is not really like that. You can also do this with others and compare notes afterwards. Other people who are interested in equines but do not know these particular animals are also very helpful for putting different slants on your interpretation. Writing brief notes is often helpful as you can easily forget what you thought previously.

2. **Free interaction with others.** The next phase is to do this observation concentrating on one equine as a focus when he is loose in a field, yard or pen with others. You will need at least thirty minutes before anything much will unravel itself, and do not be put off because you think nothing is happening, just look more closely. A pair of binoculars is useful for this, plus a thermos of coffee and a sandwich. Dress up warmly too, there is no need to be uncomfortable. You may find that they all come and show interest in you to start with, but eventually they will go off to do their own thing and you can start really observing what is going on. Take notes, and, gradually as the soap opera unfolds, you may find you become an addict!

3. **Talking to other humans.** Here the task is to talk to others about what you are seeing, or think you are seeing, as a running commentary. First do this, and then discuss it, but be careful not to develop a particularly human narrative based on what you think others want to hear, or interpreting the equine social whirl in an entirely human way (e.g. manipulating others; being deceitful, either to try to please, or to escape other problems). Make sure that you use the simplest possible explanation for what you think is happening. This is a difficult exercise, combining the first step of trying to be an observer of the complexities of equine social life (Point 2 above), with translating this into human language, which is important if you are teaching humans.

It can all be discussed after each of you have described what you think you saw, to see if everyone has come to the same understanding or quite a different one. Again, it is important to write your observations down before giving your interpretation, otherwise you will find it changes as a result of other humans ideas!

ISOLATION

One of the most obvious demonstrations of the importance to equines of learning to be a good natural psychologist, is that when they do not have the opportunity, they are often behaviourally pathological. In almost every stable yard, particularly in competitive or racing yards, there is at least one, if not many, horses who cannot be allowed to mix with others. In other words they have *not* learnt how to behave in a social group, and either put others at risk or are themselves at risk when in a group. The reason for this is nothing but mismanagement. They are social misfits. As stated, this is generally because during their lifetimes they have not had the opportunity to learn to become good natural psychologists, often because they have, for much of their lives, and particularly the formative years, been kept isolated from free interaction with other equines, or in groups that have been inappropriately structured by the carers.

Their problem is that they have not learnt the 'social contract', or 'equine etiquette', that is, what is and what is not acceptable in social intercourse in equine society. Frequently when put with others, they are frightened, and this takes the form of attacking out of defensive threat. They learn that this can get them out of the difficult and frightening situation (they are left on their own, others go away, or they are taken out of the group). Consequently, rather than learning how to ignore, co-operate, show affection for others and not be frightened of them, they learn to attack and avoid. Humans often behave in the same way when raised in isolation.

This problem is so common that rarely are many equines allowed to mix with each other. In fact it is often believed by the human owners and handlers that equines are fundamentally aggressive and nasty to each other. Such people do not pause to think how they managed to survive for a good ten million years before humans came along to save the day!

Even when individual equines have not had opportunities to learn to become natural psychologists, it is surprising how quickly they can learn, and often, given a chance, how keen they are to try.

Examples

These examples occurred at workshops in Switzerland.

1. An eight-year-old Hanoverian mare who had never been allowed to have free contact with another horse since she was weaned, was put out in her usual isolated 0.25 h grass patch, but the electric fence dividing her patch from her neighbour's was removed. The two gradually swopped areas, and over a period of thirty minutes during which they were watched by the thirty or so workshop participants, they wandered around, smelling, grazing and watching each other. Then they came up and smelt each other nose to nose, before continuing to graze 2–5 m apart.

Thus, even though the mare had had little social experience, introduction to another horse who she had previously been near and who, in a familiar place, proved not to be frightening, even welcomed. Since then they have been allowed to mix socially at least during the day when they are outside!

2. A ten-year-old Hanoverian gelding who was always kept in a small separate grass area when allowed outside during the day, was turned out with an eight-year-old Haflinger gelding who was well socialized and had lived in a group all his life. The Hanoverian immediately came up to the Haflinger and smelt him, squealed, and jumped about. The Haflinger took little notice of this but continued to stand and apparently watch the humans. The Hanoverian repeatedly came back squealed and leaped around. Eventually he started to just sniff the Haflinger, then groomed him on the neck, and then just watched him, standing next to him. Every time the Haflinger moved, he followed. It was a touching thirty minutes, watching the excitement and finally affection and delight this socially deprived horse derived from being allowed such uncontrolled social contact with another horse. It was evident how keen he was on learning from him, and how fast he learnt.

Individuals are isolated in order to protect them from being hurt, but the process of isolation increases their risk of being hurt or hurting others because of fear. Allowing youngsters to grow up acquiring the necessary social skills to mix in different groups with ease, reduces problems and risk, and makes for having an equine who will be easier to teach and more willing to learn. This is not difficult to do, it is just a question of allowing them opportunities to do what they have a tendency to want to do, that is live in a social group.

SOCIAL TRADITIONS AND CULTURE CONTROLLED BY ECOLOGY

Social traditions and cultures can be established as a result of knowledge which is dependent on the particular area (i.e. ecological knowledge, see Chapter 5).

Examples
1. What to eat, and where to find it, varies according to the area. This knowledge will be passed from one individual to another by observation, imitation and trial and error.

2. Horses (*Equus caballus*) normally defend the area immediately around the group against infiltration by others but they do not, usually, show a defence of a particular area of

ground, known as a 'territory'. However, when population densities are high, it has been reported that both stallions and mares defend a territory against infiltration by strangers (Rubenstein 1986).

Such learnt cultural differences are not restricted to a species' members' behaviour to each other, they can also be affected by their contact with other species.

Example
Zebra living with Thomson's gazelle may become more reliant on responding to the gazelles spotting predators than always being alert themselves.

A social tradition can be established as a result of learning something from humans about the environment.

Example
One common example here is that when an equine is unsure about going forward over an obstacle, or through a river, if you get off and lead, provided he has some confidence in you, he will be very likely to follow. Omeya the mother of Oberlix, would follow you anywhere. This was a big responsibility as, when crossing a bridge or a bog, we had to be quite sure that it would carry her weight as well as our own, as, come what may, she would surely follow! One day Chris was riding Omeya across the moors and found a ewe stuck in a bog. He got off and told Omeya to stay where she was (an instruction she understood). He carefully moved into the bog to release the ewe, only to find, when he was busy with the ewe, that Omeya, despite her knowledge of bogs (she had lived on Mull for five years by then, learnt about bogs and even been stuck in them), was peering over his shoulder, having tip-toed into the bog after him!

CULTURAL DIFFERENCES ESTABLISHED BECAUSE OF AN INDIVIDUAL'S BEHAVIOUR

Group differences can be the result of an individual's behaviour which is then passed on to others.

Examples
A particularly affectionate mare may influence other individuals in the group to display

such behaviour more. A particularly possessive and nervous stallion might herd his mares away from others, resulting in a group which stays away from others more. A more tolerant stallion may allow more contact with other males and even allow geldings to integrate with the herd, thus establishing a different culture in the group.

The social knowledge of domestic equines and their resulting cultural differences can often be attributed to the differences in the behaviour, attitudes and expectations of the humans having contact with them, as well, of course, as to differences in the non-social environment. Some stables are full of over-reactive horses, leaping around fearfully, biting and kicking. Another stable with the same breed (even relatives of the over-reactive horses) may have quiet relaxed horses who do not leap about, bite or kick each other or humans. These differences are particularly obvious in different racing or dressage stables (Eco Research Centre, consultancy records). Such behaviour (as it is in humans) is the result of social learning from each other and the human carers.

Example
Tests on the Druimghigha Stud over the last thirty years. The first horses purchased as adults were taught particular behaviour towards humans, that is good manners (e.g. not to push through gates, pull on lead ropes, step on human toes, to stand while being mounted and not to bite or kick humans). Subsequent generations of these equines born on the farm (fifty-six to date over five generations) have also been taught these manners. The interesting thing is that it has become increasingly easy to teach them. This is not *only* the result of improvements in teaching, but it is also, in part, that the horses have learnt from observing and imitating their mothers, fathers and grandparents. The result is that an effective 'culture' of not barging, pushing, biting, kicking humans or trying to avoid them, has been established, and such behaviour now hardly needs to be taught to the youngsters by the human handlers.

Social learning can also take place between species who spend time together, such as between equines and humans, that is equines will learn to react to the environment by observing humans.

Examples
1. Druimghigha Shindi, a nine-month-old filly was handled by an inexperienced, nervous student for three months one summer. As a result, she became very reactive, jumping away

from human contact whenever any human made a slight movement, just as the student had nervously jumped away from her. During the autumn, a quiet, confident student handler arrived, and within three months Shindi had become relaxed, even in unfamiliar situations and would stand still while being handled all over.

2. Normally, owners talk to their equines but do not really believe that they understand. The result is that the equines have no reinforcement for listening to words. At the research centre, all the equines are exposed to a restricted number of words (200) used fairly consistently and they are taught to listen to language. As a result, all of them listen and watch the humans carefully, and often (but not always) respond correctly when asked: they have learnt socially from the humans to listen to language, at least.

Humans can also learn how to behave from equines.

Example
Aderin, one of our foundation mares, a Welsh mountain pony, had quite clearly defined rules of how children should behave with her. She would not put up with being hit or pulled around, but would willingly do things if asked properly and thoughtfully. She taught many youngsters good manners at a time when it was not fashionable among western human society to teach them. She also gave many youngsters confidence in themselves.

The ability of equines to teach humans is recognized so well now that many centres are being established where equines help handicapped, criminal or mentally disturbed humans overcome their problems, not only by carrying them around, but by being reliable consistent friends and companions when the people are on the ground.

There are individual and cultural differences, therefore, in the social knowledge acquired and the resulting social behaviour between populations of these species; however there are also ground rules on how equines or humans will associate with each other, given the opportunity.

A social group is not maintained by chance: it requires organization, consequently individuals have to have some form of social understanding. In this chapter we will examine how, when, where and why these species organize their societies in their natural environments, what social knowledge they acquire and how this complements their physical and ecological knowledge. As a result of many ethological field studies on wild and domestic equine populations, we now know a fair amount about their societies. Much of the information here is from others' reported research, but some new research from our research centre is also presented.

THE EQUINES' SOCIAL GROUPS

Both humans and equines live in family groups, (Figures 6.1a and b) although there are some differences in these in different areas as a result of culture and ecology. The humans' behaviour must take this into account and their expectations must vary, depending, in particular, on the sex and age of the individuals who have different social priorities. We will first examine these.

Females' priorities in social knowledge

Females produce and look after the young, therefore, provided the necessary resources, such as food and water, are readily available and access to the young not restricted by humans, they are likely to emphasize co-operation rather than competition in their relationships with others of their own or other species, in order to benefit both themselves and their young. In part, this will be because, surrounded by their infants who have yet to learn the social norms of behaviour, a degree of tolerance is necessary for the maintenance of the group. Secondly, co-operation in protecting and overseeing their young will benefit mothers by, for example, predators being spotted earlier than with only one observer, or allowing mothers to leave infants for short periods while they go off to eat. Equine mothers are never out of sight of their infants for the first six months of their lives.

Midgley (1978) points out that social behaviour in mammals has its origin in caring maternal behaviour which is based on affectional bonds and, without which, infant survival would be so poor that the species would be extinct. Thus, social behaviour does not have its origin in competition between individuals. This will rather tend to prevent social living by splitting the group. 'Love has arisen from parental care, and is, if you will, the emotion which results in social living. It is the only way of accounting for the kind of motive love actually

Figs. 6.1a and b Family groups. a) Zebra family group: three adult sisters and the yearling foals of two of them. b) Equine family group: Oberlix (left) greets Shindi (his nine-month-old daughter) while his other daughter Shemal (on the right) has a protective eye on her younger sister. Scarlet (Dartmoor pony) and Oberlix's latest wife, Lilka (grey), are on the alert. Study of these social relations soon begins to build the narrative of the equine 'soap opera' with a new instalment every day!

is . . . Caring for the young is the only relation in which such an outgoing motive could have developed. Prolonged reliable affection, an affection which is not recognition of superiority, more a living sense of benefits to come is absolutely necessary for it.' (Midgley 1978)

Mother/young relationships and their emotional attachments are

therefore pivotal for the development of a mammalian society. The affection-ate bonds between mothers and infants are the cohesive force for mammalian societies. The resulting closeness between mother and infant allows the infant to learn a great deal from mother, both about the environment and others. Foals spend the majority of their time very near and within visual contact of their mother. Normal human babies do not attach themselves quite so exclusively to mother who does not have to be so near (Figures 6.2a and b).

Figs. 6.2a and b   Distances. a) The distances between a mare and foal for the first six months of the foal's life. b) An equivalent hypothetical construction for a human mother and baby. The point is that the mare and foal do not move voluntarily out of visual contact, even for short periods, even if there are other potential baby-sitting mares nearby. Whereas it is normal, even in tribal societies, for the human mother to leave her baby with others from time to time, often out of visual and auditory contact. Note: t = touching.

Distance between mare and foal

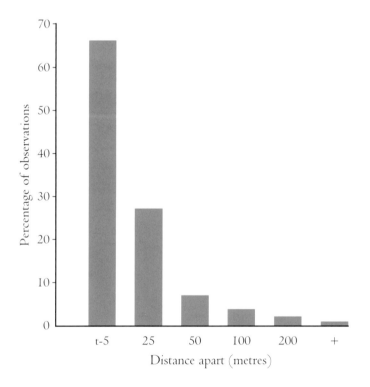

Distance between mother and baby

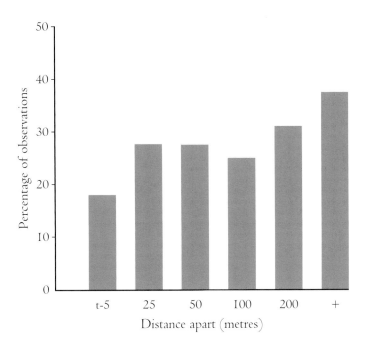

Distance apart (metres)

The interesting thing in horse societies is that this caring behaviour of females is not exclusive to mothers. Older sisters or even unrelated mares will spend much time with a foal acting as aunts. They may also protect the youngsters from any social danger from strangers or, when the youngsters become pubertal, from the stallion who lives with them who may attack both pubertal fillies and colts. We have called this the 'chaperone effect' (Figures 6.3a, b and c). Protecting youngsters is one thing, but the mares who are particularly attached to the stallion may also prevent the stallion courting and mating with strange visiting mares by behaving in the same way: placing themselves between the two, or causing all to keep moving so that the new mare and stallion cannot exchange 'love knots'. This can have the effect of preventing the stallion breeding with oestral mares. Consequently, in the experimental stud, when mares are brought to breed with the stallion, we may have to take both the mare and stallion away from the stallion's family group in order to ensure they can court and copulate when she is truly in oestrus and after they have run together for a time.

Figs. 6.3a, b and c The 'chaperone effect'. a) Oberlix, the stallion, approaches Shindi (nine-month-old filly) who champs and is slightly frightened. b) Immediately two-year-old Lilka places herself between them to chaperone her. c) Finally, Lilka steers Shindi away and Oberlix gives up and goes back to grazing.

Maternity

Maternal behaviour in humans and all other mammals is partly the result of hormonal changes, but the function of these hormonal changes is to change the feelings felt by the mother in order to improve the infant's survival. Both human and equine mothers care for their infants from birth *because they are fond of them*. If they are not fond of them then they do not care for them (with the exception of the human mother who can sometimes be persuaded she has a duty to look after her child).

With both equines and humans there are cases when things go wrong: mis-mothering' (see page 137). The mother does not show affection and care for her baby. In these cases, it is often the task of the human handler, or nurse or social worker in the case of human mothers, to awaken some affection for the infant in the poor mother. There are many ways of doing this which are similar for both human and equine mothers.

But, motherhood is difficult. First-time mothers, although they may be interested and attached to the infant, still have to learn how to be mothers. Initially, they make mistakes which can jeopardise the infant's survival. One example of this is an equine mother's pawing at the lying infant, or kicking him when he tries to suckle.

Some 'teaching' of mothers by mothers does occur in equine societies.

Example

We had a filly, Amanita, who had her first foal within her family group which included her own mother. The foal was born in the night, and Amanita had not initially stood still for her to suckle. However, 'granny' (Aisha Evans) had hovered by, and when we arrived in the morning the foal was suckling his mother, with his granny standing very close. But as soon as he had finished suckling, he went over and followed granny. Interestingly, granny (an experienced mare who had had four foals), did not continue to move off but returned to her daughter, circling around her. The grandmother was clearly very interested in the foal but she had recognized the foal as her daughter's and, to a point at least, recognized her daughter's mothering incompetence. Her presence possibly helped the young mother to relax so that the foal could suck.

Bearing in mind horses' visual-learning expertise, one might suggest that in this case the grandmother was teaching (see page 370) by encouraging observational learning in her daughter. Humans can give a helping hand to the mother to help her learn, such as relieving the milk pressure in her bag, which teaches her that suckling relieves the pressure in the udder which is painful. However, human helpers must also be aware of the damage they can do to the rapidly developing relationship between mare and newborn foal (see page 134).

Bonds between and within generations

The first affectional bonds holding the group together, therefore, are between mother and infant. In equines these are very strong. Equine infants are 'followers', never going out of sight of their mother for the first three months or so, or leaving her for more than a few minutes and then not going far away (Kiley-Worthington 1998, see Figures 6.1a and b). If they are separated, both mother and infant will become extremely upset, even after six months. Thus, **the between- (inter) generation bond is very strong** and is also crucial for the normal behavioural development of the foal. We know this because the effect of artificial weaning (usually incorrectly advocated for between three and six months) frequently results in trauma of the foal who, thereafter, may show evidence of behavioural distress (see page 180). It is often after forced weaning of this type that stereotypes such as crib-biting, wind sucking, weaving, or head throwing show a significant increase in performance (result of survey by readers of *Riding Magazine* for the Animal Behaviour Consultancy). This is particularly the case if there are others in the stable who perform these behaviours since they can also be acquired by social learning (Equine Behaviour Forum, Edinburgh 2000).

In the absence of their mother, when given a choice, the foal, up to over a year, will attach himself to other adult mares rather than others of the same age, even if he is familiar with his peers. This again indicates the greater strength of inter-generation bonds as opposed to those within generations (see Figure 6.2a). It is from older animals that they acquire knowledge: social learning. Consequently in order to have a young equine who is behaviourally normal, that is wants to learn, and does not have any pathological behaviour, it is important to ensure that the youngsters are not weaned before nine months. If possible (and the mother is well, young enough, and in foal), leave the mother to wean her foal herself as she would in the wild and before she foals again.

If the youngster has to be weaned, because of the mare's ill-health, or she is old and losing condition, then it is very important that the foal is placed with older equines, other mares if possible (see Figures 6.3a, b and c) rather than isolating the youngsters in a group together. Keeping the foals together is often practised on large studs and, as a result, the youngsters learn behaviour from each other, just like the children isolated on an island without adults, described in William Golding's *Lord of the Flies*.

The situation is different in humans when the infant, although entirely dependent on its mother for food, movement and so on, can be left for substantial periods of time by the mother. Neither mother nor infant need to be in sight, sound or touch of each other all the time. This has, through the ages, been taken advantage of by mothers hiring others to look after and even breast-feed the infant, and today by mothers going off to work. As the human infant matures, the bonds within generations become stronger. Generally, humans prefer to associate with their peer groups and spend most time with them, even if they do still retain contact with their parents. This is recognized in human institutions: play groups, schools, working environments, teenage clubs, old-people's homes and so on. We have tended to assume that because humans do this, when they become pubertal, that is they want to be with others of their own age, that equines will be the same, but it is not so. Young equines will not associate together for more than a few minutes without remixing with the adults in the group, if they have a choice. The practice of raising peer groups without adults, appears often to be at the root of later behavioural problems.

Although between-generation bonds are probably more important to equines than within-generation bonds, emotional bonds also develop between the infant and others in the group as a result of individuals becoming familiar with each other. Because of these affectional/familiarity bonds, neither colts nor fillies want to leave their natal group as they grow up. The colts as they mature become sexually interested in the mares, and a threat to the stallion, so he tries to kick them out although this may take many months.

It was always assumed that the stallion would not kick out the fillies as they matured but the few longer-term studies of horses that have been completed indicate that, if the resident stallion is the same one who either fathered the fillies, or has become familiar with them as they grew up, he will treat them like the colts, and try to get them to leave. All the four stallions we have had and monitored at the Eco Research Centre have behaved in this way.

Growing up in equine society

Equines (although they have complex societies and individual differences within them) do not dwell on their societies and how they work, as far as we know. Nevertheless, habits form within the society. One of these is to allow the growing individual much social liberty within the group, in other words to recognize that he does not yet know or practise correctly the social norms.

Example
Infants are often less able to switch attention away from 'the self' and its needs; either they must rapidly fulfil their needs (food, warmth and so on) or they perish. Thus these needs are catered for by group members, and their self-interest is tolerated, even sometimes indulged by others, for example young colts less than eighteen months old making sexual advances to mares are firmly coped with, but the mares are more tolerant than of such behaviour from an unfamiliar mature stallion.

As they grow up, the young also appear to learn to spend less time on egotistical concerns, and give more attention to the whole social and physical environment, as well as developing their role within it and this is recognized by the rest of the society.

Example
An animal who is very young and injured will make a fuss about a wound, often not making any effort to cope, to get up, walk, suckle and follow the group, but rather attracting attention screaming (if a child) or, if a foal, by just lying and not following mother. However, once they are grown, the individual will show a remarkable ability to switch off from his own pain in order, for example, to keep up with the group, sometimes coping with what must be very severe pain indeed (e.g. horses with broken, or severely infected, legs).

Another important development for the growing youngster is to develop a great awareness of the environment within which he lives and, in particular, as the result of investigating and exploring (see page 196), he learns more about the environment, and what is novel or unfamiliar. The difference in the behaviour of the young in this respect is recognized by the rest of the group.

Example

A foal sees something that is novel and stops, stares, may even leap and gallop away from it, snort and generally demonstrate that for him there is something scary around. This behaviour, will be ignored by his mother or other mature animal within the group, although other youngsters may join in, and then this becomes a game. However, when they are grown up and consequently have acquired more information about the world, responses of this kind from the same animal will be attended to and acted on by the others: looking, watching and maybe going to investigate or leaping away.

Because every member of the group learns the personality of the others, whether or not there is a response to messages will depend on the individual. One who is constantly 'crying wolf' and over-reacting will be ignored, whereas an individual whose responses are respected, will be reacted to. One of the tasks of the growing youngster is to learn about the individuals so that he knows who to watch, to follow, to avoid and when, and how, to be accepted and liked in the group.

Friendships and enemies

We all know that horses form friendships. Individuals will like some members of the group, and apparently dislike others. One way of measuring this is by measuring how much time individuals spend with each other, that is, who is their nearest and next nearest neighbour. We have had many people over the years assessing this measuring among our horses: mares, youngsters and stallions. Interestingly, the results generally confirm our own subjective opinions. In chapter 4, Figure 4.9 shows the nearest neighbour relations, and how far they were apart, for a group of our home-bred bachelors. Bachelor groups (groups of usually young or old males who have not managed to join up with any mares or fillies) have been studied much less than breeding groups to date.

Some individuals will be popular and some not so popular, but this is not clearly related to aggressive behaviour displayed to another, nor some form of 'dominance' (see page 273). Popular individuals may be quite aggressive to others, but they are still liked enough to be chosen as neighbours. Relationships are complex, just as in human societies; look at how much squabbling goes on in human families, yet it is usual that individuals have long-term and often very close relationships.

Males' social priorities

Young stallions, colts and old or mature stallions who have not obtained a harem or family group, join up in bachelor herds. Consequently these tend to be composed of all ages from puberty upwards. The groups are less stable than the family groups as stallions come and go, attempt to join harems or establish a new family. The bachelor herds also move around more than the breeding groups, and their size depends on the availability of resources (e.g. food, water, shelter) and on the number and distribution of breeding groups of females.

Fillies who have been pushed out of their maternal herd, will temporarily join up with a bachelor group. If there are other fillies there, they will join up with them, but if not, they remain with their brothers until a stallion manages to separate them, and establish a small satellite group which will finally become a new family group. It is easier for the stallion to begin to establish a harem with a filly from the bachelor group but he will have to become friendly with her brother first or she will be very difficult to separate from him and the others he is with.

Human males may associate together in bachelor groups or stay with their natal family from which they will either try and migrate to establish their own family group by attracting unattached young females (or older ones hijacked from their families) or by attracting unattached females to their natal group and continue living within it.

This establishment of a family group by either human or equine males is difficult; males do compete with other males, but females choose mates, and these are not always the winners of competitions or fights.

The stallion with an established harem may have to compete with other males to mate with the females, but the females will choose him rather than an interloper. Thus, the interloper has an extra problem as not only does he have to overcome the existing stallion but, more importantly, to establish a breeding group he has to overcome at least the adult mares' preference for their previous stallion. This is particularly difficult when he is attempting to establish a new group by trying to hijack females. Both mares and fillies will have to leave their natal group or each other, which, because of their strong emotional bonds, they are loath to do. They will await their moment and creep back to their original group. The new stallion may spend many sleepless hours trying to stop them.

The mature mares want to stay with the other mares, so it is difficult for him to separate one or two mares; it is, easier to take over the whole group by somehow getting rid of the stallion.

But, even when the stallion fights another and is replaced, the mares may take some time to accept the new stallion as part of the group and tend not to allow him close contact until he has been with them for some weeks. Consequently it may be several years before the young stallion has become a sufficient 'natural psychologist' to be able to 'have and to hold' any females. He will have to learn this from other males in the bachelor group after leaving his natal group, as well as by observing females, courting them, familiarizing them with him, and getting them to like him (see Figure 6.1b).

The male's attitude of competition for mates may be an instinctive tendency, but how, when, where and why he goes about it is acquired from the behaviour directed at him by both males and females. Fillies and mares occasionally compete for mates, but this is generally not a problem as the male can readily oblige all willing females. He will not typically have long-term monogamous relationships with one female.

Monogamous relationships, which are normal in some species (e.g. swans), may need a different type of social knowledge. It is not normal in either humans, most other primates or equines (although it has become an expectation in some human cultures).

Social knowledge necessary for sex and breeding

It is often believed that all behaviour during sex and breeding of non-human mammals at least, is innate and controlled by 'instinct'. As we have pointed out, there are instinctive tendencies in sexual behaviour in all mammals, including humans, but much social knowledge must be acquired for males to breed and mothers to raise infants.

Fillies first come into season and ovulate at about eighteen months, and can become pregnant soon after this. They come into season in temperate climates every three weeks during the lengthening days, and then less often through the rest of the year. In the tropics, they seem to come into season throughout the year, although zebras show a peak breeding season at the beginning of the rains when food is widely available.

Oestrus is diagnosed in equines mainly by smell, through smell messages (pheromones) particularly in the urine. The urine testing is often denoted by **flehmen** (see Figure 1.8). This, presumably, allows for a more thorough investigation of the smell/taste (see Kiley-Worthington 1987 and 1998).

Colts are usually able to produce sperm at around a year old, but in feral or wild populations, they are unlikely to be able to have sex until around three years old. The males of many species have been shown to have changing levels of testosterone (the male sexual hormone) depending upon the seasons and day length through the year. The breeding season corresponds to when the males' and the females' sexual hormones are highest and will correspond to favourable environmental conditions for the survival of the young when born after the normal gestational period.

Courtship and mating can be a lengthy process in equines. Although there are again instinctive tendencies for both males and females to perform a series of actions before mating, how, when, where and for how long courtship continues is the result of decisions made by the participants whose behaviour differs. Efforts are made, particularly by the male, to induce bonding, consequently demonstrations of affection such as touching, stroking, clasping, gentle nipping, licking, kissing, rubbing and many forms of embrace are frequent (see Chapter 4, Figure 4.13). Playing aggressive, sexual, chasing, leaping games are also part of it all. It is a time of high excitement with much vocalizing, squealing, snorting, nickering, neighing, shouting, laughing, crying: whatever is appropriate to the species. There is much chasing with equines and, before copulation can take place, the female has to stand willingly. The courtship of young virgin females in all these species is often particularly prolonged since their fear of the unfamiliar has to be overcome (see Figure 4.14).

Social education of stallions

It is often believed that stallions cannot control their 'instinctive' sexual behaviour, and consequently are too dangerous to be used as everyday riding horses. There are, however, parts of the world where *only* stallions are worked (e.g. Muslim countries), and other societies where both sexes have been used throughout history (e.g. by farmers employing working horses, and by some of the Native Americans). We have had six different stallions of the hot-blooded variety

(Thoroughbred, Anglo-Arab and Arab) and all of them, after being taught without violence or punishment, have learnt to control themselves in different situations and have been safe for beginners to ride out even with mares in oestrus, and with other stallions or geldings. Other stables have had the same experience (e.g. some Endurance Horse & Pony Society members in the UK; Cheval Evasion, Drome, France; Delgado Stud, Provence, France). Thus, stallions, like human males, can certainly learn to control their sexual impulses, provided they are taught how, and can even become fond of each other ! (Figures 6.4a and b.)

Figs. 6.4a and b   Stallion relationships. a) Two stallions and Shemal (on lead) out for a ride at our new mountain centre in France. b) Oberlix and Oryx. In France they have a saying: *'les freres enemis'*.

In humans, lack of exposure to females, and consequently not learning to control sexual impulses can increase the problem that males have controlling their sexual urges (e.g. in the army, until recently, or in countries where women are not present, or dressed to reduce recognition of their femaleness). Thus males of most species, including humans, have to learn to behave sexually appropriately. Normally in feral or wild equines, this is learnt by exposure to females, old and young, and other males. They learn the intricacies of being able to control their sexual urges by being severely corrected for inappropriate behaviour, that is kicked, chased away, bitten and attacked (Figure 6.5). This may begin when the colt is as young as five months old if he becomes too confident with mares other than his mother. They are, equally, rewarded for appropriate behaviour if the mares have had experience of males before. Then, when mature they may be approached, touched, smelt and generally flirted with by the mares.

In captive or domestic equines, the lack of opportunities available to become a 'natural psychologist' (that is to predict others' behaviour and understand species' etiquette) is common. This is particularly the case if a stallion required for breeding has been weaned and kept from free contact with others (the normal practice in breeding studs). As a result of not learning social and sexual equine etiquette, he cannot read the messages produced by the mares. Consequently when allowed to mix with them, he gets it wrong, and the result

Fig. 6.5 Oberlix (right) has tried to prevent Shindi (centre) from following her foal (Shenandoah) who Chris is leading. Shindi is not prepared to leave her foal and lets Oberlix know!

may be he is kicked or he kicks another. Consequently it is *recommended by the equine establishment and some of the veterinary profession* that before copulation, the mare should be strapped up by humans (with hobbles, twitches and ropes) so she can be raped by the stallion whose total social experience and understanding of courtship and mating is that he has been taught to mount and ejaculate (Fraser 1962, Morel & Davis 1993)! It is overdue that this particularly pernicious practice is seriously discouraged.

In addition, remember that if there are socially inept individuals in the stable, they are likely to be at greater risk. The risks in breeding establishments as well as competitive and racing yards are created by the husbandry and the lack of social education of the equines. This can be changed in studs by mare owners insisting on their mare running with the stallion, and not being restrained and raped.

Example

We have bred and raised three valuable premium performance-tested stallions to date. Approximately 100 mares have been covered, and we have had no serious damage to the stallions having sex while running with the mares. We have had a high percentage of mares to cover who have not previously become pregnant by normal breeding practices. Because of their experiences, these mares are often particularly aggressive to the stallion. Nevertheless, with our experienced stallions, the conception rate is 93% on first oestrus, which is much higher than normal 'in-hand' covering – 68% (Rossdale 1983).

When the male equine stays around after mating, demonstrations of an affectional bond between the breeding pair often continues, sometimes through-out life. Sex is prolonged, complex and involves above all long-term bonds of affection in equines, if they are given the chance to develop these bonds.

Equines, particularly in the temperate areas, are said to be seasonal breeders, coming into season only with lengthening days (e.g. Rossdale 1983). Mares kept with stallions do not cycle only during the spring. Those who keep their mares with stallions often have foals born throughout the year. One of ours was born two days after Christmas without the use of any light-schedule changes, hormones, drugs or surgery. Since the gestation period is eleven months, the mother conceived at the beginning of January when days are getting shorter and they are supposed not to be cycling. There is a considerable veterinary industry based on using steroids, changing day length and so on, in order to try to have foals born at the beginning of the year (e.g. Morel & Davis 1993) but one thing which is apparently overlooked, is that there is a greater possibility of having foals *at any time of the year*, provided the mares have free access to stallions, can court and be courted, develop bonds, get to like a stallion and be emotionally and sexually aroused, rather than forcibly raped; there is nothing like close contact with a stallion to ensure mares become pregnant!

Another strongly held belief is that human females are unique in having sex willingly at any time through the sexual cycle. Mares, by contrast, are said to be receptive to the males only at very particular times of the sexual cycle, that is, just before ovulation when they 'come in season'. We have some evidence to suggest that this may not always be the case, provided mares are allowed to associate with the stallion.

Example

We had a vasectomized stallion (a stallion who had had the duct taking sperm to the penis cut, but all else was normal) living with seven to nine mares for three years. During this period, all the mares had sex with him quite regularly through the spring, summer and even into the winter (particularly when they had been separated from the stallion for a day or two). At least two of the mares would have sex with the stallion, if he could be persuaded by their flirting (that is going up to him, nuzzling him, squealing, grooming and rubbing him, and turning their hindquarters towards him, urinating and even backing into him) at other times than when they should have been in season according to the recorded dates. Sex when the mares were not due to be in season was observed eighteen times with six different mares over three years. Although we did not take smears to test the oestral status of the mares, there is little reason to think that they were physiologically abnormal since they cycled regularly and conceived before and afterwards with another stallion.

There is other evidence (e.g. Skipper 1999 and Eco Research Centre Records) that some pregnant or non-pregnant mares may have sex at times other than when they are in oestrus.

The stallion may not be a provider or protector, but he is a well-known and often well-liked permanent member of their cohesive group. This suggests that we should carefully examine whether or not it is only humans who are sexually attracted to males at times when they are not ovulating.

THE DETAILED ORGANIZATION OF EQUINE GROUPS AND SOCIETIES

Dominance orders examined

It has long been believed that equines, like many other species of birds and primates arrange their social system by having dominance hierarchies (e.g. Waring 1983, Fraser 1992; reviews in Kiley-Worthington 1977, Syme & Syme 1979, Bernstein 1981). The theory behind this assumption is that individuals will inevitably be in competition for scarce resources. Hence in a social species (where there is an advantage in living in a group), if the group is to stay together there will be a need for some mechanism to reduce aggression over scarce resources, otherwise individuals may be injured and the group consequently split up.

It was suggested by Schjelderup-Ebbe (1922) who worked with chickens, that the way this was done was by individuals recognizing other individuals and developing a **dominance order** which controlled access to resources, such as food. When the dominant individual wanted some food and approached it, the subordinate individuals withdrew without fighting. This, it was argued, cut down aggression and consequently allowed competing individuals to live in groups without risk of injury to each other. This works well for hens, but unfortunately this approach has been universally adopted for other mammalian societies where it may not be relevant. This simplistic understanding of mammalian societies has also been popularized by the media, and many horse owners now assume it to be true.

The first problem is how to define a dominance order and the next, how to measure it. This is neither clear nor consistent. It has been proposed that it is a hierarchy of aggression or one that is controlled by fear. Others consider that it implies leadership, protection, or access to resources. There has been much discussion of the term, but little agreement to date (see Kiley-Worthington 1977 for review). It has recently been concluded that it is an undefined 'metaphysical concept' (Moore 1993) which makes things even more complicated!

Individuals within a group of large herbivores in their natural habitat do not need to be in competition for much of the time. Their food is equally available or not available to all of them. Consequently they may have developed a way of living together with others which concentrates, not so much on strategies for overcoming competition (because there is none, most of the time), but rather by displaying behaviours to foster group cohesion. This could be demonstrated by frequent behaviour that will help cement bonds between individuals, showing that they like each other. It could also be helped along by behaviour that is likely to deflate an emotional situation which might otherwise cause dispersion of the group, particularly aggression. One way of doing this would be for individuals to ignore aggressive attacks, another to, at times, quietly withdraw.

To clarify this situation in equines, some twenty years ago I began to study their communication in some detail. Because of the relevance of this, the most important results are presented here. In the latest study we decided to investigate in detail the relationships in a group of thirteen horses we had at the centre. This was a fairly natural type of group, with a stallion, mares and youngsters. We recorded many more behaviours than had previously been recorded. This was done to try to extract the exact meaning of movements and postures. It was important to record the identity of both the performer and the receiver of any behaviour in order to be able to assess the individual differences, that is the 'personality profiles', as well as the overall organization of the group (Kiley-Worthington 1987, Figure 6.6). To assess the meaning of the message, it is necessary to record how others interpret them, that is, the recipients' responses.

This information will give us a chance to analyse some of the visual communication in horses in detail, and may be able to tell us, not only about whether there is a dominance hierarchy or some other overall organizing system, but also allow us to ask whether equine communication has any of the characteristics of human language (see Chapter 7).

We therefore measured the behaviour that showed: 1) interest in each other (such as smelling and sniffing, touching, approaching, orientating towards another); 2) being nice to each other (such as rubbing, touching, licking, nickering and neighing); 3) ignoring behaviour directed at the recipient; 4) being aggressive or defensive (biting, kicking, head extending and ear flattening, tail swishing and intent to kick); and 5) avoiding or withdrawing. There are hierarchies in the performance of all of these behaviours, that is some individuals are more affiliative than others, some more aggressive than others, some show more interest or withdraw more than others. The interesting thing is the degree to which these different hierarchies correlate. Was the most affectionate the most, or least, aggressive? There were few correlations, but there was a correlation between the aggressive hierarchy and withdrawing least often: those that were most aggressive withdrew less often.

Rec. Response →	'Deflammatory'		'Cohesive'		'Inflammatory'	Total
	Ignore	Withdraw	App/ Int.	Affil	Aggr	
Performance ↓ Avoid % of response	306 59%	-13 0.6%	122 23%	-13 0.6%	-65 13%	519 4% of total
Approach/ Interest	+3.293 55%	+1,586 26%	853 14%	-62 1%	235 4%	6.029 45% of total
Affiliation	+1.025 41%	159 6%	148 6%	805 32%	175 7%	2,312 20% of total
Aggression	610 18%	+2.073 62%	122 4%	-25 1%	475 25%	3.305 26% of total
Total % of total	5.234 43%	3,831 33%	1,245 10%	905 7.5%	950 6.2%	12.193 100%

Figure 6.6 This table shows what responses the different categories of behaviours elicited in the responder. The vertical categories are those done by the performer, the horizontal, those done in response, by the recipient. The categories were:
a) Avoid. b) Approach and show interest. c) Affiliative/affectionate behaviour. d) Irritation or aggression. The recipient could also e) ignore the behaviour that was directed at him/her.

The + indicates that the recipients' responses of that type was significantly higher than expected, and the − that it was significantly less.

One particularly unexpected discovery here was how frequently the same category of behaviour was elicited from the respondent as had been directed at him/her. A 'be done by as you did' reciprocity. That is, if the performer was affiliiative to another, s/he was likely to receive affiliative behaviour back, and similarity with the other types of behaviour. These are in the outlined boxes. (From Kiley-Worthington 1998).

We also found that there were some correlations which indicated that certain individuals did more of everything. In other words they were more socially involved, they were 'extroverts'; while others were not very socially involved at all and were 'introverts'. Also, some were predominantly 'performers', others, 'received' more and performed less.

One of the most obvious things was how every one of these individuals behaved in a co-operative way; they were nice to others, very much more than they were nasty. This indicates that this society was *not* primarily competitive. Rather they were all making efforts to stick together and be nice to each other; they were 'stickers' not 'splitters' (Kiley-Worthington 1998). In Figures 6.7a and b, we see that the amount of behaviour related to cementing bonds and deflating potential splitting of the group, that is 'sticking behaviour' was 73% and behaviour related to 'splitting' was only 26%. Every individual showed over 60% 'sticking' behaviour (Figure 6.7b). In other words, behaviour related to group cohesion was by far the most common, that is 'make love not war' was the most common refrain!

Cohesive Behaviour 'Sticking'		
Deflamatory (withdrawing and ignoring aggression as a response)	3,625	29.79%
Cohesive behaviour (approach. show interest, affiliative behaviour)	5,379	44.11%
	9,004	73.9%
Dispersive behaviour 'Splitting'		
Inflammatory behaviour (agression and irritation: ears back, tail swishing, kicking, biting)	2,213	18%
Dispersive (avoidance as a performance)	900	8%
	3,189	26%

Thes differences are very signficant.
Significant difference: t test P>0.001 (i.e. this is not the result of chance it is a very significant difference).

Fig. 6.7a Cohesive or 'sticking' behaviour is much more common than dispersive or 'splitting' behaviour. Here the performance and recipients' responses for thirteen horses recorded for 2,500 hours are compared.

Individual differences in cohesive behaviour

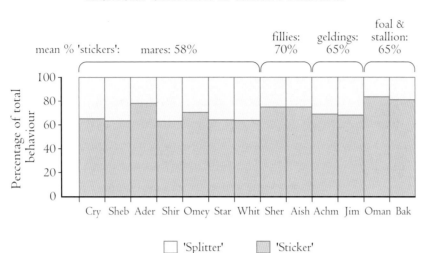

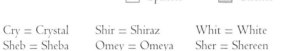

'Splitter' 'Sticker'

Cry = Crystal	Shir = Shiraz	Whit = White	Achm = Achmed
Sheb = Sheba	Omey = Omeya	Sher = Shereen	Jim = Jim
Ader = Aderin	Star = Star Dust	Aish = Aisha	Oman = Omani
			Bak = Baksheesh

Fig. 6.7b   More than 60% of the recorded behaviour for every individual was behaviour that would help the group to stick together, rather than competitive behaviour related to dominance and submission.

Another important outcome was that reciprocal behaviour was quite common. That is, 'be done by as you did' was 17% of any behaviour. In addition, 65% of friendly actions resulted in friendly actions back, that is 'do as you would be done by'.

Thus, it is fair to conclude that there are strict rules of conduct in this equine society which are based on fostering cohesion in the group rather than competition. In addition, each animal behaves differently and the only way to accurately describe them is by individual personality profiles. All of this indicates that, just as in human societies, the organization of this equine society was more complex, flexible, adaptable, tolerant and cohesive than has previously been thought.

An important way of looking at a society's overall organization is in terms of the different roles individuals have (this was suggested as long ago as 1968 by Garland). For example, one mare may be the leader, another the most

271

aggressive individual, another a performer. Our stallion Baksheesh was very socially involved in all ways (an extrovert, interacting with the others a great deal) and he would be aggressive in particular situations, but he did not have priority of access to resources (he would be attacked by a mare if he tried to take food) nor could he 'lead' them off, in any other way. In fact he usually followed. We have since done another series of studies on the next generation of this group.

Such complex societies require each individual to have a great deal of social knowledge: to be good 'natural psychologists' and be able to predict what others will do as a result of knowing the individual. Because equines' visual communication is very sophisticated (see Chapter 7) they see much that can be missed by human observers. Thus, to arrive at a more thorough understanding of their society, greater efforts need to be made to record many more behaviours than is usually the case. We still have a long way to go here.

Manipulating others, lying and deceiving (see page 358) (e.g. Bryne & Whiten 1988) are, as a general rule, unnecessary in these societies, in fact honesty is often the best policy. This may require more complex social knowledge and awareness (see Chapter 9). However, individuals do occasionally manipulate others to their advantage.

Example

When a foal is being weaned by his mother, he will go up to mother and attempt to suck. She will kick out at him, so he goes off but comes back later with an indirect approach: he smells her, licks and starts to groom her. After a few minutes he gently drops his head to try to suckle, she may kick again but, if he is persistent, eventually, often, she will give in and let him suck.

All of this may seem rather technical, and only shows what horse owners believe, that is, that individuals have personalities. Up to a point this is true, but it also shows that detailed observations can teach us more about horse societies and undermine previous beliefs concerning the overall organization of the group because what is generally believed is that horses have 'dominance hierarchies'. But, as we can see, this is not the case, relationships are more complex than this. As a result we can understand a little more of how equine societies work.

We can of course go very much further, but at least this has started the ball rolling on how equines really do organize their societies. If we know more about this, it will help us greatly improve their education. For example, rather than 'dominating' the horse to 'show who is boss' and 'be the leader', a better policy is to ensure that he likes you, and wants to stay with you and do what you ask to please you, rather than to be scared of you. It is a different mind set, but does not mean being excessively over sentimental, sloppy or soft, any more than such behaviour encourages you to be successful as a teacher in human society.

Equines (although they have complex societies and individual differences within them), do not dwell on or analyse their societies and how they work, as far as we know. Nevertheless, habits form within the society. One of these, which is striking, is to allow the individual social liberty within the group. Another is to develop a great awareness of the environment within which they live. Finally, their social behaviour is most commonly structured to keeping the group together, rather than splitting it up.

SUMMARY

1. Species are social because they have an evolutionary advantage. This may be in order to be able to find resources, or for protection against predators. But, perhaps the most important function of being social for equines (as well as humans), is to enable information about the environment to be passed on to others.

2. Equines, like humans, have instinctive tendencies to be social and associate in family groups, but the details of *how* their societies are organized vary in relation to the ecology and their lifetime experiences. In order to be accepted by other equines, they have to learn the rules of equine society, in other words they have to become good 'natural psychologists'.

3. The social knowledge that equines have to acquire during their lifetime is considerable. They recognize individuals (in some cases large numbers), and must be able to predict their behaviour. They develop different roles within the society which are moulded by their individual ages, personalities and knowledge of the environment and others.

→

4. Females have somewhat different roles from males. It is as well to remember that the glue sticking individuals together in all mammalian societies has its origin in the bond between mother and young. The male's role is one of being accepted into the society in order to be able to mate, leave offspring, and prevent the females leaving or wanting to leave. Up to a point even these generally sexually denoted roles can be changed as a result of lifetime experiences, as in humans.

5. The importance of acquiring social knowledge and becoming a good natural psychologist is illustrated by equines who have not had the opportunity to acquire 'equine etiquette' because of isolation from others during their lifetime. They behave (as humans do with similar backgrounds) in socially disruptive ways. The result is that when domesticated, the offender is isolated more. This makes the problem worse. This is particularly the case with stud stallions who, because of their lifetime experiences and lack of opportunity to learn to become good natural psychologists, are very often socially pathological.

6. A more detailed study of the social organization of equine groups when they were allowed to exercise choice in their behaviours and lived in equine societies from birth, indicated that the simplistic idea of 'dominance hierarchy' (which originated from studying chickens) is incorrect. The way in which equine societies stay together is because they foster the cohesion of the group: they are 'stickers' not 'splitters'. In other words, instead of competing, they demonstrate co-operation (affiliation), and often ignore threats and disruptive behaviour.

7. Individual equines or humans can form strong relationships with individuals from other species, as well as each other. To know what it might be like to be an equine or educate them better, it is very important to understand the complexity of their social relationships, how and when they are established, and how much social knowledge has to be acquired. Only then can a good companionship and/or a good working relationship be forged. The richness, complexity and importance of equine social knowledge enacts the daily 'soap opera' in

→

any stable yard or pasture. When people can understand and report on this in detail, they are one step nearer to understanding the social life of equines.

8. There may be lessons to be learnt for humans from the social tolerance of equines who have had the opportunity to become good natural psychologists.

7 Equine communication and language

'When I use a word . . . it means just what I choose it to mean . . .'
Humpty Dumpty in *Through the Looking Glass* by Lewis Carroll, 1871

To live in a social group, there has to be some communication. For there to be communication, there has to be some common ground, some mutual recognition of what the other is communicating. Consequently if we want to understand equines better, keep them in more appropriate environments from their point of view, and expand our associations with them in a trouble-free way, including improving their education, it is necessary to understand what they are saying and feeling, but it is equally important that they understand what we may have to say.

Although some of the classical equitation schools emphasize the importance of understanding equine communication (e.g. Podhajsky 1997), how this is achieved has not been discussed in any detail. Recently there has been a growth of interest in trying to learn a little more about equine communication and to teach people how to communicate better with their equines (e.g. Blake 1975 and 1977, Rees 1991, Kiley-Worthington 1997) and the recent type of 'horse whispering', as it has been called (e.g. Roberts 1997, Parelli 1999). But there is nothing new about horse whispering. Through the centuries, there have been good equine communicators, although they may not have told us how they did it.

Studying equines' natural communication, horse to horse, is a good place to start. Here we cannot cover the whole subject, rather we will draw attention to important aspects of communication, horse to horse and horse to human, that will help people understand their equines better.

But first we must decide *when* communication takes place. In ethology and philosophy, 'communication' is usually restricted to when there has been a *deliberate* transmitting of information to another (e.g. DeGrazia 1996). The problem here is that much behaviour among equines (or humans) is not intended as communication, yet, nevertheless, information is conveyed.

Example
A horse pricks his ears and turns his head in one direction conveying to a watching horse something like 'there is something interesting over there'. The problem is to decide whether these, or many other gestures, are made deliberately to communicate. Did he prick his ears because he was interested in something over there, or did he do it to communicate to others that there was something interesting over there, or both?

He may even sometimes be trying to deceive others in order to change their focus so that, for example, he can move closer to another individual. Here the message will be 'oh look, there is something interesting over there'. While the others look in that direction, he can sidle closer to one of the distracted individuals who would not normally allow this if he was aware of it.

This apparently insoluble problem – when is the animal doing something to communicate and when not? – has caused ethologists to concentrate their efforts when studying communication by vocalizations. Vocalizations are behaviours for which there is no other apparent explanation than communication (e.g. Catchpole & Slater 1995, Cheney & Seyfarth 1990).

But, it would be missing the point of 'what it is to be a horse' (or a human) if we were to assume that *no* communication takes place unless we have some evidence that the behaviour is intended to communicate. Equines and humans watch each other, and respond to the information so acquired. There may be many reasons why different behaviours are performed, but one behaviour has the effect of conveying information to others. **The definition of communication used here, therefore, is: behaviour which results in information being transferred between two or more sentient beings.** Whether this is done with the conscious awareness of the communicator or not will be discussed further in Chapters 8 and 9. The questions that must be addressed first are: how, what, when and where is information being transferred one to another?

Much has been discussed previously concerning the difference in how humans communicate compared to other mammals. The most obvious difference between humans and equines is that we humans predominantly use the voice to communicate, and we have 'language' which is considered unique to humans. Equines do not use their voices very commonly. In horses under normal grazing situations, 0.01 vocalizations per horse per hour (Kiley-Worthington & Randle in preparation) is the average. Equines have, however, developed their ability to communicate using visual, olfactory, taste and touch signals to an extraordinary degree.

There are two important approaches that are helpful to begin with.

1. To outline some general rules for communication, in order to help people learn equine communication themselves.
2. Only by becoming a careful, critical observer is it possible to begin to understand equine communication better.

Equines have a large number of gestures, postures and movements to convey different messages, in fact their visual communication can be similar to our verbal 'language'.

One of the characteristics of language is that it uses symbols, but equines use a type of symbol in their visual 'language', these are called **intention movements**. They are movements that are incomplete and show an intent of performing a further behaviour related to the feeling.

Example
A horse's 'intention movement to kick' is to swish his tail, or to raise the hind leg and put it down again (Figure 7.1).

Intention movements are common in both humans and equines.

Example
Equines may show an intent to be affiliative, aggressive or run away. Each has appropriate movements or postures: the affiliative intent includes approaching, ears forward, nickering, looking at the recipient. An aggressive intent includes: ear flattening, tail swishing, hind-leg lifting. An intent to run away is shown by raising the head and tail, faster breathing, staring, standing immobile and tense.

Fig. 7.1   Aisha Evans (grey, background) has just kicked out at Shindi and is still swishing her tail. Shemal (right) and Shindi (behind Shemal) have leapt out of the way but Shemal is thinking about kicking back (note tail swishing, leg lift and ear positions) displeased by her aunt's kick at her protégé. Lilka (grey, foreground) and Shezam (left) are having nothing to do with it and trot off.

Intention movements have often become **ritualized** for communication. Ritualization means that the behaviour is performed in a constant, and often exaggerated, way in order to have a particular meaning in a particular context, even though the initial reason for the behaviour may no longer be there (Huxley 1960, Morris 1956).

Example
Ear flattening (Figure 7.2) and the 'snake face' of the stallion herding mares (see Figure 4.1) are ritualized movements because they are exaggerated: the ears are flat back with the orifices rotated towards the head. When the stallion performs a snake face, the head and neck are extended forwards and moved up and down like a snake while the ears are quite flattened and rotated.

When one mare attacks another, first she flattens the ears in an exaggerated way, meaning 'go away or I will bite you', even though the ears at this point are at no risk since she is not in danger of attack at this time (Figure 7.2), so this is a ritualized intention movement.

Compared with many displays in birds for example, there are few equine

Fig. 7.2   Ear flattening. Shemal flattens her ears to Gaynor, the newcomer. Behind Shemal, Shindi has her right eye and ear on the situation and, beyond the hedge, Shezam is not missing a thing!

Fig. 7.3   Ear signals. Lilka canters along but just in front of her Shezam has his ears partly back. Is he just listening behind or not wanting Shindi, who is directly behind him, to get any closer? It turned out to be the latter as just after this shot, his ears went further back and he kicked out at her in warning.

movements and postures which have become ritualized. As a result, the messages can appear ambiguous, to humans at least.

Example

The same posture with the ears slightly drawn back is used either because the equine is listening to something behind, or as an aggressive intention movement indicating: 'Do not come any nearer' (Figure 7.3).

Although for a human, it is difficult to pick up which of these messages is intended to be conveyed, to another horse, the movement conveys a message whose meaning is dependent on other cues. In other words, the message is **context dependent**. Change the context, and the same movement or posture will have another meaning. This is very different from human language which is characterized by having **context independent** words, that is, they mean the same thing in any situation. This will give rise to a slightly different world view.

Much research on the origin and evolution of 'displays', that is behaviour performed with the intention of communicating, has been done over the years by ethologists, particularly on birds and primates, such as the origin and evolution of the smile (e.g. Andrews 1963). Other mammalian visual displays have also been studied in some depth, including the tail and ear movements and postures of equines (e.g. Kiley 1969, Kiley-Worthington 1976, 1987).

Since ritualized behaviours and vocalizations are not common, even less common for equines than for humans, everything the animal does potentially has communication value, particularly since equines are social and watch each other. But, this can lead to problems of interpretation. Take the ear movement example again.

Example

When a horse pricks one ear over to the right, is he simply seeing or hearing something strange or interesting, or is he doing this in order to convey to others that he has seen/heard something interesting, or to cause a response in others? He may be doing all of these (Figure 7.3).

First, we will outline *how* horses communicate and *what*, as far as we know, they communicate. Then we will address the question *do they have a 'language'*, and how this may or may not resemble human language, and whether this has a bearing on the development of 'mind skills' in equines. Finally, we will discuss whether there is any evidence to show that they might be able to learn to comprehend human language.

SIMILARITIES AND DIFFERENCES IN COMMUNICATION IN EQUINES AND HUMANS

Information can be conveyed from one animal to another by all of the senses. Some species specialize in the use of one or other of these, as already discussed (see Chapter 1). Figures 7.4 and 7.10 show the relative importance of the different sensory modalities used in horses. The most commonly recorded were visual but, remember, this assessment was affected by the observers' bias (they could not pick up many of the smells, for example).

We will start by considering smells and how they can be used in communication by equines, something that throws a new light on their world view.

Communication by smells

Equines have better-developed olfactory receptors and analysers (see Chapter 1) than humans do. Odours have certain characteristics which are important to outline, if we are going to begin to understand how they may affect the species' understanding.

Characteristics of smell messages

1. Unlike visual or auditory stimuli, smells can remain for a long time after they are produced. It is therefore possible to receive messages in a different time. This is also characteristic of human written language. Thus events in the past can be represented. The time can be either quite specific, for example: individual X was here Y hours ago, or not, for example, there is a general smell of new vegetation and spring in the air.

2. Odours can provide information about a different idea of space. They spread in different directions, can be carried on the wind or in water. The direction from which the smell comes can be assessed by the strength gradient and,

Fig. 7.4 The frequency of the different sensory modalities used for communication, recorded in the experimental herd. Thirteen horses were observed for 2,454 hours.

	Total number recorded	Percentage of total
OLFACTORY COMMUNICATION smelling	703	5.8%
GUSTATORY COMMUNICATION touching, licking and grooming	670	5.0%
VISUAL COMMUNICATION postures, movements of all parts of the body – head, legs, tail etc	9998	82.1%
AUDITORY/VOCAL COMMUNICATION nicker, neigh, squeal	365	3.0%
NON-VOCAL NOISES FOR COMMUNICATION snorts, sneezes, groans, grunts	512	4.2%
overall total	12,248	

Olfactory communication For example: trail following, presence or absence of others, rolling places, messages in faeces and urine. Smelling is often used with other sensory modalities, e.g. touching.

Gustatory communication This is closely related to olfaction and appears to use the varonasal gland to combine olfaction and gustation. For example, licking each other, in particular the stallion licking mares. Also possibly used when learning from others concerning food selection and discrimination.

Visual communication Every movement, posture, etc. may convey messages to another, even if it is not performed intentionally for communication to others. The involves recording postures and movements of all parts of the body.

Audition/vocal communication There are no discrete calls for specific situations with equines (see Kiley 1978). Principally they are used for retaining close contact, and finding each other again when close contact has been lost.

Non-vocal noises of communicative importance These involve hoof beats and rhythms, sneeze-snorts, grunts and groans.

consequently, trails can be both laid and followed.

3. Messages specific to individual species can be conveyed, such as 'a member of a particular species was here'.

4. Messages concerning the age, sex or sexual status of an individual, what he has been eating, where he comes from, where he has been, what he has found, and exactly who he is may also be deduced.

5. Messages with information about the emotional and/or health status of the sender can be conveyed including sexiness, aggression, fearfulness, excitement, possession of land, group membership, etc.

6. Smell messages (pheromones), particularly when used at close quarters, are often multisensory, in other words, smell, taste and touch may be confused and analysed together. (Figure 7.5a).

7. The meaning of the message can be either context independent such as a particular pheromone associated with a particular state: oestrus, for example, or it can be context dependent, that is, the same odour mean different things in different contexts (which is also characteristic of many visual and auditory displays in mammals). This is particularly the case for smells which may be related to emotional states: for example, the smell of sweat can indicate that an individual is frightened, has been running fast or is excited to greet another, is feeling sexy, or happy.

8. The importance of smells for gathering information appears to be of particular importance to equines. They leave smells everywhere they go, and investigate the environmental and each others' smells carefully. This is particularly true of stallions who when liberated into a field with mares, if they are good natural psychologists, will spend time investigating all the smells around the field – including their own (Figure 7.5b) – before going up to greet the mares directly.

9. In humans, odours can often be involved with triggering memories. Smells cannot be seen or touched, but they are perceived and analysed, perhaps this is why they are, at least in humans, often involved with 'reflective behaviour': thinking about the past or the future, planning, and so forth. Smells for equines may be involved in assessing and reassessing: 'reflecting on' the nature of the physical and social place they are in, its relationship to past experiences and possible future ones.

Figs. 7.5a, b and c The importance of touch, smell and taste. a) The stallions, Oryx, the younger, and Oberlix are fascinated by each other. Here they touch, smell and taste each other over the hedge, communicating a host of messages. b) Smelling faeces. The stallion Oryx, smells his own pile, accompanied by little Scarlet, and Gaynor. c) Here Oberlix and the Dartmoor mare, Scarlet, touch and smell each other.

It is clearly important to be aware of the importance of smells to equines, and the different roles they play, even if humans cannot perceive them.

Humans have been described as 'scent blind' (Hearne, 1994). There is a whole dimension of experience almost denied to humans (in just the same way as not having a verbal language may deny various mental experiences to equines).

The consequences of this are confusing and hamper our efforts to assess other world views.

Humans have interesting taboos about smells. They very rarely talk about individual smells, although they will wax lyrical about someone's visual appearance, or even the noises they make. It is the height of bad manners to mention another's natural smell, and this seems to apply cross-culturally. Curiously, it is acceptable to talk about another's synthetic smell: the perfume or soap they use! Even in this age of reduced sexual taboos, although smells can be very important in sex, they are rarely mentioned even in the most explicit pornographic magazines. Yet an important factor in forming friendships, or enemies, is individual smell. Babies' smells are very specific, as are those of men or women, the old or the young. Menstruation, urine, faeces, unwashed or washed skin, sweat, artificial and natural smells, are all picked up to form the perception of the world we individually inhabit. Different cultures and races have different smells. Different species have different smells. Dogs, humans and cats can all smell nasty at times. By contrast, most horse smells, are usually considered pleasant by the majority of humans: their breath, their coats, their sweat. Even the smells of their urine and faeces are bearable.

An awareness of how an individual smells often determines your behaviour to different animals and their behaviour to us. It is consequently important to understanding their reactions, and also our own.

Familiar smells

Familiar smells are extremely important for the identification of a sense of place, a 'home', a safe place. This can be easily demonstrated with infant humans and equines. A familiar-smell-bearing object such as a rug for a human, or, for equines, straw that has been in their previous stable, will often ensure that they settle down more quickly in a new place and have some sense of security in the 'unfamiliar'. If young horses are to be weaned forcibly, isolated from their mother, and probably other equines for part of the time (a widespread practice, but one that is undesirable and usually avoidable) then placing some of the bedding from the mother's stable, or something with her urine or faeces on it will often reduce the anxiety of the youngster, although not eliminate it. Similarly, odours which are unattractive, or indicate unfamiliar or frightening occurrences may keep equines away (e.g. the smell of fresh sweat on a human indicating their fear, or the smell of a frightening adult stallion on clothes or fence posts, smelt by a young colt).

For obvious reasons the majority of mammals are fussy where they make their central 'home'; where they choose to lie, and to retire to – which eventually will smell strongly of them. Although a smell of themselves may generally go unnoticed because it is constantly there, nevertheless, when confronted with a particularly pungent reminder, such as where they have lain down before, their own faeces (always smelt by stallions), a recognition of a smell of themselves cannot be avoided. Not only will this identify place (and time when left) but also it is a step towards an awareness of 'self' (see Chapter 8, page 330).

The place where equines defecate is generally chosen. Mares will wander over to a latrine area in the field, smell, walk forward and then deposit their own. Stallions defecate in piles and carry out a ritual of smelling their pile, and everyone else's, very carefully and then walking forward so they deposit their faeces right on top of the previous pile. Then they turn around and smell it again. This investigation allows them to gain considerable information. Who, when, what sex, age, direction of movement, state of sexual cycle, what has been eaten, as well, perhaps, as a strong identification of themselves (Figure 7.5b).

Flehmen
This is a behaviour performed by almost all mammals in order to carefully sample and analyse a strong or unfamiliar smell (see Figure 1.8).

Example
About twenty years ago we tested a number of horses with a whole variety of strong-tasting and smelling substances to see if flehman was confined to urine-like smells, or more frequently performed by males. It was more common in males but it was not confined to them, and neither was it confined to urine or even to the *smell* of a tested substance. The

taste of a strong unfamiliar substance, such as vinegar, lemon or garlic, also caused flehmen in both stallions and mares (Kiley-Worthington 1987).

It is well known that smells (and perhaps tastes) which have been associated with frightening, aggressive, or unpleasant situations will tend to spark off these emotions. Smells are also associated with other emotions such as excitement, conflict, frustration, happiness and joy, and they can be cues for behavioural changes. Whatever we discover in the future about this, we do now know that the smells an equine picks up will have an effect on his behaviour.

Strange smells

There are of two kinds of strange smells.

1. Unfamiliar smells of interest to equines which encourage curiosity and exploration but, at high concentrations, they generally avoid them.

Example

Hot shoeing horses for the first time often causes them anxiety because of the smell, smoke and sound of their own burning foot. An understandable anxiety: your own smell going up in smoke accompanied by crackling noises!

By smelling different things, they can of course receive particular messages, but the smell may simply generate pleasure; perhaps they are having a smell-based aesthetic experience, an appreciation of the smell for its own sake, not because it has some usefulness to them (see Chapter 11).

2. The detection of smells out of context by animals can have unforeseen consequences.

Example

We were running a teaching experiment on a young, sexually mature, wild-caught zebra stallion. I had been handling the stallion, and then, without thought, went to work with the elephants. One of the fourteen-year-old bull elephants, Nyasha, after greeting me in his usual fashion, by smelling, touching and probably tasting me (trunk to my face, neck, crotch, feet and clothes) suddenly started ear flapping and trumpeting very excitedly, accompanied by moving around. It was the smell of the zebra. But the question was, why he had reacted so strongly to this smell since he came across zebra every day in their normal free-ranging feeding activities on the 2,000 hectare (5,000 acre) ranch. The only explanation was that it was a familiar smell, although perhaps rather stronger than they had normally encountered, in a very different context: on a human handler whose individual smell was known.

For equines, smell messages can sometimes overcome visual messages. This can be confusing for humans.

Example

Oberlix, the Arab stallion, was put out in a 3 hectare (8 acre) field with Aisha Evans, a mare with whom he had been before and covered. Before they were put out, the two young geldings, Shukrune and Shanti, aged three and two were removed from the field where they had been living for around one week, sometimes with the young stallion Oryx, aged five. When Oberlix and Aisha were put out, Oberlix first investigated the faeces around the field in the usual way, then came up to Aisha and herded her around for the next four hours with a snake face. Here, he clearly smelt the young males and although he could not see them, he herded the mare away from their smell. In fact she was kept in a corner for a couple of hours!

It is also possible for smell messages to be overridden by visual or tactile ones.

Example

Oberlix, when a yearling colt, was badly attacked by a llama. His forehand muscles were ripped and bleeding. The smell of blood as well as the treatment must have been disturbing, and painful. The open wounds had to be washed, but, with careful handling by familiar-smelling people, he stood still, even though he would have been able to leap about and avoid the treatment. The way he was handled here may have been a critical factor in keeping him calm because, although there must have been smells of his own blood and sweat which could undoubtedly have reminded him of the experience and his wounds, as well as the pain, such reminders were overridden by his confidence in the handlers and their behaviour.

To date we have four other examples of horses: Druimghigha Shemal, Druimghigha Shezam, Druimghigha Aroha and Drumghigha Shindi, whose treatment of major wounds which must have been painful, was tolerated without reaction by the sufferer as a result of the visual, and presumably olfactory, messages from the familiar handlers.

Communication by taste

Smell and taste are very closely connected. We know even less about communicating with taste than with smells. Equines do lick things and individuals that interest them, here both touching and tasting. Mothers presumably learn who their infant is by taste as well as smell since they lick them after birth. Horses who become very familiar and fond of particular humans sometimes take to touching them with the nose and licking them, particularly the bare skin.

Experiments have been done to show that it is the smell of faeces that prevents horses eating adjacent grass, rather than its taste. When the grass was cut and presented to the horses away from the location where it grew they ate it, although the same horses had rejected it when in the field near the faeces (Oldberg 1972).

But, it is presumably taste which prevents equines eating many plants and foods although it is extremely difficult to separate the two.

Communication by touch

The importance of touch in demonstrating affiliative relationships differs between human cultures, and perhaps between equine cultures too, but we all use touch to demonstrate messages of friendship and to maintain and cement bonds between individuals (Figure 7.5c). Equines do not use touch in their social interactions as much as many animals, including some humans. Figure 7.6 shows that only 7% of all the social behaviours in another series of observations of the experimental herd were related to touch (Kiley-Worthington & Randle in preparation).

Equines use their noses (which are capped with sensitive hairs) to touch and feel others. Presumably they are not only feeling the texture of the other individual's skin, but also they must be able to feel the muscular contraction and hence have another way of assessing the other's general motivational state. This is probably important in courtship. It is quite likely that females may choose to mate with certain males rather than others because of the way in which they use tactile communication (as is the case with some human females).

Some humans develop tactile communication to particularly elaborate degrees. Skilled masseurs for example, are able to feel very slight muscular changes, or energy flows. This can be developed to be used on horses (e.g.

	Number	Percentage of *all* interactions (total 1,292)
Touching different parts of the body of another	40	3.00%
Licking (plus taste)	1	0.07%
Rubbing (plus touch)	5	0.40%
Nibbling (plus taste and touch)	39	3.00%
Scratching (plus touch)	7	0.54%
Total	92	7.01%

Fig. 7.6 Communication by touch in the experimental herd

Kasselle and Hannay 1995). In the same way, some equines learn a high degree of touch awareness, while others do not.

Equines learn to respond to very slight changes in weight, in the touch of the legs, or slight weight differences in even a slack rein when ridden. Equally, humans learn to receive messages from the ridden animal through touch: 'I am scared', 'I am not going to do this or that', 'I am ready for your next idea', or even 'I have an idea, and will do X'. This can be so well developed that riders are convinced that they and their horse are communicating telepathically.

Sometimes riders experience 'moments of oneness' with the horse. This often becomes an important motivation for riding. At such times, windows are opened onto other world views, even if briefly. Very good riders in the European and classical equitation schools, daily demonstrate how it is possible to tune-in to other world views with tactile communication with the horse. This is not done by violence, restraint, domination and reducing options; it is done by learning a tactile 'language' and conversing in it.

Visual communication

In my previous book (Kiley-Worthington 1987 and 1998), I outlined some obvious facial and postural expressions. We now have more information but, here, will extract only the main points to help with our present quest (Figure 7.7).

We have already pointed out how important visual communication is to equines and how acute their vision is, particularly in relation to movement (see pages 76–79).

There are many movements and postures which are used in a variety of ways, as well as for communication (Kiley-Worthington 1987 and 1998).

It has been suggested that zebras have individual stripe patterns so that other zebras can recognize them. This assumes that, without the individual patterns, zebras will be no more likely to be able to recognize other zebras visually than humans. But the visually aware zebra will be able to recognize another individual, not just by his markings, but by the way he moves, his mannerisms, the overall characteristics of his body and face as other animals do. Dartmoor ponies, black cows or buffalo recognize each other individually even though they are all of the same colour! It is the human observer who needs to note different stripe patterns to distinguish individuals. Recognizing slight differences in colour markings or acquired marks (such as ear slits) is the normal way of distinguishing individuals used by ethologists who, at least until they know the individual animals very well, are not able to recognize them by mannerisms,

Fig. 7.7 Facial expressions are important to equines as well as humans, but rarely so obvious as Obie's anticipatory raising of his top prehensile lip.

movement or overall body characteristics. Consequently, the assumption that zebras need such marking cues is a good example of the inappropriate use of anthropomorphic judgements: *unconditional* anthropomorphism.

Postures and slight movements, even changes in the tension of muscles, will be picked up by one equine from another (Kiley-Worthington 1998). Facial expressions and movements are important, and useful to humans who tend to concentrate on looking at faces. The ability to use visual cues which humans may be unable to pick up is called the 'Clever Hans effect'. It all began with a German horse called Hans who was able to tell from the slight changes in posture and movements of the human audience when he had reached the correct answer to a simple mathematical problem by beating the answer out with one of his front legs (see Candland 1993 for further discussion).

Exercise
A useful exercise is to watch a horse's face from the eyes down for a five-minute period, and make notes on what you see and how frequent the movements of the lips, mouth, nose, vibrissae etc., are. Then compare this with another horse, counting the movements if possible. Almost constant movements of the lower face will tell you of the general reactivity and awareness of the individual (provided this is not the result of some irritation), even though he may not be moving about any more than another horse. Further analysis and observation will reveal where his attention is directed from minute to minute, and help the observer concentrate on being able to pick up cues that would otherwise have been missed, and all without looking at the more obvious expressions indicated in eyes, ears or head movements.

Most postures and movements appear to convey a message concerning the general motivational state of the communicant. It is the context which gives them their more specific meaning.

Example
An upright posture with a high head and tail carriage will indicate either 'I am frightened', 'I am feeling aggressive', or 'I am feeling sexy'. The posture conveys the general message 'I am feeling excited': cues to why and what type of excitement have to be read from the situation (Figures 7.8 and 8.1). These postures are often exaggerated in the Arab horse.

The context dependence of the messages means that to understand the meaning of a message accurately, there must be a constant awareness of the environment

Fig. 7.8 Lilka's exaggerated high-posture walk indicates that she is excited. Whatever the cause it does not excite Shemal, who is walking with a very low postural tonus. Only her left ear indicates she is aware of what is going on.

all around. Human language is context independent, that is, the same statement means the same thing in any situation, although the meaning can be slightly changed by the intonation. Consequently human language users do not need to be as aware of the environment to interpret many messages.

Example
'The cat is on the mat' means the same thing in any situation, although a difference in emphasis may have a slight effect on the meaning.

All parts of the body are used in postures or movements to convey messages to another concerning the communicator's general state of awareness and excitement: the ears, nose, eyes, head, body, legs, gaits, rump and tail. These have been described so we will not go into them again here, rather the reader should refer to other texts (e.g. Darwin 1868, Rees 1983, Kiley-Worthington 1998).

Exercise

Once you have had some experience observing very carefully a group of equines in a field, for example, and assessing what is going on within their social group, it will become clear a) how difficult it is to interpret exactly what is going on and how carefully they have to be observed, b) how much information is constantly being passed from one to the other and c) how complex their social lives are (Figure 7.9).

Attempt to give a running commentary to someone else on what you think is going on in the 'equine soap opera'. The better the observer, and the more experienced, the more extraordinary is the soap opera.

Either way, it will be a surprise just how intricate the visual communication of equines is.

Auditory communication

Auditory communication can be divided up into noises made with the larynx (vocal noises) and those made without the larynx (non-vocal noises). The former are usually, but not always, made in order to communicate something to another, whereas the latter may not be made primarily to communicate, but rather be the result of circumstance.

Many olfactory or visual messages and most non-vocal noises have a function which is not associated with passing on a particular message. For example, a sneeze can clear the nose, a sigh or cough can clear the throat and lungs, and so

Fig. 7.9   Yearling Shindi smells and touches Oberlix's tail. Oberlix has one ear back indicating that he is aware of this. Shemal (foreground) is worried, unsure Oberlix is trustworthy with Shindi, her younger sister, so she is swishing her tail and shaking her head. Lilka (grey) is watchful.

on. However, for vocal noises, there is usually no functional reason to make a vocal noise other than to communicate.

Non-vocal noises

Non-vocal noises can occur through chance, such as those made by walking over sticks in a forest. They may be noises that have a function for the body, such as coughing, sighing or breaking wind but, nevertheless, they may communicate messages to others. Since equines are very aware of the environment in which they live, chance noise, footfalls for example, may convey messages to others such as what type of terrain they are walking over, who is where, what they are doing, how fast they are going, and sometimes why they are doing what they are doing.

Both equines and humans are, from time to time at least, aware that the noises they make can tell others about them. We know this since they can move without making a noise when it is important not to give their location away: when being hunted by a predator, for example. At other times they may make a considerable noise going about their daily business and thereby communicate their whereabouts to others of the group. They learn to make a noise to keep in touch with each other in an environment where they cannot see each other, or to attract attention. In stabled environments this may be chewing, groaning or sighing, coughing or just breathing noisily.

Example

When Oberlix slept in the stable next to our bedroom, he could put his head through the window and watch us, or even wake us up if he liked. Being so close to him outlined what a noise he makes in the stable, he either breathes very noisily or groans when lying down asleep, and chews, sighs or walks about in the straw when awake. Perhaps as a stallion he is particularly interested in demonstrating his whereabouts to others, including us as the nearest beings. The mares Shemal, Crystal and Omeya have all been much quieter as our nightly neighbours.

They may also make a noise by pawing, pacing up and down on a hard surface, or kicking the stable door with a front leg to attract attention from the human caretakers. Kicking the stable door is normally effective; someone usually comes up to the stable or shouts at them.

All equines **sneeze-blow** when they have irritants up their noses, such as when eating dusty hay. However, sneeze-blowing can also have a social message.

Example
When healthy, horses full of energy, are being ridden out, and want to rush off but are having to walk, one may start sneeze-blowing, and soon the group are all sneeze-blowing, one after the other. Sometimes this social sneeze-blowing results in an individual working themselves up to greater excitement, so much so that they can no longer walk, and jog around instead.

One thing that is certain is, when a bunch of horses begin to sneeze-blow, you can guarantee that they are not as relaxed as they might be, unless of course you are in the middle of a dust storm!

Exercise
When you go out for a ride with your friends, when one horse sneeze-blows, notice how many of the others start, and who does most, and relate this to their other behaviour at the time. This exercise can be useful to help understand the equine's point of view for all these different non-vocal noises.

Chewing occurs at other times than when equines are chewing food. For example, after completing some task that has been slightly frightening, or required much physical or mental effort. Voice praise given after a difficult exercise, if the equine has learnt to respond to voice praise, will, particularly with a young horse, often spark off chewing: a 'phew, thank goodness that's over' type response. But, chewing the bit also occurs in a frustrating situation, such as when the horse wishes to go forward faster or when the bit is too tight or the reins used too hard. If this is not recognized, it can quickly become a habit and can develop into a constant chewing, teeth grinding or other abnormalities. Putting on a tight drop noseband to prevent this, something which alas is commonly practised, does not remove the cause if the reins continue to be used badly and harshly. Other difficulties will inevitably result.

Sighing may also have some communicative importance, and be used with intent in equines, particularly to indicate the end of a difficult task. Sighing is common at the end of something that has required either mental or physical effort, such as after a dressage test, a training session for a young horse, or after harrowing a field.

Coughing, apart from occurring when there is an irritation in the throat, is used in humans from time to time to attract attention, and equines may learn to use it in the same way.

Snorting is one non-vocal noise that does have a specific message in equines: it is restricted to a startling or frightening situation and conveys this to others.

We have evidence, therefore, that these non-vocal noises may have messages attached, but exactly *how* they are used still remains to be investigated. From the point of view of the teacher, it is important to tune into them, and to try to assess the meaning of the message, if there is one, so that you can act accordingly.

Vocalizations

Vocalizations are made by a controlled air flow through the larynx, vibrating the vocal cords, the resulting noise is then changed by being directed through various resonating chambers. These are a) the back of the throat, b) the large nasal cavity, and c) the long mouth. Whether the mouth is open or closed, the position of the tongue controls which of these cavities the noise vibrates in, and consequently the type of sound that comes out.

Equine vocal calls, like visual cues, are not situation specific. The call given conveys the level of general excitement rather than a specific message (Figure 7.10). For example, if the equine is not very excited he will make a call that is short, lower, musical and not loud. By contrast, as he becomes more excited, whatever the situation, the call will become longer, louder, higher pitched, and

Fig. 7.10 (opposite) The changes to the sounds produced by equines are similar and are controlled not by the particular type of emotion that the subject is feeling, so much as by the general level of 'excitement', (defined here as doing more things more often, and moving around more), that is, his **general motivational state**. It all seems to rest with the degree to which he is feeling frustrated (he wants to do something, or something to happen but he is unable to achieve this) or having some conflict (he wants to do both something and the opposite as well). The classic form of this type of conflict is wanting to approach but also wanting to avoid. The squeal illustrates this well in equines, and occurs in all equines in slightly different forms; it indicates a 'stop it, I like it' sort of feeling.

Gradual increase in 'excitement'	The characteristics of the sound reflecting this motivation	Horse/ pony	Donkey	Zebra	Situation
Very high	High frequency, noisy, loud. Vocalized inspiration	Scream Occasional	Repeated scream Usual	Occasional	Extreme terror. Extreme frustra- tion/ conflict
High	High frequency, noisy, loud, mouth open, 7–9 seconds long. Vocalized inspiration	Long neigh Occasional	Loud repeated Bray Always	Squeak Occasional	Frustration/ conflict high
	Mouth open, noisy shorter	Squeal	Noisy bray	Squeal	Frustration/ conflict close greeting
Medium high	High frequency less noise, mouth open, 5–7 seconds long. Vocalized inspiration	Neigh No	Bray repeated Always	Squeak No	Frustration/ conflict medium
Medium	Low frequency, little noise, mouth shut, 3–5 seconds long. Vocalized inspiration	Nicker No	Bray Yes	Squeak No	Frustration/ conflict medium/ low
Low	Low frequency, musical, mouth shut, 3–5 seconds long. Vocalized inspiration	Quiet nicker No	Bray/ groan Breathy slight	Breathy squeak No	Frustration/ conflict low

less musical, that is, with more breathy type sounds (Kiley-Worthington 1998). So, the meaning of most of the vocal calls is also context dependent. Generally this is not the case with human language, but nevertheless there are occasions when the meaning of what has been said is dependent on the context as well as the tone in which it is given. For example, the same words used in different contexts can have a literal meaning, be ironic or sarcastic. Some other mammals (e.g. primates) have been shown to have particular calls with particular meanings – for example, vervet monkeys have an alarm call meaning 'leopard' and a different one meaning 'human' predator.

Example

A high-pitched neigh could mean something like 'I am feeling alone and isolated', 'I am feeling sexy', 'I am very frightened', or 'I am glad to see you coming'. I recorded some hundreds of calls and analysed their structure. Although one is inclined to read all sorts of specific messages into the call, for example frightened calls are louder or higher pitched than lonely ones, this was not the case when I measured the different characteristics of the calls. The conclusion was that it is impossible to know the exact meaning of a call, even of an equine you know very well, without knowing the context in which it was given. Donkeys and zebras have slightly different calls, often involving a vocalized expiration and inspiration, but nevertheless, they conform to the same pattern as horse and pony calls.

There are one or two exceptions to this, one of them is the squeal which is used in greeting, particularly (but not exclusively) between the sexes. The meaning of this call is always the same, 'I am excited to meet you', therefore it is context independent.

The interesting question is why equines have not taken what you would consider a small evolutionary step, to have particular messages conveyed by particular vocalizations, similar to human language. This involves having a particular sound occurring in a particular situation becoming associated with that situation and, consequently, indicative of it. Humans are so conditioned to this type of auditory communication, that they often believe animal calls are just a simplified type of human language: that the calls are themselves saying different things. However, so far as we know to date, the meaning of the message in the vast majority of the calls given by large mammals, can only be assessed from the context.

A context-independent language with specific words with specific meanings may tell us about the individual, and be able to describe the environment; but a context dependent 'language' entails a sophisticated level of attention to, and interpretation of, the whole world around, as well as to the individual communicator. It must involve ecological and social knowledge about the individual and his previous social interactions.

Example

A young horse walking into a strange place will snort, jump about, and show every sign of fear and uncertainty. The older experienced horses will look at him, but not respond in a similar way, rather walk along calmly. An older horse will not only have assessed the general message as something like 'I am excited, there is something scary here', but also recognized a message specific to the reacting individual in the context, something like: 'this individual is frightened, but he is inexperienced and young; there is nothing perceptible to worry about'. Thus, the behaviour of the older horse is dependent on knowing the social and physical context, and something about the individual.

Perhaps we should not underestimate the complexity of knowledge required for the correct interpretation of this type of 'language'. There may be skills and information here which we are poor at perceiving, interpreting and communicating, despite our verbal language abilities.

There are different limits on what information equine communication can transfer. For example, although they may be able to have some idea of the past and the future, nevertheless they are unlikely to be able to collect a great deal of information about it from others, at least through the traditional pathways: orally, visually, or by smell, taste or touch. But, there may be whole areas of communication which elude us, stuck as we are with a human language.

Extrasensory communication

A belief in extrasensory perception (ESP) and communication with domestic animals is at present something of a vogue, with horse whisperers and people who talk to animals abounding.

These people claim to use many different methods for their communication including telepathy, energy auras, visions and so on. To date we have no hard evidence that equines can communicate with each other or other species in other ways than by using the five senses that all mammals have. However since equines and humans have different sensitivities, it is often easy to believe that there must be some extrasensory perception going on. There may be, as a good scientist I am not prepared to deny this, but at present we can explain all the communication that goes on within their species or with us in terms of our general mammalian sensory receptors, although this may sometimes be difficult for us to understand because of our different world experiences, or different beings.

This, however, to my mind, makes the question of what it is to be an equine: equine lore, very much more interesting than if they were to have a whole range of different/magical/extra-terrestial communication and other mental abilities, because it makes the possibility of understanding them better more obtainable. If they have the same ways of communication and many of the same mental attributes that we have, then, even though they use them differently, and we will have to learn how, nevertheless, we will eventually be able to understand them better, and enrich our own lives as a result.

Exercise

Extra sensory perception (ESP)

Some Russian scientists investigated telepathy with animals. They were very clear that this had to be learnt. Try concentrating on your horse and thinking/willing him to do some very simple thing, raise his head, or walk a step left, etc. It is said that if you work at this you can get better at it. The Russians suggested that the best way to start was by sitting on a park bench, and willing the passers-by to scratch their heads. We have tried this a little, and there does seem to be some evidence that you can get better with practice – a lot of practice – but it is worth a try.

LANGUAGE AND EQUINES' ABILITY TO LEARN TO UNDERSTAND HUMAN LANGUAGE

In the 1970s the question of whether or not other mammals could learn to speak a human-type language started to be investigated. The main problem here is that non-human mammals or birds (with the possible exception of parrots) lack the muscular structure and accompanying nerves to perform careful movements of the tongue, pharynx, glottis and larynx to produce spoken language. The Gardners (psychologists in the US who were the first to research this thoroughly) recognized this, and decided to see if a young female chimpanzee, Washoe, could learn a non-vocal language that had the same characteristics as human language, but used signs. They spend some eight years teaching her American Sign Language (Gardner & Gardner 1969), and she did learn to 'speak' this, although the work was very controversial. Since then there have been a number of similar studies with apes, sea mammals and a parrot to see if they can grasp the important concepts implicit in language. The results continue to excite controversy, but all these studies have taught us more about the mental abilities of these animals; they are brighter than we thought!

Whether animals, even higher mammals such as equines, can learn to comprehend or speak 'language' revolves around the definition of language. Language is usually taken to involve more than just communicating. There are some characteristics of language which are generally agreed:

1. it uses symbols;
2. it is controlled by a series of rules (this includes semantics or grammar);
3. it is performed in order to convey some meaning to the receiver.

However, there are more detailed and rather complex characteristics that a language must have. Many people have attempted to outline what these are. Without getting heavily involved in the debate, we have simplified these characteristics from Hockett 1960 (Figures 7.11A and B).

Today, it is generally believed that although some non-human species may be able to fulfil some of these criteria in their own species language, or, by being taught by humans, fulfil more of them, nevertheless, language is unique to humans. It is also believed by many that the existence of language has been instrumental in humans' development of advanced mental abilities and consciousness. It has even been part of 'folk belief' in the Western world, that without access to human language, animals are severely mentally handicapped, that is, unable to perform a whole variety of mental tasks which are performed by adult humans (e.g. Frey 1980, Leahy 1991, Carruthers 1992 and 1996). Thus, it is argued that it is language that allows us access to information from past generations and consequently to progress in our manipulation of the world and our technical achievements. It is language which allows us to think, and to develop and swop ideas.

There may be cognitive advantages to language, in some ways. On the other hand, it must not be ignored that we are exposed to language from a very early age, and many thousands of hours are spent teaching it to us (even though we may have an innate tendency to acquire it). The result is that we have learnt to think and use our mental abilities in a particular way, and ignore others. For example, language is symbolic (each utterance represents something different) and linear (before we know the meaning of an utterance, we have to hear the whole sentence, it follows time along, one thing/statement/idea at a time). It is largely (although not exclusively as we have mentioned above) context independent. It is also stuck in one modality, usually talking (although the same structure of language can be found in visual languages developed for deaf people without speech). All of this means that, although language may have considerable cognitive advantages, it may also have some cognitive handicaps since it is very difficult for us to escape the language-based way of assessing the world. Equines (or any other species) may not have this world view, but this might not always mean that they are cognitively inferior. It might mean that they have some different cognitive abilities. One of these which is very important is that they have to be more aware of the whole environment as well as the social context in which the messages are given. They have to be aware/think of a whole batch of things at one time instead of in a linear style. Another example of the possibly different cognitive abilities is their use of smells. If not being able to use languages is a cognitive handicap, then since humans are not able to use odours except in a rudimentary way, they may also be cognitively handicapped, unable to think and perceive the world in that different fashion.

The question of whether or not equines have or could acquire at least an understanding of human language (even without teaching them to 'speak' a new language) is therefore important if we are to understand their mental abilities, and what it is to be an equine.

One thing that can be useful to help us try to understand more about the world equines inhabit, since we are unable to enter it, in some respects at least, is to try and teach some of them to enter our world in the sense of learning something about our language.

Since equines do not manipulate the world with hands (like apes and other primates do), developing a visual language for them to learn would not work. One approach might be to develop a language using rhythms and see if we could teach them that. Another method which has been developed by Savage, Rumbaugh & Brakke (1996) is teaching the subject (in this case a pigmy chimp) to recognize symbols on a computer and then build these into sentences, equivalent to a type of 'written language'. This would be possible with equines, although they would need a particularly large keyboard!

We considered that there were two ways in which it would be useful to pursue this by asking the questions:

1. Do equines in their own lives have something resembling language?
2. Can we teach them to comprehend human language, more than just responding to verbal commands correctly?

Some nine years ago we decided to begin to answer these questions using the subjects, equipment and methods that were available at the time. This research is still in progress, but there are already some interesting results that can help with our quest.

Do equines communicate among themselves with something like language?

Despite the importance which the possession of a human-type language has acquired in the debates on different species' mental abilities, there has been little emphasis on the detailed study of the natural communication in different species' societies to test how similar their normal communication is to human language (although see Cheney & Seyfarth 1990).

Method We decided to record many more behaviours than had currently been recorded in our group of experimental horses. We recorded 120 behaviours. But we also decided to record what the response of another horse was to any one of these behaviours, rather than presupposing that we knew the meaning. This has allowed us to understand a larger number of behaviours and how they are used. It has also allowed us to analyse the meaning of the messages as a result of the performance of any one of these behaviours, and behaviours in combination with one another. Consequently we have been able to assess whether the meaning of the message is different in different situations, and/or when the behaviours are in different combinations.

Results Since we have over 5,000 recordings, there is much analysis required which we are in the process of finishing (see Kiley-Worthington & Randle 2004 in preparation). However, one thing that is already clear is that equine communication fulfils many of the characteristics that define human language. This includes the fact that one behaviour (equivalent to a word perhaps) may occur in combination with very different behaviours. By analysing the recipient's response to these different combinations, we find that they mean different things. In other words, some particular behaviours at least are used like words which change meaning when in combination with different other behaviours: other 'words' (Figure 7.11B).

Can equines learn to understand language more than just obeying verbal commands?

Although humans have been in contact with equines for some thousands of years, curiously no one has looked carefully at their abilities to comprehend language, although it is part of our folk belief that these species can understand particular verbal commands. The most detailed research on language comprehension by non-primate mammals so far has been with dolphins and other cetaceans (Hermann 1980, Schustermann & Gisiner 1988).

Method We decided to employ methods developed for use with pre-verbal children (e.g. Fowler 1990). This involved:

1. Using a limited vocabulary of approximately 300 words.
2. Taking the subjects on expeditions where the words were repeatedly used to describe the environment, the subject's behaviour and that of the persons with them. When they were young, we took them (and their mothers initially) for walks around the farm and neighbourhood, to the seaside and in the woods during which we would use specific words to name objects that

Figure 7.11A

Characteristics of human language and the degree to which these are fulfilled by apes and equines (after Hockett 1960)

Characteristics	Humans	Apes (learning human language)	Equines (with each other)
1. Productivity Different components combine together at different times for different meanings	*	*	*
2. Arbitrariness Different responses to the same display	*	*	*
3. Interchangeability One display triggers another	*	*	*?
4. Specialization Displays not directly related to consequences	*	*	*?
5. Displacement Key features are not related to antecedents	*	*	*?
6. Cultural Transmissions Learn communication system from others around, and differences between populations shown	*	*	*
7. Duality Symbols to form sentences. The components of the expression contribute to the whole interpretation	*	*	*
8. Importance of word order controlling meaning	*	*	??

* Has occurred. ? May not always occur. ?? No information to date.

Figure 7.11B

Examples of '*productivity*' in equine communication: ears pricked, ears back, ears orientated or ears flat can elicit different responses when combined with other different movements and postures (from Shoise 1994. Eco Research Centre).

Performer	Recipient response
1. Ears pricked, approach, nose to nose touch	Ears pricked, chin loose, nose to nose touch
2. Ears pricked, head turn, watch	Ears pricked, chin loose, watch
3. Ears pricked, head extended, mouthing	Ears pricked, mouthing, play
4. Ears back, head extended, chewing	Ignore
5. Ears back, head extended	Ears back, withdraw
6. Ears back, chin loose, mouthing, play	Ears back, chin loose, backside turned, avoid
7. Ears orientated, chin loose, smell backside, approach	Ignore
8. Ears orientated, chin loose, rub other horse	Ears back, chin loose approach
9. Ears flat, head extended, chewing	Ears back, chin loose
10. Ears flat, head extended, approach	Ears back, chin loose, avoid

Figs. 7.11A and B The degree to which communication between equines fulfils the different characteristics of human language. These are rather complicated, but I have tried to simplify them, perhaps with some loss of accuracy.

they were showing interest in and learning about (Figure 7.12). We would use verbs, adjectives and pronouns, as well as nouns and short sentences. Now they are grown up, we use the same words when we are travelling with them, riding, competing, demonstrating, etc.

3. We also decided to study learning and teaching using words to assess whether word use would be useful for improving equine teaching. We taught the subjects (two horses, one heifer, one puppy, one llama and one elephant to date) to perform simple movements to word command. First by using the words accompanied by gestures, moulding, shaping and imitation (see Chapter 3), and finally confining the cue to the word only. We then introduced further complex problems, involving the subjects learning symbols and concepts.

During this work, we measured the cues given, the behaviour of the subject and the behaviour of the teacher and analysed this. The total amount of time we devoted to this teaching was not a great deal (350 hours).

The subjects have now grown up and learn many other things, and we are building on their understanding of words (e.g. left or right front leg) to teach them more complex movements (e.g. the Spanish walk or trot, piaffe, passage, collected and extended gaits, levade and so on – see Figures 3.18a and b).

Results Although we have not done the final tests yet, it is clear that our two equine subjects understand around 200 words, not only nouns but also verbs, pronouns and adjectives.

One of the most interesting results was the speed at which the subjects learnt when we used this way of teaching, accompanied by positive reinforcement only, that is motivating the subject to perform the response for a reward (see page 141, Figures 3.14a and b). The average number of cues given from the beginning of the teaching was only just over four for the filly. The subjects would also work for a reward in the form of giving pleasure to the teacher. (See Figure 3.20.)

They also learnt the significance of symbols, such as numbers and colours, but *further tests* will be needed here to see how far this can go (see Figure 9.2).

One of the criteria for human language is the importance of word order.

Fig. 7. 12 Shemal being shown a 'wooden table' on an expedition to teach some language comprehension.

Whether or not the subjects can learn to understand the significance of word order is one of the questions we are currently researching.

Example
'Shemal come to Marthe', or 'Marthe come to Shemal', demonstrate the importance of word order because they mean different things although the words are the same.

The subjects have also been taught to make simple movements using these words, can identify objects, and have some idea of the meaning of some verbs, pronouns and adjectives (see Kiley-Worthington & Randle 2001). Further tests still have to be done, but simple word-order meanings are being understood and responded to appropriately, so it looks as if this may not be difficult for them.

Although more tests remain to be done, we have demonstrated that:

1. equine natural communication conforms to many but not all of the criteria set for human language;

2. given enough exposure, they are able to comprehend rather more language than was previously considered (Kiley-Worthington & Randle 2002).

Apart from teaching these animals to listen to human language and respond, the other important reason for researching this area is to help humans understand and teach equines better. If they could talk to equines and ask them to do things using language, this would be much easier for the humans as they are good verbal communicators, but relatively incompetent with visual and olfactory communication.

Interestingly, those who talk to horses in the belief that they might understand (as is more generally done with pre-verbal children), have more responsive, co-operative animals than those who assume they cannot. Whether this is because of the humans' preconceived notions or the result of genuine language comprehension remains to be tested.

Verbal language as we know it does act as a 'store of historically accumulated wisdom' (McDowell 1996). It is possible that equines do have some way of acquiring historically accumulated wisdom, which to date we have no evidence of, even though they do not have human-type language. But, if this is *not* the case, then each individual equine (although they learn from each other), given the limited knowledge of each, has to learn from their own experiences and innovations; each individual in a sense, therefore, has to 'invent the wheel'. If this is the case, then innovations may be slow, since not every individual will be an Einstein. But, equally, it does *not* mean that it is impossible for these animals to learn and use a simple form of our language, given the opportunity. At present our two experimental horses have had only 350 hours of language comprehension teaching. This compares with the exposure to learning and teaching for almost every waking hour of a human infant – that is around 56,000 hours by the time they are eight years old. It is hardly surprising if the animal subjects have not yet learnt a great deal of language!

'Language' comprehension of equines has only just begun, we are simply scratching the surface. However, even now to dismiss these animals as not having some form of natural language which fulfils many of the criteria of human language, nor being able to acquire a comprehension of at least simple human language, is by no means justified.

The first experiments on equines' ability to learn to comprehend human language indicates that they *can* learn to understand simple human language.

Much more work will, I am sure, be done on the subject with greater resources than we have had available. Answers to the many questions that have arisen are very important for a further understanding of both humans and equines, and will help us to teach them in a better way.

There is another side to the idea that language is important to being able to have advanced mental skills. Rather than encouraging cognitive complexities and experiences, language could restrict these by discouraging other ways of thinking. Close and long association with equines as well as other animals has been found by many people through the ages to provide new and different cognitive experiences (e.g. Blake 1975 and 1977, Rees 1991, Skipper 1999, Sherpell 1986, Kiley-Worthington 1998). These may often be the result of encouraging different modes of consciousness (see Chapter 8).

One thing that equines definitely are doing, and which may be an advanced cognitive skill that could perhaps enrich *our* lives, is representing and experiencing a world that is *not* limited or controlled by language.

Communication demonstrates the use of associative learning, imitation and social learning, and many mental events *have* to take place for messages to be transferred. The more we learn about communication between equines, and between equines and humans, the greater the amount of information and the complexity of the messages that it seems to be possible to communicate to, and receive from, equines by humans.

In conclusion, communication, both within and between species, for humans and equines is complex and multi-sensory, often conveying messages concerning an individual's experience of the world, and not necessarily restricted to the present.

Thus, whether or not other species have language as humans know it, is far less interesting a question than whether we can use it to disclose their worlds.

SUMMARY

1. There is a problem concerning what behaviour qualifies as 'for communication' because information may be transferred without an intent to communicate. Thus, all the behaviour equines or humans perform has communicative potential.

→

2. A type of symbolism is used by equines when they perform 'intention movements' which are incomplete movements. Ritualized movements, that is movements that are emancipated from their original cause and/or exaggerated, are rare in equines.

3. Communication both between and within species for both humans and equines is complex and involves all the senses.

4. Messages conveying an individual's experience of the world are often sent, but communication in equines is not restricted to the present, particularly when smells are used. They use smells a great deal both for learning about the world and for communicating with others. These smell messages involve different ideas of space and time, consequently it is a very different view of the world from that grasped by humans who use communication by smells relatively little. Humans are cognitively handicapped compared to equines because they are unable to use odours, except in a rudimentary way.

5. Taste and, particularly, touch communication are important in equine lives, and can be developed to a sophisticated level, even between species, as with, for example, using touch for communication between a horse and his experienced rider.

6. Equines are sophisticated visual communicators and observers, often picking up cues that humans miss.

7. Auditory communication is important to equines. Particular non-verbal noises they make or are made around them will convey many messages about others and what may happen next. Their vocal communication is used rather less than some species.

8. The meaning of the message for equines is, generally, context dependent. This ensures that equines, in order to interpret the message, must have a pronounced awareness of the social and physical context in which it is given. This is not necessary for the context-independent human language. Consequently communication in equines presents a different world view.

→

313

9. How similar the natural communication of equines is to human language is being investigated. It does have most of the characteristics that define human language. However, whether or not their communication can act as a 'store for accumulated wisdom' (as human language does), we do not know.

10. The first empirical experiments on horses' ability to learn to comprehend human language show them to be able. Thus, it does not appear to be easy to dismiss language as being mentally too advanced for them to comprehend, but further research is needed.

11. Because of the ability to learn to understand words rapidly, it is clear that the thoughtful use of language is an important vehicle to help humans and equines in their search for a better mutual understanding. It is not used sufficiently in our dealings with equines. The advantage to us is that we find it much easier to use than other methods of communication.

12. Language, as it is predominantly used by humans as 'representing the world', can restrict understanding and create its own world. Hence, rather than being the vehicle to a greater understanding of the world, it can hamper and even prevent a serious appraisal and awareness of other worlds (see Chapter 9). It can even create its own world so, eventually, as is often the case today, language users believe that this is the only one available to cognitively able beings.

13. Whether or not other species have language as humans know it, is a far less interesting question than whether we can use language to disclose their worlds. This is the present task.

8 What is consciousness, and are equines conscious?

'Some argue, not especially vigorously, as they have met little opposition, that only humans have self-conscious emotions. Animals, it is said, are incapable of self-consciousness.'

Masson and MacCarthy 1994

'Operational definitions of consciousness are slippery at best, primarily because self-recognition and self-awareness. . . can be manifested in different ways in different contexts.'

Cheney & Seyfarth 1990

The previous seven chapters have outlined what we know about equine 'beings', how they learn, what knowledge they have to acquire and the complexity of their lives. We concluded, as a result of knowing all this, that equines, like other mammals, have mental lives, that is that they have many mental activities taking place. But, until now we have not mentioned the tricky question of consciousness which is usually associated with having a mental life: a 'mind'. The question of whether or not equines are 'conscious', and what we mean by this, is clearly one of the key issues concerning what it might be like to be an equine, that is equine lore. Now we have some background in what mental attributes we know equines have, we need to address questions such as: do they know what they are doing; are they self-aware or aware that others have minds, needs and desires? There are plenty of people who will say their horse thinks 'just like me', or, alternatively, 'does not think', but is this just the way the horse keepers like to see it?

Example
There was an article in *British Dressage* magazine, August 2002, which emphasized that the 'herd instinct' of horses was very strong. One of the key features of this 'herd instinct' was that horses always wanted either to be led, or to be a leader. Since the natural thing in their life (their 'instinct') was to be either submissive and needing to be told what to do, or to lead (which must involve a conflict with someone who wanted to tell them what to do), it was necessary, the writer argued, to ensure 'obedience' and 'submission' by being the 'leader' when training dressage horses, because this is 'natural' for horses.

One difficulty with this approach is what then do you do with the 'born leader' that you may encounter: have a constant conflict? We have seen that their social life is by no means as simple as this. Teaching people to underestimate equine mentality is not helpful if they are to understand how to relate well to equines. If we realize that our equines are rather more mentally complex and capable, it is clear that different individual personalities will have to be treated differently. The task of the good teacher/rider is to understand this and develop the appropriate approach for every complex individual. Luckily the good teachers do not often read such articles, it is only the beginners who may be influenced and then start off on the wrong foot!

Until recently, it was assumed that non-human mammals could not be 'conscious'. In the last couple of decades though, researchers have been thinking and experimenting with how to answer questions concerning 'consciousness'. To come to grips with this debate, you really need a whole book (e.g. DeCrasia 1996, Griffin 1992, Kiley-Worthington 2000). My task here is to summarize, as simply as possible, some of the debates as to whether equines show evidence of consciousness. This is no small task, but I will do my best!

The first thing is to understand the dichotomy between the scholars whose job it is to think about and research such things, and the people who have to deal with equines daily, who rarely doubt that they are conscious. The trouble is that few of the latter have thought very deeply about what this means. Nevertheless, people with experience of equines *do* have some knowledge about equines that others (who are primarily interested in the ideas) do not generally have. Consequently, provided the knowledgeable and experienced horseperson's understanding is critically assessed, it may contribute considerably to the debates. Such knowledge may be common sense to most horsepeople and is rarely therefore discussed. However, it is important that it is not ignored, as a trivial example will point out.

Example

Some years ago I was on the editorial board of an important international ethological journal. Scientific journals are supposed to publish the results of research in order for the scientific elite to acquire further information (albeit in a particularly curious language sometimes). I was sent a manuscript by a bright young scientist who had spend many hours watching dairy cows, and taking and testing vaginal swabs from them. He had 'proved' that when one dairy cow mounted another one, the one mounted was usually in oestrus! The fact that everyone who has kept cows for at least the last 3,000 years or so has known and used this information successfully, to know when to put the cow with the bull (or use artificial insemination), had escaped this keen young man who had had no experience of cattle at all until he performed this 'research'!

Let this be a cautionary tale for those wedded to science; some science is bad or silly science. This needs to be weeded out, just like the opinions of horse owners need to be critically assessed and weeded.

Consciousness is today a minefield, with a book a week coming out about what it is, and TV programmes often doing their best to confuse the issue by presenting one person's view as the truth. It is safe to say that at present, nobody really knows the answers to many of the questions concerning consciousness, however persuasive they may be. The important thing is that we continue to discuss it.

So far we have presented evidence to suggest that normal equines as well as humans act as a result of their awareness by:

1. acquiring and remembering information;
2. predicting, showing intent, and making decisions;
3. making choices in what they do;
4. feeling emotions, including desires and fears;
5. having beliefs about the world and expectations.

Thus, equines have physical, emotional, social and mental needs and, if we care about them, our duty must be to give them a life of quality which caters for these needs, whether or not we consider they are conscious.

Without this degree of mental awareness, they would not be able to live the lives that, as a result of many studies, we know they lead in the wild or feral state. An individual who does not have these mental attributes will have great difficulty surviving and reproducing, consequently, these attributes will be selected for. Thus, the simplest explanation is that they are 'aware', that is, have *some form* of consciousness.

'The conclusion that they [other species] are consciously aware is therefore compelling. The balance of evidence . . . is that they are and it seems positively unscientific to deny it.' (Dawkins 1989)

As long ago as 1890, the psychologist, James, decided that consciousness was necessary to organize the mind, and to prevent the 'buzzing of chaos' as a result of the plethora of stimuli and the multitude of possible behaviours, whether this was a man or a mouse, or any other mammal in between. However, the emphasis on which of these mental skills are important for a particular species to create mental order is likely to vary depending on their lifestyle.

Example
Since we humans are linear-thinking language users, it helps us to try to categorize mental events in considering 'consciousness'. If we were not, we might not do this, but rather, for example, create 'networks' concerning what consciousness is.

If we do categorize we must not lose sight of the fact that this is not the only way in which mental events work.

1. The categories we make are not discrete. They may overlap and intertwine and be mutually dependent on one another. Each category has certain characters which will overlap, merge, integrate and even depend on others, and this in turn depends on the individuals' experiences.

2. This categorization is not, and can never be, a complete explanation of consciousness. It is just an aid.

3. Division into types of consciousness (see below) is *not* the only way either humans, or equines may perceive the world, act on or explain it. Nonetheless, this categorization is one way we humans create 'mental order' but it does not mean it is the only way.

Here, I present my efforts at reducing the 'buzzing of chaos' in the mind about consciousness. It is the result of reading various other scholars' efforts from different relevant disciplines, trying to combine this with the common-sense usage of the terms, and a *critical appraisal* of what people who have equines know from experience, that is 'folk knowledge'. As a result, some of the terms may not be used exactly as particular specialists use them, However, as long as the terms are defined, and then used in this way, there is little point in debating how a term is used for improving our understanding.

UNCONSCIOUSNESS, AND SUBCONSCIOUSNESS

A living being is breathing and the heart is beating, but no responses are shown to either internal or external stimuli. Thus, the being is unable to perceive the world, or their own internal state, and is unconscious. Much of the time this definition of 'unconsciousness' works well enough.

Examples
1. Someone is lying in an 'unconscious' state having had a bump on the head after falling off a horse. Although they are breathing, there appears to be no awareness of anything around them, or of any movement their body makes.

2. A horse is under general anaesthetic and is having a surgical operation. He is breathing but otherwise not responding to having his abdomen cut open, or anything in the environment. He is 'unconscious'.

But from time to time, there are problems with these definitions

Problem 1 Recent cases of non-responsive humans (i.e. those kept alive with respirators after severe accidents) have been found to be aware and even able to communicate, by, for example, gradually using the movements of a little toe, or an eye blink, when they were showing no evidence of being conscious and were thought to be 'unconscious'.

This is relevant here because equines do not necessarily respond in ways that humans can always observe or relate to. It is, therefore, often believed that, if they are not responding, they are not conscious or aware.

Example
A 'twitch' (a piece of rope or leather twisted tightly around the nose or the ear) is often used to immobilize a horse, for veterinary care, farriery, mating, clipping and by bad

trainers and handlers whenever convenient. It is believed, even argued by veterinarians, that because the animal is immobilized, no pain is felt. It is a convenient belief because, if the animal is not feeling pain then such treatment is not 'cruel.'

But, another explanation is that use of a twitch causes immobilization *because* of the pain it generates on very touch-sensitive parts of the body. It is for the veterinarians or others to prove the animal *does not* feel pain (which is both difficult and unlikely) before assuming that, because it is convenient, there is none.

Thus, the first problem with recognizing something that we might think is obvious: 'unconsciousness', is evident.

Problem 2 The problem of 'subconsciousness'. Is this different from unconsciousness? Experiences during an unconscious state (as well as a conscious state) can, Freud (1901) suggested, be stored in the subconscious, another unaware state. These experiences can be important in affecting future behaviour, at least of humans. For example, it is considered that traumatic experiences may be stored in the subconscious. A trauma itself may have been forgotten, but continues to affect the individual's behaviour. Traumas during an equine's life (such as weaning, isolation, capture, transportation, an accident or a beating) appear, as in humans, often to be the cause of occasional unpredictable behaviour many years later in very different environments (Equine Behavioural Consultancy records). The logical position is to argue that, until it is proved to be untrue, because we are all mammals and our brains work in very similar ways, we must assume that equines also have an unconscious awareness – a 'sub-consciousness'. More evidence for this comes from the successful treatment of behavioural problems based on this premise.

UNCONSCIOUS AWARENESS, PART-TIME CONSCIOUSNESS, HABITS AND HABITS OF MIND

There are other states of consciousness where the individual reacts to things in the environment but is unaware of doing so; in humans sleep-walking is one example. Another is what is called 'blind sight' where, for example, an individual human is asked to touch something but then denies having touched it. There are many who believe that this is the normal mental state of higher mammals (except humans): they may perceive the environment and even act on it, have feelings and emotions, and behave in different ways, but they are not, and never can be, *conscious* of it. A recent quote from an elementary textbook illustrates this position. 'An eagle, for instance, not only can't remember whether it is lunch time, it can't even appreciate that it is an eagle.' [Or] 'Nothing can enable us to know what it is like to be an animal.' (Graham 1993)

Taking this view makes it difficult to explain why they do things that must imply they have some mental life (such as points 1–5 on page 317). For example, why does the eagle start hunting at midday if he is not aware that he is hungry? In order to explain behaviour that does not otherwise fit easily into such a mindless explanation, the word 'instinct', is often employed. Curiously, this is an acceptable explanation for many. The fact remains that how *instinct* operates on a day-to-day basis is very obscure. It has not been considered to date by many that perhaps the mental-event explanation of how mammals behave is simpler and more economic in its use of body resources than an instinctive explanation may be. For example, instincts are considered to be 'hard wired', that is, they are not adaptable or changeable and require the necessary hardware back up in the brain, whereas making decisions and having mental events may require less hardware, less space and less programming.

One of the main messages of the previous chapters has been to point out, with critically assessed examples, how equines as well as normal human adults must have some form of awareness, or consciousness, of their whereabouts and objects around them, because of how they live. They can perform voluntary actions, make choices, decisions and have emotions. In addition they have to acquire a considerable amount of both ecological and social information. They have desires, needs, memories and can predict events. They are, consequently, neither autistic, blind-sighted, nor are they robots – all mental states writers have attributed to equines, rather than the equivalent state of normal adult humans.

But, nevertheless, there is in normal humans, and probably equines, a state of 'unconscious awareness'.

Example
After learning some behavioural sequences, both equines and humans sometimes perform these sequences without attention: without a conscious awareness of what they are doing.

This ability has advantages since, after the recognition of objects (or patterns of responses) have been established, the attention can be directed at other new or different things, provided there is no interruption or change. This allows other information to be taken in, rather than the attention always having to be directed at performing well-established responses, thus increasing the efficiency of mental capacities.

Example
A human driving a motor car or riding a bicycle, or a schooled horse moving away from the leg or doing a half pass. While the behaviour is being learnt as a voluntary act, the 'conscious' attention must be totally directed towards the performing of the task. But after it is established, it can be performed with little direct attention, unless something different occurs, such as the brakes stop working on the car, the bicycle has a flat tyre, or, for the horse, the half pass has to be performed on very rough terrain.

It may be that equines are particularly capable of filing information away in this non-conscious way, but one thing which is clear is that, when things go wrong, such non-conscious information can be brought back into the realm of conscious awareness.

If non-human mammals are in a state of unconscious zombiism all the time, then it must be explained why they have emotions and feelings, how they learn and remember, and how the other complex behaviours I have described operate.

Example
Both humans and equines have 'instinctive tendencies' to walk, and to walk in species-specific ways (see Chapter 2), but *how* this is done has to be learnt. Walking is not simple, it involves balancing, the contraction of the correct muscles in correct sequence for the limb movements, then the proprioceptive feedback telling the central nervous system where parts of the body are at any time, so that it can send messages out about the next movement needed, followed by the consequent sequence of movements of the legs.

In humans, born at an early stage of development, walking is learnt late and slowly; even moving the arms to touch objects takes some weeks. In the precocial equine, it is learnt in the first few hours after birth, although it may take some days to perfect.

If equines are *never* able to be conscious of their limb movements, how is it that they learn to navigate difficult terrain, to move at speed over ground with different surfaces, to judge take-off and landing when jumping, change their gaits when necessary or when asked, and to modify all these things in different situations?

Although walking and running, after initial learning, can be performed without a conscious thought of *how* it is done (although there may be a conscious thought relating to *when* it is done), when a limb is injured, to maintain balance the sequence of movements and how the new movements are to be integrated has to be brought back into conscious awareness. The movement has to be changed, and decisions made on where and how to move with the injured limb.

Example

Shemal cut through a tendon on her left hind leg while we were riding around France and she could not put the leg to the ground because of the pain. She had to learn how to move about on three legs, walk with the front two and then hop on the sound hind. First she was frightened to move at all because of the pain and lack of balance, and then she made mistakes in hopping, leaving her weight-carrying hind leg too far behind, and nearly falling over. By the fourth day, however, she was much more skilled at turning, jumping forwards, balancing and so on, although the pain in the injured leg appeared to be as severe and she was still unable to put it to the ground. During this time her awareness of how she walked, balanced and moved had had to be brought to her consciousness, and decisions made on how to adapt her movement to the changing circumstances. This involved further association and trial-and-error learning which required decisions, choices and beliefs held and acted on for an activity (walking) that, until this time, had become automatic: unconscious.

Her behaviour and experiences during this trying time paralleled my own when I broke a ligament in my knee while skiing.

Both humans and equines are only too conscious of their bodies at such times because of the pain. Adapting movements to cope with the pain and restriction results in errors, frustrations, changes and, perhaps, some successes because the movement has been brought back into some form of consciousness.

Of course the change can then become a sequence of responses that occur without any conscious involvement.

Example

After a couple of weeks, Shemal became so good at hopping along on one hind foot, that she and her father escaped out of their corral to go wandering a mile or two to a field of someone else's particularly juicy lucerne!

Sometimes these new sequences become so well entrenched when the original stimulus, that is the pain, for them is no longer there, they continue.

Examples

1. As a result of a severe strain to the ankle, I developed a limp to reduce the pain when walking. At the end of two months, there was no longer any pain, but I found myself continuing to walk with a limp. To stop this I had to again consciously think how I was walking.

2. Shindi severly cut her pastern above the coronet when on an expedition. Three months later, although the wound was healed and there was no internal damage as assessed from the X-ray, she continued to trot slightly unsound. However, when particularly excited and playing chase with the other youngsters, her limp vanished. Here there apparently was a reason to move without a limp, that is, when moving fast and athletically, the movement reverted to the original balanced sequence, although whether or not she was consciously aware of this we do not know.

The subjects in these examples had formed a habit to limp, the new method of movement had become unconscious although there was no longer any pain.

Habits (see page 133) is another term for actions that are of a 'part-time conscious type'. They are rapidly established for mundane things in equines and humans, for example; how the individual walks, lies down or even performs complex learnt movements. Habits vary in how quickly they are established but, once established, one of their characteristics is that the more they are performed, the more they will be performed, that is, with performance they acquire **habit strength**, and are more difficult to change.

Examples

I. A human's daily similar sequence of movements and positioning of the towel when drying after getting out of the bath, or the similar sequence of movements of an individual horse entering his stable for the night.

2. A similar effect can be seen when mammals (including humans) make paths. Initially the path maker has to move relatively slowly, paying attention to where he is going, but once the path is made, even though it may be a very indirect route to the destination, the tendency is to follow it rather than to make a new one. The more the path is used, and the clearer it is, the more difficult it is to leave, even for short forays or to straighten out a bend. It requires less physical or mental effort to follow a made path since no decisions have to be made. Equines and humans follow their own and others' physical and behavioural 'paths' in this way, but initially the path has had to be made. All physical or mental paths are not made by humans and they all require some mental consciousness in their making.

Prey species might be expected to form habits fast.

Example

Even though the sequence of movements and decisions that the prey animal made to escape the predator may not be the best, nevertheless, if it worked and the individual is still alive, the strategy will be used again. Prey animals, usually have only one trial to learn: if they get it wrong the first time, they are dead, whereas the predator may go hungry but can try again, using the same strategy or a different one.

Forming habits prevents attention and mental effort having to be devoted to familiar tasks, so allowing it to be redistributed for new or interesting occurrences while the familiar tasks continue.

Equines characteristically form habits very fast.

Example

In the free school if a horse makes a detour in one place on the circle on one occasion (because, perhaps, there is something slightly different on the ground), he is very likely to make the same detour the next time – and many subsequent times – even if the original stimulus has been removed. This is a form of part-time consciousness. Once the habit has been established, it requires no awake-conscious attention/experience, it is repeated in the same way which allows the attention to be directed elsewhere.

In different contexts or with a change in the environment, the behavioural sequence can be bought back into the conscious domain.

Example

The task for the teacher when lungeing the detouring horse, is to make him conscious of what he is doing, attract his attention to it, make it clear that it is not acceptable, and praise him when he corrects it (see page 133).

Recent evidence (e.g. Kiley-Worthington 1996 and in the press) indicates that donkeys and zebras (even though the latter have never been domesticated), have the same facilities for quick learning and quick habit formation.

Rapid habit formation, associated as it is with quick learning, may be one of the most important reasons why horses (*Equus caballus*) have been, and remain, such an important domestic animal: they learn very fast, form habits quickly and will then continue to behave in similar ways in similar situations. Thus they rapidly learn to be handled, to be led, to enter a stable, to be ridden or driven – provided this has been done without causing fear. If fear has been induced, then the wrong habits can be as rapidly acquired, and are as difficult to change. It is, of course, not only physical habits that are adopted and reinforced by performance but there can also be **habits of mind**.

Examples

1. One habit of mind could be that the youngsters in one particular group of equines watch each other and their elders carefully and learn what to eat by imitation, whereas those in another group isolated from their elders might more frequently try to eat different things, and learn more by trial and error and less by watching or social learning.

2. The K'hung bushwoman's habits of mind: *what* she thinks about, and *how* she solves problems, are not entirely different from the female urban Londoner or the domestic Devonshire mare, but there are some differences. The K'hung bushwoman will have developed a habit of mind of assessing and acquiring detailed ecological knowledge on the whereabouts of food or water, as will the zebra who lives in her area. But neither the zebra, the bushwoman or the Devonshire mare, will have a habit of mind of reading books, doing mathematical sums, or playing on a computer which the London woman may have.

Even within our own culture, there are people with very different habits of mind; for example, some have acquired the habit of *not* learning or doing mathematics, but rather assuming they cannot understand it. Some form the habit of mind of reasoning and thinking questions through, others of doing what they have been told, others of just responding to their 'feelings'. Equally, different equines in different areas that are exposed to different conditions will not only have different knowledge, but they will also have different habits of mind. A dressage horse's habits of mind will be different from those of a Dartmoor pony, although they will have some in common, and some in common with you and me.

It should be possible to develop different habits of mind for different individuals by exposing them to different experiences. One way that has been adopted is to tutor apes to sign and comprehend human language. Chimpanzees who have had such experience have been found to perform better at learning human-designed tasks than wild or other captive chimps. This is as a result of their acquisition of the appropriate habits of mind (e.g. Premack 1988).

There is no reason why equines could not also acquire habits of mind more similar to those of the humans they associate with and who teach them, for example listening to and responding to human language (see Kiley-Worthington & Randle 1998, and page 308). This does not mean, as some have argued, that they are no longer 'equines'. It underlines their learning ability, adaptability, cognitive competence and awareness. In just the same way, the humans who associate with particular equines may also learn from them different habits of mind, for example to be more aware of the total environment around them, or to observe more closely.

Equines learn about us, including at least some of our verbal language, in all their dealings with us, but yet remain donkeys or horses, and can socialize normally with their own species as well as others, provided they have had appropriate experiences.

Humans can change their habits of mind too. They could start by changing their common belief that human mental skills and consciousness are far greater than that of any other animal, to a habit of mind of observing, looking, questioning and assessing other species' behaviour without preconceived notions.

AWAKE CONSCIOUSNESS, ATTENTION/ AWARENESS OF 'THINGS' AND EXPERIENCES

Awake consciousness is an awareness of the world as a result of being awake and receiving messages about the external world (through the senses), and about the individual's internal state (from hormones, pains, feelings and emotions). Normal adult humans and equines perceive, assess and respond to their own internal world and the external world. They have sensations and experiences and consequently have an 'awake consciousness'. Because their senses, bodies and beings are slightly different, this may differ between individuals and species. We have so far pointed out (see Chapters 1–7) where these similarities and differences may be as a result of using conditional anthropomorphism, and looking carefully at what knowledge equines need to live the way they do.

Example

One obvious species difference may be that to an adult normal human, the world is often defined by language which, in turn, defines how we think about space and time (see page 312). A horse – a visually acute animal with a sophisticated ability to see and interpret very slight visual cues – is likely to have an awake-consciousness that is defined by different ideas of space and time and, therefore, some different beliefs, intentions and memories based on vision, as well as in combination with other senses such as smell and touch. Thus, how they put the information together will vary: in other words, the way they think, and what they think about, will have some differences from the way we humans put the information together.

The conscious-awake attention experience will be an analysis of all the different sensory experiences combined, the species-specific tendencies, and the individual's lifetime experiences: his perception and learning, memories and his present feelings.

Where the **attention** is directed is a very important aspect of awake consciousness. There has to be an element of attention in order for things – external or internal – to impinge on consciousness.

In mammals, including humans, there are **orientation reflexes**: behaviours indicating to the observer where the attention is directed. Equines' orientation reflexes are particularly obvious: their anti-gravity muscles contract and as a result their body posture becomes more upright, with the head and the tail up, the head turned in the direction of the stimulus, the eyes looking and the ears pricked in that direction. If the attention is being directed behind, but the stimulus is not very strong, then the ears rotate back (see Figure 7.3).

If there is nothing much going on to hold the attention in one direction, the ears and eyes may be scanning the environment by moving backwards and forwards, just 'keeping an ear' on anything that might be of interest and need attention. Others (of the same or different species) see and assess these behaviours to identify where another's attention is directed and, consequently, what his next action might be in order to obtain social, or environmental information (Figure 8.1 and see Chapter 6).

Fig. 8.1   Knowing about others. Here Kaloon, a black Arab who has just been castrated, has come to visit. He is attracting a great deal of attention. Gaynor (left) is trying to get close to him while Shemal (third left) intercepts.   Shanti walks purposely towards the action, while Shezam, another gelding (fourth right), tries to keep the other mares away from him, and Shindi champs at him, keeping close to mother, Shereen.

Many species have inborn tendencies to perform these orientation reflexes but they also have to learn how to interpret those of other individuals.

Example

If an individual constantly 'cries wolf', that is, often over-reacts by ear pricking and showing signs of extreme attention and excitement (which is often the case with foals) the older individuals may ignore such behaviour but, if another adult behaves in this way, they will react differently. In other words, they make allowances for the age and development of the individual. To do this, they must be aware of these differences in their own and another's world view.

Equines' sophisticated awareness of visual cues leads to their use of many movements and postures to convey where the attention is directed, but because of their differences in perception we are only beginning to understand this. They also often show when they are *not* paying attention, that is ignoring something. This is another example which indicates an awareness of their own and others' attention. They can make choices in deciding whether to indicate that they are, or are not, paying attention.

Learning to perform particular responses requires motivation and attention. If teaching situations for equines, humans or other mammals are set up to attract and hold the attention of both the teacher and the student, learning is fast (see Chapter 2). However, once even complex behaviour has been learnt, there may be no further need for direct attention so it may be performed in a part-time conscious way (see page 320).

AWARENESS OF THEIR OWN BODIES

So far in this book we have argued that equines learn to do voluntary acts. They have feelings and emotions and demonstrate pain felt in particular parts of their bodies. As a result, individuals have to be aware of the different parts of their bodies, and, in particular, the difference between their body and another's, that is that their body is *theirs*.

Examples
1. Teaching a horse to cross his front legs (see Figures 3.8 and 3.10). First he will have help with words, gestures, imitation and moulding to cross his front legs which is not a movement he normally performs other than by chance (e.g. when having to turn around in a small circle). After a while he will learn to do it without the gestures and moulding, but he may not cross his leg enough. So he must learn that the leg to be crossed must be placed right over the leg he is standing on, or it will not be rewarded. He has to become aware of each front leg and what to do with it. It is not an 'on or off' response because he can do it exaggeratedly, in a half-hearted way, or not at all. In other words, he is aware of what he is doing with his legs and has to work out both the **what** it is he needs to do (knowing that) and **how** to do it. This is the same with teaching him any voluntary act (see Chapter 3, page 139).

2. Donkeys and horses are very careful about entering narrow gateways, judging the width of their bodies, and whether or not they can fit, demonstrating their awareness of their own bodies behind the point where they can see them. But, more interestingly, they can also learn when drawing vehicles (whose width is greater than their own bodies) to make allowance for this as well, going through when possible, stopping when it is not. Sometimes they make mistakes, but often they do not and some become extremely skilled at this (Figure 8.2).

Fig. 8.2 Consciousness of self and body. Shemal is very aware that the bales are too wide for the gate and that she will have to be very careful coming through. Look at her ears.

Teaching voluntary acts to equines, implies they have to have some awareness of the parts of their bodies (Figure 8.3). Thus, it is usually agreed that equines do have an awareness of their own bodies and the different parts of it almost from birth, although a human baby may take some weeks or months to mature to this stage.

This may seem obvious, but there are a large number of people who argue that non-human mammals are *not* aware of themselves in any sense, body or mind.

Fig. 8.3 Awareness of own body. Shemal, without any tack, lines herself up to the gate so that Vicki can mount. Her ears demonstrate that all of her attention is concentrated on the action.

BEHAVIOURAL SYNCHRONIZATION AND SOCIAL FACILITATION: DOING WHAT OTHERS DO

Because members of a social group will have been exposed to similar environments when together, they are likely to want to eat, drink, sleep, and will feel hot, cold or itchy, at similar times. Their synchronized daily rhythms help them to co-ordinate. This is called **behavioural synchronization**, and if it is just the result of physiological changes (feeling hungry, cold and so on) it will require no form of consciousness.

Example
Equines tend to eat at dawn and dusk – particularly in the tropics when it is hot – and have siestas in the middle of the day. Humans have the habit of eating at particular times during the day and, if a meal is late, they will feel particularly hungry.

But, an additional cue for starting or stopping different activities can be supplied by observing others performing the behaviour.

Example

There has to be a beginning and an end to each meal or bout of eating behaviour, a place where it is to be done and so forth. Neither an individual human, nor as far as we know an equine, may feel particularly like eating or drinking at a specific time, nevertheless, when one of the group starts one of these behaviours, then the others often start. Just, seeing others doing the behaviour often makes an individual feel hungry or thirsty.

This is called **social facilitation**, which, because it is the result of being in some sense aware of what others are doing, does imply some form of consciousness. One of the interesting results from our centre is that social facilitation can take place between species too.

Example

I conducted an experiment with safari-park-bred zebra, used to humans but never handled. On a day when there were insects about, so there was a tendency to shake the head to get rid of the fly irritation, I shook my head six times at one-minute intervals when standing 50 m (164 ft) from a group of four zebras. Over a half-hour period, two of the four individuals shook their heads significantly more times than they did when I did not shake my head (unpublished data 2000, Bally Vaughan Safari Park, Zimbabwe).

I felt somewhat dizzy after this, but it gave some evidence for social facilitation occurring between the zebra and me.

Prins's recent study of the African Cape buffalo (1997) is particularly interesting here. He first of all discovered the normal daily rhythms of the wild Cape buffalo. They adjourned for a siesta at midday. Before they moved off for the evening graze, many would rise and stand for a while, then lie down again. He recorded the number of individuals that rose and stood, and by taking compass readings of their orientation, found that the Manyara buffalo went off in the direction in which the majority had orientated themselves previously, that is they 'voted' on where they should go to graze. Here, the buffalo showed synchronized behaviour (all going off to graze at the same time) but they also showed that individuals were making decisions on *where* they would go to do this (social facilitation). Perhaps in this case the standing up and 'pointing' was a type of **social suggestion**.

In our association with equines, as a rule we take for granted that they are conscious in these ways, although when things go wrong we may, instead of analysing our own behaviour, consider it is just their inability to 'think' or 'be aware' in certain ways. Among philosophers and scientists, there is considerable argument about much of this. In the first place it is often believed that all the behaviour and examples I have given above can be explained by operant conditioning: stimulus response learning. Skinner (1969) believed that most human behaviour can be explained in this way too, and that the response after initial learning becomes fixed and automatic, and therefore does not require any consciousness. He even concluded: 'The real question is not whether machines think but whether men do'.

But, knowledge on these matters has progressed somewhat since the 1960s (see Chapter 3). On balance, it is necessary, as well as wise (if we want to understand equines), to consider that they are aware and conscious of things happening around them and what they are doing. In fact, every equine trainer does this, otherwise they would be unable to train.

A more contentious question is whether or not equines have, what I have called, 'reflective consciousness'; others have called this 'access consciousness' or 'reflexive consciousness' and other different terms; this is the subject of the next chapter.

SUMMARY

1. Although consciousness and what it is, is widely debated and little understood, we cannot side-step discussing it if we wish to understand something about what it is to be an equine.

2. As a result of what we now know about equines, what they learn and the knowledge they have to acquire to live the way they have evolved to live (see Chapters 1–7), we can say that equines have many similar mental events to those of humans which have been described by some as implying consciousness or awareness.

3. To try to make some sense of consciousness, we have divided it into types. a) (i) Unconsciousness, that is, being unaware of anything going on either within the body or outside it. (ii) subconsciousness: evidence for this in equines comes, at present, only from similar responses to past trauma to those shown by humans and which are

→

related to subconsciousness in humans. Assuming that these experiences will affect behaviour (although the subject may not be aware of them) is helpful in correcting behavioural problems in some equines as in humans. b) Unconscious awareness or part-time consciousness involves behaviours having become of high habit strength so they can be performed without any conscious awareness of them (such as walking, typing, performing half-passes) but, when things become difficult, can be brought back into consciousness so that decisions can be made. c) Awake consciousness (sometimes called perceptive consciousness): this is illustrated in equines by their awareness of their own bodies and that of others, and their ability to learn to perform voluntary acts and acquire knowledge. The final type of consciousness is d) reflective consciousness (considered in the next chapter).

Examples have been given to illustrate the existence in equines of these various conscious states. It must be emphasized that although we have categorized consciousness in this way, the categories interweave and overlap.

4. Equines, like humans, develop habits, or part-time conscious behaviours, and habits of mind (ways of thinking and using their minds). For both species groups, these may be different in different places or where they have had different experiences, that is, in different cultures.

Different educational experiences may be able to change habits of mind for equines, as they can for humans. This is something we should be aware of when trying to understand equines or teach them. They seem to be able to learn to think a little like us when they have a lot of contact with us. To reduce the interspecies gap and improve our teaching of them, the amount they learn and their teaching of us, we need to learn to try to assess the world a little more like them. The equines who live with us can be our tutors in such an endeavour.

→

5. More experimental and critically assessed careful observation is needed in order to be able to understand equine consciousness better. We have some information which points in many respects to the importance of *recognizing our similarities of mentality*, its complexity, and similarities in conscious experiences. But we still have a long way to go in understanding this subject in equines, as well as humans.

9 Can equines be 'reflectively conscious', or have emotions that indicate they are aware of others' minds?

We use the term **reflective consciousness** to denote what have been considered more 'advanced' cognitive states. Many have argued that without language it is not possible to have these higher cognitive states but again it is not clear either whether this is true, or where the lines between having or not having various mental states are to be drawn. At its simplest, reflective consciousness requires memories, some conscious awareness (see Chapter 8) and an emotional involvement of some sort which must involve some analysis of past experiences.

Even if equines are conscious and aware of their environment, and make decisions and choices (as we have argued they *must* be and do in order to live the lives they live) there are still problems concerning whether they have, or could have, these higher cognitive states. The questions that have to be asked are, do equines have the ability to:

1. Think?
2. Form and learn concepts?
3. Be aware that others have minds, desires and needs?
4. Be self-aware? Of course, they are not going to say to themselves as Descartes did: 'I think, therefore I am', but they might do other things that demonstrate that they are aware of their own selves including their minds.

The everyday horse owner might feel that these questions are not really of interest to them, and are either to high-flown and complicated, or unnecessary. I hope, however, that some of you will by now be convinced that actually these questions lie at the very epicentre of our understanding of equines. Even if we cannot answer them all, if we are serious about trying to get inside the equine's skin and mind we must ponder and debate them. In this chapter we show that there are some answered, but also many unanswered, questions. The important advance that has been made in the scientific fraternity in the last two decades however, is that we *can ask* these questions, not assume that we know the answer, which has been, until recently, that no non-human mammal could be reflectively conscious.

Research on the mental life and reflective consciousness of non-human mammals in the last decade or two has to date concentrated on animals who are a long way away from our everyday lives. These animals are mammals who live in a different medium from us, such as water-living sea mammals: dolphins and whales, or birds, particularly parrots, pigeons, ravens and jays (Clayton 2000). Studies on terrestrial mammals have concentrated on apes who live in remote places, such as the chimpanzees of Africa of the orang-outangs of Asia. A little work is also now beginning on the largest of all terrestrial mammals, but one that again is known to most of us only by fable, fantasy and occasional television documentaries, that is the elephants (Kiley-Worthington 2000). Most of these studies have made no effort to critically assess folk knowledge about these animals, firstly because this was considered 'unscientific', secondly because the folk who knew about these animals were generally tribal people who did not speak international languages such as English, French or Spanish, and thirdly because sometimes there was very little folk knowledge about such remote animals.

Surprisingly, the animals that we know well and are close to us, such as the horse in our fields and stables, or the dog in front of our fire, have not so far been studied in any detail in relation to what their minds are capable of, or whether or not they may be 'reflectively conscious' (although see Bekoff 1992). This is partly because we thought we knew everything there was to know about them, but it is also because examining our cultural beliefs about such animals and asking these sorts of questions concerning their mental abilities is very threatening to our lifestyle and the way we treat domestic animals. If cattle (or equines) for example are found to be as mentally able and aware as even a five-year-old child, we would have to review whether we should keep them at all, and if so how. Certainly we would neither want to kill them, even 'for their own good', nor eat them.

As a result of the research on apes and dolphins in particular, there has been some thinking on how to ask some of these questions. 1) Laboratory studies have been testing whether or not various birds and mammals may be able to think and form concepts. 2) Evidence for non-human mammals' awareness of others' feelings, desires and needs may be collected from field studies (Figure 9.1), or laboratory tests that involve deceit for example (you have to know what another wants in order to deceive). 3) Tests to see if an animal is self-aware were done by showing the subjects reflections of themselves in a mirror and seeing what responses they made to changes in their appearance; they were pioneered by Gallop (1979) and became very fashionable.

The first two of these questions are considered in this chapter as well as other types of emotions that may tell us about the awareness of self and others. Is there evidence that equines can feel something like compassion, true jealousy, embarrassment, gratitude, loyalty, pride, shyness, love or charity? To feel these emotions, the individual *must* have some awareness of self as well as of others' feelings.

Such behaviour may be rare, and its intepretation open to observer bias and preconceived notions, but now is the time to begin to search.

There are other behaviours which can throw some light on whether or not equines are aware of others' minds or of themselves, like, for example, playing; in order to play, there has to be an awareness that it is 'play'. There are rules distinguishing play from non-play. Play may involve **pretending**. In order to

Fig. 9.1   Awareness of the feelings and desires of others? Oberlix is helping Chris to shut the gate. Note that Oberlix is not wearing tack and has to have some concept of 'gate' to enable Chris to reach out and shut it. Shemal must wait quietly until it is shut and the attention of her right ear is on Chris and Oberlix, rather than her rider.

pretend it is necessary to know it is not 'real'. All this must involve an awareness of self and an awareness of others and how they might be feeling. Possession of things and stealing also demonstrates an awareness of self and others and their needs: you cannot possess without knowing that you are there and have priority, and you cannot steal (take from another) without knowing you do not possess something, but another does. Whether youngsters are consciously taught by older members of the group or not, and whether equines have anything that could be described as some simple form of a sense of humour, also bear investigating. These will be considered in the next chapter.

There is much observer bias in the literature, and sometimes another explanation for many of the examples that can be given. This is partly because looking critically for such behaviour has only just begun. But, we will start the ball rolling as far as equines are concerned, and discuss these points with examples to raise the questions, albeit there are not, so far, many answers.

CAN EQUINES THINK?

Since it is generally agreed since Bentham (1789) that dogs and horses, at least, can suffer, the question that is now more often asked, is: can they think?

If thinking is restricted to human-language users as is often argued (e.g. Carruthers 1996, McDowell 1996) then other species do not think. But, this has always seemed a strange argument to me as humans can often make decisions, or come to conclusions, without thinking in words at all. Since both humans and equines have mental experiences, if thinking involves having a mental life, then non-language-using mammals do think (e.g. DeGrazia 1996 and Lea & Kiley-Worthington 1996).

But what does thought consist of exactly? Here, thought is considered to consist of a medley of interlinked mental events: perceptions, feelings and emotions, memories and past experiences feeding back one to the other, and combining in all sorts of ways to create mental events, which are thoughts (a 'networking mentality'). Glimpses of new combinations of interlinking events may result in imagination, dreams, intuitions, or understandings of connections between things and experiences. Since, as we have shown, equines learn, have memories, past experiences, emotions and feelings and these interlink and are ordered in some way (that is, are analysed), then they must think. There may, of course, be diversity in the emphasis on the different types of these mental events, or in how they are interwoven in different individuals or species. As a result, equine thinking may be, in some respects, different from human thinking which is often, but not always, connected to language.

It may be that human language allows for more thought and the acquisition of more knowledge about past or future events, that is, different thoughts. But, as we have mentioned, (see page 314) it may inhibit other thoughts, or ways of interpreting the world.

We have already discussed (see Chapter 3) how the individual may know but be unaware of how they know. Much silent learning (see page 147) and consequently some of an equine's ecological and social knowledge may be of this type (see Chapters 5 and 6). This is sometimes called **intuitive knowledge** by humans who may say 'I just knew it would happen'. It may be that, in some cases, this can only be explained by sudden apparently self-generated ideas, or perhaps from stimuli that others may be less aware of. Or, it may be the result of perceived events without any conscious awareness (see Chapter 8, page 320). Consequently, some 'thinking' or ordering of information in the brain, may not be 'reflective' since it does not involve conscious awareness. Nevertheless, it involves sifting, sorting, fitting together and redistributing the myriad sensory and emotional experiences which can be pulled into conscious awareness.

Equines and humans learn, they have receptors, they have a brain, they have experiences, they perceive and analyse things, they have memories, they acquire knowledge, they make connections between events, they acquire a great deal of both ecological and social information and have complex social relations; consequently, they must think. The more interesting question is, **what do they think about?** We have suggested what they must be able to think about, but a great deal remains to be discovered.

One type of thought, a way in which information and feelings are shifted, reordered and redistributed, is imagination. Do equines have imagination?

Imagination

It is difficult to see how an individual could have a memory without imagination. Memories are never exactly the same as the experience, they become slightly changed, that is imagined: thus how it was believed to have been, takes precedence. Since there is no argument that equines have memories, then they must have some form of imagination: 'a free creative ordering of the contents of mind' (Flew 1983). This may be something simple, who knows, and the individual may not be aware whether it is real or imagined memory.

But how far does equine imagination go? One way of assessing equine imagination might be to assess whether they 'see things' that are not apparently there, but, it would not be surprising if equines and humans see some different things. Imagination is conjuring up, from the individual's point of view, 'as if' realities. Horses are well known for 'seeing things', they spook at the unfamiliar, or even the familiar in a different place; stopping with ears pricked, staring and sometimes snorting and jumping away. It is of course, possible that they are simply seeing things that others do not see, that is movements, insects and so on, but the interesting thing is that they will often do this when the location of an object has been changed. This may just be surprise at a familiar object in a different place, but Oberlix demonstrates one occurrence that may indicate something more than this.

Example

Oberlix is an individual I know well, and I have experienced his reaction to rocks on Dartmoor where he has been ridden and taken for expeditions, even when he was a foal. There are many granite boulders of different shapes scattered over the moor, often visible from a distance. Oberlix is familiar with lumps of granite and has never had a bad experience with one, as far as I can tell (and either I or one of our researchers has been with him every time he has encountered one). But, he sometimes shys as he comes up to either an unknown boulder, or a familiar one from a different angle or in a different light. After stopping, staring and sometimes snorting at it for a second or two, he will often go up to it without more ado.

Is this because he does not recognize it as a boulder, in which case what is he seeing it as? If it is something unfamiliar why does he not do this to all new boulders he encounters, which he does not?

But since he is so used to boulders, and he has never had a bad experience with one of them, perhaps he is seeing shapes in them that are unfamiliar and curious, or even identified frightening objects, such as potential predators. It reminds me of the faces in rocks that some see, or those pictures in which, when looked at in a particular way, whole faces or figures are suddenly discernible. Even the exercise of a cube which can be looked at either as back to front or front to back is relevant here, or the famous duck/rabbit: a drawing that when looked at in one way can look like a rabbit, and when looked at differently looks like a duck. Oberlix may be seeing alternative images in the rock shapes but, often, when he is ridden around the rock, the vision appears to vanish and he behaves normally.

This may be just unfamiliarity of shape, but why are some shapes more frightening than others? There is here an indication of another mental visual interpretation: some visual imagination. Because they are so visually aware and able, and have good memories, it would appear likely that equines have some visual imagination. How much mental imagery/imagination they use, we have no idea, but at least we can begin to critically collect possible relevant observations.

Dreaming

Dreaming can be thought of as imagination when asleep. Dogs are renowned for showing behaviour resembling the type of thing they might be doing in a dream: galloping with their legs, tail wagging, growling, whining or barking. These movements have often been explained in terms of 'reflex responses' independent of any higher mental involvement. Although why these should be 'reflex movements' without any mental experience in dogs but not humans is unclear since we do know they occur in rapid eye movement (REM) sleep when humans dream and show similar physical responses.

Since vocalizations arose in order to communicate with others (see Chapter 7), and in equines indicate general feelings (see page 299, Figure 7.10), if there are vocalizations in sleep, then the individual must be experiencing some feeling.

Feeling things during sleep is generally considered to be dreaming and may, or may not, take the form of an imagined event or series of events: a narrative.

Example

Some evidence of dreaming comes again from Oberlix who has slept at night in a stable adjacent to our bedroom with an adjoining window which either he or I could put our heads through to greet the other. As a result, we have had many opportunities to monitor his behaviour in sleep. On approximately twelve occasions I heard him nicker (low contact call, see Figure 7.10) when lying down with his eyes closed and apparently asleep. Because of the size of a horse's eyes it is relatively easy to see if there are rapid eye movements, and on four occasions I have noted this to be the case after hearing him nicker, and seeing him apparently asleep when I leaned out of the window (see also Skipper 1999). We also have similar data from four other horses now (2004).

What mental experiences equines are interweaving, and whether they remember or create narratives from it, is a question to be unravelled in the future. They certainly do not report their dreams but, perhaps, nevertheless, they have them.

DO EQUINES HAVE OR ACQUIRE CONCEPTS?

One definition of a concept is 'units of information in the mind which are recognized as a result of having more than one character in common'.

As early as the 1950s Koehler (1951) found rats and primates had the concept of numbers up to seven, at least. But it was not until the 1970s that experimental work began on whether pigeons could learn either natural concepts (such as trees) or unnatural ones (such as hats). They were shown coloured slides and had to peck if there was a tree or a hat in the picture. Other concepts such as 'same' or 'different' can also be learnt by pigeons, rats, and even horses. Pepperburg (1993) found her parrot Alex, could learn to discriminate three categories or concepts of different objects presented to her at one time. These were: shape, colour and texture. Today there are many laboratories experimentally exploring further concept acquisition in various different animals.

Little specific experimental work has been done on concept acquisition in equines although Haangi (1996) showed experimentally that horses can learn to categorize stimuli into open-centre vs. solid-centre classes and recognize 'same' from 'different' and we have indicated that they can learn numbers and colours (Figure 9.2). Also the complexity of their normal feral lives indicates that they must be able to form concepts of some sorts, e.g., recognition of the classes 'adult female', or 'young male' (see Figure 8.1).

Because of the way humans and equines are, there will be different limits, or at least different emphases on concept formation. For example, humans learn from a very young age about the concept of number and their education continues for at least fifteen years learning about quantity and how to use this in different ways to manipulate the world. Horses, because of their emphasis on visual phenomena may have elaborate visual concepts of movement, colour, texture and direction, and may use these in ways that we might normally be unable to (although we might be able to learn). They may also have a whole range of concepts relating to smells or noises and vibrations that we do not have.

One thing that we must be cautious about is the widely held belief that we cannot learn others' concepts of the world. Individuals of any species learn to learn, and with particular experience they will develop particular habits of mind; it may take some longer than others but we now have evidence that language is not crucial for concept learning.

Fig. 9.2 Oberlix touching the colour green when given the choice of four and asked to touch green from 5 m away. He has learnt the word 'green' for the colour and can pick it out from red, blue and yellow. His next task will be to identify 'same' and 'different'. He will be given several objects that are green and several that are other colours and will have to pick out the green ones.

Another test we have started is for him to identify the symbols of 1-5 and this he can do with a 90% success rate. Now we will see if he can learn the 'number concept', i.e. touch the '1' and strike your leg once, touch '2' and strike twice and so on.

Example

Equines can acquire a functional concept or category of objects which are not generally found in their natural environment. They recognize the concept of a 'bucket'. It is not only one 'bucket' they recognize, and it may be any colour, shape and size, but it is recognized because of its function: 'something to carry food or water in'. In order to perform this function, buckets must have certain characters in common, for example, they must have some area where food or water can be carried, and somewhere the equine can put his mouth to get hold of some of this. This means equines learn the concept of 'bucket' because it is functionally defined.

They can go one step further and learn to recognize subcategories of buckets: one type of bucket carries water, another one carries food, but either may be of a different colour, size, and shape. In our stables we tend to use slightly broken buckets for carrying food but the water buckets are often newer, stronger and do not leak. It does not take long before the equines who are often exposed to buckets by having regular feeds learn to recognize whether the bucket coming their way is likely to contain food or water.

Equines may also form rather different concepts from us which result in rather different solutions to problems. This is something that has struck various people who teach or study animals (e.g. Hearne 1987, Kiley-Worthington 1997).

Example
When asking an experienced Quarter Horse to cut out a steer by pointing him in the steer's direction, he will, if during his training he has been allowed and even encouraged to make decisions and use his judgement, be able to cut the steer out from the others with no further aids from the rider who simply stays in balance with him. But he may do this in rather a different way from the way the rider would have done it, using perhaps his own recognition of units of information with more than one common character, that is, a concept. Nevertheless, the job will be done, and often done more, or as, quickly as it would have been done using the human approach.

Equines, like other animals, become 'encultured' when in contact with humans or other animals, and can learn human concepts and perform various tasks in the way the humans do them. We realize they have learnt these things. In fact they are, from time to time, better at recognizing their similarity to us, than we are at recognizing our similarity to them (Brechtel & Abrahamsen 1993).

We are no nearer knowing *exactly* what concepts equines may naturally acquire nor the degree to which we can grasp each other's concepts, nevertheless, we do know they learn concepts in their own normal lives, and can learn new ones from humans.

The concept of death
Whether or not equines have some awareness of the future or any conception of death is unknown. They certainly do have an awareness of the absence of particular social partners, friends or infants. Pigs and cattle do show behavioural changes when they become aware of others dying; we know this from research conducted at abattoirs. So far this research has not been conducted on equines

at abattoirs, but there is no reason to believe that they will be very different from these other mammals in this respect. The changes in behaviour may mean they are just frightened, but the question still remains, why are they frightened if they have no concept of death or pain in others? If they see others being killed and are unaware of death or that others have feelings, then there would be no need for responses indicating fear, panic and so on.

Example
On a sad occasion one of our old mares, Omeya (aged twenty-six), was sick and lay down. After being encouraged to try to get up, she refused to do so and died. She was with two of her sons, a four-year-old colt (Oberlix) and her nine-month old last born (Oryx). Both of these colts observed and reacted to her: Oberlix snorted, stared at her and anxiously wandered around her, the younger horse, went up to her and pawed her. They were obviously aware of something strange, and particularly her unreactivity. But the problem remains, were they aware of her death?

It may be that we are not skilled at reading the subtleties of emotions in the visually communicating equines, and they do feel and show an awareness of death; but we need to observe more incidents more closely and to design experiments to help us answer this question. Just anyone's anecdotes are not sufficient.

OTHER EMOTIONS THAT EQUINES MAY EXHIBIT WHICH COULD THROW LIGHT ON THEIR AWARENESS OF OTHERS' OR THEIR OWN MINDS

Imagination and dreaming all employ memory and thinking, but there are other behaviours which generally indicate an awareness of others and the self which equines are often described as feeling. There are sometimes differing possible explanations for the behaviours we consider next, but one is that they require some 'reflective consciousness'.

Throughout this book we have argued that it is not possible to separate the mind from the body; they make up an integrated whole of a living being. Nevertheless, just as you can talk about a part of your body: 'my arm is hurting' for example, without implying that the arm is a separate entity from the whole of your body, so you can talk about the mind without implying that it is separated from the whole being. Here, when discussing whether individuals are aware of their own minds or whether others have minds, we are, again, not implying that minds are separate from bodies.

There are many types of behaviour and emotions that indicate the individual must have a concept of others, and others' minds, feelings, and desires. Firstly, it is clear to anyone who has to do with equines that they are very aware of the human's next likely actions, their intentions and, often, their feelings. If the human is frightened, for example, many equines are more likely to become excited and frightened too. An awareness of others and their intentions is also demonstrated in equine social lives (see Chapter 6). Consequently, it is sensible to conclude that the simplest explanation for these behaviours is that equines do have at least some awareness of others' mental states, or their feelings at least.

Awareness of others and their feelings is often tied up with an awareness of self. Many emotions, such as embarrassment, jealousy and shyness, indicate both. We consider here what evidence we might have that equines may feel such emotions (and some others) that imply they may have an idea of themselves and that others have desires and needs, that is, that others have some sort of a mind. Whether they can be 'reflectively conscious' rests, in part, on such evidence, however difficult it may be to collect and assess.

Love and Charity

Midgley (1978) following Eibl-Ebesfeldt (1971) makes the point that: '. . . love has arisen from parental care, and is, if you will, the emotion which results in social living . . . Caring for the young is the only relation in which such an outgoing motive could have developed. Prolonged, reliable affection, an affection which is *not* a recognition of superiority, more a lively sense of benefits to come, is absolutely necessary for it.' (Midgley 1978, page 339)

> 'Love, a disinterested fondness for others'; and 'Charity, kindness, natural affection, candour, freedom from censoriousness'.
>
> *Oxford English Dictionary*

Love, in the *Oxford English Dictionary* sense, may be the foundation stone of social living. Habits of mind may be established through an individual's life, so that how or whether love is demonstrated varies (particularly in some human societies with their games of bluff), but it arises from parental care and is well demonstrated in the societies of equines as we have seen (see Chapter 6). Not only do they show love for their own young (disinterested fondness) and for those of others, together with charity (freedom from censoriousness, kindness, natural affection), but this also develops into lifelong associations between group members who associate with the others, even when they might be disadvantaged (e.g. have to be without food or water, or, more likely, to suffer predator attack). Equines may develop very strong lifelong affections for each other, become highly distressed when parted, and recognize each other after years apart. They suffer psychologically/emotionally frequently when parted from individuals they are fond of, sometimes this grief can even lead to an individual's death; they will not eat, and become extremely lethargic, showing all the same behaviours as humans suffering from intense grief and depression. Parting horses who are fond of each other can be as traumatic as parting humans who are fond of each other.

The intricacies of human love and charity involve cultural differences. Equines may not have verbal exchanges, but they *do* have relationships involving affection and caring which are not only directed towards their own offspring. These emotions may require memory of past experiences, and predictions of future behaviour of the individual, thus requiring some sort of reflection.

The difference between 'love' and 'fondness' is not at all clear for humans, so until we have sorted this out, we cannot deny that equines might also feel love since they certainly do demonstrate fondness and affection for others.

Compassion and empathy

Equines are social species whose societies are based on keeping the group together by cohesive behaviours (see Chapter 6). In order to achieve this, they necessarily have to be aware of others' intentions, desires and needs. It would consequently be highly unlikely that they are not also aware of the suffering or pain of others. Whether they perform behaviours that identify this, is, however, not obvious. But, even though they may not respond by manipulating, that is, 'trying to help', this does not mean that they are unaware of, or unsympathetic to, the others' mental and physical states.

The aftermath of a predator's attack is likely to be the one time when members of a group might be expected to show behaviour characteristics of empathy or compassion to an injured individual. But, to date, this has not often been reported from studies conducted on wild equines such as zebra. This may be because it has not been looked for. However there are some odd incidences. When chased by predators, equines run. If a foal is left behind, the mother will go more slowly, or run back as the predators advance and try to deflect the predators attention by coming close to, and placing herself between, them and the foal, and she will attack the predators. Once the foal has been attacked, fallen and has little chance of survival, however, she usually gallops off to join the group. Apart from looking in that direction from time to time, it has not been reported that she shows other behaviour indicating compassion or even grief. Van Lawick reports one case, however, when an attack on a zebra foal by wild dogs was foiled by the family group, including the stallion, galloping back and allowing the foal to join up with the group and escape (quoted by Masson and McCarthy 1994, page 156).

Before concluding that equines do not show empathy or compassion, we must consider that: 1) little effort has been given to recording such behaviour to date; 2) it may be that equines do react to, and are very aware of, others' feelings and are compassionate, but we are unable to see or read the signs they give to demonstrate this, just as the people failed to read the signs which Clever Hans was responding to; 3) alternatively, maybe equines have a different concept of what to do when others are feeling pain or suffering. One possibility is that since they are not manipulators of the world they do not make obvious signs of helping but, just by remaining close, they are demonstrating sympathy. It is also possible that because equines are visually acute, they could be demonstrating this to others just by looking in their direction. To date, no one has measured such things with this in mind.

Sharing

Normally, even in cases where there is a scarcity of resources such as at water holes, salt licks and so on, equines, rather than fighting to try to displace another group, will hang around nearby, not necessarily in sight, until the other group moves on. Here, they appear to demonstrate a 'sharing strategy'. Sharing is more frequent when living in the 'vale of plenty' for both equines and humans. When resources become so scarce that their absence is life threatening then sharing is rare, in both equines and humans.

Example

Oberlix will share his bucket of food, even with youngsters who are often frightened of him (Figure 9.3). When only one nose can fit in the bucket at a time, Oberlix will take his nose out of the bucket to eat a mouthful and gives the sharer a chance to eat. When he is very hungry, however, he will not permit anyone to share his food, he attacks them when he takes his head out of the bucket.

The same behaviour is often shown by humans, many of whom do not share when they are short of things (even food) other than with their own offspring.

There are cultural and individual variations in sharing behaviour in both equines and humans: some never share, others almost always share.

In the rich modern human societies there is a cultural dicotomy about sharing: 'good' people give a little of their wealth or possessions to the poor. Anyone who shares it all is often considered mad or stupid!

Fig. 9.3 Oberlix sharing a bucket of food with yearling Shindi

Helping your own species and helping between species

Equines often slow up and wait for each other when injured; as we have mentioned, 'staying near' may be the equine equivalent of helping. But, it also might indicate that they are frightened of leaving a social partner, rather than actively caring. The same may often be true of humans in similar situations.

Example

There are numerous cases of horses staying with other injured horses of the group, and even with injured riders. This has been reported even when the horses have other needs such as hunger or thirst, which would normally motivate them to move off, yet they do not leave.

Horses do, however, learn to help humans in certain ways.

Examples

1. It is possible to teach an equine to place himself close, and parallel, to a gate or mounting block so that a human can get on easily. Subsequently the equine may place himself appropriately, voluntarily, when he sees that the human is going to try to mount (see Figure 8.3). This is of course operant conditioning learning, but the horse will often place himself correctly even when doing this in a new place. This involves judging the height of the human and the distance they will have to stretch over, and adjusting his position accordingly.

   When I injured my leg, I found it more difficult to clamber on to Oberlix, even when he lined himself up appropriately to the gate. After two trials in which I had to ask him to move nearer, he then made the adjustment himself.

2. Draught and carriage horses place themselves in appropriate places to have the traces attached and, in some cases, draught horses will co-operate with the human in pulling together at appropriate moments. In the modern driving competitions, the horses and humans certainly co-operate by working as a team: for example, the inside horse turns and then slows to let the outside horse make the turn; they slow up together at tricky places without human instructions, and speed up at others, taking account of the width of the vehicle behind them and judging their turning position as a result.

These behaviours are learnt by operant conditioning and/or associative learning, but the interesting thing is not only that the horses learn to do them, but also that thereafter they will do them appropriately and voluntarily, making decisions and judgements and being aware of the human's intentions and body limits, thus helping the human, but not all equines are equally good at this.

Humans also help equines in various situations.

Example

If a horse becomes tangled in wire, his immediate reaction is to struggle and panic to get out. However, horses can learn to stand still and await help when tangled, and some will also learn to call, thus summoning assistance from a human. Again this is associative learning, and learnt helplessness (see pages 172 and 210) but, nevertheless, they have had to go through various mental exercises such as: 1) controlling their natural panic, and 2) understanding the concept of help and release by 3) summoning assistance. When Shemal was stuck in the wire, out of sight of anyone in the field, she called five times. As a result, someone went up to the field, found that she had caught the wire between her foot and her shoe and released her.

Such behaviours may be rare, but if it occurs at all, it indicates that these animals have some awareness of other conscious beings, and a recognition of the differences between, for example, a human and another equine: a human can release the trapped individual, another equine is unlikely to be able to do this.

Gratitude and reciprocal altruism

Thanks for services rendered may not be something that equines show explicitly. But, in their own social lives they do reciprocate with altruistic acts: 'you scratch my back and I'll scratch yours' (figure 6.6). 'Do as you would be done by' and 'be done by as you did', (see Chapter 6) are something like gratitude, or 'be nice to me and I'll be nice to you'. Individual equines who have been helped by humans often become very attached to them. This may be only trust and amicability, but how can we separate these from gratitude in man or beast?

Reciprocal altruism is a fairly well-established way in which most human societies and many animal societies work. Some argue that it will, over time, be selected for because it will help with the survival and reproductive success of individuals (Trivers 1991) but this tells us little about its everyday importance, or lack of it, in the society. The simplest immediate explanation for reciprocal altruism is awareness of others and their individual needs and likely response. This means, of course, that they are aware of the others' mental states.

Example

One mare approaches another and begins to groom her. The second mare grooms in return. A few hours later, the situation is reversed, the recipient now goes up to the first mare and grooms her first.

The immediate cause for this reciprocal behaviour is that both feel like grooming and being groomed. They feel like this for various reasons: 1) because of an itch, 2) to establish and cement bonds between each other, or 3) just because they like each other. Again, whatever the immediate cause, there have to be mental events and awareness of others.

Loyalty

Loyalty is defined as: 'true, faithful to duty, love or obligation; faithful in allegiance'. (*Oxford English Dictionary*).

Equines do appear to show loyalty in the sense of 'faithful in allegiance' to their social partners, members of their group and friends. They may not have sovereigns or states, but they do have groups and social partners.

Examples

Mares who live in a stable group, generally will not allow any stallions but the one they live with to come near them, even if they are in season and their stallion is not there. We have taken our mares to events without their stallion and where there have been other stallions around, the mares have been extremely aggressive to them.

Curiously, since stallions are generally considered to be very competitive with other stallions for the attention of mares, stallions who do not get on with each other at all at home, will get on remarkably well away from it.

Example

On one occasion two of our stallions (Cariff and Oberlix, who lived apart at home, and who normally attacked each other given the opportunity) were aggressive towards other mares coming too close when they were together away from home. They even called to each other when parted, and greeted each other exuberantly when they met again.

Both of these animals had experience of going away to events by themselves or with others from the stables and were normally relaxed, so this response was *not* the result of being frightened or shy of others. It was more like some form of 'loyalty in alliance'.

Groups will also be extremely 'loyal' to their own group members and protect them against intruders, which is why, when new members are introduced, much time and space is required to allow the new individual to become part of the group.

Showing off and pride

Showing off involves pride which is defined as: 'an overwhelming opinion of one's own qualities.' (*Oxford English Dictionary*)

Thus, pride must demonstrate an awareness of self. Certainly there seems to be a degree of pride shown when a stallion trots in an exaggerated passage towards a mare, which is often described as 'showing off' (Figure 9.4), (e.g. Rees 1983), but it may simply be an excited reaction to particular stimuli on the part of the stallion. Nevertheless, it does involve a 'display of confidence'. Equines are aware of differences in confidence between individuals in social situations from their body postures (see Chapters 6 and 7).

Confidence in social situations involves having an opinion of one's own qualities in that situation, but whether this is ever recognized by the performer as, or ever becomes, the 'overwhelming opinion' implied by pride we do not know, although from time to time a horse is encountered whose confidence in

Fig. 9.4   Oberlix does a lovely extended passage to greet the mares. Is he consciously 'showing off' or just excited about seeing them. Either way, it certainly has the desired effect!

himself in social situations seems difficult to shake. Is this just a lack of awareness of the social innuendos? Sometimes it may indeed be so, but this is not universal in equine societies, rather the reverse (see Chapter 4 page 199), many lack confidence in social situations.

As we have already discussed, humans and equines respond to others' approval, and will work to achieve this, performing complex behaviours to do so (see page 211), and certainly respond with confidence and apparent 'pride' to the approval afterwards. Where equines are performing in circuses and other events such as dressage, show jumping, racing and other competitive sports, experienced equines will, like humans, respond to audience applause by making more effort or exaggerating certain movements. This certainly demonstrates their awareness of others' responses, even those of another species.

Example
Shemal, who was Sleeping Beauty in one of our multi-species ballets, took to eating the leafy scenery on stage. She was scolded by the stage hands for this, and ran off kicking her legs in the air. This attracted the audiences' attention and they laughed. She then repeated it, and soon there was no stopping her as she responded more and more enthusiastically to the audiences' laughter.

Suffice to say, at this stage, that individuals display obvious signs of confidence and read these signs displayed by others, although whether we can call this showing off or pride remains controversial.

Shyness
Shyness is often just a lack of confidence, or slight fear, which we know equines feel. It is read by others and may involve caution, anxiety and suspicion. It involves the same behaviour as that of humans: looking away, withdrawing, not approaching, watching the other when they are not being watched. In equines it is sometimes also accompanied by champing, particularly by young equines (see Figure 4.8).

Although it often just demonstrates slight fear, the reason it is discussed here is because it may be used to achieve certain goals as a type of 'pretend shyness'. This is used by human children who do other things in a half-hearted way when they know they are being watched, a kind of pretence of ignoring the watcher.

Again this implies some awareness of self and the other's intentions. Young equines, and even adults who want to become more integrated into the group, may champ when they are approached, approach others or are even watched by others. It may sometimes involve some form of pretence, for example, 'pretending' to be frightened to initiate a game of chase, or more contact.

Example

Shindi, a young filly, wants to eat some hay near where Oberlix is eating. She knows that if she just walks up and helps herself, he may flatten his ears and bite her, so she champs as she approaches, he sniffs her mouth but continues eating, so she begins to eat too. She was demonstrating awareness of him and his likely intentions, as well as slight fear, and achieved her goal as a result. Her actions demonstrated a type of shyness/submission, a demonstration of inferiority in order to achieve her goal.

Shyness, like jealousy may be performed to attract attention to oneself, such as mares courting stallions, who, when very interested, walk away: a sort of 'stop it, I like it' emotion (characteristic of humans also in similar situations).

Jealousy

As we have mentioned, (see page 43) you must be careful not to assume that equines feel real 'jealousy', as their behaviour may either just be frustration at not being able to acquire attention or reward, or may be redirected aggression (see page 208). Jealousy involves having some idea of being replaced in the affections of another, again implying an awareness of how others are feeling. This is not to argue that equines are not capable of feeling jealous, it is just that, so far, there is no evidence that does not have other explanations.

Shame and guilt

Many will maintain that their animals, particularly dogs, show 'shame' when they have done forbidden things, even if it is not known they have done it. But, does this indicate that they wish they had not done it for its own sake, that is real shame, or rather, are they aware they have done something that is not acceptable, and are anticipating punishment? Even if this is the case, however, it indicates some awareness of self, and of what they have done. That is, they can discriminate an action that they have done, perhaps some time in the past, that humans find unacceptable and they will be punished for, from an action that the humans will not find unacceptable. This may be the result of conditioning, but it often involves making judgements about different actions and different people.

Whether this is true shame or guilt is a difficult question to answer in the case of humans as well as other animals. It is often the case that displays of shame and guilt in humans are also related to efforts to eliminate or reduce punishment.

There are odd cases in interactions with humans where horses appear to have been 'ashamed' of what they had done to a human by, for example, knocking them over, kicking them, or hurting them in some way. They demonstrate this by watching the human and even approaching and touching or nuzzling them afterwards.

If these species are aware of some rules of their societies (which we have demonstrated they must be to be social) or even rules they have learnt when in contact with humans, then it is possible that they experience something more than just fear of punishment, but this remains a challenging question and evidence needs to be accumulated before we can even discuss it further.

Justice and resentment

In association with humans, equines can demonstrate that they know when they have broken a social rule (such as kicking a human or standing on a foot). They know they will be punished, and act afterwards by apologizing (possibly showing shame or guilt) or avoiding, withdrawing, or even attacking out of defensive threat. This is another area that has not received reliable reporting. It would be likely that they have some sense of 'just reward', justice or just punishment since they have social rules in their own societies and learn other rules of behaviour with humans. Consequently, they may have some elementary idea of rights and wrongs (see Chapter 11, see also Kiley-Worthington 2000).

Again this is an area that has not been seriously considered in any species to date, and without further evidence one way or another, we cannot make a judgement.

Deceit

Deceit, and evidence for it, has, by contrast, been considered frequently by those studying primates. It has been used as a way of assessing whether or not the animal studied has the ability to be aware of others needs and desires (e.g. Bryne & Whyten 1988). One of the best known examples is the subordinate male chimp who waits for a female behind a rock out of sight of the alpha male, in order to mate with her without the alpha male being able to see (Kummer 1982).

Example

We have seen the same type of behaviour in young stallions who will constantly try to approach and court the mares, particularly those in oestrus, but they know that if the resident stallion sees them, they are likely to be fiercely attacked. They must escape his notice, this means they are aware of him 'minding', that is having a particular mental state. Consequently, they will keep a weather eye on him and will not attempt to court the fillies if they see he is watching. When, however, they are out of his sight, they will flirt enthusiastically, but the mares are often not so keen and will frequently turn their backs, lash out and squeal (being loyal members of their group). The squeal attracts the stallion's attention, who comes rushing over as the youngster beats a hasty retreat!

Deceit is not common in equines however, although humans employ it almost every day of their lives, either in order to please someone (because they believe it to be kind), as well as to try to get the better of others.

However, it may not be a necessary or important type of strategy to adopt in equine society where there is no need to store or hide scarce resources. Of great importance, however, is cohesive behaviour: keeping the group together (see Chapter 6). Honesty may well be an equine's best policy if he wants to be able to stay in the group. Equine deceit might be ignoring aggression, which happens frequently (see page 269), or the less frequent emotional lying (see page 172) which does occasionally occur.

Possession, stealing and trespass

Because of the lifestyle of equines, there is little emphasis on possession of goods, unlike many primates, carnivores and birds where food, shelter, nesting sites and so on, are patchily dispersed, limited, and consequently often competed for.

Without an emphasis on possession and rightful ownership, it is not possible to steal. Two horses who know each other and are fond of each other may share buckets of water and feed, even when food may be scarce. More usually, however, when food is scarce, they behave like most human societies in similar conditions: defending ownership and stealing. Put a couple of buckets of food into a field with eight horses and there will be some competition, followed by ownership, and efforts at least to steal by some. This has been described as the establishment of a 'dominance hierarchy', with a 'boss' animal. We have argued that this is a product of confined conditions and the increase in aggression that results from it (Kiley-Worthington 1999, and page 269). It is not something that usually happens in free-ranging equine societies where individual personalities and roles tend to encourage co-operation in order to keep the group together, rather than competition (see page 271). But either dominance hierarchies or co-operation, may demonstrate possession and sometimes stealing. Either way, there has to be some awareness of others intentions: some degree of reflective consciousness.

Another form of possession, common in human societies, is possession of land. Feral equines are not generally territorial, that is do not defend 'their' area of land against intruders, although they know their own home areas well, and travel throughout them. But there are conditions under which they do become more possessive of land area. For example, where the population density is high, feral horses (*Equus caballus*) do take up territories of land which they defend against other intruders. The Grevy's zebras (*Equus grevii*) and the wild ass (*Equus africanus*) who live in arid savannah are also reputed to take up territories from time to time, but Burchell's zebra (*Equus burchelli*) and the mountain zebra (*Equus zebra*) who tend to live in terrain where food is more evenly distributed throughout the year, do not (Rubenstein 1986). Recent studies indicate that the degree of equine territoriality varies between populations of the same species and depends largely on availability of resources (e.g. Estes 1991). Humans behave in the same way in similar situations. The important thing here is that an intruder *knows* when he is intruding, and *recognizes possession,* so behaves differently when intruding.

Domestic and feral horse stallions (*E. caballus*) are **socially possessive**, that is they defend the area around the group of mares with which they live against intruding horses. They will chase off strange mares as well as stallions (see page 260). The mares are equally possessive of the stallion, chasing off other mares and stallions, sometimes banding together to do this, that is, forming coalitions. Both mares and stallions appear to be particularly loyal to their own groups. The stealing of mares by other stallions, or stallions by mares is a possibility, but rare.

Example

Oryx is put in a field where the senior stallion, Oberlix, has been living with his mares. Oryx does not approach the mares, rather he spends ten minutes sniffing the faeces, particularly Oberlix's piles, all around the field. When he does approach the mares, he is extremely cautious, Shiraz is interested in him but rushes at him aggressively. He appears to ignore her and walks away grazing. This goes on for a further ten minutes. Oryx makes no moves to approach the mares, they have to make approaches to him before he responds, and they are aggressive, so he moves off. When Oryx is taken out of the field and Oberlix returned, he gallops straight up to the mares, they greet him with nose to nose smelling and some squealing and then settle down to graze.

Embarrassment

This involves not only an awareness of self, but also an awareness of the way others are perceiving you. It is extremely difficult to know if equines feel embarrassment. However they do, from time to time, behave similarly to humans who are embarrassed, although they do not, as far as we can see, blush, but then blushing cannot be seen in dark-skinned people. Equines with their awareness of others' feelings, displayed by visual signals, may not be 'blushing', but doing something else with a similar cause, which, to date, we have not identified. Things like, a slight wrinkling of the nose, turning the head away, or shaking the head in certain contexts might indicate some form of embarrassment to another.

Example

Oberlix, is on the lawn near the table where we are sitting. He starts to eat the dog food from a plate on the ground, but he knows this is forbidden as he has previously been told not to do it, and was scolded when he did. He is aware that we are watching, I scold him verbally, he kicks his legs up in our direction (he also knows that kicking at people is severely reprimanded). He misjudges his speed, the slipperiness of the ground, and falls over. We laugh. He gets up, looks at us, and then sneezes, and quickly starts 'displacement eating' (incomplete grazing, with apparently great concentration on the very short grass that normally he would not eat). Here, the sneezing appears to be a transitional/displacement behaviour but has social significance. The eating of the very short grass with much energy is not typical in this situation either. Was he embarrassed, aware of the social faux pas? He had done two forbidden things, eaten the dog food and made a feigned threat, and had then fallen over! He showed his social disturbance by 1) looking at us, presumably to assess our reactions, and 2) performing displacement and transitional type behaviours.

An alternative explanation is that he was just frustrated because he was told off for eating the food. If it was this, and there were no social innuendoes, why did he bother to look at us, kick out or perform displacement activities after falling over? It is of course possible that this was chance, but in a socially aware being such as a young stallion, it seems unlikely. We decided to test this and set up the dog food with an electric fence wire in it so he would get a small shock when he touched the food, and with no one watching. He touched it and jumped back staring at the dog food with ears pricked, snorted (a startle-type response) and walked off. Thus, being watched and laughed at, as one breaks the rules and falls over, resulted in different behaviour from just being negatively reinforced. It indicates that he may have felt something like embarrassment, and it certainly showed his awareness of us and our reactions to his behaviour.

There are many examples quoted in equine literature of equines' embarrassment, but without a critical analysis of each we do not know if there is not another simpler explanation. Nevertheless, because of their complex social systems and their awareness of their own bodies and those of others, 'something like embarrassment' is an emotion equines might experience.

SUMMARY
1. Equines are conscious, aware of their own bodies and parts of their bodies, and demonstrate this daily in their learning how to do various actions with humans, the first step in something like reflective consciousness.
2. In answer to the questions at the beginning of the chapter. a) Equines think, that is, they combine information from perceptions and from past experience and analyse it all. Exactly what they think about, how

→

far they can develop this skill, and whether their thinking is very different from our non-verbal thinking, we do not know. Dreaming and imagining, involving the sifting, sorting and selecting of information and experiences, are types of thinking, and it does seem likely, at least until proved to the contrary, that equines dream and imagine even if this is different or less sophisticated than our dreaming and imagining. b) Equines can form simple concepts, and learn human ones. Learning human-type concepts is something that they probably get much better at with practice and exposure to humans.

3. Equines certainly have an awareness of others' bodies, and they must be aware that others have desires and needs just because of the information they acquire during their lives in order to survive and live socially.

4. They have beliefs about things, which are sometimes quite complex, for example in their understanding of others' intentions.

5. The ways generally used to assess whether or not a species has an understanding that others have minds, have been: a) whether they show evidence of deception or b) compassion and sympathy. We have examined if equines show behaviour characteristic of these and other states, which have no other explanation. At present the evidence for a) and b) is slim, but is this because: (i) we have only just started looking, (ii) being deceitful is not part of the equines' world, or (iii) they are showing sympathy and compassion in different ways?

6. One of the interesting things about the debates concerning whether or not equines could be reflectively conscious, is that it makes us think much more carefully about what this means. There appears to be no direct yes or no answer. It may be that it is more about establishing the right 'habits of mind' in individuals. The cultures and lifetime experience of an individual may or may not encourage the reflective consciousness of that individual. The culture may be as powerful an influence on the development of reflective consciousness as the mammalism species to which the individual belongs.

10 Reflective consciousness. Other behaviours indicative of awareness of others' minds and self-awareness

Further to the subjects covered in Chapter 9, there are other types of behaviours or emotions which indicate or imply an awareness of others and the self. The only ones to date that have received any discussion in relation to non-human mammals, are playing and teaching. We will consider what evidence there is for these in equines.

PLAY, PRETEND, AND TEASE

Play has for a long time been recognized as something that many animals, as well as humans, do (e.g. Hinde 1970). It is generally defined as an incomplete behaviour, detached from 'serious' aims and ends, and performed for the pleasure the activity itself gives.

Ethologists have suggested various functions for play ranging from a 'spontaneous and rewarding activity with its own motivation' (Martin & Caro 1985), to 'an unmotivated behaviour occurring when the animal has nothing else to do' (Loizos 1966, Poole & Fish 1975). Most ethologists consider that its function is to allow the individual to learn to perform particular behaviours, or to learn about particular things in the world that will be important to his survival in the future. For example, a kitten plays with objects in a way that will help him to catch mice. A foal runs and leaps around to help him develop his athletic abilities, to balance, to become fast and physiologically fit enough to escape predators. Play may also enhance the flexibility and innovation in behaviour (reviewed by Wemelsfelder 1993).

It may or may not be a necessary behaviour for physical survival but, because of its role in encouraging flexibility, creativity, diversity, individuality and innovation of action, it may be particularly important for acquiring knowledge, and for the individual's mental development.

A function of play which is rarely suggested for animals (although frequently for children), is that it is done 'for fun', it has value in itself, that is, intrinsic value to give pleasure, joy and delight to the player, and often the observers too (Figure 10.1).

Equines, like all other mammals play and the youngsters play more than the adults, but detailed studies of play have not to date been made. Therefore, we will discuss equine play in the light of how other species' play (where play has been more thoroughly studied) is discussed.

There is **object play** (such as picking things up and throwing them around, chasing sticks, leaping up and down on banks, or over streams, rushing around trees or the field, and standing around investigating, chewing or manipulating some object). Object play in equines, often involves athletic galloping, turning,

Fig. 10.1 Gallop play. Lilka galloping for the fun of it.

leaping, kicking and rearing about. Then there is **social play**, that is playing with others. There are two important aspects here: 1) each game has a set of rules to define it as a game (rather than 'real') which each player must know or learn; 2) It must be pleasurable for all participants, or it ceases to be play.

There are **rules for play**, and individuals must adapt their play to their play partner for, if the rules are breached then it is no longer play.

Consequently, social play must involve learning about individuals and predicting their behaviour, that is, becoming good natural psychologists (see Chapter 6).

Examples

1. Two colts (three-year-old Shere Khan and two-year-old Karma) are playing. They are having a fast, rough chase-each-other-about-in-the-field game which leads to leap-up-and-box-each-other-with-the-front-legs, followed by another chase game. Shere Khan comes across a foal (Christmas) and goes up to her and smells her; she leaps about and he trots relatively quietly after her. He has adapted his game to the individual and is less rough. Thus, some understanding of another's abilities, and what is 'pleasurable' – or at least not painful – to another, is necessary, that is, an awareness of others' desires and emotions, including what might cause them pain.

2. Shirac and Shergar who lived together were playing stand-up-on-your-back-legs-and-box-each-other. Shirac is hurt by one of Shergar's front legs hitting his head. It ceases to be play. Shirac makes it clear the game is at an end. He stops leaping and does not respond to Shergar's leaps. Shirac then, with apparent fury, lashes out with his teeth and front legs; Shergar withdraws as the game is clearly at an end – the rules have been broken.

When playing aggressive games, although one player may bite or pull at parts of another roughly, it may be acceptable within the context of the game although the same behaviour out of the play context would not be, but if it becomes too unpleasant, then play will cease, or it will turn into a real fight.

Play may involve **pretence**. To pretend it is necessary to be aware of oneself. (Adam & Bekoff 1997)

Example

Pretending to chase seriously is a game played by both young and adult equines. Shiera (aged four) and Shirac (aged two) gallop about at top speed, one taking the lead and then

Fig. 10.2. Teasing play. Lilka pushes Shezam, who is reluctant to participate in the game.

the other. Then, Shirac becomes trapped in a corner. Shiera gallops past him but she does not attack him (which might be the case if the chase were serious). He then comes out of the corner and chases after her; the roles have been reversed.

Play also may involve **teasing and annoying** another (Figure 10.2). It is acceptable to annoy in play, that is to tease, pull, bite, tussle, kick and so on, up to a point. In part it appears that the behaviour is performed in order to get a reaction. If this goes too far, the recipient may become seriously aggressive. Then the performer's task is to **appease**, in order to continue the game, or to try to introduce another type of game with that individual. Adults often become too annoyed too quickly, or are too unreactive for too long, so they are not the preferred playmates for young humans or equines.

Examples

Colts and stallions will play long fighting games (Figure 10.3), or games of sex: mounting and courting each other. Batchelor groups composed of several youngsters, will spend much time playing chase, and leaping and cavorting in between – their games often resembling a dance. Foals will play the same games, play mounting and leaping-about-on-mother are favourites but mother gets bored with this, and the foals will end up playing this type of game with the stallion who is often more tolerant of their antics.

Fig. 10.3 Aggressive play. Oryx and Shukrune play biting games.

Play between species also occurs, dogs with horses, donkeys and cats, zebras and gnu, humans and horses. Horse play is indeed rough play so when young horses play these games with humans, humans may well get hurt. Nevertheless, because it is play, the equines can easily be taught the rules of the game the human wants to invent. Just as equines learn the rules of the game with a foal who will more easily get hurt, the main rule being 'don't be so rough as you are with others of your own age' a rule for a game with a human could be for example, 'gallop at the human and rear up, but do not touch them'.

These types of games that have been learnt by the horse with the human are sometimes used for performances at various events.

Example

Grab-the-arm-with-your-teeth-but-do-not-touch-any-flesh (i.e. grab only clothing), is a game it is necessary to teach a young stallion for when he is being led around; colts and young stallions usually want to grab something in their teeth. If they are not taught the rules of the game by the human, it may result in the horse setting the rules, which may be unpleasant for the human. The horse's preferred version of the rule in this instance may be 'grab anything you can, hold on and shake'. The human will shout and try to hit, and this allows the invention of other games, such as ways-of-trying-to-get-away, by, pulling, leaping about, rearing out of reach, and then rushing again to grab the human. The result, from the human's point of view, is an unmanageable young stallion who has to be trussed up with restraints before he can be led, and all because the human taught him the wrong game, without knowing that he was learning from them!

Social play is therefore, an awareness of others' bodies, minds and intentions. Without awareness, it is not possible to play, and there would be no social play if there were no awareness of others minds, desires and needs, that is, reflective consciousness.

TEACHING

Active teaching (as opposed to observational learning) of one animal by another of the same species has received very little attention to date. Caro and Hauser (1992) argue that when teaching: 'An animal modifies its behaviour, to no immediate benefit to itself, only in the presence of a naïve observer, and with the result that the observer gains knowledge or learns a skill with greater efficiency than otherwise.'

This rules out ambiguous cases of teaching, such as weaning and fighting because, although it can be argued that the animal may learn not to suckle, or not to attack certain individuals when they attack, it is not because he is 'being taught for his own good' but because, in these cases, the 'teacher' benefits.

And, the catch-22 is the same with observational learning as with communication (see page 276), that is, it is not possible to know if, for example, a mare is doing something *because* she is being watched by, and teaching, her infant, or if she is doing it for herself anyway.

Example
A mare is eating while being watched by her infant. The mother is aware of being watched. Does she emphasize particular movements or avoidance of certain plants rather more than she would otherwise? So far no one knows, but it could indeed be measured and assessed.

Thus we do not know if the mare is 'actively' teaching her foal, or if the foal is learning only by 'observing' mother doing what she usually does, that is by social learning.

Equines have little need to teach complex manipulative skills to their infants but, by contrast, if their foal is to survive, they do have a genetic vested interest in them acquiring ecological knowledge (see Chapter 5) and social knowledge (see Chapter 6). Thus, the mother may have an instinctive tendency to help them learn this, that is, to teach them. Equines are sophisticated visual communicators (see Chapter 7) who learn about the world and its occupants by observing and experiencing it (see Chapter 3). These abilities might lead to more active teaching as the recipient would acquire information fast and with slight cues. On the other hand, it might lead to little need for explicit active teaching (in Caro and Hauser's sense) as other equines will learn anyway by observation, imitating each other and other species. At present we do not know the answer to this. But explicit teaching as we see in chimps and humans, does not appear to take place in equines. Yet, again, no one has looked very carefully.

HUMOUR

Humour involves various acts that might be identified as 'humorous', and certainly must involve an awareness of others and what makes them laugh, so it is worth considering here.

A definition of humour is not easy. It usually involves the occurrence of something unexpected: a mismatch between the expected and the observed. It is not just surprise (see page 198) because it must also cause some sort of pleasure. The mismatch may be between something obviously happening, a mental mismatch, or a mistaken assessment. The *Oxford English Dictionary* defines humour as: 'a state of mind, mood, facetiousness ["addicted to or marked by pleasantry"] comicality.' *The Dictionary of Psychology* (Drever 1960) defines it as: 'Character of a complex situation exciting joyful and in the main quiet laughter, either directly, through sympathy or through empathy'. Neither of these definitions is adequate.

Laughing, an expression of pleasure and humour, has, like crying, been considered one of the distinctive attributes of humans. It is generally true that other species do not vocalize in a particular way to represent their understanding of the humour of a situation. This is not, however, to say that there may not be other ways in which different species display their appreciation of humour. In equines this may be visually, or by smell; they may have smell jokes, a difficult concept for us!

There are, however, other situations than humorous ones when we laugh, and this is usually culturally dependent. We laugh when frightened, embarrassed, happy, nervous, and so on. Not only, therefore, is humour difficult to define, but its obvious expression, laughter, is not confined to humorous situations. Thus the message portrayed by laughter appears, like many vocalizations of animals (see Chapter 7), to be context defined. It is necessary, before understanding the meaning of another's laughter, to make a full assessment of the context in which the laughter is occurring. Laughter, then, may be one of the few human vocalizations that is particularly important in awakening the recipient's awareness of the context, encouraging them to analyse the social and ecological situation.

That humans find this difficult is illustrated by the number of times you hear the question 'what are they laughing at?', and the number of people who seem not to have some 'sense of humour'. Another common occurrence is an inappropriate response to laughter, indicating that the recipient has mistakenly interpreted the meaning, as, for example, when you think someone is laughing at you, but in fact he is laughing at something else which has nothing to do with you.

Humans have various sorts of humour that can be divided into particular categories: slapstick, that is, the slipping-on-a-banana-peel type of humour; verbal joke telling; and ironic or satirical humour, among others.

Since equines do not use verbal language, we will consider whether or not they show any evidence of appreciating slapstick-type humour. But, the first problem is since it is difficult to know what might be equivalent to a laugh for them, how do we know whether there is a response to humour, that is, whether they are able to understand jokes or play jokes on each other? What we can do is look at any equine behaviour directed towards humans that might be related to humour.

Examples

1. Do equines show a response to human laughter? Yes they do, they learn rapidly that human laughter, and chuckling, indicates pleasure. As a result, chuckling and laughter can be used as a reinforcer when teaching (see page 118). This is associative learning: the

human laughs and they associate this with giving the human pleasure. Children often learn humour in a similar way.

Equines must understand something about humour to get the humans to laugh *again*. Repeating the same behaviour may work for a time, but eventually it is no longer funny, but performing a novel behaviour may be. Again, this is something they learn quickly in performances. If they raise a laugh (or a clap) they will tend to do the same again, when it ceases to raise a clap or a laugh they quickly learn to do something different. There is some indication that Oberlix and Shemal have learnt to perform novel behaviours to raise a laugh.

2. Oberlix has learnt to yawn when anyone asks him (Figure 3.21). This generally makes people smile, chuckle and laugh. If he yawns once when he sees some people looking at him, they laugh and he repeats it. He will go on thereafter until they cease to laugh. When I have been conducting workshops, he may be standing behind me as I lecture, and on eight occasions so far, he has started to yawn and received a round of applause from the audience who were listening to me. He repeats it again and again, to the point of totally disrupting the lecture!

3. An indication of performing behaviour to raise a laugh from humans is when Oberlix gives a little kick/buck as he comes down the centre line at the end of a dressage test. This nearly always raises a laugh or an obvious response both from the audience and his rider. Another interesting thing is how he knows that it is the last time he has to come down the centre line as we have had to come down it before during the tests on several occasions, and neither he nor I know the tests by heart!

4. Shemal has performed in various ballets and plays. She has become very aware of the audiences' response, and will often act up to this. Thus, if being applauded and laughed at for eating the scenery (made of leaves), for example, she will shake her head, trot off to the next clump, repeat this, and get more laughter. She will then be stopped by someone and told off for doing this. She will then gallop off shaking her head, bucking and leaping around the ring: this earns her more and louder laughter. If she kicks her heels up at the person ticking her off (something she knows, and everyone else knows, is against the rules), she receives more laughter and is loudly applauded. Once this happens the whole performance begins to resemble a human comedy act which gets slightly out of hand!

Oberlix and Shemal have learnt this by association, but they do new things frequently; they have a definite awareness of causing pleasure. Thus, by causing laughter, they have learnt something about humour, in much the same way as children do.

So there is some evidence then that equines are, at least, able to learn something like humour when in association with humans. So far, no one has looked at how we might be able to assess humour, or a lack of it, in their own societies.

The final question on reflective consciousness, which we have already discussed indirectly, is: to what extent are equines aware of themselves? We have already argued that equines must be aware of their own bodies since they lead the lives they do, and learn the things they do, particularly those with humans. But are they aware of their own minds, desires and needs, their emotions, their intentions, their lives? This is called 'introspective self-awareness'.

INTROSPECTIVE SELF-AWARENESS

Are equines able to reflect on themselves? Gallup's (1979) much quoted way of approaching this question was to show apes their reflection in a mirror and see how they responded to it, and then to alter the individual's appearance to see if they showed any evidence of having noticed the change. If they did, they were self-aware, if they did not show they recognized a difference, they were not self-aware. Since apes and humans are very closely related (both are manipulators of the world, and consequently may have much in common in their world view), apes might be expected to react to changes in their appearance much like human children do, that is, by touching the changed area. Gallup marked some chimps faces with coloured marks and then, giving them a mirror, found that they touched the mark. Consequently he concluded that the chimps were self-aware.

However, when such experiments were done with elephants (Povinelli 1989), the elephants used the mirror to allow them to see around corners they would not otherwise have been able to see around, and move objects using the mirror, rather than touching themselves. It was concluded that elephants were therefore not self-aware! The extraordinary naïvety of this assumption is worrying. It is difficult to move objects using mirror images, and particularly difficult if they are completely out of sight, but the elephants learnt to do this. Consequently, they must have been aware that the image was their body, and how they must move their trunk (back to front) in order to move objects seen in a mirror out of sight. Rather than proving that the elephants show no self-awareness, this indicates that elephants are able to reflect and use parts of their body to achieve certain goals even in a mirror image. But, they are not particularly interested in their own images and any changes that may have happened to it. *Their* self-image may have more emphasis in their interaction with others and with the whole living world: a different world view. This is another example of assuming that the only 'advanced' way of thinking and experiencing the world is the way humans do it. It points to a serious concern for the respectability of some scientific judgements!

Because of the use of large mirrors in arenas which allow the human to see what they look like, and correct faults, when they are riding, horses are often exposed to mirrors and their own reflection. As a result there are many anecdotes about horses reacting to mirrors (e.g. Skipper 1999). Generally, when inexperienced, they react to their reflection 'as if' it were another horse, and greet it, vocalizing, ears pricked and approaching, followed by nose to nose sniffing. After a few minutes however, they tend to show no further *very obvious* interest in the reflection, but they do watch it, and also the reflection of the rest of the world in the mirror. Some keep an eye on the reflection of the door when they cannot see it directly, and by this means assess what other individuals are coming or going, and react to their presence or absence accordingly in the mirror image. They also turn around to see the real being from the image, thus demonstrating an awareness of what the image is of; that is, the fact that it is *an image*. Here, they may or may not be all that interested in their own appearance, but, like the elephants, they *have* learnt to use the mirror as an extra eye, a different approach to 'self'. There are many experiments that could be done, but so far this has not been an area of enquiry. At the research centre, we have a few observations.

Example

Our horse subjects have seen reflections of themselves in large glass windows. Both Oberlix, the stallion, and his daughter Shemal reacted to their image by calling to it, trotting up to the window, sniffing and even squealing at it. However, within about three minutes, they walked off, although often staying within sight of the image and continued to graze, doze and so on. Oberlix on three separate occasions positioned himself near the reflection in order to doze close by, in much the same way as he might with another horse. However, it is difficult to believe that he had no recognition of the reflection as himself because he stopped giving his attention to the reflection much more quickly than he would have done to another horse. In addition, he would have been aware of the reflection of everything else around in the garden, including people, dogs, distribution of the plants, and so on, cues that in such a visually alert animal are more than likely recognizable as reflections: 'same but not solid'. His interest in being near the reflection indicated his preference for being near another horse, even if it was only a reflection, or may be it indicated his narcissism! Either way, it is certainly not possible to conclude that he had no recognition of himself. It may be that he is aware of himself, and occasionally reflects on himself in some form, but he is not of central interest to himself. It may be the whole world around and his involvement with it that is his central concern, a different type of world view.

Reflective consciousness coming, as it must, from co-ordinations between mental events, must arise from time to time in equines when decisions and choices are made involving memories, perceptions and imaginations. The question is not 'does it exist?' so much as where and when might it be demonstrated in equines as well as humans?

Tools, their making and use

The making and using of tools is another way in which it is now widely believed we can assess whether or not the species has some introspective self-awareness as an individual has to have some idea of function, of structure and of what can lead to what, in order to make or use a tool. As we have mentioned, humans are world manipulators and they have the physical apparatus to make this relatively easy, that is, hands with opposable thumbs. Some apes and birds have also been shown to be able to make and use tools, both in their own environments and in experimental ones. Elephants are also able to manipulate things with their trunks and become extremely able at making tools to help them achieve ends, such as appropriately shaped sticks to scratch themselves with and the use of ropes and chains to attach to logs, lift them and move them around for their human handler when working in forests.

Equines, as we have pointed out, are not world manipulators, they have other skills: running, jumping, being aware of many things at once etc. However that is not to say that they never make or use tools. A well-known example is the horse who has learnt to let himself out of his stable by undoing the bolt on the door, and another is horses like ours who learn how and when to be able to creep under or over electric fences. However, one of the best examples of tool making and using comes from one of our traveller student's horses: Gaynor, a big old cob mare who came to live with us one summer. She was used to being tethered and had taught herself how to use the tether to scratch her hind leg pasterns where she often had mud fever and it was very itchy (Figures 10.4a, b and c). In this case the mare had to have a considerable grasp of basic physical principles of direction of pull and amount of pull and its consequences and so on. She also had to have taught herself exactly how to manipulate the rope or chain when it was tied around her neck; a rather tricky operation since pressure will cause the loose collar to rotate around her neck if it is not in exactly the right direction.

Tool use may take on a rather different aspect in equines, but it is not something that has been studied much to date. It would be unwise, however, to assume that these animals do not have the mental apparatus to make or use tools until a great deal more study has been done. Since they learn to imitate humans, there is another likely road for their development of tool use when in the company of humans.

It is clear that different individuals have different consciousnesses about different things and environments. Yet the culture and experiences that an individual has, affects the type of consciousness they have and the knowledge they have about the world. For example, within any one culture the experiences and consciousness of a young child, a female, a male, or a disabled person, will be different. They will be aware of different things in their environments which will be of different importance to them and interpret them accordingly.

Jackson (1992) points out that there may be much about the world that lies beyond the understanding of humans. Nagel (1974) states: 'the wild extends beyond the limits of our minds'. But, can we not expand the boundaries of our minds, and cannot other species too? Recently there has been a recognition that it is possible for humans to change their level of consciousness in different ways. This can be done with drugs but also in ways which develop different habits of

Figs. 10.4a, b and c Tool use and self-awareness. An interesting incident, not uncommon in travellers' horses. Over years of being tethered, Gaynor has found out that she can scratch her itchy heels with the rope. To do this she has to manipulate herself into the right position, get the rope around her heel, then keep the tension correct between her collar (where the rope is attached) and her heel. She is using the tether rope as a tool, showing that she is self-aware, and demonstrating her ability to manipulate the available resources to satisfy her needs. In this case she has taught herself, although she may have seen others doing something similar at some time. a) Using the chain as a tool, Gaynor adjusts her hind legs to get it in the required position. This requires knowledge of basic physics. b) Gaynor has managed to manoeuvre the chain over her left hind leg and adjust the tension. c) Everything set to start scratching.

mind, such as: awakening the consciousness of the way the body is held and moved (e.g. the Alexander technique, judo, yoga); ways of improving, developing and using the imagination and its awareness (Shamanistic journeys); traditional eastern techniques for controlling and concentrating the mind in meditation, or fighting symbolically or in reality without weapons (e.g. kung fu); feeling energy differences in human beings and other animals (auras); or channelling energy through to another (reiki). What all these disciplines (and there are many more) have in common is that their aim is to change the type of consciousness in order to be able to achieve an improvement of some sort in your own or others' lives, or deaths (e.g. Rinpoche Sogyal 1992). Many of these techniques have achieved these aims for many people so cannot be dismissed. Whatever else they do, they change the level or type of consciousness and the field of attention; they encourage different habits of mind.

These different schools of thought illustrate that there are many types of consciousness. Consequently, making judgements concerning the level of consciousness, even within humans, seems to have little meaning. It will have even less meaning between species since each species' type of consciousness is likely to be different. Equines who have had much to do with humans will be more able to tune in to the teacher's particular consciousness, so are good subjects to begin this study. We may need interpreters who are familiar with both species to begin with, but at least we can start the quest for such understanding and experiences.

Rather than emphasizing species differences – particularly that between humans and other mammals – a more constructive way to begin to seriously understand the world of different animals starts with appreciating similarities which, as we have seen, are numerous between equines and humans, and to respect differences. But, again, we must be careful not to bring a catalogue of preconceived notions and folk beliefs to this study, nor to interpret the world in unquestioning human terms.

One of the exciting reasons for developing our interactions and lives with other species is the widening of the horizons, enrichment of our own lives and the resulting different consciousnesses that may arise. We may learn different ways of perceiving and interpreting the world, different ways of interacting with others: different languages, different habits of mind, different consciousnesses.

The everyday feats of different individuals of different species will not only teach us more about that species, but, also, more about ourselves.

The only valid conclusion appears to be that the separations between the consciousness that humans and equines have is a great deal more fuzzy than it is sometimes believed or argued. One of the overriding problems here is ignorance but, unlike trying to consider what future generations of humans would prefer, we do not need to be bound by such ignorance, the animals are here for us to ask.

This of course is the challenge of good equine education, it is not only about the easiest and pleasantest way for both us and the equine we are teaching, it is fundamentally about allowing them and us to have different, new and enriching experiences as here and there we have a glimpse of different ways of interpreting the world. This is surely why Podhajsky said 'My horses, my teachers'. Let us not lose sight of this, it is why we enjoy teaching them so much and why we will get better at it. In the past, it has been the odd practically able, but perhaps not very articulate, person who 'had a way with horses'. Now we can explain much more about how to teach and what it might be like to be an equine and allow anyone interested to progress in their way.

SUMMARY
1. Equines certainly have an awareness of others' bodies, and they must be aware that others have desires and needs just because of the information they acquire during their lives in order to survive and live socially.
2. Equines play. They play with objects and socially. For play to be play there need to be rules; it must be clear when it is play, and when it is not. This indicates that they must have some awareness of others' minds: a 'theory of mind'.
3. There are other emotions and behaviours which could be used to answer the question of equines' awareness of others' minds. For example, there is some evidence that they can learn something about humour, and perform novel acts to give pleasure to humans, but we do

→

not know if they do this in their own societies. They do seem to be able to learn the appropriate habit of mind to be humorous when given the opportunity, albeit in a simple form.

4. They learn socially as we have already stressed (see Chapters 3 and 6), but whether individuals actually teach others rather than the pupils' just learning from observing we do not yet know.

5. We have to conclude that the jury is still out on whether or not equines have a fully developed reflective consciousness. There is evidence, supported by rational arguments that indicate that they have an awareness of their own bodies and others', that they know about others' intentions, desires and needs, and that they can learn different habits of mind, one of which may well be a more sophisticated reflective consciousness.

6. If equines are able to attribute mental states to others, including other species, they can understand something about a human teacher's mental state, as well as that of other equines. This underlines how careful we must be when teaching equines, to convey what we want them to learn.

7. There is no unequivocal evidence that demonstrates that equines are aware of themselves and their own mind. There is evidence that they are aware of their own bodies, and that they appear to perform behaviours that must imply that they are aware of themselves (e.g. imitation of novel acts), but such a question has barely been researched in equines to date.

8. They, like humans, also develop habits, and habits of mind, and these may be different in different places or where they have had different experiences, that is in different cultures. Different educational experiences may be able to change their habits of mind as it can for humans. They seem to be able to learn to think a little like us when they have a good deal of contact with us. The better carer or teacher should try to think a little like them. Our tutors must be equines who already live with us and with whom we already have some mutual understanding.

11 Do equines have an aesthetic sense or appreciation, and are they moral agents?

An area which has received very little consideration to date for animals is whether they are capable, not just of appreciating things because they are useful to them, or satisfy some need, but whether they appreciate things for their own sake, that is do they have an **aesthetic sense**? We need to make detailed behavioural recordings before we can settle this debate.

Another interesting question which is now debated by those who study these things is whether, in view of what we know about equines' mental abilities, equines are, or could be, **moral agents**. To be a moral agent it is necessary to be able to make moral decisions, that is to know 'right' from 'wrong'. But what does this mean?

In this chapter we use what we have discovered about equines' mental abilities, and consequently what it might be like to be an equine, to address these questions. But first we need to briefly outline what we are talking about in more detail. I must also point out that, as usual, philosophers differ widely on how they define aesthetic senses and moral agency, so this is one point of view that I have argued as a result of studying equine lore over the last fifteen years, but much remains to be discovered and questioned further.

AESTHETIC SENSE

Since equines have a knowledge and awareness of their environment and others in it, it is likely that they appreciate certain things within it and, in this sense, 'value them'. But first we need to define what we mean by this. This is tricky. There is little agreement on the definition. But the primary task here is to point out why this question is worth asking in order to help us understand equines better, and to be able to improve their living and learning conditions with us.

What are aesthetic experiences?

The Greeks used the term 'aesthetic experiences' to mean 'sense experiences' (e.g. Plato and Aristotle). There is no doubt that equines have sense experiences and so, in the Greek sense, they must have aesthetic experiences. But, although this is a nice simple argument, it does not seem to answer the question.

If aesthetic experiences are more than having pleasure from certain feelings, what are they? Many have argued that they must involve some 'disinterestedness' which means that aesthetic appreciation is an appretion without any usefulness to the subject, but how are we to know (for humans as well equines) if this is really the case? If we can assess a human's real or not so real aesthetic appreciation (or lack of it) by closely observing his behaviour, then we may be able to do the same for horses when we know them well (for examples see Chapters 5 and 8).

But, the question remains whether equines have the mental apparatus to make judgments concerning beauty or otherwise. Equines certainly have feelings and we also suggest that they are capable of some type of mental reflectivity (see Chapters 9 and 10).

What might equines' aesthetic experiences be?

We have seen how sensitive to context these animal groups are (see Chapters, 6, 7 and 8), illustrated by how the meaning of messages changes according to the context. It is therefore likely that context will be an important factor in aesthetic experiences in these animals.

Another possibility is that mammals such as equines, who are very visually orientated and have emotional experiences are likely to seek out pleasurable visual experiences, for their own sake, even though there may have been some original evolutionary reason for encouraging such choices as some argue.

Example

If horses choose to stand in areas with views (which they do, see Chapter 4) and give up the proximity to food or shelter to do this, even when they have never been chased by predators, then the view will be having an effect on them and giving them some pleasure, whether or not this is because it is appreciated for itself or because it might give the equine a better chance of seeing predators coming.

Seeking out good views, mountains, sunsets and so on by humans is considered to be for aesthetic reasons: because they give a pleasurable visual experience without necessarily having instrumental (useful) value, although they too may originally have given pleasure because they were helpful to spotting predators coming.

If equines are unable to have mental experiences, to choose, to make decisions, to think or have imagination or memory, then it might be assumed that aesthetic experiences would not be possible. But we know that equines do have these mental experiences (see Chapters 2 to 10). Presumably, these mental abilities have been selected for to help them survive. One way of ensuring that the right choices are made in what either the human or non-human mammal does, is to ensure that they have pleasurable experiences. In other words, appreciating things for themselves or having an aesthetic experience can be considered a useful survival strategy, and may be an 'instinctive tendency'.

Of course, equines' judgements and awareness of pleasure or beauty may be different from ours. After all they have somewhat different perceptive skills and views of the world (horses are more visually and smell orientated than humans who are primarily auditory, language-orientated creatures, see Chapter 7).

Aesthetic judgements and experiences are thought to be affected by past experiences. Thus, equines will learn, by observational learning, or even by being taught (by other equines or humans) a series of visual rules in order to discriminate between 'beautiful' (nice) and 'not beautiful' and 'ugly' (nasty). Thereafter the individual might use these rules to make aesthetic judgements. A detailed study of equines' visual awareness and apparent appreciation (or lack of it) of their environments, can result in humans' greater visual appreciation, or at least it has for me.

Learning from equines' different types of aesthetic appreciation may rest on improving our awareness of smell, for example. Brady (1999) suggests how we could learn to become more aware of the aesthetics of smell.

At a simpler level, humans and equines also appreciate the same things, for example loud sudden noises are unpleasant, bird song is pleasant. Certain colour combinations or combinations of shapes may be universally appreciated such as sunsets, cloud formations, tree movements in the breeze. There may even be ways in which our taste can be educated by other animals, and we might begin to appreciate things we have hardly noticed before by being a better observer and watching them closely. I have, indeed, had some of these experiences. They have come from watching and recording behaviour, from teaching equines and trying to develop more appropriate teaching methods.

As a result of a long association with, and study of, equines, my appreciation of some things in the environment has changed: silence, object shapes, wind-induced movements in vegetation and landscapes, for example, which has led to different or enhanced aesthetic experiences. There is no reason to doubt that equines who have much to do with humans may well have their view of the world, and their aesthetic appreciation of it, changed too. One example of this is their response, often involving pleasure and relaxation, to certain types of human music.

I have also had experiences of what one could call violating an equine's idea of 'good taste', causing an unpleasant, perhaps aesthetically unpleasant, experience to an equine.

Example

On one occasion, I was in the truck with a particularly beautiful Arab mare, Omeya. Tired after a long day, I absent-mindedly stretched my leg and unsavoury-smelling sock-covered foot in the direction of her head. She moved her head slightly sideways so that she could look at me with her right eye, curled up the top of her nostril and then raised her head and looked out of the window in a rather directed way. I looked to see if there was anything particular that had attracted her attention, which there appeared not to be. I was then overcome by my lack of understanding of her sensitivity to smells, and her sense of 'good taste'. The unpleasant smell of the foot near her face had resulted in behaviour that had a very particular meaning to me, and would have conveyed some message to other horses whatever it might be!

How do we know when equines are having aesthetic experiences?

There are, I suggest, ways in which we can accumulate information concerning the possibility of animals having aesthetic experiences and appreciation, although systematic experimentation has not yet been conducted. One way to accumulate this information is to make much more careful observations and recordings of animals' visual choices, and indications of pleasure from other sense experiences which are appreciated for their own sake.

Another approach is to develop preference tests for experiences: do they prefer certain visual or auditory experiences, independent of any instrumental value it might have?

Example

Give a couple of stabled equines a tape recorder, teach them to switch it on or off with their nose or foot, and then play different types of music (or even just horse noises) to them, and record how long they listen before turning it off. After a while, it would be possible to introduce several tape recorders playing different types of music or noises, and see which one they prefer to switch on and keep on. Do the particular subject equines prefer birdsong to reggae, or West African drum music to Bach? Such questions are worth asking and can be answered.

Another way of assessing their aesthetic appreciations is to live with equines twenty-four hours a day and, as a result, become more familiar with them and be able to critically assess their responses in a variety of environments and situations. There is some evidence to suggest that they will tend to look at sunsets, seascapes, the movement caused by the wind in the trees and so on. This is backed up by the fact that stabled equines with views of the natural world, show less evidence of behavioural distress than those kept in enclosed stabling (Kiley-Worthington 1998), but more experimental work needs to be done.

Whatever the results of our observations, to assume that aesthetic experiences are denied to equines (or other mammals) is not possible. They have the sensory, emotional and cognitive abilities to have these experiences. Of course they are not going to discuss at length the aesthetic value of particular views, or landscapes, smells or tastes as some humans might, but to deny them aesthetic experiences, knowing what we do about them, would seem very foolish. What these experiences are is a much more difficult question which requires a great deal more thought and experimentation. But, this is equally true for human individuals who have very different aesthetic tastes and needs.

It is tempting to contemplate that equines are likely to consider much of the world much of the time disinterestedly since they are not (as humans are) planning, building, manipulating and using objects in it. Rather they are 'being' in it, sensing it and, at least some of the time, able to 'reflect on it' in some way (see Chapter 10), that is having some form of aesthetic experience much of the time.

EQUINES AS MORAL AGENTS

Equines may not reflect on the rights and wrongs of their behaviour at length or in great depth (there are also plenty of humans who do not), but the possibility that they qualify as moral agents is something which needs serious consideration, particularly by those involved with animal welfare.

The arguments concerning what moral agency must consist of are various, and we have discussed many of the approaches very briefly.

Equines as well as humans, may not merely be objects of moral concern, but moral agents. A brief summary of why is given in Figure 11.1.

1. Their behaviour is not governed by 'instinctive attitudes' any more than that of humans. They show flexibility of behaviour and are confronted by dilemmas and make choices, consequently they can be thought of as 'free agents'.
2. They learn the difference between right and wrong behaviour in different situations, and with different species, including humans.
3. They have feelings, are aware of others and can suppress their own desires from time to time.
4. They at least understand cause and effect in learning and to this degree they reason, have memories and beliefs, and work for goals.

→

5. They do not have human language, but the degree to which this disqualifies them from moral agency is not clear.
6. They have a form of social contract, and learn the rules which include reciprocity and demonstrating affection.
7. The way in which humans relate to non-humans is structured (often the product of erroneous beliefs) so as to militate against observing behaviour which would be interesting to study in order to answer further questions concerning the possibility of these animals' being moral agents.
8. If equines are able to be reflectively conscious, which, it is argued, may be inescapable if they are able to learn to perform voluntary actions and remember, then it is *possible* that these species groups qualify as moral beings even on the grounds of 'being able to evaluate, revise and abandon reason, recognise qualities of mind and character, use relevant skills and develop virtues' (MacIntyre 1999).

Fig.11.1 Qualifications required for moral agency fulfilled by equines

The applied consequences of the possibility of equines being moral agents

If then, equines' natural lives are not 'solitary, poor, nasty, brutish and short' (Hobbes 1651), but rather their lives are social and they have a degree of freedom of choice, appreciate in some way a quality of life, sometimes behave rationally, and may be moral agents, then it behoves us humans to treat them with equal consideration as that given to other moral agents, that is, humans. This requires, first, the dropping of the inappropriate or false preconceived notions generally held by most humans concerning their cognitive inferiority. But it also requires serious further investigation of current folk beliefs concerning equine treatments, including redesigning their husbandry and their education to ensure that they develop virtues and live lives where they can flourish as the beings they are, with or without humans. I have outlined how we may be able to achieve this in terms of:

1. Ensuring that the equine can at some stage in his life at least, perform all the behaviour in his repertoire that does not cause suffering to others (see Figure 4.4, page 184). In this figure we have attempted to measure 'behavioural restraint' in different types of environments in which equines are often kept, and the fulfilment of their various needs. In other words, **the relative quality of their lives.** The natural world, it must be pointed out, is not the freest environment. As you can see from the lower part of the figure, there are restrictions there that sometimes the domestic animal does not have.

2. If they are to have a life of quality, their whole being requires that their physical, social and intellectual/cognitive needs are fulfilled (see Figure 4.4).

We now know enough about their physical and social needs to ensure that we can give equines lives which will allow them to flourish. To do this, however, some preconceived notions that are held by many humans may have to be reviewed.

As a result of this investigation, we can now outline with more authority what an equine's intellectual/cognitive needs may be, and why. The idea that equines have some mental attributes that have previously been assigned only to humans, such as reflective consciousness, aesthetic experiences and moral agency, can no longer be so easily dismissed. There are many more questions to be asked in this domain, but we are now better equipped to ask them.

If we are to give equines the benefit of the doubt concerning whether or not they have cognitive abilities that previously have been considered unique to humans, then the question arises as to whether or not our conventional husbandry and treatment of them is acceptable or justifiable. We need to design their environments to fulfil all their needs better in order to allow them to have a life of quality.

One solution which some individuals who are concerned about the quality of life for domestic animals take, is not to have them as domestic animals under any form of control by humans. In today's world this solution is not often a possibility because of the lack of available land. It is important, however, that some wild populations are retained.

But if their needs are properly catered for, contact between species can be an enriching experience for both species involved. Consequently, thoughtfully managed, the life of domestic equines could be of a higher quality than that in the wild and give them opportunities to enrich their own lives and those of the humans they have to do with, so that all have a life of quality, a virtuous life in the Aristotelian sense.

To ensure that this is the case however, we must use what we know about equine lore, and think very carefully about the environments we keep them in, how and what we teach them or allow them to learn, how we relate to them and our expectations of them.

The good news here is that this does not have to be either difficult or expensive, it only needs motivation.

SUMMARY

1. To have aesthetic experiences it is necessary to have the mental ability to have more than a sense experience. It must involve some appreciation of the object disinterestedly, 'for itself'.

   Whether equines have such aesthetic experiences has not been established, although it has been shown that they have the necessary mental abilities to be able to do this by perceiving and sensing acutely sights, sounds, odours, tastes and touch, and making choices and decisions, and thinking and having memories). Incidences from the behaviour of equines suggest that they do have such aesthetic experiences 'for themselves' although these may be different from those of humans.

2. It is suggested that this could be carefully assessed by more detailed observation, (particularly as a result of living with equines) as well as with experimental tests.

3. It is possible that equines, because they are not manipulators of the world and consequently have to accept it as it is, are having aesthetic experiences, appreciating things as they are, more than the manipulating human primate who can alter things with the instrumental or potential instrumental value of objects and sensations.

→

4. It is also argued that because of equines' mental attributes including the possibilities of their having reflective consciousness, and the need for them to acquire a social contract, they may well be considered moral agents.

5. The consequences of considering that equines possibly have aesthetic appreciation and may be moral agents, rather than just beings of moral concern, has very considerable effects on the way we should keep and educate them. This, together with all the other considerations of what we know about equine lore is discussed in more detail in the final chapter.

12 Applying equine lore to how we keep equines

So far we have considered what equines know, how they learn, and what their mind is capable of, as far as we know. We are most likely to have a better idea of how and why equines do things, and what it might be like to be an equine by first considering our mammalian similarities. Secondly, we must take account of the differences in our world views. We have investigated both our similarities and differences in the previous eleven chapters and suggested that when trying to understand an equine (or any other mammal) the first step is to use a 'conditional anthropomorphic' approach.

A conditional anthropomorphic approach can be used to re-examine how we keep our equines, and how we train them. Are we keeping and training equines in a way which is conducive to their learning and wellbeing as a result of what we now know about equine lore? Which types of husbandry are likely to fit better with equines and which are unacceptable? In particular, can we, as a result of knowing more about equine learning, the information they have to acquire and their mental abilities, develop better methods of teaching them? Can we therefore combine science and rational, critical thinking with folk knowledge to improve the lives and learning of equines? If so how?

These are the questions addressed in this Chapter and Chapter 13. Much of this has been stated already in the text, but it is summarized here.

As a result of what we have discovered in Chapters 1–11, we can outline their general needs from the equines' point of view (Figures 12.1 and 12.2). There may be many ways in which these criteria can be fulfilled so that the equines have better lives and flourish, as well as the humans who have to do with them, just like there are many different ways in which humans can live and be taught and still have lives of quality. It is not a question of opening the stable door and waving good-bye to your friends as they gallop off into the gloaming; in fact, they may well be back looking hungry and bedraggled as the night advances and the rain falls!

We will outline some ideas of how to improve the husbandry of equines so that the criteria in Figures 12.1 and 12.2 are better fulfilled.

Fig. 12.1 A summary of what we know are all the needs of equines as a result of this study.

Physical needs (see Chapters 1, 2 and 5)

Food Not just a correct nutritional diet, but one that is also psychologically sound for equines.

Water Clean water and the opportunity to learn about what water to drink.

Shelter The opportunity to learn about where to shelter as well as the provision of some shelter appropriate to climate (see Chapter 5).

Physical health/lack of pain and disease Appropriate veterinary care but not overprotection. Psychological correlates of the prescribed veterinary treatment must be taken into account (see Chapters 1 and 2).

Good feet Appropriate care of the feet and the opportunity for the equine to use them appropriately (see Chapters 1 and 2).

Exercise Equines are evolved to constantly move quietly and sometimes to run fast. Sufficient constant movement must be allowed for (see Chapter 2).

Social needs (see Chapters 6 and 7)

Equines are social animals Equines must have constant access to others of their own species.

They live in family groups Their inter-generation bonds are very strong. They should have access to others of different sexes and ages.

Sex and courtship are an important part of their lives They should have the opportunity to experience and perform appropriate actions.

Young equines have to learn the social contract and acquire much social knowledge All equines should be raised in a way that ensures they are able to do this, both males and females.

→

A foal's most important relationship is with his mother Mares should be allowed to wean their offspring naturally. Artificial weaning causes trauma to the foal and mother alike.

Social play is important for equines They must have the opportunity to be able to exercise this.

Emotional needs (see Chapter 4)

Equines form strong long-term bonds of affection They must have the opportunity to do this with their offspring, their social partners and those of the other sex.

They must have the opportunity of experiencing and expressing the whole range of emotions: aggression, sex, affiliation, pleasure, joy etc.

They must not be kept in environments where they show evidence of prolonged negative emotions: distress, frustration, conflict, fear, or aggression. However, short periods of stress may be beneficial in order for them to be able to experience more.

Cognitive or intellectual needs (see Chapters 3 and 1–11)

Skill stimulation Equines need to be able to exercise and stimulate all the skills they have for using all the sensory modalities: sight, hearing, smell, taste and touch.

Learning Equines require an environment that is sufficiently changing and stimulating to allow them to exercise their abilities to learn new things and acquire ecological, social and perhaps even conceptual information.

Memory Equines need situations that stimulate memory, not just fearful situations/memories.

Problem solving Equines require situations that stimulate their problem-solving abilities.

Rational thinking Equines require situations that stimulate their rational thinking and a cause/effect understanding of the world.

Innovation Equines need situations that stimulate innovation and new/creative solutions to problems.

'Mental habits' can be established and can then facilitate further cognitive development and experiences.

Fig. 12.2 Detailed outline of the equines cognitive/mental abilities, as far as we know

Body knowledge (see Chapters 8 and 9)

1. They are aware of their own bodies and they can identify parts of them and learn to do particular things with different parts.
2. They are aware of when others have similar bodies, e.g. another equine or another species.
3. They are athletic movement specialists, able to move at speed, over distances, and perform many acts of balance and agility.

Learning (see Chapter 3)

1. They learn by imprinting or early learning, Pavlovian conditioning, instrumental learning, trial and error, imitation, associative observation and social learning, and cognitive or silent learning.
2. They learn to perform particular complex actions by acquiring declarative (learning that) and procedural (learning how) knowledge.
3. They can learn fast, often in one trial.
4. They remember well for years.
5. They are particularly able at associative learning.
6. They form habits and habits of mind (that is, particular ways of using the mind) easily.
7. They can learn concepts and symbols.

Ecological knowledge (see Chapter 5)

1. They have to acquire a great deal of knowledge about the environment to live the way they do when wild. They need to become field botanists, zoologists, geologists, meteorologists, geographers and field ecologists, or 'natural historians'.
2. Partly because they are a prey species, they are particularly aware of the environment around them.

Social knowledge (see Chapter 6)

1. In order to be able to live in social groups they have to have a social contract. Each individual needs to learn this, and become a natural psychologist.
2. They must learn normal behaviour for the class of individual (e.g. male, female, young) as well as the individual personalities in the group in order to predict and react appropriately to their behaviour.

→

3. To remain in the social group they need to cement bonds between individuals by being nice to each other and deflating potential disagreements. They must learn to co-operate.

4. Their social knowledge is acquired through their lives as the result of social learning so there are cultural differences between populations.

5. Individuals who have not had an opportunity to learn 'equine etiquette' because of being isolated from groups have not learnt the social contract and are unable to live in the group.

6. One of the most important reasons for living in a social group for equines may be in order to pass on knowledge, particularly about the environment, to each other.

Communication (see Chapter 7)

1. Equines are sophisticated visual communicators and able to pick up very slight visual cues.

2. They have an elaborate communication system concerning smells which presents a different world view.

3. They can acquire information and communicate between each other and other species with tastes, touch and audition.

4. Most of their communication is context dependent, rather than the context independence of human language. This ensures close attention to the surrounding environment.

5. Equines learn quickly to respond to visual cues from humans, and also word commands particularly when given with expression in the voice.

6. If taught, they can also learn to comprehend individual words independent of other cues, that is they can learn to understand simple human language.

Emotions (see Chapters 4 and 9)

1. Equines are highly emotional beings. They have a particularly low threshold for fear which presumably helps with survival, and their response is, when in doubt, run. They particulary fear unfamiliar or unpredictable situations and objects.

2. They show similar behaviour to humans or other mammals which indicates that they feel also aggression, fondness, lust and sex, frustration, distress, grief, happiness and joy, pain and other emotions.

3. They may feel emotions implying some knowledge of others' minds such as compassion, sympathy, embarrassment, shyness, deceit and shame. To date,

→

behaviour indicative of these feelings has not been looked for seriously; we need more information.

4. They can predict others' behaviour by observing them and consequently have some idea of others' feelings, including humans.

Consciousness and reflective consciousness (see Chapters 8–11)

1. Equines are conscious of being in the environment, and awake and reacting to it.
2. They learn to do voluntary acts and therefore have intentions, desires, work towards goals, understand cause and effect.
3. They are conscious of their own bodies and those of others.
4. They learn to do complex activities which then can be performed without conscious awareness which allows their attention to be directed to other things.
5. They make choices and have beliefs about things.
6. They remember past events, make simple plans, and can predict some future events.
7. They have memories and consequently must have some form of imaginative experience.
8. Whether they can reflect on past events and pass on knowledge to others concerning them we do not know.
9. They may be aesthetically aware and make judgments since they are so environmentally aware.
10. They have a social contract and might be considered moral agents.
11. They appear to have many of the mental skills that humans have, although as a result of their different beings they will have a different world view.

Figure 12.3 A list of some of the most important problems facing horses in conventional husbandry and training, and how to improve these.

---

1. Overexcitement

Causes One of the most common causes of this problem is fear, others are insufficient exercise and insufficient stimulation: boredom. The equine has not had sufficient experience with particular procedures, or he has had bad experiences with them and people have negatively reinforced them. Bad handling, and insufficient exercise and intellectual work.

Improvements Allowing him time and always being relaxed with him. Reduce hard food, or cut it out altogether, but ensure he always has access to high-fibre food; give more exercise. Spend more time taking him about, introducing new things quietly. Praise and reward him when he is quiet. Let him live and work with other equines particularly older more experienced ones so that he can learn by observation.

2. Lethargy, lack of energy

Causes Boredom and insufficient stimulation in the work and living environment.

Improvements Ensure he has a more interesting life by having more or different social interactions, has access to high-fibre food all the time but not too much hard food. Give him new things to learn for positive food rewards, such as ground work, harness work, etc.

3. Overeating, getting too fat

Causes Insufficient exercise and other stimulation, overfeeding.

Improvement Increase the number of things he does, and the amount of exercise he has. Let him live outside with company, but with access to only a little grass.

4. Lack of appetite

Causes Poor quality food, stress, too much work or being asked to do things that are too difficult for him.

Improvements Let him go outside with company, and ensure he has some grass. Feed small feeds frequently, and always remove any leavings. Reduce or change his work.

5. Performing a stereotype or an abnormality
A stereotype is a behaviour that is repeated in the same way over and over again and is apparently purposeless (e.g.

→

---

weaving, windsucking, crib-biting, head throwing, tongue rolling, head nodding etc.). Abnormal behaviours are also included in this group (e.g. box walking, pacing up and down, box kicking, standing immobile for prolonged periods).

Causes Trauma, boredom, overfeeding, shortage of fibre, too little exercise. His physical, social or intellectual needs are not fulfilled.

In young equines (up to around five years old) changing the conditions he is kept in, in order to more closely fulfil his needs (see Figure 12.1), can cure the behaviour. Once the behaviour is well established (over eight years old) it is impossible to cure completely, although the amount it is performed can be reduced considerably. In older equines, the behaviour will have generalized to occur in almost every type of situation: too much stimulation, frustration or when there is not enough.

Improvements Increase the stimulation of his life, put him out more and with others, ensure that: he has always some high-fibre food to eat, he has different work to do, he has sufficient exercise and has little time while in a stable or a dull field and he is not fed high levels of high-concentrate food. Give him more and different hard work with more time away from the stable or paddock, and teach him different things.

What is *not a cure* is to put on further restraints (e.g. straps around the neck, electric wires, drugs, or having surgery such as cutting the neck muscles) to prevent the equine performing the behaviours. These unethical procedures do not address the cause.

6. **Performing an undesired behaviour** (e.g. not being caught, biting or kicking, attacking people, avoiding people, refusing to enter the stable or field, standing still in one place for prolonged periods).

Causes Overstimulation, fear or boredom may be the original cause. In some cases he may have formed a habit to perform a particularly undesirable behaviour. These are all learnt behaviours often taught by the handlers rewarding the behaviour in some way. The likelihood of performing inappropriate and particularly aggressive behaviour increases the more inappropriate the environment, that is the needs (see Figure 12.1) are not fulfilled.

Improvements a) Look carefully at whether or not the conditions in which he is kept fulfil all his needs: physical, social, intellectual and emotional, and change them if they do not. b) Ensure that the handlers are neither frightened nor causing him any discomfort. c) Start a retraining schedule, rewarding him for *not* doing the undesired behaviour. d) Ensure the handlers improve their handling by studying it carefully and if necessary attending courses, as well as gaining practical experience.

→

7. Cannot get on with other equines

Causes Lack of social experience, and the equine has learnt to attack or to avoid others in order to reduce his fear.

Improvements When in the stable, allow others to come up to the stable door and contact him. Reduce the partition between the stables so that the neighbours can see and touch each other. Put him out in a large field with one other older socially experienced horse and leave them. After this introduction has been achieved and the two can be together, take that companion out and introduce another. When he has several horses he can run out with, introduce one and then another so they form a group. Leaving the problem horse with just one equine he gets on with, without further social education will cause a very strong attachment to that one horse which may become a problem. Change the group structure slowly so that he eventually gets used to the majority of the equines in the stables.

This social education is vital and relatively quickly learnt in a young horse (Figure 12.4). The older the horse and the less social contact they have had, the more difficult social integration will be and the slower it will have to progress, but it is always possible to improve.

8. There are many problems with reproduction, many of them based on the lack of social education and how to behave in sexual situations, e.g. the mare does not conceive

Cause Once the normal physiological investigations of the reproductive tract have been carried out and no abnormalities are found, the problem is likely to be behavioural. One of the major causes of lack of conception is fear and stress. Mares have frequently never had access to mature stallions in their lives.

Improvements Allow the mare to run out with a stallion and a group of mares when she is *not* in season in order to learn about the stallion, sex and courtship (see Figure 4.14). Leave her with a socially educated stallion when she comes into season so she can be courted. Eventually, provided there is no very serious physiological problem, she will conceive.

There are very many other problems that I have encountered over the years being a behavioural consultant, but they can usually be placed in one of the above categories.

Fig. 12.4 Social experience is as essential to the equine as to the human. Young Shindi (left) learns what to eat and how to behave from her elder sister Shemal (right).

IDEAS FOR IMPROVING THE HUSBANDRY OF EQUINES

Nearly everyone who has a horse and cares for him will consider that the way they look after him is the best possible way, but sometimes they will add the codicil 'in the circumstances' to this. These 'circumstances' are not often clear, but such people will often say that if they had more time/money/facilities they would change this or that. Generally however, it is not a question of these three things, but a question of inclination. If the person wants to improve the life of their equine, they can, in just the same way as they can improve the life of their child or partner without the time, money or facilities — if they really want to.

Perhaps, however, the equine's life is acceptable to him, in whatever the conditions in which he is living, and this is the first question to ask, now we have much more information on how to answer it. From the equine's point of view, if things are wrong, and his life is in some way or another inadequate then, just like humans, he will show signs of **prolonged distress** (see Figure 4.3, and the following exercise).

Exercise
Walk around your own or a friend's yard, or the yard where you ride. Watch each horse for five minutes and record how many are sick, lame or on some form of medication. Also look carefully at their behaviour and record any performance of the behaviours listed in Figure 4.3 and how many times it occurs during the five minutes. Work out how frequently the equine will be doing it per hour based on this five-minute measure. From this you can work out how frequently there is some evidence of distress in those equines. This exercise can also be done with equines at pasture or in different types of stabling.

There are many possible causes for each of the behaviours that indicate that all is not well with your equine, that is whether or not he has enough exercise, his diet is appropriate, he has a social life, he has enough mental stimulation and so on. But one of the most obvious causes is too much restriction on what he can do (see Figure 4.4).

Exercise
Assess honestly 1) the degree of behavioural restriction and 2) the fulfilment of all your equine's behavioural needs, by the type of husbandry and the type of work you do with your equine, as we have done in Figures 4.3 and 4.4 with ours, and see how they score. You may find you give different scores and score more different behaviours. Our example is only a trial. The important thing is to do it honestly.

Horses kept in stalls for long periods of time will be more behaviourally restricted than ones kept at pasture. But that does not mean that stalls are always bad and pasture always better.

Example
Equines were the major source of power for transport and agricultural work 150 years ago; they were usually out working for around eight hours a day, and then kept tied in stalls when they had time off. In their stalls they had just enough time to rest, eat their high-fibre and energy foods, and sleep. As a result, it appears that stereotypes were rare in working equines, as indeed they are today where equines still work, e.g. Egypt and Tunisia. Keeping equines in stalls may not be the best environment but, provided other things are

appropriate, the stalls may not be the most important thing to change.

By contrast, many recreational/competitive equines today are kept and raised in small paddocks or pastures where they are fed on high-quality food, often kept isolated from others, and may be pampered and protected, yet they frequently develop stereotypes, a sign of behavioural distress. This may be a result of having insufficient stimulation of one sort or another (exercise, problems to solve, choices to make) or inappropriate physical conditions (too much high-energy food without sufficient exercise, and too little fibre) (see Figure 4.4).

So it is not just the type of husbandry itself that ensures that the equine has a life of quality and shows no distress, so much as the husbandry combined with all the other factors in his life. A little thought and a few changes within the husbandry system can make an enormous difference to the life of your equine, it *does not* depend on time, money or facilities.

Many people who keep their horses at livery yards are frightened to suggest changes that they would like on the grounds that the yard owners must know best, and that their horse might be thrown out if they make 'trouble'. Now is the time, however, to begin to tactfully make suggestions about changes that you would like to see in the husbandry of your horse since there are now many livery stable clients who are becoming more aware that all may not be well for the horse when kept in the conventional way, however clean and tidy the yard may be! If they wish to retain their clientele, livery-yard owners will be forced to consider questions concerning the improvement of their husbandry from the equines' point of view and for the first time, perhaps, discuss the issues with their clients.

The next step in rethinking the husbandry of equines is to consider whether just showing no evidence of distress, and reducing the equine's behavioural restriction a little, is really sufficient for him to have a **life of quality**. Perhaps the equine should have more than a life just free of pain and suffering.

We have argued that we can find out what this life is for the equine as a result of knowing more about what it might be like to be an equine, and outlined their various needs.

If the equines are behaviourally restricted with a score above, say, 10–12 for an unfulfilled need, or show evidence of distress in any way (such as overexcitement, aggressiveness, boredom, refusing to do things, spooking or leaping about, showing any stereotype, needing drugs, or being sick or lame much of the time (see Figures 4.3 and 4.4), then:

1) reduce the behavioural restrictions;
2) work out why they are distressed;
3) change the husbandry, handling and teaching to put this right, or at least reduce the abnormality.

The cognitive enrichment, or fulfilment of the 'mind needs' of equines in association with humans can be assessed a little further. A first attempt is made in Figure 12.2. Does he demonsrate that he may feel pleasure?

Exercise

Watch your horses at pasture for thirty minutes after you put a group out, and count the number of times each individual rushes around, leaps about, play bites or chases another. Can you suggest other behaviours which might indicate that they are feeling pleasure?

All equines who have a life of quality are relaxed, well-natured beings, who, provided they have not had bad previous experiences will be curious and interested in humans. If they are frequently excited, jumpy, scared, aggressive, lethargic or uncooperative, then their environment and/or the teaching is not right. There are no exceptions to this rule. Even though an equine might have had a bad past experience, (such as a trauma at weaning, or being frightened of loading into a vehicle, or having been beaten), it is *not possible* to pass the buck. It is of course necessary to take the individual's past experience into account, and continue to change his conditions to ensure that the behaviours become less frequent. **What is not acceptable is to ignore the husbandry conditions when treating any behavioural problem,** as, alas, is too often done.

There are many different types of stabling and ways of keeping equines indoors and out, from the donkeys of Lamu who wander around eating the organic wastes wherever they find them, to the competition horse living in the fashionable indoor-stabling system, often for years at a time. Here he has little or nothing to see other than the animal in the next stable, few if any changes in sounds, smells, tastes or tactile stimuli, little to eat for most of the time since he is fed high protein/carbohydrate food which he finishes in an hour or two, and no way in which he can exercise himself, acquire information, make choices and decisions or have problems to solve. The surprising thing is that equines kept in such situations, although they almost all show evidence of distress, survive and behave the majority of time as we would wish, even if they do have coughs, go lame and have colic frequently! This says a great deal for the adaptability of equines. Humans placed in similar conditions for years at a time often do not survive or behave acceptably.

I have been very critical of the conventional 'top end of the market' husbandry practices where the equines are severely restricted, overprotected and often treated like precious motor cars rather than intelligent living beings, but there are many ways in which such environments can be rendered much more acceptable for the equines. It is clear from what we now know about equine lore and equine needs, how such environments can be changed. Here are a few suggestions.

1. Construct ways in which the equines can at least see and experience the outside by:

   a) Ensuring they are out in even muddy paddocks for part of the time (preferably with others).

   b) Being able to put their heads out to the outside, even if this is only to see and experience the wind and weather, the trees and sky. This can often be easily arranged by cutting out a portion of the back wall of the stable or by having windows put in so that they can see out, or leaving the end doors of an enclosed stabling system open, rather than sliding them shut.

2. Ensure that they have sufficient exercise and are out of the stabling for at least three hours a day by:

   a) Taking them out regularly for work for *at least* one hour a day moving at *at least* 10 km an hour on average. One one-hour walk will not be sufficient to keep the equine either physically or mentally happy if he is shut up the rest of the time.

   b) Taking them for walks while they graze and experience the weather and the environment.

   c) At least once a week ensure that they are doing a different type of exercise from the rest of their work: a jumping horse should do some flatwork and progress with this; a dressage horse could go for a long-distance ride of at least, say, 15 km (10 mls) at a reasonable speed of at least 10 km (6 mls) an hour; a long-distance horse should do some flatwork or liberty work; a driven donkey could be ridden or given some liberty work; and zebras in a zoo should be given some exercise by, for example, being taught to run around their area before they receive their food.

3. Construct ways in which they can have the same type of time budgeting as they would have in a wild or feral situation by:

   a) Ensuring they have enough high-fibre food available all the time. If they eat too much and become too fat, make them work to obtain the hay/silage/straw by either putting it in a net with very small holes so it takes them a long time to eat, or put it slightly out of reach so each mouthful has to be stretched for, or some activity performed to obtain it, e.g. stepping on a particular rock or a panel to lower it for a short period etc.

   b) Ensuring that they have enough to do and are not standing in their stables without having options. Give them a paddock or yard to run out into, or others to meet, people to teach and more exercise.

4. Construct ways in which they can have more contact with other equines by:

   a) Putting them out into paddocks together, preferably for long periods. This is not difficult in the summer when every type of equine can live out night and day and can still be easily brought in when required for work. In the winter, it is better that they run out in a manege, paddock, yard – or even a small muddy area – for a few hours each day, rather than being shut in all the time.

   b) Taking down the bars between the stables so that they can see, touch and smell their neighbours over the partitions. If they do not get on well with their neighbours, do this slowly and open up a small area at a time until they do. Only pathologically distressed animals will continue to be aggressive to their neighbours. Even stallions can be kept near other horses in stable blocks.

   c) Keeping them in groups in yards where they can have their own small subdivision (where they are tied or enclosed) for feeding, or other individual care.

   d) Frequently work the horses in groups: at liberty, or being ridden: riding on the flat; jumping, both free and ridden; and riding quietly out for periods, including stopping and waiting while the riders have picnics or meals in pubs.

5. Increase their cognitive/intellectual stimulation by giving them lessons that teach them different things at least twice a week, using only positive reinforcement by:

a) In the stable, teaching them to respond to word commands 'go to the back of the stable', 'come here', 'lift the bucket', 'put your head down', 'shake hands' and so on (see Chapter 3). This is to increase the stimulation in the stable.

b) Learning new movements while loose in the school, or dressage movements, even if they are not required for any competition, and work in hand can be done at almost any time and in any place.

c) Go to different places to have different experiences and learn about different things, e.g. through water, up steep slopes (see Figure 5.7) or learning to balance at higher speeds when going downhill. Gymkhana games can be good lessons to use here. They must get used to the equipment used and the format of e.g. the sack race, the egg and spoon race, or bending etc. quietly before they take part in races.

d) Teach them to listen more carefully to language and teach them to make discriminations or understand concepts (see page 345).

e) Give them problems to solve in the stable, e.g. they can have their food if they lift a lid, or push something and this can gradually be made more complicated so that eventually they do a series of different things correctly before obtaining a reward. This can be constructed and then the animals left to work it out. In zoos, such ways of giving the animals something to do is now called 'environmental enrichment' and is a necessary part of the designing of the husbandry for any good modern zoo.

f) Teach several of the horses in riding schools, for example, to work in harness so they can take the muck out and spread it on the fields, harrow the school, weed the vegetables or do other work around the stable yard. This also allows the humans to have new and different experiences with their equines, while, at the same time, getting a job done that you might otherwise have to pay someone else to do (Figures 12.5a, b, and c).

g) There are many more ways in which anyone (who takes the time and trouble) can give their equine more to think about, and new problems to solve in his daily life, in or out of the stable.

6. Increase your equines' possibilities of acquiring knowledge about the world and different environments by:

a) Taking them to different places for competitions or rides.

b) Leaving them staying with friends in different places for short periods, or take them on holiday with you.

c) Constructing their paddocks so that they have many different types of areas within them: e.g. boggy areas, trees and forest, bushes, open grassland, tufted sedges, stony areas or rocks and so on.

d) Taking youngsters out and about with older equines to learn about the world as they grow (rather than being stuck in a place devoid of cognitive interest and stimulation) in order to establish the right 'habits of mind'.

7. Understand better what it might be like to be an equine, and ensure that his needs (see Figures 12.1 and 12.2) are fulfilled.

No matter what the equine – donkey, mule, zebra, pony or horse – is kept for and expected to do, nor what level he is working at – from first lessons to international standards, whether this is racing of any kind, dressage, driving, travelling, trotting, breeding, long distance, jumping, teaching, working, pulling, showing or just being looked at – there is no need to keep any equine in the types of conditions which do not fulfil his needs). Even if the system is set up in a conventional way (which not fulfil their needs), it is possible with a little thought and energy to change the system so that it is better from the equines' point of view.

Although there are today many behaviourally pathological horses who, because of their past bad experiences, may find it difficult to adapt to different more acceptable conditions, my experience over the last thirty years has been that even the most pathological of such individuals can improve when appropriate husbandry changes are made. Most importantly, *we do not have to have more pathologically raised equines in the next generation because we now know how such problems are caused, and can prevent their establishment, provided changes are made in many types of horse husbandry. It just needs to be done.*

Figs. 12.5a, b and c
A different experience.
a) Oberlix, between races and dressage tests, working with a spring tyne harrow. b) Crystal and Cariff rescue a broken down car stuck in a field. c) Oryx digging potatoes with Chris and Vicki.

Remember, the golden rule is: anyone can improve their equine's life, if they want to, it does not need money or facilities. It does need motivation and an ability to try to understand their point of view. This will also make your life easier and you a much better horse handler, driver or rider, at whatever level you are working and for whatever reason: fun or to earn a living, or for competition from preliminary to international level.

SUMMARY

As a result of having studied equine lore, what it might be like to be an equine, and carefully considering equines' mental abilities, or skills that at this stage we cannot assume equines do not have, we can draw up a list of their general physical, social, emotional and cognitive needs. If we wish to improve their lives and have animals that are more fun to be with, have fewer problems and have more fun themselves, then there are ways in which we can change both the husbandry and the teaching of equines to ensure this improvement. These involve the following.

1. There are inadequacies in equine husbandry systems that we can appreciate when we understand equine lore. In this chapter we have suggested a few ways in which changes can be made. It must be emphasized that these changes do not have to rely on money or time; they simply need thought and motivation. If we wish to provide environments for our equines so that they can have lives of quality, then it is necessary that we make such changes. The advantages are that it will not only be better for our equines, but also better for us because we will have animals who have happier, longer, healthier lives with many fewer problems of any sort, including behavioural ones.

2. Reducing their behavioural restrictions, giving them choices in where they go and what they do in their husbandry. They have somewhat different needs from humans but we have many in common. Thus, all aspects of their lifestyle as a horse must be catered for (for example

→

not feeding them nutritionally adequate foodstuffs that do not cater for their psychological need to eat for many hours a day).

3. Not overprotecting them so that they are unable to develop their own abilities to look after themselves and make their own choices.

4. One indicator that things are wrong for the horse is when they show behavioural distress. This can be easily measured. When this is the case, then things must be changed, if it is believed that equines are sentient/feeling creatures.

5. Equines must also be able to demonstrate their emotions, particularly positive ones of pleasure and joy.

6. They must be allowed sufficient social contact of mixed ages and sex groups to allow them to acquire the necessary social knowledge to be good natural psychologists and be able to live in a group.

7. They must be given sufficient mental stimulation to allow them to fulfil their behavioural needs.

All of the equines' needs can be fulfilled to a very much greater degree than is normally the case with the conventional husbandry and teaching or training of equines. The advantages of changing these methods are very considerable in allowing both the equines and the humans with them to have enriched lives of quality as a result of their association, rather than ones fraught with expense and problems. It can all be done, if you want to do it.

Further detailed methods and examples can be found in Kiley-Wothington (2004).

13 Applying equine lore to handling and teaching equines

Having considered how to think about improving the environments in which we keep equines as a result of having a better grasp of equine lore, the next question is how we should behave when we are with them in order to help them learn the things we would like them to learn so that we can have a mutually enriching relationship.

Over the years that I have been teaching teachers, it has become evident that a little effort put into reflecting on how to teach whatever is required and to consider the equine's point of view is invaluable. Although many people are sympathetic to this idea in principle, when they begin to try to teach an equine (or another species of animal), they often find it difficult to relate to the animal and to try to understand his similar yet different point of view. It is rare for teachers of equines to critically examine their own behaviour; if things do not go smoothly, they tend to consider the animal at fault. By contrast, this is not the present cultural approach towards teaching children; human teachers must consider their method and approach rather than blaming the children for not understanding, and they have to attend long and thorough courses to enable them to do this before they are permitted to teach. The arguments for this difference of approach are often related to the incorrect idea that the behaviour and even learning of equines is controlled by instinct, whereas that of human infants is controlled by their past experience. We have discussed why this approach is wrong (see pages 107–112).

Everyone wants a quick fix. They want to be taught in one easy lesson how to back a horse, make the horse lie down, stand still, jump better and so on. In fact the English word 'break' (to teach an equine to carry someone on his back) still sums up the current approach. It implies that all that has to be done is to force the animal into submission in some way. The current vogue of 'natural horsemanship' usually shows and tells people how to do it otherwise successfully. But, when they go home to try it themselves, it rapidly becomes apparent that they really have not grasped the similarities and differences in the perception and analysis of the world between themselves and their equine student. Even among those disposed to approach handling and educating equines differently, the human teacher rarely displays an awareness of the equine's mind that is so crucial to developing a pleasant relationship and teaching. Perhaps it is because of this that so many dogmas arise. People try one for a bit, then jump to another, rarely getting down to the hard work of trying to catching a glimpse of that different world view.

The first experience for both the equine and the human must be just becoming aware of that other being, how they behave, that is learning about the other's mind and body. Be assured the equine will be learning about you, whether or not you are bothering to learn about him. The first step in developing a relationship is to be together, watching and appreciating each other.

The next step which develops from being together is the touching of each other. It is a good idea to wait until the equine makes the first move to smell and touch you. Touching equines is generally called *handling*. A knowledge of equine lore helps greatly in understanding how to handle and the best way to help the equine learn what you would like him to learn about a human.

As we know, equines and other mammals are emotional beings (see Chapter 4) just like humans; they form relationships and develop likes and dislikes for others. If you do not have the motivation to work at your relationship with an equine, then you will not do either the equine or yourself any good by continuing to deal with him.

Consider carefully your behaviour before you restrict, restrain, or try to teach a young horse. Remember, he will learn the wrong thing just as quickly as the right, and relearning the right after the wrong takes much effort.

HANDLING

Handling, from the animal's point of view, involves learning to do nothing and standing still while various curious things are done to his body: being touched by a human, stroked, groomed, scratched, and so on.

Handling is as important a skill as riding well. But it is rarely given the attention it needs at all levels, from the zoo keeper, through the donkey driver and weekly rider to the serious professional. It is something that any motivated human can and must learn if they are going to be involved with equines. Like riding, skiing, writing, or playing music, it is not something you are 'born with', although some may find it easier than others. To learn to do it well, you have to think and work hard at it.

Knowing about how equines learn, and how they perceive the world allows us to develop some general rules. Not all good handlers and educators are good at articulating these, but the rules are easy to learn, although they are not always so easy to put into practice! (Figure 13.1)

Fig. 13.1 Rules for better handling

1. The most important thing is to consider carefully *what you do* before you do it. Until you have a great deal of experience, it is very foolish to act without consideration. Because both the horse and the human are good natural psychologists and respond to visual information, the equine will respond to the emotion the human is feeling, and vice versa. Thus, if the horse is excited and rushing about, the human is likely to be tense which adds to the horse's excitement.

2. It is very important to self-analyse and to be self-critical. If you do something and it does not seem to have the desired effect, rather than assuming that the

→

horse is crazy or stupid, or that it is the horse's breed or 'instinct' (see page 107), assume you are doing the wrong thing with this horse at this moment. Reappraise the situation and try another approach. If you do not, then you are just a bad teacher.

3. Posture, movements of parts of the body and muscular tension are important in conveying to the equine what you are feeling (see Chapter 7). Convey pleasure in his company, delight in his appropriate responses. Any tenseness will indicate wariness and this will keep the equine away and make him restless.

4. Use the voice with expression to convey your delight, to calm him, and to attract his attention away from something scary or new for him, for example touching his legs or rubbing his stomach.

5. Positively reinforce the appropriate behaviour, e.g. standing still while being touched or rubbed all over. If he stands still, you praise him and give him a food reward. When he moves you say 'no' and try again, without haste or irritation, until he stands and you praise him.

6. Be sure you are in control of your emotions, whether this is fright or irritation. If you lose your temper or become irritated, things will only get worse. If frightened, only do as much as you feel confident doing, and make sure you do not get hurt. If you get hurt, it makes your problem, and the equine's, worse. There are no 'Brownie points' gained for gritting your teeth and carrying on regardless – so-called 'courage'. If you are really frightened, recognize it and go and do something else until both the equine and yourself calm down. Then try something less difficult. Do not reward him with a positive emotional reaction (smiling or laughing) if he has not given you what you *really* want, or you will teach him to do the wrong thing.

7. Make up your mind how you would like your equine to behave and then work towards that aim. If you do not mind him dancing around as you get on, or jumping about afterwards, then he can easily learn to do these things. On the other hand if you really dislike this behaviour, he can easily learn to stand still whenever you ask and stay there until you ask him to walk on again. It is up to you to teach him what you would like.

8. Make sure you have a schedule for advancing his learning. Do not just repeat old things, go on to the next stage. For example, if you like him to stand still while you mount, and he does, then make him line himself up to a gate or a mounting block (so that you can get on more easily) or stand still in more difficult conditions when others are coming and going. There is no end to

→

education. The idea is to make your life easier, to enable both of you to enjoy yourselves more together, and also to ensure that he has sufficient cognitive/mental exercise, which is often neglected in equines (see page 394).

9. Do not rush in to try to do everything at once. If you are teaching him to lift up his foot, rub his legs first and get him used to this, then pick the foot up, even if only for a second, and tell him how marvellous he is. Gradually increase the time he has his leg held up, and do not fight to hold it up whatever happens; the horse can learn that fighting works in certain circumstances, so do not fight. Instil confidence instead. This applies equally to farriers and veterinarians who are often in a hurry. If they are trying to rush and upsetting your animal by restricting him, shouting, hitting, twitching, grabbing, etc., stop them. Take a little time and show them that it is not necessary. It is quicker for them and nicer for everyone in the long run another way. There are very very few occasions when a twitch or severe restraint is really necessary if you handle well and take a little time, even when the treatment may cause pain.

Fig. 13.2 It is best to begin handling equines as foals. Note the relaxed body posture, encouraging the foal to make contact. One-month-old Shella being handled for the first time.

Handling and first education of older naïve equines

It is best to begin handling equines when they are foals (Figure 13.2), but there are many equines who are not handled as foals, such as animals caught from the wild or ones that have been left alone at pasture. Handling these equines is more difficult than teaching them about humans when they are young, but it is not particularly taxing if approached properly. The same general rules apply, but the first thing is to get the animals used to the presence of humans by doing nothing. Exciting curiosity without frightening is important. The best way is to have the animal in a small enclosed area where there is nothing to eat or drink. Take a good book and go and sit in the middle of the enclosure together with a small pile of food or hay and a bucket of water. Take no notice of the equine, even when he comes up to the food or water and, gradually, through curiosity, he will begin to want to investigate you. Lucy Rees made a television documentary in the 1970s comparing her co-operative approach to handling and training a wild-caught mustang in the US, with a Western cowboy's approach. She used the 'do nothing' method, and there were pictures of the wild horse coming up to smell and investigate her. In the meantime, the cowboy and his horse were having a bad time; he threw blankets and sacks on the horse who pulled back and cavorted around with terror. Two weeks later, Rees's wild mustang was wandering in a headcollar along a river bed in the sunset with Rees sitting bareback on him, while the cowboy had given up!

This approach is particularly important with wild-captured animals, including zebras. First they must get used to the humans and their activities they can see and hear around their enclosure. Then, eventually, when they have ceased to be frightened, the handler sits on the barrier and slowly descends into the enclosure and continues to, apparently, pay little attention to the animals, until the animals begin to be curious.

At some point it will be necessary to teach the equine about restraint, so that he can be tied up and led, but only after they have become familiar with humans (see Kiley-Worthington 2004).

The education of adult previously unhandled equines needs to be tailored to their experiences as well as the development of the skills that will be required. In this way they can be helped to develop the right habits of mind.

One very important, often neglected and easy to use, cue to help with teaching is the voice. This is an area our research centre has been considering and experimenting with for some time. We will discuss the use of the voice in more detail.

WHAT IS 'NATURAL'?

What is 'natural'? If you really believe that you should only do to the equine what is natural, then why are we educating them at all? It certainly is not natural for them to learn to carry people on their backs, wear harness, bridles or saddles, or have much to do with humans at all. Consequently, if we sincerely believe they must only be taught to do what they do naturally, then we should have nothing to do with them (except hunt them perhaps), but just leave them to live their natural lives. There are some who take this stance, but I suggest it is misguided.

What justifications are there for using equines?

There are various justifications for using equines, and teaching them different things. We will examine the main ones briefly.

1. Some maintain that equines are sentient, feeling creatures, but very inferior to humans both mentally and in terms of our moral concern and, consequently, we are justified in using them as we like, provided this use does not cause them to suffer. According to this view, equines have the same kind of status as valued slaves. This is the view held by many people who own, love, and are involved with equines. As I have argued elsewhere, there are problems both for the humans' rational thought and the equines' wellbeing with this approach (Kiley-Worthington 1998). But here, what concerns us is whether or not they are seriously inferior to us mentally. If not, then this argument will not apply.
2. Even though it is not natural, it is necessary for the equine to be educated and live with humans because of the pressure on land and resources. This is an important argument because, if we were to open all the gates and doors and let equines gallop off into the wilderness, they would quickly become

much less numerous and eventually extinct (like their wild cousins have become in Europe and are in the process of becoming in Africa and Asia). This is not because they cannot survive, but because of the demand for land by human beings and the shrinking of the wild. Consequently, equines must retain some instrumental (useful) value for humans, to avoid extinction.

3. Learning is natural. Consequently, whatever equines learn is natural. A comparison in this respect of an equine learning to carry someone on their back or pull a wagon, with an activity that humans perform (which we consider beneficial, although not natural in the sense of being something that all humans do) is learning to write. It is not natural for humans to learn to write, but is considered important for the individual. Consequently, limits do not have to be imposed on teaching an equine only movements that he may do anyway in his natural life. Since it is natural to learn, it is reasonable to suggest that, just as for humans, if he learns new and different things he may have a life of greater quality and a greater range of experiences (see Introduction). Humans have enriched lives by learning new and different things and having to do with equines. It should be that the equine also has an enriched life by having to do with us humans. Thus, there are no limits to what he can be taught, provided it causes no pain or suffering to him or to others, and enhances his quality and length of life.

The wild is not such a marvellous place sometimes. When equines are domesticated, we can improve on the wild existence by, for example, ensuring that no equine dies of starvation, is hunted and eaten, and that their diseases and wounds are treated. But, to ensure that they have a life of quality, a *better* life than they would have in the wild, we must *also* ensure that all their needs are fulfilled, whether these are their physical, emotional, social or cognitive/intellectual ones. It is not good enough to assume that the way we have developed to keep them – sometimes for our own convenience, sometimes for our own inconvenience (which makes us feel we are doing the right thing) – is the best, or even good enough.

We need not therefore reject using something that may not have been in the species' evolved experience to help us develop our relationship with them, *provided* it does not cause suffering. Thus we humans can benefit our relationship with equines by learning more about visual communication from them, equally they can learn more about auditory communication from us.

DON'T WHISPER, TALK!

It is important to recognize that equines rarely use only one sense at a time to assess the situation they are in. Visual signals are important, as we have stressed, but their meaning is tempered by the smells and noises around, being touched or touching and/or tastes. As we have repeatedly stated, the meaning of a message to an equine is generally context dependent, unlike human language which is context independent (see page 299, Figure 7.10). Equines can learn something about our language, for example that particular noises are signals that can have particular meanings independent of the context, but it does not come easily to them.

There has recently been much emphasis on the use of visual cues (body language) to help train equines. Here, the human trainer becomes aware of the importance of changes in their body posture to convey messages to the equine. This is an important first step to increasing an awareness of how important the trainer's behaviour is for effective equine teaching.

Over the last fifteen years or so, many 'natural horsemen' have demonstrated how quickly horses respond to the body position and movement cues given by the trainer. This is no new idea, it has been known and used for centuries by good equine educators worldwide, often to a much greater level of sophistication, in, for example, some circuses. The importance of this development now for the horse-owning public is that it is attracting attention. But, so much attention has been drawn to the use of body language that the use of the voice (something we humans are particularly good at, and something which, again, has been used for centuries by humans with horses) is ignored. The use of the voice is even frowned on by the exponents of body language (e.g. Roberts 1999, Parelli and their followers). Many people argue that, again, it is not 'natural' for the equine to listen to the voice and understand the message so conveyed and, consequently, this is not a good way of teaching equines. This approach needs very careful assessment.

The use of the voice is not going to cause the animal to suffer physically at least, and rarely psychologically, and then only after he has learnt a considerable amount about it, but, will it be helpful? From our human point of view it is much easier for us to use the voice than to learn to use subtle visual cues and consequently it could be very useful. But, it can be argued, if it is very difficult for the equines to learn to understand what the voice is saying, it may not be useful to them. The first thing, therefore, is to study whether or not an equine can learn to understand messages via the voice and language, and how far he can go with comprehending human language. Only then can we answer this. To date, serious study of the comprehension of language has been confined to dolphins (e.g. Hermann 1980 and 1990), chimps (e.g. Gardner 1969, Savage-Rumbaugh 1996) and one parrot (Pepperburg 1993).

There are different possible experimental methods to help us answer this question. The one we adopted is to use the routine for language teaching that is often used by mothers when they begin to teach preverbal infants something about language. It is the emotional exchanges and resulting interest in learning between the pupil and the teacher in the normal world in which they associate, that is used to encourage the child to learn to understand and talk. Normal mothers and their infants have strong emotional bonds: they like each other and both learn quickly how to cause the other pleasure, or annoyance. Consequently, to help the infant or horse learn, the mother praises the child when they have achieved something, that is, the voice is used as a positive reinforcer (see page 118) which helps motivate the child. Demonstrations of pleasure by the child, help or motivate the mother to teach better.

First, simple words are introduced accompanied by visual cues such as gestures or movements, and sometimes helped by shaping and moulding (see Chapter 3, pages 124–126). Watching the teacher and imitating them is another important cue for the child or horse. Praise is conveyed by using appropriate intonation and words ('yes, yes, good boy', and chuckling), often with touch messages (hugging, stroking, patting, etc.), or visual demonstrations of pleasure by the teacher such as facial expressions (e.g. smiling and nodding).

The method used by a mother to teach a child to listen and begin to understand language can have much in common with the teaching of an equine by a human (see pages 156–161). This is quite different from the normal experimental situation to test an animal's ability to learn, in which the subject is often isolated in an alien environment and where there is no emotional interactivity.

When we consider the normal everyday way in which equines are taught by humans, it is generally in a one-to-one relationship with much emotional interactivity. In fact, it is very like that of infants with their mothers. The difference is that the human teacher does not often bother to teach them to understand language, although they may use the odd word command.

Some ten years ago, we adapted Fowler's method for use when teaching our young horses (as well as elephants, dogs, llamas and cows). There were three main reasons for this; as we have mentioned before they were:

1. In order to learn more about equines' (and other species') abilities to comprehend language when they were given some structured teaching.
2. To learn more in general about teaching equines.
3. To discover whether or not the use of the voice and their ability to learn something about language could help improve the teaching of equines.

There were two points that quickly became apparent in these experiments:

1. Many of us have an equine because we want a companion and friend. One of the functions of this companion may be that we will tell him all our problems. In a sense, he may act as a psychotherapist, appearing to listen and sometimes even responding to our chatter. There is nothing wrong with this, of course, but the only thing we must be aware of is that if we want to use language in order to help him understand simple concepts, ideas and commands, we must make a distinction in how we talk to him on different occasions so he knows when to listen.
2. Few people really believe that equines can understand or learn to understand language, consequently they do not take the trouble to use it simply and consistently. We talk to each other about our horses, ponies and donkeys in their presence without taking any trouble over the words and language we use; tacitly assuming they will not understand. We are much more likely to take the trouble to simplify the language we use to a child who we believe will, eventually, learn to understand.

One important consequence of the way we use language when with equines is that many equines learn *not* to listen to language or word commands, but to wait until they are visually or physically asked to do something (e.g. tied, led, pulled, pushed or a gesture is used). A similar thing happens if you are initially trying to understand an unknown language. After a while, if nothing is explained and you are given no help with your efforts to understand what is going on, you, like the equine, will not bother to listen any more, and as a result not learn the language. This is equally true with humans trying to learn something about how equines communicate from time to time. Consequently, if you want the equine to learn to perform movements, or listen carefully to language, a distinction must be made between:

1) asking, or talking to, the equine when you are teaching him to listen and understand and;

2) talking about or to, him without expecting his understanding.

We will now discuss the potential uses of the voice and language with equines.

The use of the voice to convey emotions to the equine

Most people use their voices in this way, even if they are not thinking about the consequences. Here it is the intonation, the emphasis and the tone of the voice rather than the individual words which convey meaning to the equine. Consequently, it does not really matter what you say, it is how you say it.

There are some general rules that help in this context.

1. To get the horse to move on, the tone will be shorter and sharper, the frequency and amplitude higher.

2. To quieten the horse, a calm, leisurely use of the voice, with a lower amplitude and frequency is required. If words are used, then they are lengthened and repeated in a singsong way.

These rules are based on the changes in the calls of many mammals as they become more excited (Kiley 1972), and they make sense to humans who react in the same way.

To praise the equine, the voice has to convey the speaker's real pleasure, not just a 'good boy' but 'goooooood booy' chuckle, chuckle, smile and nod. Often, rather than words, different noises will be used: clicking the tongue to encourage the equine to move faster is a favourite, and low quiet noises to slow or quieten them. Different teachers often have their own particular non-verbal noises which they use when with their horses. Sometimes it is surprising how good the equines are at learning what these mean. From time to time, I have found certain noises disturbing rather than settling: for example, the 'shhhhh' noise which is expected to quieten an individual, made me (and my horses when it was tried on them) extremely uneasy, although horses accustomed to it may quieten.

It is possible to convey many emotions with the voice, as we well know: pleasure, irritation, anger, fear, among others. These different expressions, often associated with visual cues (such as facial expressions), the equine will learn about and respond to rapidly, if they are made obvious, direct, clear and consistent. Whether they also comprehend more subtle emotions such as embarrassment and humour, we do not yet know (see page 348 *et seq.*).

In the first instance the voice and the expression you wish to convey must be paired with visual cues about what you are feeling, but associative learning is rapid so, after only a short time, the visual cues will no longer be necessary, just an expressive voice when out of sight; even a tape recording may do. At the beginning it is also useful to be overdemonstrative with the emotion, so if you are pleased, you show it both with your body, your movement, your facial expression and your voice; as they learn to listen, it will no longer be necessary to exaggerate.

One instance when this can be used is when beginning to harness-train a lively youngster. Here the constant use of the voice from behind, calming him – telling him that you are there, he is not alone in this present scary world, that there is really nothing to worry about – makes a very considerable difference to his ability to keep fear in check at least, and sometimes even to stay calm, and accept the new and frightening things. This will of course have much more effect if the equine has first learnt to listen carefully to the voice. That is, he has learnt that he can at least predict behaviours and understand emotional states by listening to the voice.

Example

Much to my surprise, when I used my voice with force and expressed my fury, the two adult stallions, Oberlix and Oryx, who had managed to get out together with the mares nearby, stopped in their tracks before seriously attacking each other. They stopped long enough to allow us to go up to them and lead them away. I did not think that in such an intense emotional state, they would listen, but they did. . .that time! This again illustrates how we tend to underestimate the potential for utilizing the voice in our relationships with equines. Without it, in this case, there would have been a serious fight as it was in a restricted area, and someone would probably have been badly injured.

As with all learning, however, it is vital that the voice is used consistently and directly, and not just repetitively. Constantly shouting at donkeys, mules, ponies or horses switches them off so they no longer listen, just as with humans. Constant praising, patting and cuddling also loses its meaning, again, just as for humans.

Words to convey particular messages or commands

With some teaching, equines can rapidly learn the individual meaning of many words. The first group with which it is easy to start is commands: 'walk', 'trot', 'canter', 'halt', 'come here', 'go out', 'go left', 'go right', and so on. It is remarkable how quickly they will learn these words if they are initially carefully paired with visual cues. Within ten minutes of starting a youngster working loose in the school, if well taught, he will understand 'walk', 'trot', 'halt' and 'come here'. Of course he may not remember all these words independently of the visual cues for a while, but he will be hearing and learning by association. (See Kiley-Worthington [2004] for further details and methods.) The visual cues can then be gradually reduced.

Expression in the voice is useful, just as with a child. As usual it is important to be clear and concise and to ensure the same word is used for the same activity each time, thus if you want a horse to go right, say: 'go right' do not sometimes say: 'go over there'. This is quite difficult for humans to do, as we often substitute words which have the same meaning. It requires some thought and attention to help them understand.

Two of the most important words are 'yes', and 'no'. When the equine understands these (they are really not difficult to teach, a little exaggeration in your emotional response is initially helpful) then an enormous stride has been taken. All you have to do when teaching even something difficult and advanced, is to say 'yes, yes' when he begins to do the right thing, and he will continue to do it, and 'no' when he tries something else, so he stops doing it. The 'yes' and 'no' have to be used immediately he starts to do something, almost before he does what you think he is going to do.

Learning to perform simple movements to word command requires no particularly advanced mental skills, it is learning to perform a voluntary act in order to achieve a reinforcement (see page 139). However, it helps a lot if the teacher is aware of exactly *what* the horse may be feeling and his next likely action, and takes this into account so that the command can be given at the right time.

Example

When Shindi was first loose schooled aged eighteen months, to start with she would not walk quietly around the ring. She trotted, cantered, slipped, tried to get out to join her friends, then stopped, turned and charged off in the other direction. My job as the teacher was first to keep her going around the circumference of the circle in the same direction without stopping, not to ask her to calm down and walk about quietly as I knew, initially, this would be very difficult for this reactive filly. Once she had grasped the idea of keeping going around the circle in the same direction at a trot or canter, had begun to balance herself and consequently did not keep frightening herself by slipping, and was showing an inclination to want to stop, this was the time to ask her to walk. This approach resulted in her wanting to do what was asked for from the beginning. So she found the whole lesson fun, once she understood what was required, rather than an exercise in obedience, domination by the human and mental confusion.

In performance, good circus performers must act on the messages they are receiving from the horses (or other animals). They are doing a show and it must be seen to be impressive, not that an animal is disobedient or the act disorganised – unless that is the point of the act. As a result, the circus presenter must incorporate movements or behaviours which are not a scheduled part of the act as if they were. Consequently, the format changes in line with what the animals want to do at that time rather than the presenter insisting on submission and obedience when in the public eye. It is a pity that this approach is not more widely used by teachers outside performance to encourage an animal's innovation and more active participation.

It is quite remarkable how few people praise their horses when they have done the right thing, but nearly all of them tell them off for doing the wrong thing! The voice is the best way of indicating praise, once the horses have learnt about the voice expressing pleasure, joy and so on, because it can be done anywhere, any time, in or out of sight, near or far. It is the easiest and most immediate way to reward and communicate with a horse.

We have learnt a lot recently from educational psychologists concerning the education of children using a positive, non-confrontational, interactive approach to teaching. We should be doing this much more with equines, if we want them to go further faster with their education and learning. By contrast, there is a general belief when training horses on the lunge for example, that it is vital to get the animal to do what you ask at all costs. If he does not want to walk, then you go on and on at him until he does walk, often becoming frustrated and irritated along the way, which the horse reads from the body language, and makes him less likely to want to go quietly. But the good teacher's job is to assess when the equine is likely to want to do what you ask and then ask and obtain the correct response, then everyone is happy.

Using such a co-operative approach does not mean that you allow disobedience or the lack of a quick response when, perhaps for matters of safety, you need it. In fact if the equine has been taught in such a co-operative interactive way, he will quickly recognize urgency and necessity in your voice and act accordingly; see the example on page 425 of how the voice stopped the two stallions fighting.

A word is used to denote exactly what response is required, paired with visual cues and cues from touching, physically aiding the equine to begin to respond in the desired way.

Example

Teaching a donkey to lift a front leg. First, you arrange the situation so he is likely to do this. If he is used to having his feet cleaned, the same cue, touching the lower leg, for example, can be used. The word command is given simultaneously as the leg is touched. When he lifts the leg, or even begins by shifting his weight to the other leg, he is verbally praised. The next time, he must lift the leg right off the ground before he is praised, and then given a food reward. Then the teacher gestures towards the leg, but does not touch it, as she gives the verbal command. Next, the teacher stands in front of the donkey, and simply looks at the leg as the verbal command is given. Finally, all the teacher has to do is say the words 'lift your left leg' and he will understand it, even if the teacher is looking in another direction. Whether or not he will lift the leg will depend on if he wants to or not, he always has a choice! So the teacher's job, as we have repeatedly stated, is to ensure that he *does* want to.

Head shaking, leg crossing, lying down, Spanish walk and trot, piaffe, passage, flying changes: whatever you want to teach can be taught in this way (see Kiley-Worthington 2004). If it is not done exactly as you would like or the dressage rules demand, then all that is necessary is to teach him in the same way to alter the response as required (see Learning 'that' and 'how', page 153).

Example

When Oberlix does not lift his hind legs enough in the piaffe, I ask him with my voice to lift them more and touch his hind leg with a whip. If he lifts one leg higher at least once, I stop and praise him. We repeat the exercise and when he performs three higher lifts, I excitedly acknowledge this with 'yes, yes', and reward him with my voice and a piece of apple. After five more trials, he understands not only the 'knowing what' to do, which he already knew, but also the 'knowing how', that is, how I want it done. Eventually, provided you are vigilant, the habit can be established so that the behaviour is always performed as you want it to be done.

It is not necessary to have spent years studying how to teach equines, or to ride very well, before you teach your equine these types of movements, all that is necessary is that *you observe and act appropriately, and that you understand and apply the rules of good teaching* (see page 164). If this is done, anyone can progress with teaching almost any horse these movements in as little as half an hour. A young horse may try things out at times when you do not require them, so remember, it is just as important to teach him *not* to do them at the wrong place or time.

Teaching must be progressive and to achieve this, the teacher must set the situation up correctly, observe the pupil closely, change the approach as required and react positively as soon as he begins to give the correct response. The next time he performs the exercise, he will have to do it a little better, and it must improve with each successive performance. Once an equine has learnt to learn and listen to the voice, it should not take him more than about thirty minutes teaching time before he understands some simple command words, when they are paired with slight visual cues. If it takes you longer, then it is because the teaching method is not as observant and reactive as it could be, so analyse your own behaviour. This way rapid improvements can be made.

The next stage is to introduce positional words such as 'left', 'right', 'on', 'off', 'in', 'out', 'behind', 'in front' and so on, in relation to doing particular things. It will take many repetitions in different situations before the equine has grasped the general meaning of these propositions. One of the most important things about this exercise is that it really makes you concentrate on what you are doing and what messages, both visual and verbal, you are giving to the equine.

Whether or not your equine grasps the exact meaning of the words, he will grasp that you are paying a lot of attention to him and trying to communicate seriously with him, rather than just bossing him around in a rather confusing muddled way. We have three horses now who we have worked with carefully in order to see if they can recognize these types of words and their meanings, and they certainly can do this without us consciously using any visual cues. But, whether they are responding to some subliminal visual cues, like Clever Hans, we do not yet know since we have not done the 'double blind' tests. This means that we are not seen, so we must either be behind a blind, or use a tape recorder.

There are some important points which we human language users do not often consider. The context in which equines are asked to do something, particularly when learning something rather difficult such as lying down or doing the Spanish trot, is important, not only from the point of view of everything conducive to the equine performing the behaviour, but also that they will quickly associate a particular action with a particular context, and then it works well there, but not in other places. Consequently there has to be a second stage where they are taught to generalize the response to different situations.

Example

Shemal was taught to lie down when she was around nine months old, and for four years would do it to the word command, without any visual cues. During a rehearsal for a ballet we were putting on, Oberlix who had to come up to her and smell her face on the ground, struck out with his front leg while she was lying flat (because there was another stallion near, and I had failed to take this into account), and cut her lip slightly. Nine months later, she still took over fifteen minutes before she would lie down at all, and as soon as she was down she would be up again. Here I made a very silly mistake, and it took many hours to reverse what she learnt in one trial, that is, lying down when asked is dangerous, even after four years of having no bad experience. However, she has no problem lying down in the field or stable when she is with Oberlix, it is lying down when she is asked to do so that is the problem, that is, it is *context dependent*. Now, one year later, she has got over this, but we must still be more careful than we were before when and where we ask her to do it.

The more complex comprehension of language by equines

Our subjects already associate the word with the written symbol for the numbers 1–5. We ask them to go and touch one of the five numbers displayed and they get it right too many times for it just to be chance. But the next step is to test whether they can learn to associate the word with the written symbol and with the concept of the number. This will be tested by asking them to paw out the number associated with the symbol of the number, thus, for example, they touch the 2, then they must paw twice with a hoof; the exercise is the same with the other numbers. It is very early days with these experiments, and it would be better to have more subjects, (although if one horse can do it, there is no way we can then maintain that horses *cannot* do it). It will also need to be tested without the presence of anyone who knows the answer, otherwise they may just be responding to cues they have been given, however inadvertently.

Another question is: can the equine subjects learn to understand concepts defined by language? For example, the name of 'yellow' for yellow objects, the name of 'green' for green ones, etc. They can in fact learn to do this (see Figure 9.2). But have they understood the greenness of green, as it were? The next stage is to test whether they understand that all green things have this in common (the same) and non-green things do not have this character (different). To do this we need to give them a range of green-coloured objects with a few non-green ones and ask them to sort out the green from the not green. Again, so far we have not done this experiment. There is a problem with colours though, as green can be of many shades. To score correctly, the equine will have to acquire our concept of green first and he may see more or fewer shades, we do not know.

Whether they can understand other aspects of human language (e.g. word order, see Figure 7.11A and pages 309–310) needs more research, but by using interactive co-operative teaching, we may be able to answer such questions a lot more easily than in a laboratory, and have a lot more fun doing it too.

By teaching this type of thing, can we learn more about equines and their view of the world? This certainly has been the case for me. One thing that has become very evident is how fast the equines learn such 'unnatural' things in an interactive teaching situation. Each subject has, to date, had 350 trials for each of the simple actions we have taught. Rats and pigeons in a laboratory situation take very much longer to learn these discriminations (sometimes thousands of trials for one act). This does not tell us that equines are particularly bright (see page 108), but it does tell us that this type of teaching is successful and quick.

The conclusion is that the use of the voice and language can be very helpful and important when educating equines. It must be carefully used, and the equine helped to listen and understand but this can be done starting simply.

If you get into the habit of talking in this way to equines (and other species) it is remarkable how quickly they learn, how much easier it makes the teacher's life, and how much greater the enjoyment.

REDUCE RESTRAINTS

In order to ensure that the equine is not frightened, wants to do what is asked, and is enjoying his lessons and his work, extra restraints *must not* be used. If the teacher needs, as work progresses, to use more restraints rather than less, then it is no longer co-operative teaching, it becomes domination and obedience training, because the animal has no choice. This is not the way to ensure either a human or an equine enjoys learning, nor is it particularly safe. Equines, although larger than humans, can be trussed up with a whole range of bits, pieces of leather and rope in order to be physically restrained (Figure 13.3). As a result, they do not kill very many people, even if they are terrified or patholog- ical because they can always be forcibly restrained, but they can damage themselves and people badly (and frequently do) as a result of such treatment, but this does not have to be the case.

One of the best lessons in reducing restraints for me came from the teaching work with African elephants. Elephants, are much larger than equines and very difficult to restrain. When riding them, for example, there are no bits or reins, indeed no way of stopping them if they do not want to stop. You can only ask them to stop or stop them by using an ankus (which can hurt). If an elephant is frightened and does not want to stop or turn, then there is nothing you can do but pray. Elephants, like any other animal, are very likely to hurt themselves or others or become aggressive when frightened (see page 202).

Training any mammal with fear, pain and domination and keeping them in environments where their needs are not fulfilled is very dangerous because they

Fig. 13.3 Grade A showjumping at Exeter where the competitors are mostly professional riders, yet martingales, running reins, drop nosebands and boots were worn by almost every horse in the class. Restraints such as those pictured compensate for bad training and riding. Action from animal liberation movements can be justified in this case!

may well react to this with defensive threat and, if they are large, kill the trainer. But, unfortunately, using fear, domination and pain is the traditional way of training Asian elephants and, as a result, many trainers (mahouts) are killed. In Kerala, South India, even though they have a very active elephant welfare group, 500 elephants have killed 100 mahouts in the last ten years; there must be something wrong.

As a consequence of these facts, we used the co-operative teaching method with our experimental group of African elephants in Zimbabwe, using positive reinforcement, and spending time just talking to the elephants and handling them gently. So far we have had no accidents, and the elephants have learnt a great deal very fast. The key to this teaching is ensuring that this very large and potentially dangerous animal enjoys his life, his needs are fulfilled, he likes and trusts his handlers and teachers, and his fear and frustration are reduced. That is training co-operatively. In this way no restraints are necessary, and if some animals already have restraints, their use is reduced during training. If this is possible with the much larger elephant, then it must be possible with equines.

Most owners of equines are not going to be able to spend the majority of their lives with them, nor be in any sense professional riders or trainers. Consequently, I realize that some safety factors are necessary, but these must be constantly reviewed, rather than just there because everyone uses them.

Some branches of the 'natural horsemanship' movement are also interested in reducing restraints, and often substitute complex equipment with relatively simple ropes or halters. On closer inspection, however, it is often the case that such halters or configurations of ropes can have very severe effects when pulled (e.g. the 'Be Nice' halter, the Parelli halter and the Roberts loading halter). The conventional approach to a horse who cannot be led or ridden without the handler/rider having some problem, is to add to the restraint by using increasingly severe bits; restrictions to prevent them opening their mouths, such as drop nosebands (which are used by almost 100% of dressage riders); pieces of leather to stop them raising their heads (martingales), forcing them to lower their heads (running reins), and so on. The power of the folk culture concerning what is correct for equines is so strong that many people who put these and many other restraints, on their horses, when questioned, do not know why they do, other than they were 'told to' or 'everyone does' (see Figure 13.3).

As many experienced teachers know, the problems experienced by the riders reflect their own inabilities. What they need to do is to learn more about their equines and how to handle or ride them. Nevertheless, often one is left with the problem of safety. If a particularly severe bit is not fitted to that particular horse, the rider may have an accident. There are often other solutions here, but let us stick to pointing out that increasing restraint may not always be the best answer. Perhaps it is necessary, as with the elephants, to think much more carefully about how and why the equine is responding in the way he is and then try to correct this by changing the person's behaviour and re-education of the equine.

Ideally, with co-operative teaching, what you are aiming for in the end is a symbiotic relationship with the equine in everything you do. First his husbandry system is examined to see if restraint can be reduced there, then the way he is taught and worked is examined to see how you can progress to less restraint. In the end, you should be able to have your horse follow you, or ride him anywhere, safely, without a bridle, headcollar reins or even a rope around his neck. The saddle is not so much a restraint for the horse as comfort for the rider but, again, ideally it should not be necessary.

'Work in the round pen' (where a special pen is made to restrain the horse) is no less restraining than work on the lunge; one method uses a pen around which the horse is chased, the other method uses a line to stop the horse running off. But progress can be made with a horse, after starting him in either of these ways, towards being able to perform this work genuinely at liberty. The same is true of any type of riding or driving: it may be necessary to start with some restraints, but these should gradually be reduced, until it is to be hoped, we can manage without any at all.

This is the final aim of co-operative teaching: to be able to ride, drive, walk, or do anything else with your equine without any form of restraint, although it may be necessary to have reins attached to a headcollar in case of an emergency. It will also be necessary to accustom the equine to tack, so start with a bridle and bit and, gradually, when he understands the words and touch aids and has the habit of carrying himself well, remove the bit.

Not all of us will be able to achieve this all the time but, it is something to work towards. It may indeed be necessary, in order to reduce a rider's fear, to have something that can be used in an emergency for safety but, if it is necessary to introduce gadgets to stop the horse, to shut his mouth, to stop his head moving up or down, and so on, then, all this tells us is that the horse has a bad teacher and rider, and there is no co-operation between horse and rider.

SUMMARY

1. An understanding of equine lore can help dramatically in educating our equines. The most rational approach and the one taken here is to develop co-operative teaching based on how we conduct good relationships with other humans.

2. As a result of knowing more about how they learn, it is clear that a much quicker way of teaching equines than has often been the conventional practice, is to use the voice, assume they can learn to understand simple language and adapt similar methods for teaching young children, including using much praise, very little negative reinforcement or punishment, and giving them a host of different experiences.

→

3. Finally, if we wish to develop a symbiotic relationship with our equines, we can demonstrate this by gradually reducing the physical restraints used on them until we can work them from the ground, ride or drive them, or perform any other activity with them, without restraints. This may be an ideal, but perhaps one that is worth working towards even if few of us are likely to achieve it.

Fig. 13.4   Doing something useful. Shemal carries hay to some of the other stock through the Devon woodland.

Further detailed methods and examples can be found in Kiley-Worthington (2004).

14 Conditional anthropomorphism revisted, and conclusions

Throughout this book, we have pointed out what we know about equines' behaviour and their minds and how to use this to improve their husbandry and education. However, in the nature of things, this will not always have been done well; everyone makes mistakes with equines: you and I, present and past handlers, we can all cause problems. Blaming 'others', be it another human, the horse or his genes, for his unpleasant or desired behaviour, will not make the problem go away. The one way in which it can get better, whenever it was established, is by the present handler or teacher thinking carefully about the problem and how s/he and the present environment in which the equine is living, may be part of it. It is crucial to assess how he lives and is kept and how he is handled, ridden or being taught. The first obvious change that can be made is to analyse your own behaviour first and change it where it may be wanting.

Behavioural problems in equines are the result of inappropriate environments and/or bad education of the horse. Only a very small percentage of them are related to abnormality or damage to the brain, because those who are likely to have such problems have been heavily selected against (they will have died *in utero*, or very young) as we do not know or care as much about equine neuro-medicine as we do about that of humans. Equines are considered to be more disposable so mentally or physically handicapped animals are allowed to die or are culled.

When confronted by a behavioural, and sometimes a physical, problem of a horse, it is important first to try and understand the fundamental cause and then, by removing the cause, work on achieving a cure. This may seem to be common sense, but an in-depth assessment of the cause for that individual by looking at their total environment is necessary. This approach when treating humans' mental disorders was first publicised by R. D. Laing (1960), and has been, at least in part, adopted by psychiatrists and psychotherapists. For the treatment of equines it is invaluable.

The truth is that we do know how the vast majority of equines' misbehaviour problems are caused, and we definitely can design environments and educational strategies which ensure that they do not occur in the next generation, if we really want to. We do not need further money spent on research in order to try to justify particular husbandry practices because they are traditional or convenient. This does not mean we should not use the horse in certain ways, except if the nature of the work means that they will suffer. It does mean we need to question, and maybe change, some of our traditional establishment practices, at least for some equines.

We can do this if we use a conditional anthropomorphic approach, that is recognize our mammalian similarities then mould this to benefit equines by using our awareness of what we know of our species differences and the slightly different worlds we live in.

Everyone wants an instant fix: 'my pony knocks my son with his head when he is just talking nicely to him, what do I do?' Think about it, think about what you know about equines, about his life, about how your son is behaving, about how the equine learns, and then change things to ensure that the pony does not want to do this. This approach is about solving it for yourself, thinking about it, trying things, and not just listening to someone else who may or may not have the solution. There are no magic solutions. The answers involve looking carefully at whether or not his needs are fulfilled in the way he lives, is kept or taught. We have examined what these are, with the knowledge we have, in Chapters 1–12 of this book. To summarize:

Ensure that the way he is kept, the food he is given to eat, the company he keeps, and the things he is asked to do fulfil all his needs. If they do not, work out practical ways within this situation that will more closely fulfil:

1. his physical needs (see Chapters 1 and 2);
2. his social needs (see Chapter 6);
3. his emotional needs (see Chapters 4, 7 and 9);
4. his cognitive/intellectual needs (see Chapters 5, 6, 8–11);
(See Figure 12.1).

Observe, self-analyse and put effort and time into changing things. If we understand why he is not doing what is required, we can make sure this does not happen again. But, it may require time and, certainly, motivation before there is improvement. We all make mistakes, but we can learn from them.

Example

Some twenty-five years ago, I loaded my young Anglo-Arab stallion Baksheesh (three years old) into a trailer for the first time. He was kept with mares, easy to handle, and confident and relaxed with humans. He walked into the trailer quietly and well. The trailer did not have a canvas over the roof, and he was able to stick his head up through the roof trusses; when he did, he hit his head and was hurt and frightened. I was young and inexperienced but, nevertheless, the reason for the problem I had loading him thereafter was quite obvious. It did not need an 'expert' to tell me the reason, nor did it need an 'expert' to tell me how to put it right. All I had to do was to convince him this would not happen again. It took me a while to do this, largely because I was lazy and did not do enough loading and short journeys in a trailer with a roof. It was a stupid mistake and I was slack about correcting it, although it was obvious what I had to do. When we make mistakes, the first step is to admit them and try to put them right.

Equines do not come from Mars; how they think, what they know, how they learn, what they need, is not a complete mystery. They are very similar to us, which is why we like them. But in some ways they are different. If we critically assess what we observe, and review what is generally known about equines, we can learn more about their world view which will help us solve behavioural problems but, in addition, it can enrich our own lives and appreciation of the world.

Equines and humans are the result of a fusion of both the body and the mind. There are problems which have their origin in the mind (psychological problems) but which show themselves physically. There are also problems which have their origin in the body (physical problems) but which show themselves in behavioural problems: 'mind' problems. Thus, if the equine is constantly frustrated, frightened, worried or anxious he is likely to become physically ill, as well as behave in undesirable ways. If he is frequently physically ill, it is not helpful just to treat the disease with the appropriate medicines. It is crucial that the entire environment is looked at and assessed for its appropriateness (or lack of it) for both the equine's body and mind needs.

Veterinarians are skilled at identifying and treating physical illnesses, but not necessarily their relationship to psychological problems which may be the cause. Thus, first, when trying to understand a behavioural problem, try to understand the *cause* by looking at all aspects of the animal's life. There is always a cause, it is never 'just chance'.

One thing that is, in the great majority of cases, not appropriate, is the use of drugs to try to overcome equine behavioural problems. Very occasionally, the use of a tranquilliser will give some helpful results, but the equine still has to learn not to behave in the way he generally does in that situation without the tranquilliser. It is just a matter of taking the time and developing the skill to understand the animal's world that will help you make progress, whether this is trying to handle a wild zebra, loading a Thoroughbred who has been in a crash before, teaching an Arab to pull a set of harrows that he ran away with last time, or teaching a horse to stand still and wait while you get on.

There are many ways of making life more enjoyable for a horse, particularly when you remember that his joy will not only come from associating with other horses, or running around loose, but also from associating with humans who like him and who he also likes and trusts, learning new things and performing to attract praise from people, particularly those he knows and likes.

Equines, just like humans, are all individuals, the result of their nature and their nurture. As a good carer and educator, you have to constantly adapt, invent, try out, and rethink. That is the challenge, excitement and fun.

Equines teach us to know ourselves better. They can teach us new things. They have taught me an enormous amount about many things in the world – to view them in new ways and 'being in the world' – opening many mental doors. The more you learn about them and what it might be to be an equine, the more options of world views you have, and the more delight in being alive.

Almost every day I am taken by surprise by something that happens in the equine soap opera enacted in our fields, the result of a different world view, or a different way of doing something. One thing that is clear is that they have taught me (through the experiences of living with them, teaching them and studying them empirically) not to be so sure that the general belief that humans are cognitively/mentally superior to other mammals can always be assumed.

By their sheer physical beauty, energy, strength, athleticism, and particularly their mental attributes, they have enormously enriched my life, and will continue to do this every new day, as many other people also find.

15 Main summary of the different world view of equines: equine lore

Chapters 1–13 of this book have concluded with summaries for easy Chapter reference. The summaries are on the following pages: Chapter 1, pages 80–82; Chapter 2, pages 105–106; Chapter 3, pages 162–163; Chapter 4, pages 216–217; Chapter 5, page 240; Chapter 6, pages 273–275; Chapter 7, pages 312–314; Chapter 8, pages 334–336; Chapter 9, pages 363–364; Chapter 10, pages 380–381; Chapter 11, pages 390–391; Chapter 12, pages 410–411; Chapter 13, pages 434–435.

The following is a list of the main points of those summaries.

1. Equines are athletic movement specialists and their first response to the unfamiliar is to flee. They can run fast and far and perform amazing feats of balance over difficult terrain and jumps, and carry or pull a high percentage of their body-weight. Thus, their idea of space and distance is different from ours.

2. They are highly adaptable and tolerant animals and consequently have been able to survive often in extremely difficult surroundings when domesticated.

3. They are acutely aware of what is happening all around them at any time, having a scanning attention, and even when attending to one thing, they are aware of other changes around them. In effect they are often doing two things at a time.

4. An acute awareness of smells opens up a different world view from the human one involving messages concerning past and future events and detailed social information.

5. They are very visually acute particularly to slight movements, and can predict next actions and emotional states from visual cues involving slight muscle movements and tensions. They can pick up these messages between species too, particularly from humans.

6. They acquire an enormous amount of information in order to become good natural historians/ecologists so that they know: what to eat and where to find it, how to recognize and predict the behaviour of other species, where to go and how to find their way around, what places to avoid, and where to find shelter at different times of the year.

7. They are social co-operative-living creatures. Their social life has rules, the most important one being to ensure that the social group sticks together. They have to become good sociologists/natural psychologists in order to to get on with others, predict others' behaviour and know and understand individuals' different personalities and roles.

8. The bonds between generations are very strong, youngsters spend more time with their elders than with siblings so, consequently, are able to acquire more reliable information by social learning and observation.

9. They show fondness for individuals, often forming life-long associations, and particular loyalty to their familiar group.

10. They learn about other species, including their different world views, for example they can learn to comprehend some human language.

11. They are sensitive to others and their feelings.

12. They learn very fast, often in a single trial. They can learn complex series of movements and to use concepts and symbols.

13. The meaning of the messages in their communication is context dependent, thus to interpret the specific message they have to absorb cues from the environment. This is unlike the context independent human language.

14. They are not manipulators of the world, and so may demonstrate feelings such as compassion and sympathy in different ways from those humans might expect.

15. They experience mental events, they learn, remember, make choices and decisions, have beliefs, have some awareness of others' minds and feelings, are conscious and conscious of their own bodies.

16. They have some form of aesthetic appreciation and moral agency although this needs further investigation.

17. Whether they reflect on things or are conscious of their own minds remains an open question.

Postscript

We moved to a new location on 25th December 2003 in La Drome, France. We have a Research and Education Centre here and an ecological farm and wildlife reserve on 172 hectares (425 acres) of mountains, forest, streams, ponds, cliffs, screes, grassland, and arable acres. We have gites to hire, and less-expensive bunk accommodation, plenty of superb riding country for which you can bring your own horses or ride ours. We have a small cafe/restaurant serving food from our farm. The Druimghigha horses and their humans continue to be studied, and teach people, and we run courses in equine lore and education, teach people how to do research, have meetings, conferences and take students of many types, and occasionally have young horses for sale. We run courses on valuing the environment and studying ecology for amateurs and professionals in English and French.

Anyone interested in any of the holidays/courses is invited to write to the centre: Eco Research et Education Centre, La Combe, Bezaudun sur Bine, 26460 Drome, France. Tel: 00.33.1475532027; email: eco-ferme.mkw@wanadoo.fr; website: www.eco-etho-recherche.com.

Fig. 13.4 Our new home in La Drome, france. Onyx, Lilka, Shemal and Oberlix (carrying the camera) have made themselves quite 'at home'.

Bibliography

Anon, 'L'equitation, le cheval et l'ethologie', Colloque du 18 Sept 1999 a l'ecole National d'Equitation, Belin, Paris.

Adam, C. and M. Bekoff (1997) *Species of Mind*, MIT, Cambs, USA

Andrews, R. J. (1963) The origin and evolution of the calls and facial expressions of the primates, *Behav.*, 20, 1–109

d'Arcy, W. Thompson (1942) *On Growth and Form*, Cambridge University Press, Cambridge (reprinted 1963)

Ardrey, R. (1966) *The territorial imperative*, Fontana, Collins, London

Bagemehl, B. (1999) *Biological Exuberance, Animal Homosexuality and Natural Diversity,* St Martins Press, NY

Barney, E. B., B. Landjerit and R. Wolter (1991) Shock vibration during the hoof impact on different track surfaces, pp97–106 in *Equine Exercise Physiology 3*, eds. S. G. B. Persson, A. Lindholm and L. B. Jeffcott, ICEEP publ., Davis.

Baron-Cohen, S. (1993) From attention-goal psychology to belief-desire psychology: the development of a theory of mind, and its dysfunction, pp59–82 in *Understanding other Minds*. eds. S. Baron-Cohen, H. Tager-Flusberg and D. J. Cohen. Oxford University Press

Bateson, P. P. G. (1966) The characteristics and context of imprinting, *Biol. Rev.* 41, 177–220, ch8, p2

Bavidge, T. and G. Ground (1994) *Can we understand animal minds?* Routledge, London.

Bekoff, M. (1992) Scientific ethology, animal consciousness, and animal protection: a principled plea for unabashed common sense. *New Ideas in Psychol.* 10, 79–94.
(2000) *The Smile of the Dolphin*. Remarkable accounts of animal emotions. discovery Books, USA

Bennett, J. (1988) *Thoughtful Brutes*, Proc. and Addresses of American Philosophical Association, 62, 199

Bentham, J. (1789) *Introduction to the principles of morals and legislation*

Berger, J. (1977) Organisational systems and dominance in feral horses in the Grand Canyon, *Behav. Ecol. and Sociobiol.*, 2, 91–119

Berlyne, D. G. (1960) *Conflict, arousal and curiosity*, McGraw Hill, London

Bernstein. I. S. (1981) Dominance: the baby and the bathwater. *Behav. Br. Sci.*, 4, 419–29

The Bible

Bindra, D. (1959) *Motivation, a systematic reinterpretation*, Ronald Press, NY

Bitterman, M. E. (1984) Learning in man and other animals, in *Perspectives in Psychological Experimentation: Towards the year 2000*, eds. V. Sarris and A. Parducci, Erlbaum. NY

Blake, H. (1975) *Talking with horses, study of communication between man and horse*, Souvenir Press, London

(1977) *Thinking with horses*, Souvenir Press, London

Bonner, J. T. (1980) *The Evolution of Culture in Animals*, Princeton University Press, Princeton

Borgese, E. M. (1968) *The Language Barrier: Beasts and Men*, Holt, Rinehart & Winston, NY

Bortof, H. (1996) *The wholeness of Nature. Goethe's way of science*, Floris books, Edinburgh

Braddon-Mitchell, B. D. and F. Jackson (1996) *Philosophy of mind and cognition*, Blackwell, Oxford.

Brady, E. (1999) Sniffing and savoring: the aesthetics of smell and taste, *Philosophy & Geography*, 4

Brechtel, W. and A. Abrahamsen (1993) *Connectionism and the Mind*, Blackwell, Oxford

Bristol, J. (1982) Breeding behaviour of a stallion at pasture with twenty mares in synchronised oestrus. *J. Reprod. Fert.* Suppl. 32, 71–7.

British Horse Society (1982) *Horse Management*, BHS, Stonleigh

Broom, D. M. and K. G. Johnson (1993) *Stress and Animal Welfare*, Chapman & Hall, London

Bryne, R. (1998) *The Thinking Ape*, Oxford University Press, Oxford

Bryne, R. and A. Whiten (1988) *Machiavallian Intelligence. Social Expertise and the Evolution of Intelligence in Monkeys, Apes and Humans*, eds. R. Bryne and A. Whiten, Oxford University Press, Oxford

Buckingham, S. H. W. and L. B. Jeffcott (1991) Skeletal effects of long term submaximal exercise programme on standard-bred yearlings, pp411–418 in *Equine Exercise Physiology 3*, eds. S. G. B. Persson, A. Lindholm and L. B. Jeffcott, ICEEP publ. Davis

Budiansky, S. (1996) Don't bet on faster horses, *New Scientist*, 10th August. pp29–31

Burger, U. (1959) *The way to perfect horsemanship*, J. A. Allen, London

Burghardt, J. M. (1991) Cognitive ethology and critical anthropomorphism. A snake with two heads and hog-nosed snakes that play dead, in *Cognitive Ethology*. ed. C. A. Ristau, Erlbaum, Hillsdale

Butler, P. J., A. J. Woakes, L. S. Anderson, K. Smale, C. A. Roberts and D. H. Snow (1991) The effect of cessation of training on cardiorespiratory variables during exercise, pp71–76 in *Equine Exercise Physiology 3*, eds. S. G. B. Persson. A. Lindholm and L. B. Jeffcott, ICEEP publ., Davis

Candland, D. K. (1993) *Feral Children and Clever Animals*, Oxford University Press, Oxford

Caro, T. H. and M. D. Hauser (1992) Is there teaching in non-human animals? *Quart. Rev. Biol.*, 67, 151–74

Carroll, L. (1871) *Through the Looking Gass*, Macmillan, London

Carruthers, P. (1992) *The Animals' Issue. Moral theory in practice*. Cambridge University Press, Cambridge

(1996) *Language, thought and consciousness. An essay in philosophical psychology*, Cambridge University Press, Cambridge

Catchpole, C. K and P. J. B. Slater (1995) *Bird Song. Biological themes and variations*, Cambridge University Press, Cambridge

Chambers, T. (1993) Recognition of pain and distress in horses. Brit. Vet. Ass. Roadshow, *Pain in Practise*, BVA, Plymouth

Cheney, D. L. and R. M. Seyfarthe (1990) *How Monkeys see the World*, University of Chicago Press, Chicago

Chomsky, N. (1988) *Language and Problems of Knowledge*, MIT Press

Clark, S. R. L. (1977) *The Moral Status of Animals*, Oxford Univeristy Press, Oxford.

(1982) *The Nature of the Beast: Are Animals Moral?* Oxford University Press, Oxford

(1997) *Animals and Their Moral Standing*, Routledge, London

Clayton, N. and A. Dickinson (1999) Episodic-like memory during cache recovery by scrub jays, Nature 395, 272–278

Clutton-Brock, T. H., F. E. Guinness and S. D. Albon (1982) *Red Deer. Behaviour and the Ecology of Two Sexes*, Edinburgh University Press, Edinburgh

Collingwood, R. G. (1938) *The principles of art*, Oxford University Press, Oxford

Crook, J. H. (1987) The nature of conscious awarenes, in *Mindwaves. Thoughts on intelligence, identity and consciousness*. eds. C. Blackmore and S. Greenfield, Blackwell, Oxford

Dantzer, R. (1986) Behavioural, physiological and functional aspects of stereotyped behaviour: a review and a re-interpretation, *J. Anim. Sci* 62, 1776–1786.

Darwin, C. (1868) *The Expression of the Emotions in Man and Animals*, John Murray, London

(1887) *The Descent of Man and Selection in Relation to Sex*, John Murray, London

Dawkins, M. S. (1993) *Through Our Eyes Only? The search for animal consciousness*, W. H. Freeman, Oxford

Dawkins, R. (1986) *The Blind Watchmaker*, Longman, Harlow

(1989) *The Selfish Gene*, Oxford University Press, Oxford

Dawson, F. L. M. S. (1984) Equine Reproduction, in *Horse Management*, ed. J. Hickman, p1–54, Academic Press, London

Declaration of Human Rights, (1948) United Nations, Geneva

DeGrazia, D. (1996) *Taking Animals Seriously*, Cambridge University Press, Cambridge

Dennett, D. C. (1991) *Consciousness Explained*, Little, Brown & Co., Boston

(1996) *Kinds of Minds*, Phoenix, London

Descartes, R. (1641) *Meditations on Philosophy*, Michel, Paris

Desmond, A. (1980) *The Apes Reflection*, Quartet Books, London

Dickinson, A. (1994) Instrumental conditioning, pp45–79 in *Animal learning and cognition*, ed. N. J. MacIntosh, Academic Press, San Diego

Drever, J. (1960) *A Dictionary of Psychology*, Penguin, London

Dreyfus, S. H. I. and S. T. Dreyfus, (1980) Making a mind versus modelling the brain, *Daedalus*, ed. 117, 15–43

Dunnett, M. (1989) Language and Communication, in *Reflections on Chomsky*, ed. A. George, Blackwell, Oxford

Dunbar, I. (1998) Groups size and brain size in primates. Seminar, Dept. Psychology, University of Exeter, 1998

Eibl-Ebesfeldt, I. (1971). *Love and Hate*. trans. G. Stachan, Collins, London

Erasmus (1704) from *The Oxford Dictionary of Quotations* (1999) Oxford University Press, Oxford

Estes, R. D. (1991) *The Behavior Guide to African Mammals*, Russel Friedman, South Africa

Evans, H. (1987) *The criminal prosecution and capital punishment of animals* (first edition, 1906) Faber and Faber, London

Feist, J. D. and D. R. McCullogh (1976) Behaviour patterns and communication in feral horses. *Tierpsychol*, 2. 41, 337–371

Fillis, J. (1969) *Breaking and Riding*, trans. M. H. Hayes, J. A. Allen, London

Fisher, J. A. (1986) Taking Sympathy Seriously: A Defense of Our Moral Psychology Towards Animals, *Environ. Ethics*, 198, 197–215

   (1991) Disambiguating anthropomorphism: an inter-disciplinary review, *Perspectives in Ethology*, 9, 124–35

Flew, A. (1983) *A dictionary of philosophy*, Pan, London

Fodor, J.A. (1975) *The Language of Thought*, Scranton, Cromell

   (1987) *Psychosemantics. The problem of meaning in the philosophy of mind*, MIT, Camb, Mass.

Fouts, R. and S. Mills (1997) *Next of Kin*, Penguin, London

Fowler, W. (1990) Early stimulation and the development of verbal talents, pp179–210 in *Encouraging the Development of Exceptional Skills and Talents*, ed. M. J. A. Howe

Fox, M. W. (1968) (ed.) *Abnormal Behaviour of Animals*, W. B. Saunders. NY

Franchini, M. (2001) *Les Indiens d'Amerique et le cheval*, Zulma, Paris

Fraser, A. F. (1968) *Reproductive Behaviour in Ungulates*, Academic Press, London

   (1992) *Horse Behaviour*, CAB, Wallington, USA

Fraser-Darling, F. (1954) *A Herd of Red Deer*, Cambridge University Press, Cambridge

Freud, S. (1953) *Standard Edition of the Complete Psychological Works of Sigmund Freud* Vol. 6, Hogarth Press, London

Frey, R. G. (1980) *Interests and Rights: The Case Against Animals*, Oxford, Clarendon

Gaita R. (2000) *The philosopher's dog*, Routledge, London

Galef Jr., B. J. (1986) Tradition and Social Learning in Animals, pp149–163 in *Animal Intelligence. Insights into the Animal Mind*, eds. R. J. Hoage and L. Goldman, Smithsonian Institution Press, Washington

Gallistel, C. R. (1996) Representations in Animal Cognition: An Introduction, in *Animal Cognition*, ed. C. R. Gallistel, MIT, Cambridge, Mass

Gallup Jr., G. G. (1979) Self-awareness in primates, *American Scientist*, 67, 86–87

Gardner, R. A. and B. T. Gardner (1969) Teaching sign language to a chimpanzee, *Sci.*, 165, 664–672

Garland, J. S. (1968) Structure and function in primate society, *Folia Primatologia*, 8, 89–120

Gibbon, J. and R. M. Church (1990) Representation of time, *Cognition*, 37, 23–34

Goldsmith-Rothchilde, B. von (1976) *Sociale organization und verhalten eines Camargue-Pferde-Bestandes*, Lizentiat, Bern

Goodall, J. (1990) *Through a Window: My Thirty Years with the Chimpanzees of Gombe*, Houghton Mifflin, Boston

Graham, G. (1993) *Philsophy of mind*, Blackwell, Oxford

Gregory, R. L. (1958) Eye movements and the stability of the visual world, *Nature*, 182, 1214–1216

Griffin, D. R. (1984) *Animal thinking*, Harvard University Press, Cambridge, Mass
(1992) *Animal Minds*, University of Chicago Press

Grove, A. J. and G. E. Newell (1942) *Animal Biology*, University Tutorial Press, London

Groves, C. P. (1974) *Horses, asses and zebras in the wild*, David and Charles, London

Guérinière, F. R. de la (1733) *The School of Horsemanship*, trans. T. Boucher (1994), J. A. Allen, London

Haagni, E. B. (1994) Serial reversal discrimination learning using shape cues in horses (*Equus caballus*), *Equine Research Foundation*, California
(1996) Conditional discrimination learning in the horse (*Equus caballus*), *Equine Research Foundation*, California.

Hamilton, W. D. (1963) The evolution of altruistic behaviour, *American Naturalist*, 97, 354–356.
(1964) The genetic evolution of social behaviour, *J. Theor. Biology*, 7, 1–52.

Harnad, S. (1987) editorial comment in Macphail 1987

Harris, R.C., D. J. Marlin and D. H. Snow (1991) Lactate kinetics, plasma ammonia and performance following repeated bouts of maximal exercise, pp173–178 in *Equine Exercise Physiology 3*, eds. S. G. P. Persson, A. Lindholm and L. B. Jeffcott. ICEEP publ., Davis

Hauser, M. (1996) *The evolution of communication*, MIT, Cambridge, Mass.

Hayes, K. J. and C. Hayes (1954) The cultural capacity of chimpanzees, *Human Biology*, 26

Hearne.V. (1987) *Adam's Task, Calling Animals by Name*, Heinemann, London
  (1994) *Animal Happiness*, Harper Collins, NY

Hebb, D. O. (1949) *The organisation of behaviour*, Wiley

Hegel, G. F. W. (1807) *Phenomenology of mind*

Heidegger, M. (1969) *Identity and Difference*, Harper & Row, NY

Herman, L. M. (1980) *Cetacean Behaviour: Mechanisms and Functions*, Wiley, NY

Herman, L. M and P. Morrel-Samuels (1990) Knowlege Acquisition and Asymmetry betwen language Comprehension and Production, in *Intepretation and Explanation in the Study of Animal Behavior*, eds. M. Bekoff and J. Jamieson, Vol I, p287, Boulder, Westview

Hermann, L. M. (1987) Receptive competencies of language trained animals,. *Advances in the study of behaviour*, 7, Academic Press, NY

Herrnstein, R. J. (1979) Aquistion generalisation and discrimination reversal of a natural concept. *J. Expt. Psy. Animal Behav. Proc*, 5, 116–129

Heyes, C. M. (1997) Theory of mind in nonhuman Primates. *Behav. & Brain Sci.*, 21, 101–148

Hickman, J. (1984) *Horse Management*, Academic Press, London

Hinde, R. A. (1970) *Animal Behaviour*, McGraw-Hill, London

Hoage, R. J. and L. Goldman (eds.) (1987) *Animal Intelligence. Insights into the Animal Mind*, Smithsonian Inst, Washington

Hobbes, T. (1651) *Leviathan*

Hockett, C. F. (1960) Logical considerations in the study of animal communication, pp392–430 in *Animals Sounds and communication*, (eds) W. E. Lanyon and W. N. Tavolga, American Inst. Biological Sci. Washington, DC

Horak, V., P. Draber, J. Hanak and S. Matolin, Fibre composition and tubulin localisation in muscle of Thoroughbred sprinters and stayers, pp262–268 in *Equine Exercise Physiology 3*, eds. S. G. B. Persson, A. Lindholm and L. B. Jeffcott, ICEEP publ., Davis

Houpt, K. A. (1979) The intelligence of the horse, *Equine Practise*, 1, 20–26

Houpt, K. A, D. M. Zahorik and J. A. Swartzman-Andert (1990) Taste aversion learning in horses, *J. Anim. Sci*, 68, 2340–2344

Howe, J. (1997) *IQ in question. The truth about intelligence*, Sage, London

Hughes, B.O. and I. J. N. Duncan, (1988) The notion of ethological "need". Models of motivation and animal welfare, *Anim. Behav*, 36, 1696–1707

Hull, C. L. (1945) The place of innate individual and species differences in a natural-science theory of behavior, *Psychological review*, 52, 55–60

Hume, D. (1778) *Treatise on Human Nature*, ed. C. R. Selby-Bigge, Oxford University Press, Oxford

Humphrey, N. (1976) The social function of intellect, in *Growing points in ethology*, eds. P. Bateson and R. Hinde, Cambridge University Press, Cambridge

(1986) *The Inner Eye*, pp93–4, Faber & Faber, London

Husserl, E. (1965) *The Crisis of the Sciences as Expression of the Radical Life-Crisis of European Humanity*, Harper Row, NY

Hutt, C. (1966) Exploration and play in children, *Symp. Zoo. Soc*, 18, 61–81, London

Hutt, C. and S. J. Hutt (1965) The effect of environmental complexity on stereotyped behaviour of children, *Anim. Behav*, 13, 1–4

Huxley, J. H. (1960) *Ritualisation*, Royal Society, London

Imam, S. A. H. A. A. (1983) *Mis-en-Main without a bit*, Imam Hazaribagh

(1987) *The Centaur. A critical analysis of horsemanship plus relevant equitant history*, Indian Heritage, Hazaribagh

Iwanowski, G. (1987) *You and Your Horse*, Shutter and Shooter, Johannesburg

Jackson, J. (1992) *The Natural Horse. Lessons from the wild for domestic horse care*, Northland, Flagstaff, Arizona

James, W. (1890) *The principles of psychology*, Henry Holt, NY

Jerison, M. (1973) *Evolution of brain size and intelligence*, Academic Press, London

Johnson, B. (1995) *The skilful mind of the guide dog*, G. D. B., Herts

Johnson-Laird, P. (1973) Visual perception of biological motion and a model for its analysis. *Perception & Psychophysics*, 14, 201–11.

Jolly, A. (1996) Lemurs social behaviour and primate intelligence, *Sci.*, 153, 501–506

Jung, C. G. (1931) *Die Psychologie der unbewusten Prozesse, The Oxford Dictionary of Quotations* (1999) Oxford University Press, Oxford

Kant, I. (1963) *Lecture in Ethics: Duties to Animals and Spirits*, trans. Infield, Harper & Row. NY

Kasselle, M. and P. Hannay (1995) *Touching Horses. Communication, health and healing through Shiatzu*, J. A. Allen, London

Keiper, R. R. (1969) Causal factors of stereotypies in caged birds. *Anim. Behav*, 17, 114–119

Kellog, W. N. and C. A. Kellog (1933) *The ape child*

Kennedy, J. (1992) *The New Anthropomorphism*. Cambridge University Press, Cambridge

Kiley, M. (1969) *Some Dislays in Ungulates, Canids and Felids with particular reference to causation*, D. Phil, Sussex University

(1972) The vocalisations of ungulates. Their cause and function. *Zeit. Tierpsychol*, 31, 171–222

Kiley-Worthington, M. (1976) The tail movements of ungulates, canids and felids with particular reference to causation and their function as displays, *Behav*, 6, 115–138

(1977) *The behavioural problems of farm animals*, Oriel Press, Stockton

(1987) *The behaviour of horses in relation to management and training*, J. A. Allen, London

(1990) *Animals in Circuses and Zoos. Chiron's World?* Little Eco-Farm Publishing, Basildon

(1998) Competition and Cooperation. A detailed study of communication and social organisation in a small group of horses (*Equus caballus*), *Eco Research Centre*, ISBN 367-2045, paper 024

(1998) *Equine Welfare*, J. A. Allen, London

(2000) *Right in Front of Your Mind, Equine and Elephant Epistemology*. M.Phil thesis in Philosophy, University of Lancaster

Kiley-Worthington, M. (in press). *L'elephant, l'homme et le cheval*, Zulma, Paris

Kiley-Worthington, M. and H. Randle (1997) Animal educational psychology. A comparative study of teaching four mammals of different species, *Eco Research Centre*, 013

(1997) Animal Handling and Animal Educational Psychology. Symposium Comparative Psychology, Montreal and *Eco Research Centre*, 012a

(1997) An investigation into the effectiveness of improved handling and teaching techniques in five large herbivores, *Eco Research Centre*, 012b.

(2004) *Equine Education*, Whittet Books, Stowmarket.

Kiley-Worthington, M. and D. Wood-Gush (1987) Stereotypies in Horses, in *Current therapy in equine medicine*, ed. N. E. Robinson, Saunders, London

Kingsley, C. (1880) *The Water Babies*, Methuen, London

Klingel, H. (1975) Die soziale Organisation der Equiden. *Verh. Dtsch. Zool. Ges.*, pp71–80

Koehler, O. (1951) The ability of birds to count. *Bul. Anim. Behav.*, 9, 41–45

Kohler, W. (1925) *The mentality of apes*, Vintage. NY.

Krebs, J. R. and Dawkins. R. (1984) Animal signals: mind reading and manipulation, in *Behavioural Ecology. An Evolutionary Aproach*, 2nd edn., pp380–402, eds. J. R. Krebs and N. B. Davies, Blackwell Scientific Publications, Oxford

Kummer, H. (1982) Social knowledge in free ranging primates, in *Animal Mind-Human Mind*, pp113–130, ed. D. Griffin, Springer, Berlin

Laing, R. D. (1960) *The Divided Self*, Penguin, London

Lawrence, M. (1980) *Flyers and Stayers. The book of the greatest rides*, Harrap, London

Lea, S. E. G., (1995) The ability of pigeons to recognise three dimensional photographs, seminar in Dept. Psychology, University of Exeter

Lea, S. E. G., A. Lohman and C. M. C. Ryan (1993) Discrimination of five dimensional stimuli by pigeons, seminar, University of Exeter

Lea, S. and M. Kiley-Worthington (1996) Do Animals Think? in *Unsolved Mysteries of the Mind*, ed. V. Bruce

Leahy, M. P. T. (1991) *Against Liberation: Putting Animals in Perspective*, Routledge, London

Leakey, R. (1981) *The making of mankind*, Abacus, London

Lee, R. B. and I. de Vore (1968) *Man the Hunter*, Chicago University Press, Chicago

Lieberman, P. (1976) Comments on Mounin's paper, *Current Anthropology*, 17, p14 (quoted by Desmond)

Lijsen, H. J. (1993) *Classical Circus Equitation*, J. A. Allen, London

Lilly, J. C. (1961) *Man and Dolphin*, Gollanz, London

Linden, E. (1986) *Silent partners. The legacy of the ape language experiments*, New York Times Books

Locke, J. (1960) *An essay concerning human understanding*

Loizos, C. (1966) quoted by Wemelsfedler (1993) p106

Lorenz, K. (1996) *On Aggression*, Methuen, London

Lorenz, K. Z. (1981) *The Foundations of Ethology*, Springer-Verlag

Lyons, W. (1980) *Emotions*, Cambridge University Press, Cambridge

McDowell, J. (1996) *Mind and World*, Harvard University Press, Cambs, Mass

McGinn, C. (1989) *Mental Content*, p62, Blackwell, Oxford

MacIntyre, A. (1999) *Dependent Rational Animals. Why Human Beings Need the Virtues*, Duckworth, London

Macphail, E. M. (1998) *The evolution of consciousness*, Oxford University Press, Oxford

Manning, A. and M. S. Dawkins (1998) *An Introduction to Animal Behaviour*, Cambridge University Press, Cambridge.

Martin & Caro (1985) quoted by Wemelselder (1993), p106

Masson, J. and S. McCarthy (1994) *When Elephants Weep. The Emotional Lives of Animals*, Jonathan Cape, London

Maynard-Smith, J. (1989) *Did Darwin get it right? Essays on games, sex and evolution*, Penguin, London.

Merkens, H.W., H. C. Schamhardt, G. J. V. van Osch and J. van Bogert (1990) Ground reaction force analysis of Dutch Warmblood Horses at canter and jumping, pp128–135, in *Equine Exercise Physiology*, eds. S. G. B. Persson, A. Lindhom and L. B. Jeffcott, ICEEP Publ., Davis

Meyer-Holzapfel, M. (1968) Abnormal behaviour of zoo animals, in *Abnormal Behaviour of Animals*, ed. M. W. Fox, W. B. Saunders, London

Midgley, M. (1978) *Beast and Man: The Roots of Human Nature*, Cornell Press, Ithaca, NY (1992) *Science as Salvation. A modern myth and its meaning*, Routledge, NY

Miller, R. (1999) L'impregnation comportementale du poulain nouveau-ne, pp13–21, in *L'equitation, le cheval et l'ethologie*, Colloque du 18 Sept 1999 a l'ecole National d'Equitation, Belin, Paris.

Miller-Graber, P., L. Lawrence, J. Foremen, K. Bump, M. Fisher and E. Kurz, Effect of dietary protein level on nitrogen metabolites in exercised Quarter horses. pp 305–314, in *Equine Exercise Physiology*, eds. S. G. B, Persson, A. Lindholm and L. B. Jeffcott, ICEEP publ., Davis

Mohr, E. (1971) *The Asiatic Wild Horse*, J. A. Allen, London

Moore, A. J. (1993) Towards an evolutionary view of social dominance, *Animal Behav.* 46, 594–596

Morel, M. and G. G. Davis (1993) *Equine reproductive physiology, breeding and stud management*, Farming Press, Ipswich

Morgan, L. (1894) quoted by Dawkins (1993)

Morris, D. (1957) "Typical intensity" and its relation to the problem of ritualisation, *Behav.*, 11, 1–12

Moss, C. (1975) *Portraits in the Wild. Behaviour Studies of East African Mammals*, Houghton Mifflin, Boston

Mugford, R. (1992) *Dog Training the Mugford way*, Ebury Press, London

Naess, A. (1984) A defense of the deep ecology movement, *Envir. ethics*, 6, 265–70

Nagel, T. (1974) What is it like to be a bat? *Philosophical Review*, 83, 435–50

Noske, B. (1989) *Humans and Other Animals*, Pluto Press, London

O'Hear, A. (1997) *Beyond evolution, human nature and the limits of evolutionary explanations*, Clarendon Press, Oxford

Oldberg, F. (1972) ch. 7, presence of faeces

Oliveira, N. (1976) *Reflections on Equestrian Art*, J. A. Allen, London

Oxford English Dictionary (1986) Oxford University Press

Parelli, P. (1999) Natural Horsemanship, in *l'Equitation, le cheval et l'ethologie*, Colloque du 18 Sept 1999 a l'ecole National d'Equitation, 23–34, Belin, Paris, and demonstration

Patterson, F. and E. Linden (1981) *The Education of Koko*, Holt, Rhinehart & Winston, NY

Pearce, J. (1987) *Introduction to Animal Cognition*, Harvester, Hove, UK

Persson, S. G. B., P. Lindholm and L. B. Jeffcott (1991) *Equine exercise physiology 3*, ICEEP, Davis

Pepperburg, I. M. (1993) Cognition and communiation in an African Grey parrot (*Psittacus erithacus*), Studies on a non-human, non-primate, non-mammal subject, in *Language and Communication, A Comparative Perspective*, eds. H. L. Roitblat, L. M. Herman and P. E. Nachtigall, Lawrence Erlbaum Assoc.

Petersson, H. K., H. F. Hintz, H. F. Schryer and G. F. Combs Jr. (1991) The effect of vitamin E on membrane integrity during submaximal exercise, in *Equine Exercise Physiology 3*, eds. S. G. B. Persson, A. Lindholm and L. B. Jeffcott, ICEEP publ., Uppsala

Piaget, J. (1953) *The origins of intelligence in children*, International University Press, NY

Piaget, J and B. Inhelder (1969) *The psychology of the child*, Basic Books, NY

Plato, The Republic, in *The Oxford Dictionary of Quotations* (1999) Oxford University Press, Oxford

Pluvinel, A. de (1989) *Le Maneige Royal*, trans. H. Nelson. from 1626 edn., J. A. Allen, London

Podhajsky, A. (1967) *The Complete Training of Horse and Rider*, trans. V. Williams, J. A. Allen, London

(1997) *My Horses, My Teachers*, trans. E. Podhajsky, J. A. Allen, London

Poole, T. and J. Fish (1975) An investigation of playful behaviour in *Rattus norvegicus* and *Mus musculus*, J. Zoo. Lond. 175, pp61–71

Povinelli, D. J. (1989) Failure to find self-recognition in Asian elephants (*Elephas maximus*) in contrast to their use of mirror cues to discover hidden food. *J. Compar. Psych,* 103, 122–131

Premack, D. (1988) Does the chimpanzee have a theory of mind revisited, in *Machiavallian Intelligence,* eds. R. Bryne and A. Whiten, Oxford University Press, Oxford

Premack, D. and G. Woodruff (1978) Does the chimpanzee have a theory of mind? *Behav. & Brain Sci.,* 4, 515–526

Prins, (1997) *The Cape Buffalo,* Methuen, London

Rachels, J. (1990) *Created from Animals: the Moral Implications of Darwinism,* Oxford University Press, Oxford

Radner, D. and M. Radner (1989) *Animal Consciousness,* Prometheus Books, NY

Randle, H. and M. Kiley-Worthington (1997) Social relations in a small group of African elephants. (*Loxondonta africana*), *Eco Research Centre,* occas paper 008

Rees, L. (1983) *The Horse's Mind,* Stanley Paul, London
(1991) *Riding: The True Techniques,* Stanley Paul, London

Rendell and Whitened (2001) *Social Learning in Certaceans,* (ms. for comment *Brain and Behavioural Sci.*)

Rendle, C. (1996) Appropriate harness and implements for working equines, Symposium on Working Equines, Rabat, *Eco Research Centre, Paper 15b*

Rinpoche, Sogyal (1992) *The Tibetan Book of Living and Dying,* Rider, London

Ristau, C. A. (ed.) (1991) *Cognitive Ethology,* Erlbaum, Hillside

Roberts, M. (1992) *The man who listens to horses,* Hutchinson, London
(1999) *Shy Boy,* Harper Collins, London

Roitblat, H. L. (1987) *Introduction to comparative cognition,* W. H. Freeman, NY

Rollin, B. (1989) *The Unheaded Cry. Animal Consciousness, Animal Pain and Scientific Change,* Oxford University Press, Oxford

Romanes, G. (1883) *Animal Intelligence,* Kegan Paul & Co., London

Romer, A. S. (1954) *Man and the Vertebrates,* Pelican, London

Rossdale, P. D. (1983) *The Horse from Conception to Maturity,* J. A. Allen, London

Rousseau, J. J. (1762) *The Social Contract,* Routledge, London

Rubenstein, D. I. (1986) Ecology and sociality in horses and zebras, in *Ecological Aspects of Social Evolution,* pp282–302, eds. D. I. Rubenstein and R. W. Wrangham, Princeton University Press

Russell, B. (1921) *The analysis of mind,* Allen & Unwin, London

Ryle, G. (1949) *The concept of mind,* ch8, p7, Penguin, London.

Sainsbury, D. W. B. (1984) Housing the Horse, in *Horse Management*, ed. J. Hickman, p63–91, Academic Press, London

Salt, H. (1980) *Animal Rights*, Cetaur, London

Sartre, J-P. (1962) *A sketch for the theory of the emotions*, trans. P. Mairet, Methuen, London

Savage-Rumbaugh, S. and K. E. Brakke (1996) Animal language. Methodological and interpretive issues, pp269–288, in *Readings in animal cognition*, eds. M. Bekoff and D. Jamieson, MIT Press, Cambs., Mass

Schmidt, J. (1991) *Animal Welfare Science*, Academic Press, London

Schjelderup-Ebbe, T. (1922) Beitrage zur Social psychologie des Huashuhns, *Z. Psychol*, 88, 225–252

Schott, H. C., D. R. Hodgson, W. M. Bayly and P. D. Gollnick, (1991) Renal responses to high intensity exercise, pp361–367 in *Equine Exercise Physiology 3*, eds. S. G. B. Persson, A. Lindholm and L. B. Jeffcott, ICEEP publ., Davis

Schulsterman, R. J and R. Gisiner (1988) Artificial language comprehension in dolphins and sea lions: The essential cognitive skills, *Psychol. Rec*, 38, 311–48

Selye, H. (1950) *The Physiology and Pathology of Stress*, Acta Inc, NY

Seyfath, R. M. and D. L. Cheney (1988) Do monkeys understand their relations? in *Machiavellian intelligence: social expertise and the evolution of intellect in monkeys, apes and humans*, eds. R. W. Bryne and A. Whiten, Oxford University Press, Oxford

Schafer, M. (1974) *The Language of Horses*, J. A. Allen, London

Sheldrake, R. and M. Fox (1997) *Natural Grace*, Cox and Wyman, Reading

Sherpell, J. A. (1986) *In the company of animals*, Blackwell, Oxford

Shettleworth, S. J. (1998) *Cognition, Evolution and Behavior*, Oxford University press, Oxford

Simpson, (1976) quoted by Wemelsfelder, (1993) p106

Sisson, S. and J. D. Grossman (1938) *The anatomy of vertebrates*. W. B. Saunders, London

Skinner, B. F. (1938) *The Behavior of Organisms; an Experimental Analysis*, Appleton-Century-Crots, NY

Skinner, (1969) from *Oxford Book of Quotations* (1999) Oxford University Press, Oxford

Skipper, L. (1999) *Inside Your Horse's Mind*, J. A. Allen, London

Stich, P. S. (1983) *From Folk Psychology to Cognitive Science*, MIT Press

Sutherland, N. S. (1989) *MacMillan Dictionary of Psychology*, London, MacMillan

Svenson, E. (1994) *Handbook of Donkeys*,. Donkey Sanctuary, Sidmouth

Swift, S. (1996) *Centred Riding*, J. A. Allen, London

Syme, G. T. and C. A. Syme. (1979) *Social Structure in farm animals*, Elsevier, Amsterdam

Tellington-Jones, L., and S. Taylor (1992) *The Tellington-TTouch*, Cloudcraft Books, Berks

Terrace, H. S. (1978) Apes who "talk". Language or projection of language by their teachers, pp19–42, in *Language in Primates*, eds. de Luce and Wilder

Tinbergen, N. (1956) *The study of instinct*, Oxford University Press, Oxford

Thorpe, W. H. (1963) *Learning and Instinct in Animals*, Methuen, London

Toates, F. (1994) Motivation, CAEC meeting, Provence, France

(1995) Animal motivation and cognition, in *Comparative Approaches to Cognitive Science*, eds. H. Roitblatt and J-A Meyer, MIT Press

Tolman, E. C. (1932) *Purposive Behavior in Animals and Men*, Century, NY

Trivers, R. L. (1991) The evolution of reciprocal altruism, *Quart. Rev. Biol.*, 46, 35–57

Tschiffely, A. F. (1933) *Tschiffely's Ride. 10,000 miles on horseback through South and North America*, Heinemann, NY

Turnbull, C. (1982) *The Forest People*, Paladin, London

(1984) *The Mountain People*, Paladin, London

Tyler, S. (1972) *Behaviour and Social Organisation of New Forest Ponies*, Animal Behav. Monograph, 5, 85–196, Bailliere Tindall, London

Vicchio, S. J. (1986) From Aristotle to Descartes: making Animals Anthropomorphic, pp187–206 in *Animal Intelligence. Insights into the Animal Mind*. eds. R. J. Hoage and L. Goldman, Smithsonian Institution Press, Washington

de Waal, F. (1996) *Good Natured. The Origins of Right and Wrong in Humans and Other Animals*, Harvard University Press

Walker, S. (1983) *Animal Thought*, Routledge, London

Wanless, M. (1987) *Ride with your mind. A right brain approach to riding*, Methuen, London

Waring, G. (1983) *Horse Behaviour*, Noyes Press, NY

Wasserman, E. A. and S. C. Astley (1994) A behavioural analysis of concepts: its application to pigeons and children. *Psychol. of Learning & Motivation*, 31, 73–132

Watanabe, S., S. F. G. Lea and W. H. Dittrich (1993) What can we learn from experiments on pigeons concept discrimination? in *Vision Brain and Behaviour in Birds*, eds. H. P. Zeigler and H-J. Bischof, MIT, Cambs.

Watson, J. B. (1919) *Psychology from the Standpoint of a Behaviorist*, Lipincott, Philadelphia

Watson, L. (1999) *The Organ of Jacobson*, Allen Lane, Penguin, London

Welsh, B. L. (1964) Psychological response to the mean level of environmental stimulation – a theory of environmental integration, in *Medical Aspects of Stress in a Military Climate*, US Gov. Washington

Welsh, D. A. (1973) *The life of Sable Island wild horses*, Ph.D. thesis, Dalousie, Canada

Wemelsfelder, F. (1993) *Animal Boredom towards an empirical approach to animal subjectivity*, Proefschrift Leiden

Whiten, A. and J. Prener (1991) Fundamental Issues in the Multidisciplinary Study of Mindreading, p1–18, *Natural Theories of Mind*, ed. A. Whiten, Oxford University Press, Oxford

Wickler, S. J. and W. Troy (1991) Blood volume, lactate and cortisol in exercising Arabian equitation horses, pp397–401 in *Equine Exercise Physiology 3*, eds. S. G. B. Persson, A. Lindholm and L. Jeffcott, ICEEP Publ., Davis

Williams, M. (1960) *Adventures unbridled*, Methuen, London

Wilson, E. O. (1975) *Sociobiology*, Belknap Press, Cambs. Mass.

Wittgenstein, L. (1953) *Philosophical Investigtions*, Oxford

Woolf, V., from *Oxford Dictionary of Quotations*, Oxford University Press, Oxford

Wright, M. (1975) *The Jeffery Method of Horse Handling*, Williams, South Australia (1983) *The thinking horseman*, Edwards printing, Tamworth, NSW

Wynne-Edwards, (1962) *Animal Dispersion in Relation to Social Behaviour*, Oliver & Boyd Hafner Publ., London

Xenophon, 350BC (1972) *The Art of Horsemanship*, J. A. Allen, London

Young, J. Z. (1950) *The life of vertebrates*, Oxford University Press, Oxford

Zeuner, F. E. (1963) *A history of domestic animals*, Hutchinson, London

Zhahavi, A. (1975) Mate selection – a selection for a handicap, *J. Theor. Biol*, 67, 603–605

Bibliography

Index

Note: Page numbers in **bold** refer to
llustrations; those in *italic* to boxes

abattoirs 347–8
adaptability of equines 46–8
　methods of enhancing 53–4
Aderin 14, **17**, 18
aesthetic sense 383–7
affection 100, **212**, 213, 213–14, 349–50
aggressive behaviour 203–8
aggressive play 368, **369**
Aisha Evans 14, 20
Alia 14, **17**
alternative therapists, equine 42–3
altruism, reciprocal 354–5
AMSLAN (American Sign Language) 126
anaerobic respiration 61
annoyance 207–9, 368
anthropomorphic judgement *82*
anthropomorphism, conditional 35, 41–6,
　130, 167–8, 192, 392, 437–40
anti-weaving bars **104**, 187
anticipation 193–4
anxiety 193–4
apes 300, *307*, 338, 374
appetite 92, *398*
Aristotle 38
arm gestures 124
ass, wild 51–3, 93
associative learning 87, 142–3, 147
attachment 100
attention 328–30
auditory communication *283*, 295–301
auditory cortex 74
avoidance learning 130–2
awareness
　conscious 315–19
　of others 165, 339–40
　of self/own body 287, 330–1, **332**,
　　339–40, 374–80
　of 'things' and experiences 328–30
　unconscious 320–7

bachelor groups 259, 260
bacteria, gut 60
Baksheesh 14, 15, **17**, 19

ball kicking 150, 151, **152**
bantams 138
Bavridge, T. 37
behavioural problems 436–7
　causes 99, 104–5
　conditional anthropomorphic approach
　　to 437–8
　in conventional husbandry systems
　　398–400
　use of drugs 439
behavioural restriction 181–6, 402–4
　assessment and reduction of 183–6
　breeding/courtship 181–2, 264–6
behavioural synchronization 332–4
behaviours
　'essential for life' 83
　'luxuries' 83
beliefs
　of convenience 209
　cultural 80
　false 27
　folk 32, 33, 39–40, 80, *81*, 110, 303
birds 76, 345
bits 124
　chewing 195, 297
Black Bess 98
'blind sight' 321
body awareness 330–1, *332*, *395*
'body language' 420
body shape 58–9
body-weight 56–7
　and brain size 68
body/mind relationship 38
bogs, familiarity with 231
boredom 103, 187–93
Bortoft, H. 27
botanical knowledge, of horse 229–33
brain 66–8
　auditory cortex 74
　body-weight ratio 68
　comparison of species **67**
　corpus callosum 77
　visual cortex 76–7
breeding 65–6
　courtship behaviour 181–2, 214–15
　problems *400*

restriction of normal behaviours 181–2,
　264–6
　social knowledge needed for 261–2
breeds, variation in reactivity/emotions 171
buffalo 234, 333
bullfighting 169

care of horse, *see* husbandry
Cariff 15, 21
caring behaviour 251–3, **254**
Caro, T.H. 370
carriage driving horse 98
Carroll, Lewis 276
caution 199
Chaka (elephant) 158–61
'champing' 200–1, 358
'chaperone effect' 253, **254**
Charge of the Light Brigade (Tennyson) 33
charity 349–50
Cheney, D.L. 315
Cherif 15
chewing
　bit 195, 297
　wood 188
　see also champing
Christmas Time 15
circus performers 426
classical schools of equitation 169–70
Clever Hans 293
clicker training 115–17
coat, maintaining 99–102
cognition, and language 303–4, 312, 341
'cognitive map' 146, 223
cognitive (mental) needs 45–8, *186*, 191,
　394
cognitive (silent) learning 147, 150, 342
colic, causes 84, 87, 91
colours, learning 345, **346**, 430
colts 65, 262
　see also stallions
commands 158
　words as 425–30
communication 99, 102, 268, 272, *396*
　auditory 277, 278, 295–301
　by smells 282–90
　by taste 290

by touch 290–1
context dependence/independence 177, 293–4, 300–1
definition 277
extrasensory 301–2
frequency of use of different modalities *283*
ritualized 279–81
visual 278, 291–5
companionship **212**
compassion 350–1
concepts
    acquisition of 345–7, 430
    of death 347–8
    definition of 345
conditional anthropomorphism 35, 41–6, 130, 167–8, 192, 392, 437–40
conditioned response, generalization 121–4
conditioned stimulus 112
conditioning 93, 108, 112
    clicker training 115–17
    instrumental (operant) 139–41, 334
    Pavlovian 138–9
consciousness 315–19, *397*
    awake 328
    changing levels of 377, 379
    definitions 315
    reflective 334, 337–40, *397*
    of self and body 330–1, **332**
    types of 379
    see also unconsciousness
co-operative (interactive) teaching 156–61, 427–9, 433–4
corpus callosum 77
coughing 298
courtship 181–2, 214–15, 262, 264–5
crib-biting 46, **104**
crying 209
Crystal (*Crysthannah Royal*) 15, **17**, 20
cultural beliefs 80
cultural habits 86
cultures 144–5, 169, 170–1, 243, 246–7
curiosity 196–8

Dartmoor ponies 230
Darwin, Charles 38
Dawkins, R. 318
death, concept of 347–8
deceit 273, 359–60
Declaration of Human Rights 83
declarative knowledge 153–5, 220
defaecating behaviour 72, 167, 287
defensive threat 202–3
dehydration 60–1
depression 209
Descartes, R. 38
desensitization 113–14
developing countries 44–5
digestion 60
dislike 205–9

displacement activities 102, 178, 195, 362–3
distances
    perception of 225
    travelled by horses 98
distress 103, 180–7, 402
dogs
    brain 67
    dreaming 344
    shame/guilt 358–9
dominance hierarchies 267, 361
donkeys 111, 300
    adaptability 44–5, 47
    co-operative teaching 427
    size and weight 56
    trial and error learning 146–7
    vocal communication *299*, 300
dreaming 97, 344
drinking 92–4
drugs, use of 439
Druimghigha Osnan 22
Druimghigha Shindi 15, **18**, 25
Druimghigha Shirac 148
Druimghigha Stud 15–16, **17–18**
dualism 38

ear signals 279, **280**, 281–2
earthquakes, horses' sensitivity to 75
eating 84–92
    selection of foods 84–6, 87, 90–1
    stabled horse **89**, 90–1
    time spent by horses 88–9
Ecclesiastes 83
ecological knowledge 219–20, *395*
    acquiring 220–1
    field botany 229–33
    field geology 226–8
    geography 221–6
    meteorological 236–9
    of other species 233–6
education 27
    vs training 30
elephants 237, 288–9
    learning experiments 158–61
    response to mirrors 374–5
    tool making 376
    training 431–2
embarrassment 362–3
emotional needs *185–6*, *394*
emotions 165–7, 348–9, *396–7*
    arguments against existence in animals 165–6
    arguments for existence in animals 168–70
    conveying with voice 423–5
    general 176–95
    indications of the end of 195
    obstacles to understanding in others 170–5
    reflective 175, 216

shared 166–7
specific 195–215, 349–63
thresholds for 174
empathy 350–1
endurance, of horses 61–2, 98
endurance horse
    feeding 92
    route following 224
environment, awareness of 218–20
environments, for domestic horse 225
Equidae 50–3
Equus, interbreeding 53
Equus africanus (wild ass) 51–3
Equus burchell 51
Equus caballus 53
Equus grevyi 51, 93
Equus zebra 51
Erasmus 337
evolution 38, **52**, 53–4, 168
excitement 176–7, *398*
exercise tolerance 61–2
expectation 193–4
experience, social 84–6, 90, 143–5, 242, 247–50, 256–7, *400*
experiences
    different 407–8, **409**
    shared 166–7
    social 84–6, 90, 143–5, 242, 247–50, 256–7, *400*
exploration 196–8
extinction 112–13
extrasensory communication 301–2
eyes 76, 78

facial expressions 173, **174**, 204, 279, 292
fear 198–201
    high levels of 200
    horses' response 168
    thresholds 174
feeding 87, 90–1, 92, 406
females, *see* mares
feral horses 183, *184–6*
    adaptability of 47
    drinking 93
    ecological knowledge 223
    health 91
    knowledge of living environment 224
    territoriality 361
    time budget **89**
field botanists 229–33
field geologists 226–8
field zoologists and ethologists 233–6
fighting games 368, **369**
fitness 98
flehmen posture **70**, 287–8
foals
    bottle-reared 138
    handling 136–7, 414–16
    imprinting 134–8
    predator's attack 351

relationship with mother and other
females 251–3, 272
social learning 256–7
weaning 182, 256–7, 286–7
folk beliefs 32, 33, 39–40, 80, *81*, 110,
303
folk knowledge 32–3, 40–1, 168
folk psychology 39
food
acceptance 87
aversions 86–7
processing 90–2
as rewards 115, **118**, 120, **160**
selection 229–33
sharing 351–2
force, use of 133
reducing restraints 431–4
Freud, S. 320
friendships 259–60
frustration 177–9

gaits 63–5
Gardner, R.A. and B.T. 302–3
gazelle, Thomson's 233, 247
'General Adaptive Syndrome' 176, 180
generalization 121–4
generalization gradient 122
genetic factors 44, 171
geographical knowledge 221
geological knowledge 226–8
gestures, use of **123**, 124
giraffe 138
gnu 233
Goethe 40
gratitude 354–5
grazing
knowledge of plants 229–33
observing horse 226
selective 84–6, 90
grief 209
grooming
mutual 100
self 99–102
Ground, G. 37
groups, *see* peer groups; social groups
guanaco, learning experiments 157–61
guilt 358–9
gustatory communication *283*
gut, digestion 60

Haagni, E.B. 345
habits 133–4, 324–6
habits of mind 134, 155, 326–7, 350
habituation 113–14
halters, training 131–2
hand gestures 124
handling 414
foal 136–7
older naïve equine 417
rules for better *414–16*

happiness 210–13
harness work 407, **409**
Hauser, M.D. 370
hearing 74–5
heifer, learning experiments 157–61
helping, others 353–4
helplessness, learnt 210
hierarchies, social groups 267, 361
hobbies 102–3
'home', recognition of 286–7
homosexual courtship 214
'horse whispering' 42–3, 276, 420
human-horse comparisons 50–65, *80–1*
adaptability 53–4
body shape 58–9
brain 66–8
communication 282–302
gaits 63–5
perception of space and distance 62–3
physiology 59–62
size and strength 56–7, *58*
skeleton and muscles 55–6
human/horse relationship
mother/child 27–8
overprotection 91, 103–4, 182, 210
humans 50
crying 209
drinking 93–4
evolution 54
hunter gatherers 88–9
imprinting of foal on 136–7
laughter 371–3
learning from equines 33–4, 249,
379–80, 439–40
leisure time 102–3
observation of equines 161, 163, 295
rules for good teaching 164
sleep 97
smell sense 284, 286
stereotypic behaviours 45–6
use of voice 115, **118**, 132–3, 213,
420–1, 423–7
humour 371–4
hunter gatherers 88–9
husbandry of horses
behavioural problems *398–400*
behavioural restriction 183, *184–6*,
402–4
improving quality of life 401–10
modern systems 99, 182, 210
and quality of life 388–90, 419
hybrids, *Equus* 53

imagination 129, 342–4
imitation 126, **127**, 145–6, 150, **163**
imprinting 134–8
on humans 136–7
incest taboo 206
information, methods of gathering 40
injuries, limb 323

insight learning 147–9
'instinct' 44, 261, 316, 321
'institutionalized' individuals 104
instructions
use of different types 122–4, **141**, 158
words as 425–30
instrumental (operant) conditioning
139–41, 334
intelligence 108–12
and brain development 67
comparisons of species 109
definition 109–10
intention movements 278–9
interactive (co-operative) teaching 156–61,
427–9, 433–4
intuitive knowledge 342
investigation 196–8
IQ tests 109–10
irritation 207–9
isolation 244–6

Jackson, J. 377
James, W. 318
jealousy 43, 358
joy 210–13
Jung, C.G. 241
justice 359

Kathiawar 13–14, 18
knowing, 'that' and 'how' 153–5, 220–1
knowledge
intuitive 342
see also ecological knowledge; social
knowledge
Koehler, O. 345
Kohler, Wolfgang 147–8

language 111, 165, 293–4, 302–12
characteristics 303, *307*
cognitive advantages of 303–4, 312,
341
context dependence/independence
293–4, 300–1
in equines 305–6, *307–8*
equines' understanding of 28, 155, 306,
308–12, 421–3, 430–1
learning 249
words as messages/commands 425–30
lateral movements, learning 154
latrine areas 287
laughter 371–3
learning 30–2, 395
associative 142–3
avoidance 130–2
basic rules of *150–1*
cognitive/silent 147, 150, 342
concepts 345–7, 430
conditioned 93, 108, 112, 115–17
definition 108
folk beliefs 110

food selection/acceptance 84–6, 87, 90–1
habit formation 133–4, 324–6
of human language 28, 155, 306, 306–12, 308–12, 421–3, 430–1
humans, from equines 33–4, 249, 379–80, 439–40
imitation 126, **127**, 145–6, 150
imprinting 134–8
insightful 147–9
maze tests 110
motivation 130, 154
of movement 322–3
Pavlovian 138–9, 150
reversal 132–3
social 143–5
studying of 161
'that' and 'how' 153–5, 220–1
trial and error 146–7
learning curve 108, **109**
lethargy *398*
liking 205, 214, 259–60
Lilka 15, **18**, 25
Liloni 15, **18**
livery yards 403
llamas 234, 289
loading, into trailer 131–2, 438
loose schooling 426
love 213–14, 349–50
loyalty 355–6
lungeing 427
Luxor 15, **18**
lying down **89**, 94–7

McCarthy, S. 165, 315
McDowell, J. 218
malimprinting 137–8
mammals, characteristics of 49–50
Man *vs* Horse race 62
manipulation, of others 272
manners, horses' 144–5
mares
    breeding behaviour 181–2, 261–2, 264–6
    caring behaviour of 251–3, **254**
    ecological knowledge 221
    maternal behaviour 251–2, **253**, 255–6
    pregnancy 65
    relationship with offspring 272, 370–1
    relationships with stallions 207
Masson, J. 165, 315
mating, *see* breeding
maze, performance in 110
memory 128–9, 342–3
mental (cognitive) needs 45–8, *186*, 191, *394*
metronome 75, 76
Midgley, M. 218, 250–1, 349
migrations 224
military, use of donkeys and mules 111

mind of horse 35, 37–9
    capacity for thought 341–4
    human assumptions about 28–9
    mental needs 45–8, *186*, 191, *394*
mirrors, responses to 374–5
mismothering 137–8
monism 38
monkeys 300, *307*, 338, 374
moral agency
    consequences for care and education of equines 388–90
    of horses 382, 387–8
mothers, *see* mares
motivation
    for learning 130, 154
    and praise 213
moulding 126, **127**
movement 61–2, 98–9
    intention 278–9
    learning 322–3
    restriction of 99
mules 111
muscles 55–6
music 76, 386
mutual grooming 100, **212**

Nagel, T. 42, 377
Namibian desert horses 47
'natural', defined 418
'natural horsemen' 28, 420
nature *vs* nurture 44–5, 107, 171
needs
    cognitive (mental) 45–8, *186*, 191, *394*
    emotional *185*–6, *394*
    physical *393*
    social *185*, *393*–4
negative reinforcement 114–15, 124
neigh 298–300
nicker *299*
noises, non-vocal 296–8
noses, and communication 290
numbers, learning concept of 345, **346**
'nutritional wisdom' 85

Oberlix 15, **18**, 22
observation of equines 161, 163, 295
observational learning 143
odours, *see* smells
oestrus 65, 261–2, 284
olfactory communication 282–90
Oliver **212**
Omani **17**
Omeya 15, **17**, 19
operant (instrumental) conditioning 139–41, 334
orientation reflexes 328–30
Oryx 15, **18**, 24
Osnan 22
ostrich 234
overexcitement *398*

overprotection 91, 103–4, 182, 210
ownership 360–2

Paddy **17**
pain 196, 323–4
panic 199, 200
pasture-kept horse, behavioural restriction *184*–6
paths, making 325
Pavlovian learning 138–9, 150
pawing 178, **179**
peer groups 257, 259, 260
Pepperburg, I.M. 345
perceptions, space and distance 224–5
performing, pleasure of horse in 211, 213, 373
pheromones 284
phobias 131
physical needs *393*
physiology, human/horse comparison 59–62
piaffe, teaching/learning 125–6, 155, 428
pigeons 345
plants, horses' knowledge of 229–33
play 339–40, 365–70
    between species 369–70
    function of 365–6
    object 366–7
    and pretence 367–8
    rules for 367
    teasing and annoying 368
pleasure 211–13
Podhajsky, A. 380
positive reinforcement 115, **118**, 213, 423–4, 426–7
    secondary 159–60
possession 360–2
praise 115, **118**, 159–60, 213, 423–4, 426–7
preconceived notions 170
predator's attack 351
preferences, individual 213–14
pregnancy 65
pretence/pretending 339–40, 357–8, 367–8
pride 356–7
primates 50, 54
    vocal communication 300
    see also apes; humans
Prins 333
procedural knowledge 153–5, 220–1
protected environments 219–20, 238
protection of horse 91, 103–4, 182, 210
Przewalski's horses 53
psychology, folk 39
punishment 120–1

quality of life (domestic equine) 388–90, 419
    improving 401–10

racehorses
    conventional husbandry of 46
    speed 61, 62, 98
ragwort 86
rape 215
rearing 132–3
Rees, Lucy 417
reflections, responses to 374–5
reflective consciousness 334, 337–40, *397*
reflective emotions 175, 216
reinforcement 114–20
    delayed 119–20
    negative 114–15, 124
    partial 117–19
    positive 115, **118**, 213, 423–4, 426–7
reinforcers, secondary 115–16, 159–60
relaxation 179, 195
reproduction, *see* breeding
resentment 359
respiration 61
response
    conditioned 121–4
    defined 112
resting behaviour 94–7
restraints, reducing 431–4
restriction, behavioural, *see* behavioural restriction
reversal learning (unlearning) 132–3
rewards
    food 115, **118**, 120
    praise 115, **118**, 159–60, 213, 423–4, 426–7
    use of different types 159–60
rhinoceros 50–1
rhythm 75–6
riding
    important of touch/weight 291
    justification for use of equines 418–20
    tuning in to horse's sensitivity 73
ritualization 279–81
river crossings 227, **228**
rocks, horses' knowledge of 226–7
'rodeo' 169
rolling 102
round pen 115, 433–4
routes, learning/following 223–5
rubbish tips, donkey living on 44–5, 47

Schjelderup-Ebbe, T. 267
science, approach of 34–5
sea, experiences of 227
self-awareness 287, 330–1, **332**, 339–40
    introspective 374–80
    and tool use 376–7, **378**
self-fulfilling prophecies 170
self-grooming 99–102
Senecio jacobea (ragwort) 86
senses
    aesthetic 383–7
    'extra' 79–80, 301–2

hearing 74–5
    smell 69–73, 282–90, 385
    taste 69, 70, 290
    touch 73–4, 290–1
sentience 166
sex 65–6, 214–15
    misdirected 214–15
    restriction of normal behaviours 181–2, 264–6
    see also breeding; courtship
sexual dimorphism 59
Seyfarth, R.M. 315
shame 358–9
Shanti 25
shaping 124–6, 154
shared experiences 166–7
sharing 351–2
Sheba **17**, 20, 94–5
Shebat 21
Shella 15
Shemal 15, **18**, 23
Shenandoah 15, **18**
Shere Khan 23
Shereen 14, 15, 21
Shergar 24
Sherpell 169
Shezam 15, 25, **95**
Shiera 23
Shindi 15, **18**, 25
Shiraz 14, **17**
showing off 356–7
Shukrune 24, **100**, 145–6
shying 120–1, 342–3
shyness 357–8
sighing 297–8
sight, *see* vision
silent learning 147, 150, 342
size 56–7, *58*
skeleton, comparison of horse and human 55–6
skin irritation 178
Skinner, B.F. 27, 117, 334
sleep **89**, 94–7
    dreaming 344
    rapid eye movement (REM) 97, 344
smell, sense of 69–73, 282–90, 385
smells
    and communication 282–90
    familiar 286–7
    strange 288–9
    taboos 286
    unpleasant 385
'snake face', of stallions 173, **174**, 204, 279
sneeze-blow 297
snorting 298
'social contract' 242–3
social facilitation 333
social groups 250–3, **254**
    behavioural synchronization 332–4

bonds between and within generations 256–8
    differences 247–50
    friendships and enemies 259
    growing up in 258–9
    male priorities 260–1
    organization 267–73
    reasons for living in 241–4
social isolation 244–6
social knowledge 243–4, *395–6*
    for breeding 261–2
    females' priorities 250–3
social learning/experience 84–6, 90, 143–5, 242, 247–50, *400*
    foals 256–7
social needs *185*, *393–4*
social possessiveness 361–2
social traditions 243, 246–7
space, perception of 62–3, 224–5
Spanish walk, teaching/learning 119, 153
spare time 102–3
speed, of equines 61, 62, 98
spooking 120–1, 342–3
squealing *299*, 300
stable management, *see* husbandry of horses
stabled horse
    behavioural restriction 183, *184–6*, 402–4
    feeding/eating 87, 90–1
    improving quality of life 405–7
    lying down 95
    time budget **89**
stabling
    improvements to 405–7
    types and design **104**, 188, **189**
stallions
    aggressive behaviour 203–4, 206–8
    behaviour towards each other 355–6
    breeding behaviour and restriction of 181–2, 214–15, 254–5, 261–2, 264–6
    defaecating behaviour 167, 287
    herding of mares 173, **174**, 204, 279
    importance of smells 71–2, 284, **285**, 287, 289
    possessiveness 361–2
    showing off/pride 356–7
    'snake face' 173, **174**, 204, 279
    social behaviour 257–8, 260–1
    social education 262–6
    young 360
standing **89**, 94–7
startle 198
stealing 360–1
stereotypes 45–8, 104–5, 187–90, 256, *398–9*
stimulus
    defined 112
    generalization 122–4
    habituation to 113–14

strength of 124
stimulus-response learning 139–41, 142, 334
stimulus-stimulus (associative) learning 142–3, 147
stress, prolonged (distress) 180–7, 402
subconsciousness 320
submission
  'champing' 200–1, **358**
  dominance hierarchies 267, 361
substrates, horses' knowledge of 226–7, 231–2
successive approximations (shaping) 124–6, 154
surprise 198
suspicion 199
swimming 93
Syringa 14, 19

taste
  and communication 290
  sense of 69, 70
teaching 370–1
  co-operative 156–61, 427–9, 433–4
  reducing restraints 431–4
  rules for good 164
teasing play 368
telepathy 301–2
temperature control 60–1
Tennyson, W. 33
territoriality 361

thinking
  equine capacity 341–4
  and human language 303–5, 312, 341
Thomson's gazelle 233, 247
thought, *see* thinking
threat, defensive 202–3
time, spare/leisure 102–3
time budgets 88–9, 94–5
tools, making and use 376–7, **378**
touch, sense of 73–4, 290–1
toys, equine 190
trailer loading 131–2, 438
transitional activities 195
trial and error learning 146–7
twitch, use of 319–20

unconscious awareness 320–7
unconsciousness 319–20
urination 72
use of equines, justification of 418–20

views, appreciation of 384
vision 76–9, 225
visual awareness 225, 383–4
visual communication *283*, 291–5
vocalizations *283*, 298–301
  in sleep 344
voice (human), use of 115, **118**, 132–3, 213, 420–1, 423–7

walking, learning 322–3

water, drinking 92–4, **228**
weaning of foals 182, 256–7, 286–7
weather, knowledge of 236–9
weaving **104**, 187
whip, as conditioned stimulus 112
wild ass 51–3, 93
wild horses, *see* feral horses
Wittgenstein, L. 42
wood chewing 188
Woolf, Virginia 337
words, teaching equines 425–30
working horses, nineteenth century 190–1

Xenophon 169

yarded horses 89, 99, *184–6*
yawning **163**, 373
young
  care of 251–3, **254**
  see also foals

zebras 51, **52**, 61, 93, 233, **251**
  adaptability 47
  in captivity 190, 192
  emotions 171
  learning 139, 147, **197**
  living with other species 233–4, 247
  stripe patterns 292–3
  territoriality 361
  vocal communication *299*, 300
zoo-kept animals 219–20, 238

Non-restraint riding: Shemal and Vicky, Oberlix (Shemal's father) and Chris, with Fats the collie.